The VISUAL HANDBOOK

of Energy Conservation

A Comprehensive Guide to Reducing Energy Use at Home

CHARLIE WING

The Taunton Press

The Taunton Press, Inc., 63 South Main Street, PO Box 5506, Newtown, CT 06470-5506

email: tp@taunton.com

Editor: Christina Glennon

Copy editor: Seth Reichgott

Indexer: Jay Kreider

Cover design: Jean-Marc Troadec

Cover and interior illustrator: Charlie Wing

Interior design: Nick Anderson

Layout: Charlie Wing

Library of Congress Cataloging-in-Publication Data

Wing, Charles, 1939-

The visual handbook of energy conservation : a comprehensive guide to reducing energy use at home / Charlie Wing.

   pages cm

  Includes index.

ISBN 978-1-62113-956-0 (paperback)

1. Dwellings--Energy conservation--Handbooks, manuals, etc. I. Title.

TJ163.5.D86W575 2013

690.028'6--dc23

Printed in the United States of America

10 9 8 7 6 5 4 3 2 1

The following names/manufacturers appearing in the *Visual Handbook of Energy Conservation* are trademarks: BoilerMate™, Energy Star®, Home Energy Saver™, Kill A Watt®, Mickey Mouse™, Minnie Mouse™, TJI®, Tyvek®, West System®

Homebuilding is inherently dangerous. Using hand or power tools improperly or ignoring safety practices can lead to permanent injury or even death. Don't try to perform operations you learn about here (or elsewhere) unless you're certain they are safe for you. If something about an operation doesn't feel right, don't do it. Look for another way. We want you to enjoy building, so please keep safety foremost in your mind whenever you're working.

For Paul Kando and Beth McPherson
Friends of the Earth—they walk the walk

Acknowledgments

Although I take credit for devoting a year of solitary days to creating this book, I must acknowledge certain people without whom it never would have come to be. First, my best friend, Wid, for staying the course and sustaining my life in spite of my neglect. Second, my faithful agent, Ray Wolf, for browbeating the finest building and remodeling publisher into taking a chance on my idea. Third, the staff at Habitat for Humanity/7 Rivers Maine for allowing me the chance to create and deliver much of this material in the form of weatherization training to hundreds of their volunteers. Finally, a diverse group of energy educators, auditors, and enthusiasts for contributing more than they will ever know: Doug Fox of Unity College, Jeffrey Granger of Granger Technologies, and Paul Kando, Topher Belknap, and Guy Marsden of Maine's Midcoast Green Collaborative.

Contents

Introduction

Long, long ago, in 1972, I conducted a seminar at Bowdoin College which treated "the house" as a subject in physics: building loads, strength of materials, structural analysis, heat flow by conduction, convection, and radiation, ventilation by natural convection, passive solar heating, electrical circuits, and acoustics.

A sort of "Physics for Poets," the seminar proved immensely popular—at least with the students. They lovingly called the seminar "Hammer and Nails." The rest of the faculty was somewhat less enthusiastic. Before offering the seminar a second time, I was advised by the Dean of the Faculty to change its title to "The Art of the House," in order to counter faculty sentiment that the course was "too practical." Too practical? That was exactly the point! If my seminar was deemed too practical, then how would one characterize most of the other Bowdoin courses?

As I said, the seminar proved popular with the students, but that proved to be the lesser gratification. As the seminar progressed, word spread among Maine's back-to-the-land community. This was the 1970s, and throngs of young, idealistic, war-protesting couples were flocking to Maine to homestead. One by one, then by twos, these bright-faced energetic couples appeared, asking if they might just sit in the back of the room and listen. When the 90-minute sessions ended, the Bowdoin students retired to their card games, or to a hockey game, or to their rooms, but the homesteaders wouldn't leave. They pressed to the front with question after question. They wanted to know, they needed to know—not for a grade or for a degree—but for life.

That is when I discovered my purpose in life: to share my understanding of how things work with people who truly want to understand. That is when I left my teaching position at Bowdoin to co-found Shelter Institute, the first owner-builder school in the nation.

At Shelter, I refined the Bowdoin seminar into a 45-hour course. Over the next three years I conducted the course some thirty times to students, not only from Maine but also from all over the United States. It was gratifying to provide something people thought worthy of serious money, three weeks of precious time, and thousands of miles. Increasingly, however, I was bothered by the tiny percentage of people I was able to reach. What about those who couldn't get three weeks off from jobs, or who had children to care for, or who simply couldn't afford the course? That is when I decided a book could spread my words more efficiently.

Actually, I wasn't the one who decided I should turn my course into a book. It was John Cole, editor of the alternative weekly *Maine Times*. John was author of a half-dozen books and the self-appointed spokesman for what he termed "the post-industrial age." I was dubious, having been told by every high school and college English instructor that I couldn't write. Not all put it in so many words, but my poor grades seemed a clear message.

But John was insistent. "If Wing can't do it, I will write it for him," I heard him tell the Editor in Chief of Atlantic Monthly Books. In the end, John and I wrote *From the Ground Up* together. Fifteen chapters based on my fifteen lectures interspersed with fifteen marvelous chapter introductions by John—a little sugar to make the medicine go down. John's instincts proved right: I could write (at least about a subject I loved), and the book sold 75,000 copies.

Forty years and thirty books later, I am finally ready to tackle a subject I have too long put off. The homesteaders have built their homes, raised their children, and many gone to Florida. Post and beam is in, and organic farming is going commercial. One problem, however, remains. Like prodigal children, we are burning through our inheritance. For millions of years the earth deposited carbon compounds in a vast savings account. Then, less than 200 years ago (a blink of the eye in the vast scale of time), someone cracked the safe. Since then we have been spending that inheritance without consideration of the earth or of future generations. We all complain about fuel prices, but most of us still live in drafty, poorly insulated homes.

In 1977, at the time of the first energy crisis, Jimmy Carter went on the radio to pronounce energy conservation "the moral equivalent of war." In the decades since, the U.S. government has spent hundreds of millions of dollars trying to reform our spendthrift ways—trying to get us to insulate and tighten our homes, trying to get us to use less hot water, trying to get us to give up shamefully inefficient incandescent light bulbs, trying to convince us to purchase more expensive but far more efficient appliances. Yet little has changed. Do we not care? I do not believe that to be the case.

I believe it is simply a matter of understanding. I think it is as if we were being told to repair our own automobiles. Sure, we know how to drive; we know how to turn the engine on; we even know how to refill the fuel tank. But repair a sputtering engine?

It is the same with our homes. We think of them mostly in architectural terms, as beautiful spaces in which to live and entertain. Sure, we know how to open and close the doors and windows, turn lights on and off, adjust the thermostat, even replace burned-out light bulbs. But, like our automobiles, our houses are actually complex systems: structure, sheathing, cladding, insulation, ventilation, wiring, plumbing, heating, and cooling. These elements are intertwined. You cannot modify one without considering the others.

I have come to believe that understanding is the key to action. If you understand why your basement is damp, even moldy; if you understand how and where hidden air leaks are robbing your home of valuable heat; if you understand how an electric heat pump can provide heat for even less cost than oil or gas; if you understand that an improvement having a five-year payback is exactly the same as a bank account paying 20% interest, then I believe you will take control of your home and take responsibility for what you are doing to the earth. As a bonus, you will also feel more secure, be more comfortable, and have more money in your pocket.

I have tried to make this book informative yet a pleasure to read. It contains physics, but you won't know it. I further believe the saying, "A picture is worth a thousand words," to be an understatement, so I have striven to deliver understanding through illustration.

Whether a frustrated homeowner struggling to pay your utility bills, a young person studying to be a carpenter or architect, an energy auditor looking for ways to explain conservation to your clients, or just someone who likes to understand how things work, I hope you find in these pages something worthwhile. I will be gratified if you do.

Charlie Wing
New Limerick, Maine

About Energy

What exactly is energy? We know it is something we can buy; we know it has something to do with heat; we also know it sometimes has something to do with motion. To answer this question, we first examine the *three faces of energy.*

We also know that *temperature* is, in some way, a measure of energy. But why does the temperature of boiling water not continue to rise as we continue to heat it? The answer lies in the difference between *specific* and *latent heats.*

The primary focus of this book, however, is heat loss and heat gain. Real understanding of these phenomena requires a solid understanding of the nature of *heat transfer.*

The United States is one of only three countries yet to completely replace the old English (foot, pound) System with the Metric System. We still calculate our heat energy in British Thermal Units (Btus). Unfortunately, most scientific and engineering information, in both print and on the web, is in metric units. We therefore have listed a comprehensive table of *unit conversions* between the two systems.

Finally, to give you a better "feel" for the quantities of energy we will be dealing with, we present an amusing and enlightening illustration titled "*How Big Is a Btu?*".

The Three Faces of Energy

Energy is the subject matter of a scary-sounding college physics course titled "Thermodynamics." Separating the term into its two Greek roots, *thermo* and *dynamics*, tells us it is all about moving (*dynamics*) heat (*thermo*). Heat, of course, is the primary subject of this book. Specifically, we are interested in our homes losing less heat in the winter, gaining less heat in the summer, generating and removing heat more efficiently, and paying less for it. Let us begin, however, with a wider look at the many different forms of energy. We will calculate in the International (Metric) System, but you can convert to English units using the table on p. 7.

Potential Energy

Potential energy is the energy possessed by a mass due to gravity and the height of the mass above a reference plane, usually the ground. The formula is:

PE = mgh

where:

- PE = potential energy in Joules
- m = mass in kilograms (1 kg = 2.2 lb.)
- g = acceleration of gravity, 9.8 meters/sec^2
- h = height in meters (1 meter = 3.28 ft.)

By definition, 1 Joule = 1 kg-m^2/sec^2.
In the English units Americans are more used to:

1,000 J = 0.948 Btu
1 Btu = 1,055 J

Kinetic Energy

Kinetic energy is the energy possessed by a mass due to its velocity. The amount of kinetic energy a mass possesses is calculated with the formula:

KE = ½mv^2

where:

- KE = kinetic energy in Joules
- m = mass in kilograms
- v = velocity in meters/sec

Note that kinetic energy is also measured in Joules.

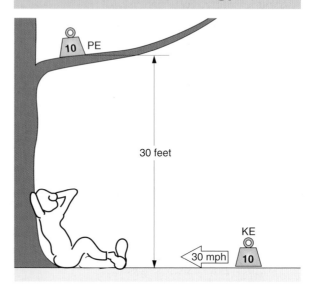

Potential vs. Kinetic Energy

Question (see illustration): Which has more energy:
(A) a mass weighing 10 lb. (4.54 kg) sitting on a limb 30 ft. (9.14 m) above the ground, or
(B) the same mass sliding across ice at 30 mph (13.41 m/sec)?

(A) has potential energy, due to its height above ground, but has zero kinetic energy because it is not moving. Its energy is:

PE = mgh
    = 4.54 kg × 9.8 m/sec^2 × 9.14 m
    = 406.7 kg-m^2/sec^2
    = 406.7 J

(B) has kinetic energy, due to its velocity across the ice, but has zero potential energy because it is at ground level. Its energy is:

KE = ½mv^2
    = 0.5 × 4.54 kg × (13.41 m/sec)^2
    = 408.2 kg-m^2/sec^2
    = 408.2 J

Internal Energy

The third form of energy, internal, is energy in a mass.

Sensible heat is internal energy created by the rotation and vibration of atoms and molecules. It is "sensible" because its transfer results in a temperature change that can be sensed by a thermometer. As we will see on p. 6, internal energy can be transferred within a mass or between masses by three processes: conduction, convection, and radiation. The direction of transfer is *always* from higher to lower temperature.

In addition, molecules consist of atoms bound by interatomic forces. Molecules are broken apart and rearranged into different molecules during chemical reactions. Even molecules are bound together, this time by intermolecular forces. These forces are:

- weak or nonexistent in gases
- moderate in liquids
- strong in solids, particularly crystals

Interatomic and intermolecular forces result in two additional types of internal energy:

Latent heat is the energy required to either break or form intermolecular bonds when a substance changes phase. It is "latent" because it happens without a change in temperature. Most substances exist in three phases or states—sold, liquid, or gas—depending on their temperature. Water provides the example we are most familiar with:

- When freezing or melting, water changes phase from liquid to solid or vice-versa. During this phase change, energy is removed or added to the water without a temperature change. The amount of energy removed or added is its *latent heat of fusion.*
- When condensing or evaporating, water changes phase from gas to liquid or vice-versa. During this phase change, energy is also removed or added without a change in temperature. The amount of this energy is water's *latent heat of vaporization.*

Chemical energy is the energy of interatomic and intermolecular bonds released during chemical reactions. Combustion, a chemical reaction, releases internal energy in the form of heat.

Three Laws of Thermodynamics

The three principles, or laws, of thermodynamics are simple and readily understood.

First Law

We have already seen that a substance (or a system of substances) can possess three types of energy: potential, kinetic, and internal. The First Law says that, while energy can change from one form to another, it can be neither created nor destroyed. The First Law is also called the Law of Energy Conservation. That is not to say, however, that energy cannot be added to or removed from a system.

Second Law

The Second Law says that, while energy can be neither created nor destroyed (First Law), the quality (ability to perform work) of the energy in a system naturally deteriorates over time.

A spring-driven clock provides a good example. When wound, the clock spring possesses potential energy. As the clock runs, the spring unwinds, converting potential energy to kinetic energy. And while the gears turn, friction converts their kinetic energy into internal (heat) energy.

High-quality energy is said to have low entropy (disorder), while lower-quality energy has higher entropy. For this reason, the Second Law is also known as the Law of Increased Entropy.

Third Law

The Third Law has little application in the non-scientific world. It states that the entropy, or disorder, of a system approaches zero as its temperature approaches Absolute Zero (-273.15°C or -459.7°F). Another definition of Absolute Zero is the temperature (a measure of the concentration of internal energy of motion) at which all motion (and therefore all kinetic energy) ceases.

Temperature

Temperature

As we have seen, absolute zero is the temperature at which atoms and molecules have zero internal energy of motion. At any temperature above absolute zero, the atoms and molecules, of which all things consist, are pushing, pulling, bumping, gyrating, and vibrating. What we call "temperature" is a measure of the intensity of this agitation. Just as couples doing the jitterbug require more space than couples doing a slow dance, the more molecules are agitated, the more space they occupy. That expansion with temperature is the basis for most thermometers.

The two common temperature scales, Celsius (also called Centigrade) and Fahrenheit, are defined by the two points at which water changes phase: first at the melting point (0°C and 32°F), when solid water (ice) turns into liquid water, then at the boiling point (100°C and 212°F), when liquid water turns into gaseous water (water vapor).

The difference in energy content between the melting and boiling points of water is arbitrarily divided into 100 Celsius degrees and 180 Fahrenheit degrees. Fahrenheit and Celsius temperatures are related by the following formulae:

$$°F = 32° + (1.8 × °C)$$

$$°C = 0.556 × (°F - 32°)$$

Alternatively, you can use either the table or the chart below.

Equivalent Temperatures

°F	°C		°C	°F
-459.7	-273.15	Absolute Zero	-273.15	-459.7
-20	-29		-30	-22
0	-18		-20	-4
10	-12		-15	5
20	-7		-10	14
32	0	Water Freezes	0	32
50	10		10	50
68	20	Room Temperature	20	68
100	38		40	104
212	100	Water Boils	100	212

Fahrenheit—Celsius Conversion

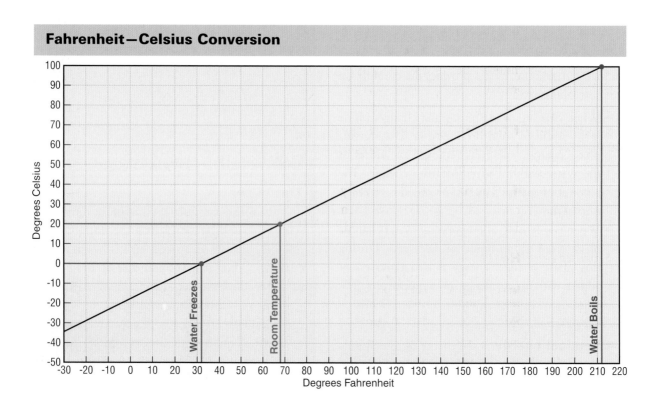

Specific and Latent Heats

Specific Heat

Specific heat, in its full definition, is the ratio of the amount of heat required to raise the temperature of a unit mass of a substance by one unit of temperature to the amount of heat required to raise the temperature of a unit mass of water by the same amount.

Since the specific heat of water is 1.00 in both systems, the definition becomes: the number of calories required to raise the temperature of 1 gram of a substance by 1°C, or the number of Btus required to raise the temperature of 1 pound of a substance by 1°F. The table below lists specific heats of a few common substances.

A Few Specific Heats

Substance	Metric cal/g/°C	English Btu/lb./°F
Water	1.00	1.00
Lead	0.03	0.03
Glass	0.20	0.20
Wood	0.40	0.40

Latent Heat

Latent heat is defined as the amount of heat absorbed or released by a unit mass of a substance changing its state. In metric, latent heats are expressed in cal/g; in English they are expressed as Btu/lb. The two latent heats are:

Latent heat of fusion—the quantity of heat absorbed or released by a unit mass when changing from solid to liquid or liquid to solid.

Latent heat of vaporization—the quantity of heat absorbed or released by a unit mass when changing from liquid to vapor (gas) or vapor to liquid.

A Few Latent Heats

Substance	Fusion Metric cal/g	Fusion English Btu/lb.	Vaporization Metric cal/g	Vaporization English Btu/lb.
Water	79.7	144	539	970
Steel	69.1	124	1520	2736
Lead	5.9	10.6	208	374

Three States or Phases of Water

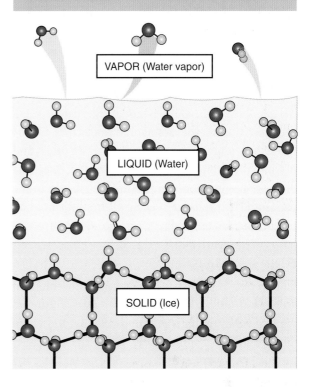

VAPOR (Water vapor)

LIQUID (Water)

SOLID (Ice)

Heating Water from 0°F to 250°F

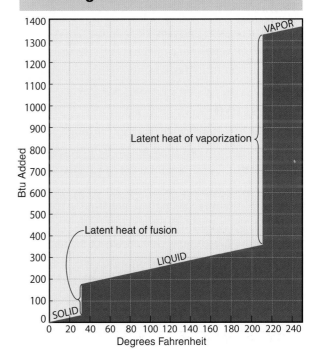

Heat Transfer

All heat flow mechanisms—conduction, convection, and radiation—obey the hot-to-cold principle.

Conduction

Conduction is the transfer of heat through solid materials. A cooking pan handle provides a familiar example. The handle is not in the flame, yet it becomes warm. The atoms and molecules of the metal pan and handle are jostling each other and passing their internal energy down the line. The intensity of vibration (temperature) is greatest in the pan, so the net transfer of energy is from the hot pan toward the cooler handle.

Conduction

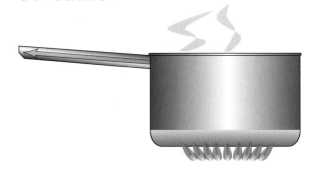

Convection

Convection is the mass (not internal) movement of atoms and molecules in a liquid or a gas. Examples include wind, updrafts in thunderclouds, and warm air rising from a wood stove. When the molecules move from a warmer area to a cooler area, there is a net transfer of heat in the direction of the motion.

The middle illustration shows a wood stove in a room in winter. Room air contacts the stove, is heated, and expands. Air in contact with the cold window gives up heat, contracts, and falls like a lead balloon to the floor. The movement of air (convection) results in a net transfer of heat from the hot stove to the cold window.

Convection

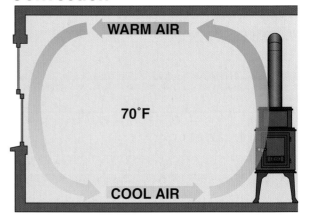

Radiation

Radiation is transfer of energy through space. Sunlight and heat felt from a fire are both examples of radiation. While not intuitive, all matter in the universe continually both emits and receives radiation. The intensity of emitted radiation is proportional to the emitting object's surface temperature raised to the fourth power, so an object having twice the surface temperature of another emits sixteen times as much radiation. The woodstove in the illustration is warmer than the surrounding room surfaces, so there is a net transfer of heat by radiation from the hot stove to the cooler room.

Radiation

Unit Conversions

English to Metric

Multiply	By	To Get
ENERGY		
Btus	1,055	Joules
Btus	252	calories
Btus	0.252	kilocalories
Btus	0.252	Calories (food)
Btus	0.293	Wh
Btus	0.000293	kWh
calories	3.97×10^{-3}	Btus
kilocalories	3.97	Btus
Calories (food)	3.97	Btus
Watt-hours (Wh)	3.412	Btus
kWh	3,412	Btus
MASS		
grains	0.0648	grams
ounces	28.35	grams
pounds mass (lbm[1])	453.6	grams
pounds mass (lbm[1])	0.4536	kilograms[2]
tons, short US	907.2	kilograms[2]
tons, short US	0.9072	metric tons
LENGTH		
inches	2.54	centimeters
feet	30.48	centimeters
yards	0.914	meters
miles	1.609	kilometers
AREA		
square inches	6.452	square centimeters
square feet	0.0929	square meters
square miles	6.4516	square kilometers
VOLUME		
cubic inches	16.387	cubic centimeters
cubic feet	0.0283	cubic meters
cubic yards	0.7646	cubic meters
gallons, US liquid	3.785	liters
gallons, US liquid	0.8327	gallons, imperial

Metric to English

Multiply	By	To Get
ENERGY		
Joules	9.48×10^{-4}	Btus
calories	3.97×10^{-3}	Btus
kilocalories	3.97	Btus
Calories (food)	3.97	Btus
Watt-hours (Wh)	3.412	Btus
kWh	3,412	Btus
Btus	252	calories
Btus	0.252	kilocalories
Btus	0.252	Calories (food)
Btus	0.293	Watt-hours (Wh)
Btus	2.93×10^{-4}	kWh
MASS		
grams	15.43	grains
grams	0.0353	ounces
grams	2.2×10^{-3}	pounds mass (lbm[1])
kilograms[2]	2.205	pounds mass (lbm[1])
kilograms[2]	1.102×10^{-3}	ton, short US
metric tons	1.102	ton, short US
LENGTH		
centimeters	0.3937	inches
centimeters	0.0328	feet
meters	1.094	yards
kilometers	0.6214	miles
AREA		
square centimeters	0.1550	square inches
square meters	10.764	square feet
square kilometers	0.3861	square miles
VOLUME		
cubic centimeters	0.0610	cubic inches
cubic meters	35.315	cubic feet
cubic meters	1.308	cubic yards
liters	0.2642	gallons, US liquid
liters	8.39×10^{-3}	barrel, US liquid

[1] The English unit of mass is pounds mass, lbm. Weight is mass x gravity, and the English unit of weight is the pound, lb.

[2] The Metric unit of mass is kilograms, kg. Weight is mass x gravity, and the English unit of weight is the Newton, N.

How Big Is a Btu?

Wooden match
1 Btu

16-oz. cola
770 Btu

Glazed donut
715 Btu

1-lb. lump of coal
10,000 Btu

Gallon of heating oil
138,690 Btu

Bag of wood pellets
320,000 Btu

Barrel of oil
5,800,000 Btu

Cord of hardwood
24,000,000 Btu

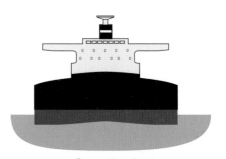

Super oil tanker
11,600,000,000,000 Btu

How Many Btus per Hour?

Sleeping
290 Btu/hour

Walking
830 Btu/hour

Running
2,400 Btu/hour

Candle
430 Btu/hour

100-Watt bulb
340 Btu/hour

900-Watt Toaster
3,070 Btu/hour

Wood Stove
10,000 – 50,000 Btu/hour

20 mpg automobile @ 60 mph
336,000 Btu/hour

Energy Fuels

2

Where are *fuel prices* headed? If you believe fuel and heating equipment manufacturers and dealers, we will soon run out of every fuel but theirs. Even if we don't run out, they would have you believe fuel prices are rising exponentially. We present graphs of the prices of the major fuels—natural gas, propane, oil, electricity, and wood—from 1976 to 2013. As the saying goes, "The best predictor of the future is the past."

The price you pay for fuel is not the whole story, however. *Heating equipment efficiency* is the percentage of fuel energy content that ends up heating your home rather than escaping up the chimney. We offer a table of average equipment efficiencies, including those of older equipment, to help you to decide if you need to replace your existing system.

Gallons, cu. ft., ccf, therms, kWh, cords, face cords, lb., tons—fuel is sold in a bewildering array of units. To compare prices we need to know the *energy content of fuels*. A comprehensive table on p. 17 shows the number of Btus in the customary selling unit for each fuel.

Of course, the bottom line in comparing fuels and heating systems is the cost per Btu delivered into the home. We demonstrate the simple formula for *calculating cost per MBti* (million Btus).

For those lacking a calculator, we offer a *graphical cost per MBtu*.

Fuel Prices

In selecting the most economical fuel with which to heat a home, four issues must be addressed:
- current price per unit of fuel
- likely fuel price escalation
- energy content per unit of fuel
- conversion efficiency from fuel to heat.

The graphs on the facing page address the first two issues; pp. 14–15 aid in answering the last two. First, however, a look at the five primary residential heating fuels: natural gas, electricity, #2 fuel oil (heating oil), propane, and wood.

Natural Gas (50%) is a naturally occurring gas mixture found in association with petroleum and coal. The practice of *fracking* (hydraulic fracturing of underground rocks) promises to release vast amounts of gas not previously recoverable. With increased supply, prices are expected to remain relatively low and stable well into the future. Natural gas is available wherever utility gas lines exist, primarily in metropolitan areas. Elsewhere, natural gas may be available as compressed natural gas (CNG), which is similar to propane.

Electricity (35%) is price-regulated by public utility commissions. Because rate changes require lengthy hearings, and because electric utilities purchase fuel to generate electricity in long-term contracts, the price per kWh remains remarkably steady. And because electricity can be generated in so many ways and with so many different fuels, the real price (price adjusted for inflation) has actually decreased over the past 30 years. Unique among fuels, when powering a heat pump the effective price of electricity can be half or less than its nominal price.

#2 Fuel Oil (6%) is the primary heating fuel in the Northeast but is rarely used elsewhere. With the rapidly increasing cost of drilling new wells and demand from developing countries, the price of oil is expected to rise more rapidly than that of other fuels.

Propane (5%) is a byproduct of the refining of oil and the processing of natural gas. It exists as a gas at atmospheric pressure but is easily compressed at low pressure for storage and transport. An odor is added

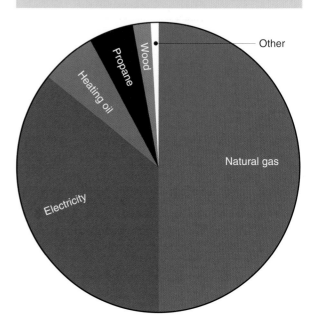

Primary Residential Heating Fuels

to the gas as a safety factor in case of a leak. Because it is a byproduct of oil and natural gas, it tends to track those more common fuels in price. With the development of new natural gas supplies by fracking, propane should remain a reliable and economical heating fuel. Note, however, that pricing is often tiered by amount consumed. Check with your propane dealer.

Wood (2%) was the only fuel available to the Colonists. In fact, due to the vast amounts burned in New England, the percentage of cleared land was once twice what it is today. With availability of coal and oil, wood burning was relegated to heavily wooded rural areas. Recently, with the development of higher-efficiency woodburning stoves, furnaces, and boilers, and particularly the availability of wood pellets, woodburning is seeing a resurgence. As you can see from the table on p. 17, the fuel content of wood species varies enormously. Further complicating the calculation of heating cost is the great difference in heating efficiency between green (unseasoned) and dry wood. For this reason, we have included only wood pellets (2% moisture content) in the fuel price graphs.

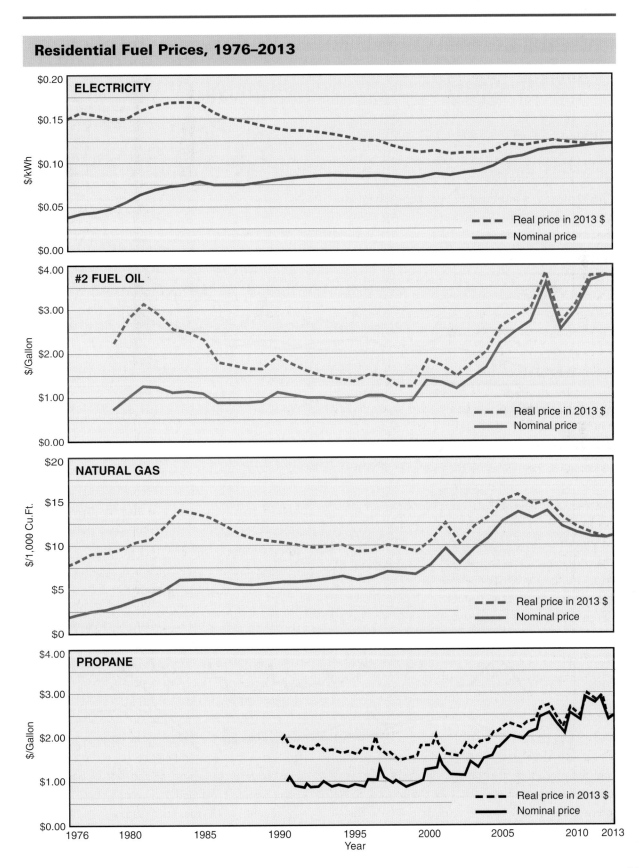

Nominal Energy Prices per MBtu, 1976–2013

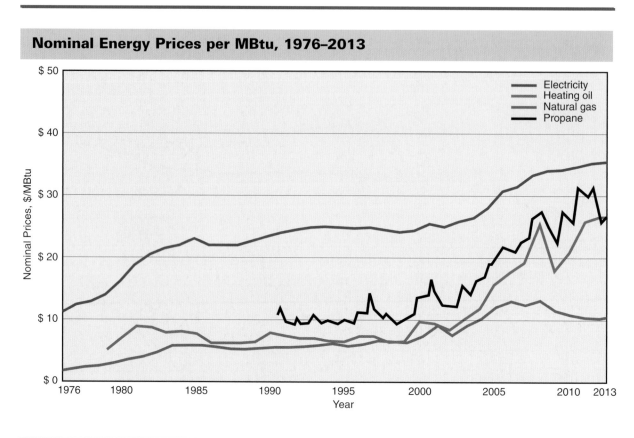

Real (Inflation-Adjusted) Energy Prices per MBtu, 1976–2013

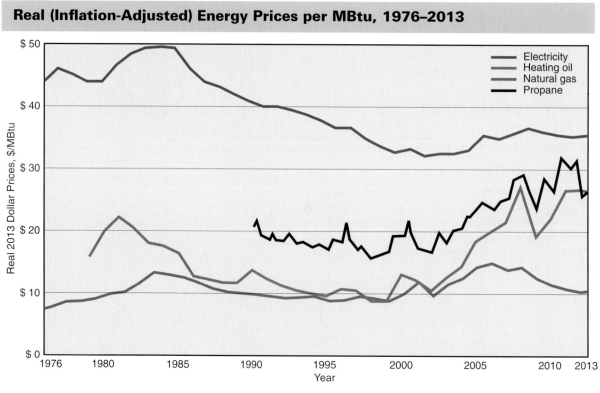

Nominal Delivered Energy Prices per MBtu, 1976–2013

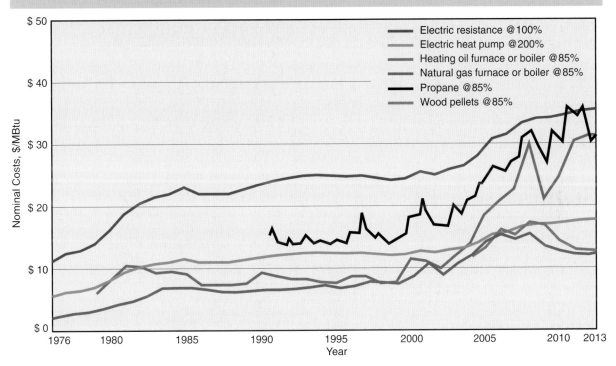

Real (Inflation-Adjusted) Delivered Energy Prices per MBtu, 1976–2013

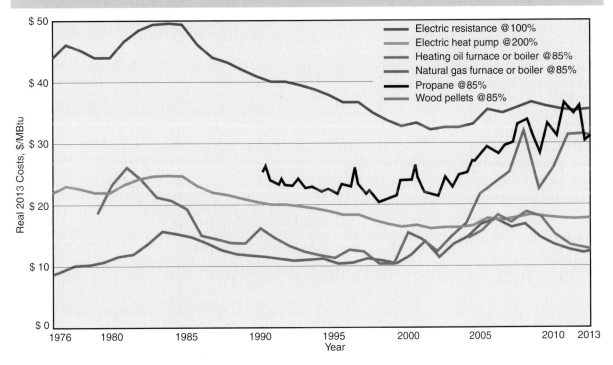

Heating Equipment Efficiencies

Boilers generate hot water, which is piped through finned convectors to heat the house. Many boilers also contain tankless coils (heat exchangers) for supplying domestic hot water. Many factors conspire to decrease a boiler's annual fuel utilization efficiency, AFUE:

1. Burner firing rates and aquastat temperatures are often purposely set too high by service technicians fearing calls at night from cold customers.

2. Even when set to just meet demand on the coldest night, the firing rate and temperatures are necessarily too high for the rest of the heating season.

3. Tankless water heaters demand hot boilers all summer, even when no space heating is required.

Furnaces don't contain tankless water heating coils, but they suffer from the same overfiring problems as boilers. In addition, uninsulated and leaky ducts waste up to 25% of their heat.

Electric baseboards and electric furnaces require no venting because they generate no combustion gases. As a result, their steady efficiency and AFUE are both 100%. Seasonal efficiencies of heat pumps, however, depend on the temperature of outdoor air (air-source heat pumps) or the temperature of the earth (geothermal heat pumps). Both of these vary with location, so it is difficult to assign seasonal efficiencies. The values in the table at right are nominal values. Better estimates can be given by local equipment dealers and installers.

Wood heating efficiency depends not only on the design of the stove or appliance but also on the species of fuel wood (see the table on facing page), moisture content, and knowledge of the operator. The values listed in the table assume the fuel to be seasoned (maximum moisture content of 20%), mixed hardwood burned at a fast rate without smoke.

Wood Pellets eliminate most of the uncertainty in seasonal efficiency. The pellets are engineered to have a uniform energy content of 8,000 Btu/lb. and a moisture content of only 2%. In addition, the pellets are burned in an ideal geometry with optimum air flow. Labeled AFUEs are, therefore, quite accurate.

Heating Equipment AFUEs

Fuel type	AFUE
Oil boiler	
Pre-1980	65%
Average new	83%
Energy Star® min.	85%
Oil furnace	
1960–69	65%
1970–74	72%
1975–83	75%
1984–2013	80%
Energy Star min.	85%
Propane or natural gas boiler	
Pre-1980	70%
Non-condensing new	79%
Energy Star min.	85%
Propane or natural gas furnace	
1960–69	60%
1970–74	65%
1975–87	68%
1988–2013	78%
Energy Star min.	85%
Electricity	
Baseboard or central	100%
Heat pump, avg. new	225%
Heat pump, Energy Star min.	250%
Wood, cord	
Box stove	40%–50%
Air-tight stove	60%–75%
Catalytic stove	70%–80%
Max. efficiency stove	90%
Conventional fireplace	10%
Rumford fireplace	20%
Russian fireplace	90%
Wood boiler, avg. efficiency	45%
Wood boiler, max. efficiency	60%
Wood pellets	
Pellet stove, min. efficiency	78%
Pellet stove, max. efficiency	85%

Energy Content of Fuels

Fuel is sold in a bewildering array of units. To compare the heating values of fuels we need to know their energy content in Btus. The table below lists the number of unburned Btus in the most common retail unit for each fuel. These quantities can be plugged into the formula on p. 18 to calculate the cost in dollars per million Btu (MBtu).

Firewood, due to its extreme variability, requires a separate table, at right. In the table, species are divided into two groups: hardwoods (deciduous) and softwoods (evergreen). Within groups, they are listed in order of heat content per cord.

Although softwoods are listed, they are generally avoided for serious heating for two reasons:

1. Their low energy density and rapid combustion result in too rapid a burn.

2. They contain a high percentage of resin (pitch), which results in smoke and dangerous creosote.

Firewood is most often sold by the cord, a stack measuring 4 ft. × 4 ft. × 8 ft., or 128 cu. ft. Beware of "face cords," which measure 4 ft. × 8 ft. × ? ft.

The table specifies "dry cord." The moisture content of wood is the weight of water contained as a percentage of the weight of oven-dry wood. "Dry" wood contains no more than 20% moisture. Vaporizing the water in firewood lowers its combustion temperatures and reduces the amount of heat produced.

Energy Content of Fuels

Fuel		Btu per	Unit
Oil	#1 (kerosene)	134,000	gal.
	#2 (residential)	139,000	gal.
Gas	Natural	103,000	ccf
	Propane	91,600	gal.
Electricity		3,412	kWh
Wood	Firewood–see table at right		
	Pellets	8,000	lb.

Energy Content of Firewoods

Species	Dry Cord Weight, lb.	Heat Content MBtu/Cord
HARDWOODS		
Eucalyptus	4,560	34.5
Shagbark Hickory	4,327	27.7
Eastern Hornbeam	4,016	27.1
Black Locust	3,890	26.8
Bitternut Hickory	3,832	26.5
Honey Locust	4,100	26.5
Apple	3,712	25.8
Beech	3,757	24.0
Red Oak	3,757	24.0
Sugar Maple	3,757	24.0
White Oak	3,757	24.0
White Ash	3,689	23.6
Yellow Birch	3,150	21.8
Grey Birch	3,179	20.3
White Birch	3,192	20.2
Black Walnut	3,120	20.0
Cherry	3,120	20.0
Sycamore	2,992	19.1
Red Maple	2,900	18.1
Quaking Aspen	2,400	18.0
Aspen	2,295	14.7
Butternut	2,100	14.5
Willow	2,236	14.3
SOFTWOODS		
Western Larch (Tamarack)	3,221	28.7
Douglas Fir	3,075	26.5
Ponderosa Pine	2,520	21.7
Eastern Larch (Tamarack)	3,247	20.8
Western Red Cedar	2,000	17.4
Norway Pine	2,669	17.1
Hemlock	2,482	15.9
Spruce	2,482	15.9
Eastern White Pine	2,236	14.3
Balsam Fir	2,236	14.3
Eastern White Cedar	1,913	12.2

Calculating Cost per MBtu

The only way to compare heating costs is on an apples-to-apples basis, in this case cost-per-million Btus of delivered heat:

$$\text{Cost per MBtu} = \frac{10^8 \times P}{F \times AFUE}$$

where:

P = price of one unit of fuel, $
F = Btu content of the same unit of fuel
AFUE = annual fuel utilization efficiency, %

The tables on p. 17 list the Btu contents of fuels in their usual unit quantities. Typical AFUEs for heating systems also are listed in a table on p. 16, as well as discussed in Chapter 4. Note that all new heating equipment is required by the US Department of Energy (DOE) to display a label listing its tested AFUE.

Sample Calculations

Example 1: What is the cost of electric resistance heating, in $/MBtu, at $0.12/kWh? In the formula, P = $0.12/kWh, F = 3,412 Btu/kWh, and AFUE = 100%.

$$\text{Cost per MBtu} = \frac{10^8 \times 0.12}{3,412 \times 100} = \$35.17$$

Example 2: What is the cost of heating, in $/MBtu, with a pre-1970 oil boiler at an oil price of $3.89/gal.? In the formula, P = $3.89/gal. and F = 139,000 Btu/gal. From the table on p. 16, AFUE is assumed to be 65%.

$$\text{Cost per MBtu} = \frac{10^8 \times 3.89}{139,000 \times 65} = \$43.05$$

Example 3: What is the cost of heating, in $/MBtu, with an air-source heat pump of HSPF 8.2 at an electric rate of $0.15/kWh? In the formula, P = $0.15/kWh and F = 3,412 Btu/kWh. AFUE is 100 × HSPF/3.4 = 251%.

$$\text{Cost per MBtu} = \frac{10^8 \times 0.15}{3,412 \times 241} = \$18.24$$

Increasing AFUE Alone

The cost-per-million Btu formula can also be used to calculate the savings realized from increasing just the heating-system efficiency. Provided the type of fuel remains the same, however, the table on the facing page is more convenient because it shows the projected reduction in annual heating bill as a percentage of the existing bill.

Example 1: Your present natural gas heating bill is $2,000 per year. What savings would be realized by installing a new gas furnace if the AFUE is increased from 65% to 80%? From the table, the annual savings would be 18.8% of $2,000, or $376.

Example 2: How long would it take for a flame retention head burner to pay back its cost if the burner increases the estimated AFUE of a boiler from 60% to 75%? The present fuel bill is $2,400 per year, and the new burner costs $600. From the table, the annual savings would be 20% of $2,400, or $480. The $600 cost would be paid back in $600/$480 = 1.25 years. This is equivalent to receiving 80% interest on your $600 investment.

Example 3: How long would it take for an $8,500 Energy Star-rated air-source heat pump to pay for itself if replacing electric baseboard heat, where the present heating bill is $3,200 per year? Consulting the table on p. 16, we see the present AFUE (Electricity, baseboard) is 100% and the proposed AFUE (Electricity, heat pump, Energy Star min.) is 250%. From the table on the facing page, we find that the annual savings are 60% × $3,200 = $1,920. The payback will occur in about $8,500/$1,920 = 4.4 years.

Percentage Fuel Savings from Increased Efficiency

From AFUE, %	60	65	70	75	80	85	to AFUE, % 90	95	100	150	200	250	300
50	16.7	23.1	28.6	33.3	37.5	41.2	44.4	47.4	50.0	66.7	75.0	80.0	83.3
55	8.3	15.4	21.4	26.7	31.3	35.3	38.9	42.1	45.0	63.3	72.5	78.0	81.7z
60	0.0	7.7	14.3	20.0	25.0	29.4	33.3	36.8	40.0	60.0	70.0	76.0	80.0
65	—	0.0	7.1	13.3	18.8	23.5	27.8	31.6	35.0	56.7	67.5	74.0	78.3
70	—	—	0.0	6.7	12.5	17.6	22.2	26.3	30.0	53.3	65.0	72.0	76.7
75	—	—	—	0.0	6.3	11.8	16.7	21.1	25.0	50.0	62.5	70.0	75.0
80	—	—	—	—	0.0	5.9	11.1	15.8	20.0	46.7	60.0	68.0	73.3
85	—	—	—	—	—	0.0	5.6	10.5	15.0	43.3	57.5	66.0	71.7
90	—	—	—	—	—	—	0.0	5.3	10.0	40.0	55.0	64.0	70.0
95	—	—	—	—	—	—	—	0.0	5.0	36.7	52.5	62.0	68.3
100	—	—	—	—	—	—	—	—	0.0	33.3	50.0	60.0	66.7
150	—	—	—	—	—	—	—	—	—	0.0	25.0	40.0	50.0
200	—	—	—	—	—	—	—	—	—	—	0.0	20.0	33.3
250	—	—	—	—	—	—	—	—	—	—	—	0.0	16.7
300	—	—	—	—	—	—	—	—	—	—	—	—	0.0

Percentage Fuel Savings from Increased Efficiency

From AFUE, %	60	65	70	75	80	85	to AFUE, % 90	95	100	150	200	250	300
50	16.7	23.1	28.6	33.3	37.5	41.2	44.4	47.4	50.0	66.7	75.0	80.0	83.3
55	8.3	15.4	21.4	26.7	31.3	35.3	38.9	42.1	45.0	63.3	72.5	78.0	81.7z
60	0.0	7.7	14.3	**20.0**	25.0	29.4	33.3	36.8	40.0	60.0	70.0	76.0	80.0
65	—	0.0	7.1	13.3	**18.8**	23.5	27.8	31.6	35.0	56.7	67.5	74.0	78.3
70	—	—	0.0	6.7	12.5	17.6	22.2	26.3	30.0	53.3	65.0	72.0	76.7
75	—	—	—	0.0	6.3	11.8	16.7	21.1	25.0	50.0	62.5	70.0	75.0
80	—	—	—	—	0.0	5.9	11.1	15.8	20.0	46.7	60.0	68.0	73.3
85	—	—	—	—	—	0.0	5.6	10.5	15.0	43.3	57.5	66.0	71.7
90	—	—	—	—	—	—	0.0	5.3	10.0	40.0	55.0	64.0	70.0
95	—	—	—	—	—	—	—	0.0	5.0	36.7	52.5	62.0	68.3
100	—	—	—	—	—	—	—	—	0.0	33.3	50.0	**60.0**	66.7
150	—	—	—	—	—	—	—	—	—	0.0	25.0	40.0	50.0
200	—	—	—	—	—	—	—	—	—	—	0.0	20.0	33.3
250	—	—	—	—	—	—	—	—	—	—	—	0.0	16.7
300	—	—	—	—	—	—	—	—	—	—	—	—	0.0

Graphical Cost per MBtu

The graphs on these two pages offer an alternative to calculating the cost/MBtu equation. Three examples will illustrate the method.

Example 1: I have an ancient (about 1965) oil furnace, and the last time I filled the tank I paid $3.89/gal. Considering the efficiency of my old furnace, what am I actually paying per MBtu for my heat?

Solution: According to the equipment efficiency table on p. 16, the 1965 furnace AFUE is about 65%. From $3.89 on the green oil price scale on the bottom, draw a vertical line to the point representing AFUE 65%. From that point draw a horizontal line across to the vertical Cost/MBtu scale. Answer: $43/MBtu.

Example 2: For the same furnace as Example 1, I am considering installing an inexpensive pellet stove. What would be the most I could pay for pellets and still save on my heating bill?

Solution: According to the equipment efficiency table on p. 16, the AFUE of an inexpensive pellet stove is probably about 78%. Using the graph from Example 1, extend the horizontal line representing the price of $43/MBtu to the right to the point representing AFUE 78%. From that point drop a vertical line to the brown pellet price scale. Answer: $530/ton.

Example 3: My natural gas furnace was installed in 1982. I now pay $1.20/ccf for gas, and my annual heating bill is $1,200. Would it pay to replace the furnace with an Energy Star-rated heat pump if my electric rate is $0.12/kWh?

Solution: According to the equipment efficiency table on p. 16, the AFUE of a 1982 gas furnace is about 68%. From $12 on the natural gas scale on the bottom, draw a vertical line to the point representing AFUE 68%. From that point, draw a horizontal line to the vertical scale at left. Answer: $17/MBtu. From the equipment efficiency table again, we get AFUE 250% for an Energy Star heat pump, so draw a vertical line from $0.12/kWh to the AFUE 250% line. From that intersection, draw a horizontal line to find about $14/MBtu. Expressed as a percentage, the savings would be ($17 - $14)/$17 = 17.6%. Annual savings would thus be 0.176 × $1,200 = $211.

Graphical Example 1

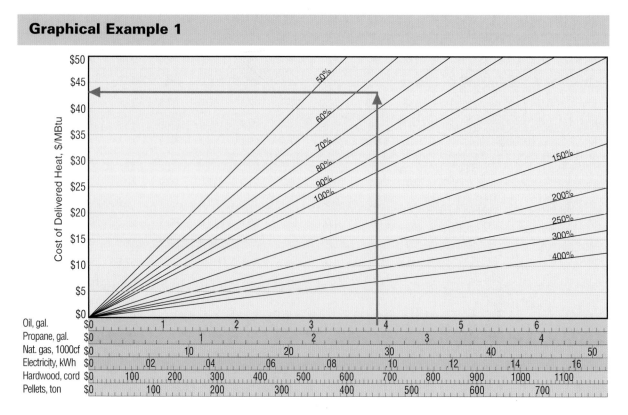

Graphical Example 2

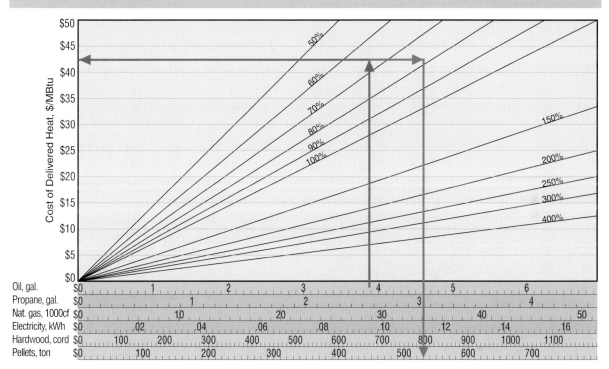

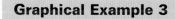

Graphical Example 3

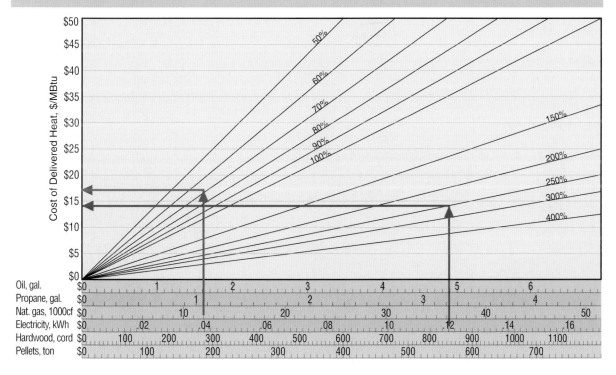

Climate

3

Unless you live in Hawaii or San Diego, more than half of your annual energy budget probably goes to heating and/or cooling your home. Heating consists of supplying Btus of heat energy to keep interior temperatures above too-low outdoor temperatures. Cooling consists of the opposite: removing Btus of heat energy to keep your home cooler than too-warm outdoor temperatures. Climate thus directly impacts our energy bills. This chapter contains climate data, which, in addition to helping you choose a more amenable neighborhood, will enable you to calculate heating and cooling loads and create an even more amenable microclimate.

We begin with *heating degree days*, useful in predicting heating costs and in selecting appropriate levels of insulation. Next are *cooling degree days*, used analogously for cooling. *Design temperatures*, the highest and lowest expected temperatures in a location, are used to size heating and cooling equipment. *Relative humidities*, either too low or too high, can add to your annual energy bill due to the need to either humidify or dehumidify your home. *Precipitation*, in the form of rain and snow, is more a nuisance than an energy factor, but we include it because it so affects our moods.

Solar radiation is perhaps the single most important climate factor. It affects not only our heating and cooling bills but also our moods. Winter heat gain is determined by *solar radiation received on windows*. Solar water heaters and photovoltaic panels depend on *radiation on south-facing surfaces*.

Do you love the four seasons, or would you rather have endless summer? The *first and last frost dates* determine where in the spectrum your site lies.

Birds know it; the animals of the forest know it: We show you how to take advantage of *trees for shade and shelter*. And *shelterbelt design* shows how to control the wind for advantage in both winter and summer.

Finally, you may be surprised at the power of common topographic features in creating locally enhanced *microclimates*.

Heating Degree Days

Heating Degree Days, Base 65°F

State, City	July	Aug	Sep	Oct	Nov	Dec	Jan	Feb	Mar	Apr	May	Jun	Ann
Alabama, Birmingham	0	0	1	133	359	590	691	514	339	154	31	1	2823
Alaska, Fairbanks	121	283	615	1287	1882	2199	2315	1926	1670	999	504	179	13980
Alaska, Juneau	257	288	453	704	953	1125	1219	1010	973	728	529	335	8574
Arizona, Flagstaff	33	56	224	554	850	1085	1099	930	880	668	446	174	6999
Arizona, Phoenix	0	0	0	14	121	304	290	169	100	28	1	0	1027
Arkansas, Little Rock	0	0	13	124	400	666	775	563	369	150	24	0	3084
California, Los Angeles	1	0	2	21	121	234	252	205	200	141	78	19	1274
Colorado, Denver	1	9	136	436	826	1078	1111	892	788	524	267	60	6128
Colorado, Colorado Springs	19	20	172	483	848	1100	1130	917	827	576	312	76	6480
Connecticut, Hartford	3	12	120	413	697	1054	1218	1024	844	486	195	38	6104
Delaware, Wilmington	1	2	49	297	564	872	1029	864	687	376	132	15	4888
DC, Washington	0	7	19	205	477	775	917	742	563	272	73	5	4055
Florida, Miami	0	0	0	0	4	38	52	39	15	1	0	0	149
Florida, Orlando	0	0	0	2	40	142	202	128	57	9	0	0	580
Georgia, Atlanta	0	0	11	126	352	600	692	523	346	150	26	1	2827
Idaho, Boise	12	15	110	398	768	1083	1095	807	672	451	245	71	5727
Illinois, Chicago	6	9	112	401	759	1151	1333	1075	858	513	232	49	6498
Indiana, Indianapolis	2	4	77	335	659	1020	1192	957	724	394	141	16	5521
Iowa, Des Moines	1	6	103	386	804	1227	1385	1090	826	439	153	16	6436
Kansas, Topeka	1	1	73	287	665	1030	1174	898	647	336	106	7	5225
Kentucky, Louisville	0	1	36	240	527	838	992	779	569	280	84	6	4352
Louisiana, Baton Rouge	0	0	2	49	212	397	457	326	185	57	4	0	1689
Maine, Caribou	58	103	344	691	1039	1505	1719	1466	1254	805	417	159	9560
Maine, Portland	19	37	199	523	790	1152	1346	1141	985	649	361	116	7318
Maryland, Baltimore	0	1	42	296	570	862	1000	816	648	349	120	16	4720
Massachusetts, Boston	4	8	84	344	604	932	1104	951	815	503	233	48	5630
Massachusetts, Worcester	9	20	158	478	764	1119	1284	1094	952	601	278	74	6831
Michigan, Detroit	5	12	121	426	742	1099	1270	1074	886	527	219	41	6422
Michigan, Sault Ste. Marie	91	107	320	642	979	1383	1606	1399	1253	798	434	212	9224
Minnesota, Duluth	69	106	331	682	1124	1587	1771	1422	1244	787	421	180	9724
Minnesota, Int'l Falls	55	102	360	723	1217	1744	1946	1531	1298	775	378	140	10269
Mississippi, Jackson	0	0	7	102	315	528	611	440	272	115	11	0	2401
Missouri, St. Louis	0	1	46	246	583	949	1097	844	613	294	79	6	4758
Montana, Great Falls	52	73	291	592	967	1247	1327	1065	964	657	410	183	7828
Montana, Missoula	55	62	276	637	985	1287	1291	1019	852	596	384	178	7622
Nebraska, North Platte	6	14	158	481	902	1222	1312	1013	853	519	240	46	6766

State, City	July	Aug	Sep	Oct	Nov	Dec	Jan	Feb	Mar	Apr	May	Jun	Ann
Nevada, Las Vegas	0	0	1	57	318	571	574	375	244	83	16	0	2239
Nevada, Reno	12	22	130	416	732	987	984	756	683	502	285	91	5600
New Hampshire, Concord	22	44	212	548	835	1220	1402	1183	997	623	302	90	7478
New Jersey, Newark	1	6	42	269	543	872	1030	869	697	375	126	13	4843
New Mexico, Albuquerque	0	0	29	248	614	898	914	670	525	294	85	4	4281
New Mexico, Roswell	0	0	18	144	485	755	775	542	378	182	51	2	3332
New York, New York	7	2	43	261	525	844	1009	853	695	372	127	16	4754
New York, Syracuse	10	25	158	460	748	1113	1296	1131	959	579	258	66	6803
North Carolina, Greensboro	0	1	32	232	480	742	851	679	501	245	77	8	3848
North Dakota, Bismarck	19	44	256	625	1112	1539	1711	1329	1109	660	305	93	8802
Ohio, Columbus	3	7	80	347	654	982	1154	940	731	415	152	27	5492
Oklahoma, Tulsa	0	0	29	152	468	782	898	658	437	179	38	1	3642
Oregon, Eugene	45	31	115	370	594	780	769	615	564	443	308	152	4786
Oregon, Salem	39	34	116	376	592	771	765	623	574	452	301	141	4784
Pennsylvania, Philadelphia	1	2	39	269	545	857	1020	858	681	362	113	12	4759
Pennsylvania, Pittsburgh	6	13	105	397	677	996	1163	979	788	462	200	43	5829
Rhode Island, Providence	3	9	101	377	637	961	1125	965	817	494	221	44	5754
South Carolina, Columbia	0	0	8	121	325	552	628	485	321	131	23	0	2594
South Dakota, Rapid City	16	21	190	521	934	1233	1314	1061	925	595	313	88	7211
Tennessee, Nashville	0	0	24	189	460	744	859	664	462	217	56	2	3677
Texas, Austin	0	0	2	32	205	406	475	319	163	44	2	0	1648
Texas, Brownsville	0	0	0	6	69	186	206	125	45	7	0	0	644
Texas, Dallas	0	0	7	62	281	527	605	415	238	75	9	0	2219
Texas, Houston	0	0	1	37	189	367	427	298	156	48	2	0	1525
Utah, Salt Lake City	3	3	89	379	747	1067	1108	857	665	448	215	50	5631
Vermont, Burlington	17	38	203	538	834	1240	1457	1273	1063	642	283	77	7665
Virginia, Norfolk	0	0	8	152	375	631	759	638	488	247	66	4	3368
Virginia, Richmond	0	1	27	225	470	748	873	705	528	254	80	8	3919
Washington, Seattle	52	50	139	362	571	735	729	593	564	423	266	131	4615
West Virginia, Charleston	8	3	62	309	560	837	977	794	604	330	141	19	4644
Wisconsin, Madison	12	33	183	504	892	1298	1490	1203	978	576	261	63	7493
Wyoming, Casper	16	25	233	582	975	1262	1312	1073	921	661	393	118	7571

Cooling Degree Days

Cooling Degree Days, Base 65°F

State, City	Jan	Feb	Mar	Apr	May	Jun	Jul	Aug	Sep	Oct	Nov	Dec	Ann
Alabama, Birmingham	1	3	16	51	167	351	476	455	280	69	9	3	1881
Alaska, Fairbanks	0	0	0	0	0	20	42	11	1	0	0	0	74
Alaska, Juneau	0	0	0	0	0	0	0	0	0	0	0	0	0
Arizona, Flagstaff	0	0	0	0	0	23	64	36	3	0	0	0	126
Arizona, Phoenix	2	15	74	226	478	745	910	859	667	336	51	1	4364
Arkansas, Little Rock	1	1	14	52	188	408	542	502	296	72	8	2	2086
California, Los Angeles	4	6	6	15	19	58	135	175	154	81	22	4	679
Colorado, Colorado Springs	0	0	0	1	5	74	176	116	32	0	0	0	404
Colorado, Denver	0	0	0	2	23	136	261	217	57	0	0	0	696
Connecticut, Hartford	0	0	1	5	38	144	277	220	68	5	1	0	759
Delaware, Wilmington	0	0	2	9	62	215	368	317	135	16	1	0	1125
DC, Washington	0	0	4	21	107	304	456	407	200	28	4	0	1531
Florida, Miami	133	154	236	315	442	510	568	568	517	433	291	194	4361
Florida, Orlando	62	60	129	201	373	485	539	543	484	319	154	79	3428
Georgia, Atlanta	0	1	11	52	170	354	463	430	262	58	8	1	1810
Idaho, Boise	0	0	0	3	31	122	297	275	74	5	0	0	807
Illinois, Chicago	0	0	1	9	48	159	279	233	91	10	0	0	830
Indiana, Indianapolis	0	0	2	10	69	221	331	272	122	14	1	0	1042
Iowa, Des Moines	0	0	1	12	60	219	353	285	110	12	0	0	1052
Kansas, Topeka	0	0	3	22	85	278	419	357	166	26	1	0	1357
Kentucky, Louisville	0	0	6	24	109	287	421	374	189	29	3	1	1443
Louisiana, Baton Rouge	11	15	55	119	298	457	534	523	389	157	48	22	2628
Maine, Caribou	0	0	0	0	7	39	80	56	9	0	0	0	191
Maine, Portland	0	0	0	0	7	51	144	120	24	1	0	0	347
Maryland, Baltimore	0	0	4	11	71	236	372	311	129	13	0	0	1147
Massachusetts, Boston	0	0	1	4	32	139	282	235	76	7	1	0	777
Massachusetts, Worcester	0	0	0	0	7	64	166	122	12	0	0	0	371
Michigan, Detroit	0	0	0	6	42	145	254	208	75	6	0	0	736
Michigan, Sault Ste. Marie	0	0	0	1	6	20	56	50	12	0	0	0	145
Minnesota, Minn.-St. Paul	0	0	0	4	41	146	259	190	56	3	0	0	699
Minnesota, Int'l Falls	0	0	0	1	17	47	91	67	10	0	0	0	233
Mississippi, Jackson	0	8	32	82	228	419	524	505	338	99	25	4	2264
Missouri, St. Louis	0	0	7	32	114	316	461	396	196	36	3	0	1561
Montana, Great Falls	0	0	0	1	7	47	105	107	19	2	0	0	288
Montana, Missoula	0	0	0	0	3	33	111	99	10	0	0	0	256
Nebraska, North Platte	0	0	0	4	22	139	279	234	70	2	0	0	750

State, City	Jan	Feb	Mar	Apr	May	Jun	Jul	Aug	Sep	Oct	Nov	Dec	Ann
Nevada, Las Vegas	0	1	20	98	323	602	796	739	474	157	4	0	3214
Nevada, Reno	0	0	0	0	11	72	204	164	41	1	0	0	493
New Hampshire, Concord	0	0	0	2	18	82	173	133	33	1	0	0	442
New Jersey, Newark	0	0	2	10	70	236	394	347	42	18	1	0	1220
New Mexico, Albuquerque	0	0	0	6	70	297	417	343	148	9	0	0	1290
New Mexico, Roswell	0	0	1	47	194	391	488	431	228	32	2	0	1814
New York, New York	0	0	2	10	63	214	379	331	134	16	2	0	1151
New York, Syracuse	0	0	1	4	29	105	203	158	48	3	0	0	551
North Carolina, Greensboro	0	0	4	25	97	263	398	345	172	24	3	1	1332
North Dakota, Bismarck	0	0	0	2	18	80	180	161	30	0	0	0	471
Ohio, Columbus	0	0	2	9	61	198	305	254	109	12	1	0	951
Oklahoma, Tulsa	0	1	10	50	163	385	568	524	277	64	6	1	2049
Oregon, Eugene	0	0	0	0	5	21	95	88	32	1	0	0	242
Oregon, Salem	0	0	0	0	7	25	95	98	31	1	0	0	257
Pennsylvania, Philadelphia	0	0	2	10	70	234	395	351	152	19	2	0	1235
Pennsylvania, Pittsburgh	0	0	2	8	41	143	244	203	78	6	1	0	726
Rhode Island, Providence	0	0	0	3	25	122	265	223	71	5	0	0	714
South Carolina, Columbia	2	4	20	69	211	390	519	467	296	76	15	5	2074
South Dakota, Rapid City	0	0	0	2	13	86	227	208	59	3	0	0	598
Tennessee, Nashville	0	0	9	37	136	321	453	416	229	46	5	0	1652
Texas, Austin	7	18	59	147	323	495	605	610	439	207	51	13	2974
Texas, Brownsville	54	76	179	287	457	545	601	603	494	332	166	80	3874
Texas, Dallas	3	7	10	72	265	478	621	601	376	118	15	2	2568
Texas, Houston	15	21	63	147	328	485	573	563	412	196	65	25	2893
Utah, Salt Lake City	0	0	0	4	34	183	387	347	105	6	0	0	1066
Vermont, Burlington	0	0	0	3	23	96	192	139	35	1	0	0	489
Virginia, Norfolk	1	2	8	35	119	303	453	400	235	45	10	1	1612
Virginia, Richmond	0	1	8	33	107	277	415	367	187	33	6	1	1435
Washington, Seattle	0	0	0	0	5	19	65	65	19	0	0	0	173
West Virginia, Charleston	0	0	7	25	76	182	300	254	114	17	3	0	978
Wisconsin, Madison	0	0	0	6	33	123	214	154	48	4	0	0	582
Wyoming, Casper	0	0	0	0	3	64	182	152	27	0	0	0	428

Average and Design Temperatures

January Temperatures

State, City	Average, °F	Design, °F	State, City	Average, °F	Design, °F
Alabama, Birmingham	42.6	10	Nebraska, North Platte	23.0	-20
Alabama, Mobile	52.5	10	Nebraska, Omaha	24.9	-10
Alaska, Anchorage	15.8	-8	Nevada, Reno	34.0	-5
Alaska, Juneau	21.6	7	New Hampshire, Concord	22.2	-15
Arizona, Flagstaff	28.5	-10	New Jersey, Atlantic City	33.6	5
Arizona, Phoenix	53.9	25	New Jersey, Newark	31.3	0
Arkansas, Little Rock	42.4	5	New Mexico, Albuquerque	36.6	0
California, Los Angeles	52.1	35	New York, Albany	22.2	-10
Colorado, Grand Junction	26.1	-15	New York, Buffalo	24.5	-5
Colorado, Denver	31.9	-10	New York, New York	33.8	0
Connecticut, New Haven	30.5	0	North Carolina, Asheville	35.8	0
Delaware, Wilmington	33.3	0	North Carolina, Raleigh	41.1	10
DC, Washington	37.2	0	North Dakota, Bismarck	12.2	-30
Florida, Jacksonville	53.1	25	Ohio, Cleveland	28.0	0
Florida, Miami	67.8	35	Ohio, Columbus	28.3	-10
Georgia, Atlanta	43.8	10	Oklahoma, Tulsa	38.9	0
Idaho, Boise	32.7	-10	Oregon, Baker	24.0	-5
Illinois, Chicago	25.0	-10	Oregon, Portland	41.0	10
Indiana, Indianapolis	29.1	-10	Pennsylvania, Philadelphia	32.3	0
Iowa, Davenport	23.0	-15	Pennsylvania, Pittsburgh	29.0	0
Iowa, Sioux City	18.0	-20	Pennsylvania, Scranton	25.7	-5
Kansas, Dodge City	30.1	-10	Rhode Island, Providence	29.9	0
Kansas, Topeka	27.0	-10	South Carolina, Columbia	46.2	10
Kentucky, Louisville	35.2	0	South Dakota, Rapid City	22.0	-20
Louisiana, New Orleans	53.9	20	Tennessee, Memphis	39.9	0
Maine, Portland	23.4	-5	Texas, Amarillo	36.0	-10
Maryland, Baltimore	34.6	0	Texas, Corpus Christi	56.0	20
Massachusetts, Boston	31.3	0	Texas, Dallas	44.1	10
Michigan, Detroit	25.9	-10	Texas, Houston	53.3	20
Michigan, Grand Rapids	22.4	-10	Utah, Salt Lake City	31.0	-10
Minnesota, Duluth	8.4	-25	Vermont, Burlington	19.1	-10
Minnesota, Minneapolis	16.0	-20	Virginia, Richmond	38.5	15
Mississippi, Vicksburg	46.0	10	Washington, Seattle	41.0	15
Missouri, Kansas City	26.9	-10	West Virginia, Charleston	35.1	0
Missouri, St. Louis	32.3	0	Wisconsin, Milwaukee	22.3	-15
Montana, Billings	24.0	-25	Wyoming, Cheyenne	28.2	-15
Montana, Butte	15.0	-20			

July Temperatures

State, City	Average, °F	Design, °F	State, City	Average, °F	Design, °F
Alabama, Birmingham	80.0	95	Nebraska, North Platte	74.0	85
Alabama, Mobile	81.5	95	Nebraska, Omaha	75.3	95
Alaska, Anchorage	59.0	69	Nevada, Reno	66.2	95
Alaska, Juneau	56.0	69	New Hampshire, Concord	67.1	90
Arizona, Flagstaff	72.4	90	New Jersey, Atlantic City	72.2	95
Arizona, Phoenix	89.6	105	New Jersey, Newark	77.0	95
Arkansas, Little Rock	80.5	95	New Mexico, Albuquerque	76.4	95
California, Los Angeles	68.3	90	New York, Albany	73.4	93
Colorado, Grand Junction	79.0	95	New York, Buffalo	71.0	93
Colorado, Denver	70.6	95	New York, New York	74.5	95
Connecticut, New Haven	76.1	95	North Carolina, Asheville	74.2	93
Delaware, Wilmington	74.0	95	North Carolina, Raleigh	76.2	95
DC, Washington	77.0	95	North Dakota, Bismarck	67.8	95
Florida, Jacksonville	83.0	95	Ohio, Cleveland	69.8	95
Florida, Miami	82.0	91	Ohio, Columbus	75.0	95
Georgia, Atlanta	77.5	95	Oklahoma, Oklahoma City	80.0	101
Idaho, Boise	70.8	95	Oregon, Baker	66.0	90
Illinois, Chicago	71.2	95	Oregon, Portland	63.8	90
Indiana, Indianapolis	73.4	95	Pennsylvania, Philadelphia	77.0	95
Iowa, Davenport	75.0	95	Pennsylvania, Pittsburgh	70.2	95
Iowa, Sioux City	75.0	95	Pennsylvania, Scranton	71.8	95
Kansas, Dodge City	80.0	95	Rhode Island, Providence	70.1	93
Kansas, Topeka	79.0	100	South Carolina, Columbia	79.6	95
Kentucky, Louisville	75.9	95	South Dakota, Rapid City	73.0	95
Louisiana, New Orleans	81.3	95	Tennessee, Memphis	82.2	95
Maine, Portland	65.6	90	Texas, Amarillo	78.5	100
Maryland, Baltimore	74.8	95	Texas, Corpus Christi	84.0	95
Massachusetts, Boston	71.1	92	Texas, Dallas	85.0	100
Michigan, Detroit	70.0	95	Texas, Houston	82.1	95
Michigan, Grand Rapids	72.0	95	Utah, Salt Lake City	73.5	95
Minnesota, Duluth	65.9	93	Vermont, Burlington	67.3	90
Minnesota, Minneapolis	70.6	95	Virginia, Richmond	76.0	95
Mississippi, Vicksburg	81.0	95	Washington, Seattle	63.0	85
Missouri, Kansas City	80.0	100	West Virginia, Charleston	73.0	95
Missouri, St. Louis	76.9	95	Wisconsin, Milwaukee	68.2	95
Montana, Billings	72.0	90	Wyoming, Cheyenne	65.9	95
Montana, Butte	62.0	95			

Relative Humidities

January Average Relative Humidities

State, City	Morning, %	Afternoon, %	State, City	Morning, %	Afternoon, %
Alabama, Birmingham	80	64	Nebraska, North Platte	80	66
Alabama, Mobile	83	65	Nebraska, Omaha	75	63
Alaska, Anchorage	75	73	Nevada, Reno	79	50
Alaska, Juneau	78	74	New Hampshire, Concord	76	59
Arizona, Flagstaff	74	50	New Jersey, Atlantic City	79	59
Arizona, Phoenix	64	32	New Jersey, Newark	73	59
Arkansas, Little Rock	80	65	New Mexico, Albuquerque	68	39
California, Los Angeles	71	61	New York, Albany	78	64
Colorado, Grand Junction	78	62	New York, Buffalo	79	73
Colorado, Denver	63	49	New York, New York	68	60
Connecticut, Hartford	72	57	North Carolina, Asheville	85	59
Delaware, Wilmington	76	60	North Carolina, Raleigh	80	55
DC, Washington	71	56	North Dakota, Bismarck	76	71
Florida, Jacksonville	88	58	Ohio, Cleveland	79	70
Florida, Miami	84	60	Ohio, Columbus	78	68
Georgia, Atlanta	81	58	Oklahoma, Tulsa	78	63
Idaho, Boise	80	70	Oregon, Eugene	92	80
Illinois, Chicago	78	70	Oregon, Portland	85	76
Indiana, Indianapolis	81	71	Pennsylvania, Philadelphia	74	60
Iowa, Des Moines	77	70	Pennsylvania, Pittsburgh	77	66
Iowa, Sioux City	78	71	Pennsylvania, Williamsport	77	62
Kansas, Dodge City	76	61	Rhode Island, Providence	72	57
Kansas, Topeka	78	66	South Carolina, Columbia	83	54
Kentucky, Louisville	78	65	South Dakota, Rapid City	69	64
Louisiana, New Orleans	85	68	Tennessee, Memphis	78	65
Maine, Portland	76	61	Texas, Amarillo	71	53
Maryland, Baltimore	73	57	Texas, Corpus Christi	87	70
Massachusetts, Boston	69	58	Texas, Dallas	79	63
Michigan, Detroit	80	70	Texas, Houston	86	68
Michigan, Grand Rapids	82	73	Utah, Salt Lake City	79	69
Minnesota, Duluth	78	72	Vermont, Burlington	73	64
Minnesota, Minneapolis	76	69	Virginia, Richmond	80	57
Mississippi, Jackson	86	68	Washington, Seattle	82	75
Missouri, Kansas City	77	67	West Virginia, Charleston	78	63
Missouri, St. Louis	81	68	Wisconsin, Milwaukee	76	70
Montana, Billings	65	57	Wyoming, Cheyenne	58	51
Montana, Missoula	85	76			

July Average Relative Humidities

State, City	Morning, %	Afternoon, %	State, City	Morning, %	Afternoon, %
Alabama, Birmingham	86	62	Nebraska, North Platte	83	57
Alabama, Mobile	90	66	Nebraska, Omaha	85	63
Alaska, Anchorage	74	63	Nevada, Reno	60	18
Alaska, Juneau	79	67	New Hampshire, Concord	84	51
Arizona, Flagstaff	67	37	New Jersey, Atlantic City	83	57
Arizona, Phoenix	43	20	New Jersey, Newark	72	51
Arkansas, Little Rock	86	58	New Mexico, Albuquerque	59	27
California, Los Angeles	86	69	New York, Albany	81	55
Colorado, Grand Junction	48	22	New York, Buffalo	79	55
Colorado, Denver	68	34	New York, New York	75	55
Connecticut, Hartford	79	51	North Carolina, Asheville	95	65
Delaware, Wilmington	79	54	North Carolina, Raleigh	89	58
DC, Washington	76	53	North Dakota, Bismarck	84	53
Florida, Jacksonville	89	59	Ohio, Cleveland	82	57
Florida, Miami	83	63	Ohio, Columbus	84	56
Georgia, Atlanta	88	59	Oklahoma, Tulsa	81	57
Idaho, Boise	54	21	Oregon, Eugene	87	39
Illinois, Chicago	82	60	Oregon, Portland	82	45
Indiana, Indianapolis	87	60	Pennsylvania, Philadelphia	78	54
Iowa, Des Moines	83	61	Pennsylvania, Pittsburgh	83	54
Iowa, Sioux City	86	63	Pennsylvania, Williamsport	87	55
Kansas, Dodge City	76	50	Rhode Island, Providence	77	56
Kansas, Topeka	85	63	South Carolina, Columbia	88	53
Kentucky, Louisville	85	58	South Dakota, Rapid City	74	41
Louisiana, New Orleans	91	68	Tennessee, Memphis	84	60
Maine, Portland	80	59	Texas, Amarillo	73	46
Maryland, Baltimore	80	53	Texas, Corpus Christi	93	62
Massachusetts, Boston	74	57	Texas, Dallas	79	53
Michigan, Detroit	82	54	Texas, Houston	92	63
Michigan, Grand Rapids	84	56	Utah, Salt Lake City	52	22
Minnesota, Duluth	85	63	Vermont, Burlington	78	53
Minnesota, Minneapolis	81	59	Virginia, Richmond	85	56
Mississippi, Jackson	93	64	Washington, Seattle	82	49
Missouri, Kansas City	85	64	West Virginia, Charleston	90	60
Missouri, St. Louis	83	60	Wisconsin, Milwaukee	82	64
Montana, Billings	64	32	Wyoming, Cheyenne	70	38
Montana, Missoula	78	31			

Precipitation

Rainfall

State, City	Inches/year	Rainy Days	State, City	Inches/year	Rainy Days
Alabama, Birmingham	45.2	127	Nebraska, North Platte	19.7	84
Alabama, Mobile	66.0	122	Nebraska, Omaha	30.3	99
Alaska, Anchorage	15.7	117	Nevada, Reno	7.3	50
Alaska, Juneau	55.2	221	New Hampshire, Concord	38.1	126
Arizona, Flagstaff	18.1	72	New Jersey, Atlantic City	40.3	112
Arizona, Phoenix	7.7	36	New Jersey, Newark	43.5	122
Arkansas, Little Rock	50.5	105	New Mexico, Albuquerque	8.5	61
California, Los Angeles	14.9	35	New York, Albany	34.4	135
Colorado, Grand Junction	8.6	73	New York, Buffalo	38.3	169
Colorado, Denver	15.4	89	New York, New York	44.9	120
Connecticut, Hartford	45.2	127	North Carolina, Asheville	38.1	125
Delaware, Wilmington	42.1	116	North Carolina, Raleigh	41.8	112
DC, Washington	39.3	112	North Dakota, Bismarck	15.8	96
Florida, Jacksonville	53.0	116	Ohio, Cleveland	37.2	156
Florida, Miami	58.5	129	Ohio, Columbus	37.8	137
Georgia, Atlanta	50.3	115	Oklahoma, Tulsa	38.1	90
Idaho, Boise	11.8	90	Oregon, Eugene	47.8	137
Illinois, Chicago	35.3	126	Oregon, Portland	37.5	151
Indiana, Indianapolis	40.2	126	Pennsylvania, Philadelphia	40.9	117
Iowa, Des Moines	32.4	108	Pennsylvania, Pittsburgh	37.0	153
Iowa, Sioux City	27.7	99	Pennsylvania, Williamsport	38.7	141
Kansas, Dodge City	20.6	78	Rhode Island, Providence	45.8	124
Kansas, Topeka	34.6	97	South Carolina, Columbia	48.7	109
Kentucky, Louisville	43.6	125	South Dakota, Rapid City	16.1	96
Louisiana, New Orleans	61.1	114	Tennessee, Memphis	52.3	107
Maine, Portland	44.2	129	Texas, Amarillo	19.9	69
Maryland, Baltimore	40.9	113	Texas, Corpus Christi	30.4	77
Massachusetts, Boston	42.2	126	Texas, Dallas	33.3	79
Michigan, Detroit	29.6	136	Texas, Houston	47.8	106
Michigan, Grand Rapids	35.5	145	Utah, Salt Lake City	15.6	91
Minnesota, Duluth	26.1	134	Vermont, Burlington	34.1	154
Minnesota, Minneapolis	27.3	115	Virginia, Richmond	42.7	113
Mississippi, Jackson	49.2	110	Washington, Seattle	34.0	150
Missouri, Kansas City	36.0	106	West Virginia, Charleston	43.5	151
Missouri, St. Louis	37.1	111	Wisconsin, Milwaukee	33.9	125
Montana, Billings	14.6	96	Wyoming, Cheyenne	14.5	96
Montana, Missoula	13.4	123			

Snowfall, Inches

State, City	Annual Avg.	Storm Max.	State, City	Annual Avg.	Storm Max.
Alabama, Birmingham	1.9	13.0	Nebraska, North Platte	30.4	17.7
Alabama, Mobile	0.5	6.0	Nebraska, Omaha	29.9	18.9
Alaska, Anchorage	69.5	35.7	Nevada, Reno	24.6	36.4
Alaska, Juneau	99.0	45.9	New Hampshire, Concord	64.3	28.0
Arizona, Flagstaff	54.9	50.6	New Jersey, Atlantic City	16.1	21.6
Arizona, Phoenix	0.0	1.0	New Jersey, Newark	27.0	27.8
Arkansas, Little Rock	5.1	18.3	New Mexico, Albuquerque	11.1	18.9
California, Los Angeles	0.0	3.0	New York, Albany	40.1	46.7
Colorado, Grand Junction	25.1	23.6	New York, Buffalo	91.1	81.5
Colorado, Denver	68.0	60.4	New York, New York	26.9	26.9
Connecticut, Hartford	48.6	21.0	North Carolina, Asheville	15.6	33.0
Delaware, Wilmington	21.0	22.2	North Carolina, Raleigh	7.0	20.3
DC, Washington	16.6	32.4	North Dakota, Bismarck	41.9	28.3
Florida, Jacksonville	0.0	1.9	Ohio, Cleveland	55.4	22.2
Florida, Miami	0.0	0.0	Ohio, Columbus	27.6	20.4
Georgia, Atlanta	2.0	10.3	Oklahoma, Tulsa	8.6	14.1
Idaho, Boise	20.9	23.6	Oregon, Eugene	6.8	29.0
Illinois, Chicago	38.2	23.0	Oregon, Portland	6.5	27.5
Indiana, Indianapolis	22.7	16.1	Pennsylvania, Philadelphia	20.8	30.7
Iowa, Des Moines	33.2	21.5	Pennsylvania, Pittsburgh	29.3	30.2
Iowa, Sioux City	21.2	22.9	Pennsylvania, Williamsport	36.1	24.1
Kansas, Dodge City	20.0	20.5	Rhode Island, Providence	35.5	28.6
Kansas, Topeka	21.2	22.1	South Carolina, Columbia	1.9	16.0
Kentucky, Louisville	16.2	22.4	South Dakota, Rapid City	39.1	32.2
Louisiana, New Orleans	0.2	8.2	Tennessee, Memphis	4.6	18.5
Maine, Portland	71.4	27.1	Texas, Amarillo	15.5	20.6
Maryland, Baltimore	20.8	28.2	Texas, Corpus Christi	0.0	5.0
Massachusetts, Boston	41.8	27.6	Texas, Dallas	2.7	7.4
Michigan, Detroit	32.9	24.5	Texas, Houston	0.4	20.0
Michigan, Grand Rapids	71.6	28.2	Utah, Salt Lake City	57.9	23.6
Minnesota, Duluth	39.8	36.8	Vermont, Burlington	73.4	29.8
Minnesota, Minneapolis	49.5	28.4	Virginia, Richmond	13.9	21.6
Mississippi, Jackson	1.4	11.7	Washington, Seattle	7.1	32.5
Missouri, Kansas City	17.0	25.0	West Virginia, Charleston	34.0	25.6
Missouri, St. Louis	19.8	20.4	Wisconsin, Milwaukee	40.2	26.0
Montana, Billings	56.5	42.3	Wyoming, Cheyenne	51.2	25.2
Montana, Missoula	46.3	28.3			

Solar Radiation Received on Windows

Clear-Sky Solar Radiation Received on Windows on December 21

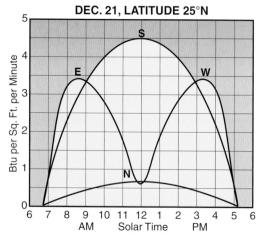

DEC. 21, LATITUDE 25°N

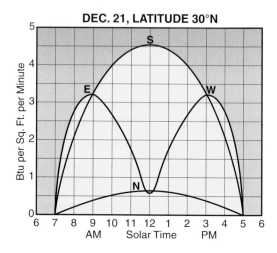

DEC. 21, LATITUDE 30°N

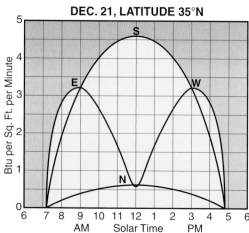

DEC. 21, LATITUDE 35°N

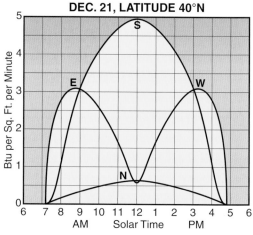

DEC. 21, LATITUDE 40°N

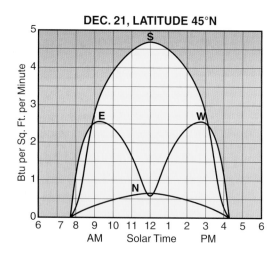

DEC. 21, LATITUDE 45°N

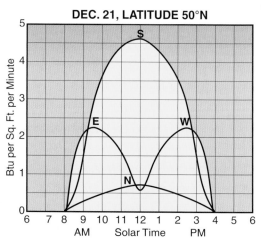

DEC. 21, LATITUDE 50°N

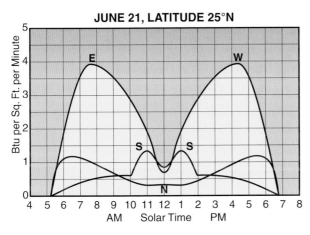

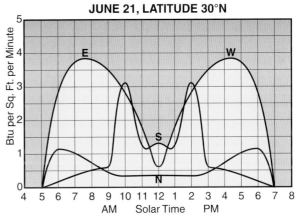

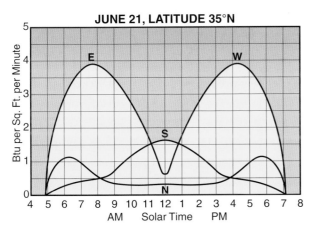

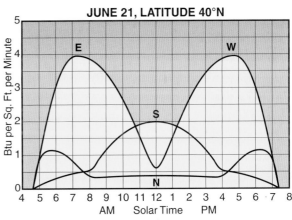

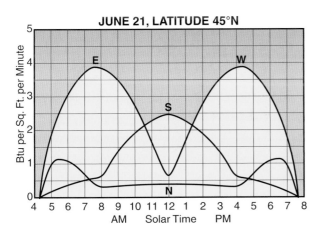

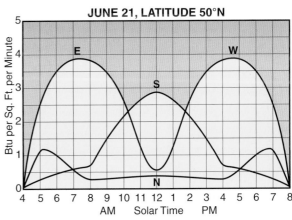

Radiation on South-Facing Surfaces

Average Daily Solar Radiation

To calculate the effects of solar radiation on annual heating and cooling bills, we need the average values of radiation received. Monthly values for south-facing glazings in 35 locations are listed in the table below and on the following pages. Values for slopes of 0° (horizontal), 30°, 60°, and 90° (vertical) are given to allow calculations for skylights and sunspaces.

Average Daily Solar Radiation on South-Facing Surfaces, Btu per sq. ft.

State, City	Slope	Jan	Feb	Mar	Apr	May	Jun	Jul	Aug	Sep	Oct	Nov	Dec
AK, Fairbanks	Hor	70	279	858	1417	1756	1940	1635	1336	677	316	99	22
13,980 HDD	30	504	791	1600	1840	1883	1939	1674	1555	956	679	469	252
74 CDD	60	809	1110	1962	1884	1715	1692	1483	1495	1041	887	721	416
	Vert	901	1152	1849	1527	1255	1190	1064	1154	905	883	787	471
AR, Little Rock	Hor	729	964	1318	1675	1944	2069	2054	1900	1627	1274	898	688
3,080 HDD	30	1058	1254	1520	1704	1801	1836	1857	1858	1802	1639	1306	1043
2,086 CDD	60	1164	1285	1414	1407	1351	1315	1355	1469	1606	1653	1431	1174
	Vert	1020	1051	1033	872	732	681	712	851	1094	1314	1241	1048
AZ, Phoenix	Hor	1093	1502	1918	2367	2666	2725	2400	2253	2091	1664	1248	1031
1,027 HDD	30	1706	2092	2295	2430	2436	2364	2143	2195	2355	2217	1916	1683
4,364 CDD	60	1928	2203	2157	1976	1747	1601	1518	1705	2094	2261	2140	1946
	Vert	1703	1809	1548	1140	827	704	738	934	1386	1790	1864	1753
CA, Davis	Hor	581	942	1480	1944	2342	2585	2540	2249	1833	1281	795	544
2,749 HDD	30	873	1299	1803	2047	2216	2326	2337	2269	2133	1748	1225	859
1,237 CDD	60	981	1379	1740	1735	1689	1675	1721	1835	1967	1828	1386	991
	Vert	879	1163	1313	1101	921	839	885	1078	1384	1503	1236	905
CA, San Diego	Hor	976	1264	1577	1710	1817	1880	2016	1839	1644	1330	1046	903
1,063 HDD	30	1455	1676	1822	1719	1667	1657	1803	1777	1773	1680	1513	1395
866 CDD	60	1612	1785	1684	1400	1240	1182	1297	1386	1575	1670	1646	1577
	Vert	1408	1399	1205	848	674	619	669	789	1052	1307	1413	1402
CO, Boulder	Hor	740	988	1478	1695	1695	1935	1917	1618	1518	1142	819	670
5,487 HDD	30	1247	1418	1836	1791	1618	1772	1787	1628	1755	1567	1326	1188
691 CDD	60	1471	1538	1797	1535	1272	1332	1366	1342	1625	1650	1535	1434
	Vert	1355	1318	1375	1003	759	750	780	843	1168	1371	1392	1344
DC, Washington	Hor	585	846	1178	1484	1646	2054	1947	1701	1351	1034	777	541
4,055 HDD	30	884	1144	1394	1539	1559	1864	1802	1700	1521	1360	1195	857
1,531 CDD	60	997	1205	1329	1306	1216	1379	1362	1386	1387	1400	1352	989
	Vert	895	1014	1004	852	720	752	762	853	987	1145	1206	904
FL, Apalachicola	Hor	1078	1340	1623	2025	2242	2176	1992	1866	1693	1539	1226	972
1,415 HDD	30	1549	1722	1830	2007	2010	1870	1752	1771	1809	1916	1736	1432
2,642 CDD	60	1678	1733	1656	1592	1426	1272	1231	1351	1558	1876	1859	1577
	Vert	1435	1374	1152	903	692	606	615	740	1007	1434	1566	1371

Average Daily Solar Radiation on South-Facing Surfaces, Btu per sq. ft.

State, City	Slope	Jan	Feb	Mar	Apr	May	Jun	Jul	Aug	Sep	Oct	Nov	Dec
FL, Miami	Hor	1263	1531	1808	2003	2032	1955	1977	1870	1646	1432	1303	1174
149 HDD	30	1748	1913	1990	1933	1784	1651	1698	1733	1705	1690	1751	1672
4,361 CDD	60	1848	1879	1753	1487	1237	1101	1152	1282	1426	1596	1816	1800
	Vert	1539	1444	1167	801	594	534	553	666	888	1180	1483	1527
GA, Atlanta	Hor	839	1045	1388	1782	1970	2040	1981	1848	1517	1288	975	740
2,827 HDD	30	1232	1359	1594	1805	1814	1801	1782	1795	1656	1638	1415	1113
1,810 CDD	60	1360	1389	1475	1478	1349	1281	1294	1410	1461	1638	1545	1247
	Vert	1189	1130	1068	899	725	659	680	811	990	1292	1332	1107
IA, Ames	Hor	640	931	1204	1484	1767	1992	1973	1693	1351	1008	688	526
6,791 HDD	30	1105	1375	1486	1575	1704	1841	1859	1728	1571	1398	1129	933
830 CDD	60	1320	1516	1459	1366	1354	1400	1438	1442	1469	1485	1318	1131
	Vert	1230	1320	1134	918	818	800	834	918	1076	1250	1207	1068
ID, Boise	Hor	522	858	1248	1789	2161	2353	2463	2095	1679	1156	666	452
5,727 HDD	30	888	1279	1575	1945	2106	2184	2336	2180	2036	1690	1128	805
807 CDD	60	1058	1421	1568	1708	1674	1657	1800	1834	1947	1844	1336	980
	Vert	989	1247	1233	1148	991	923	1008	1156	1440	1578	1237	931
IL, Chicago	Hor	353	541	836	1220	1563	1688	1743	1485	1153	763	442	280
6,498 HDD	30	492	693	970	1273	1502	1561	1639	1503	1311	990	626	384
830 CDD	60	538	715	924	1098	1196	1198	1274	1252	1212	1020	687	417
	Vert	479	602	712	746	734	707	754	806	887	846	610	373
IN, Indianapolis	Hor	541	788	1148	1447	1808	2014	1995	1789	1491	1078	648	478
5,521 HDD	30	819	1065	1368	1507	1721	1837	1855	1801	1711	1450	974	750
1042 CDD	60	927	1124	1311	1286	1343	1371	1408	1477	1576	1511	1092	864
	Vert	835	950	998	848	788	759	792	911	1128	1247	974	791
KS, Dodge City	Hor	953	1204	1590	1988	2073	2426	2393	2146	1815	1399	1031	854
5.037 HDD	30	1598	1718	1938	2083	1952	2177	2193	2148	2090	1917	1661	1492
1,481 CDD	60	1872	1848	1866	1755	1491	1569	1614	1728	1913	2003	1908	1783
	Vert	1706	1562	1396	1100	831	798	839	1014	1335	1639	1709	1652
MA, Boston	Hor	511	729	1078	1340	1738	1837	1826	1565	1255	876	533	438
5,630 HDD	30	830	1021	1313	1414	1677	1701	1722	1593	1449	1184	818	736
777 CDD	60	970	1101	1281	1226	1335	1303	1340	1331	1352	1244	931	875
	Vert	895	950	996	831	810	759	791	857	993	1044	842	820
ME, Caribou	Hor	504	846	1351	1473	1745	1767	1874	1657	1226	773	405	390
9,560 HDD	30	963	1362	1808	1613	1721	1668	1804	1736	1474	1103	654	765
191 CDD	60	1201	1570	1865	1441	1406	1315	1441	1492	1419	1199	766	966
	Vert	1156	1417	1510	1006	887	803	882	991	1080	1038	711	942

Average Daily Solar Radiation on South-Facing Surfaces, Btu per sq. ft.

State, City	Slope	Jan	Feb	Mar	Apr	May	Jun	Jul	Aug	Sep	Oct	Nov	Dec
ME, Portland	Hor	578	872	1321	1495	1889	1992	2065	1774	1410	1005	578	508
7,318 HDD	30	1015	1308	1684	1602	1836	1853	1959	1830	1870	1427	941	941
347 CDD	60	1223	1456	1684	1403	1468	1423	1526	1341	1582	1537	1099	1160
	Vert	1149	1279	1326	953	889	824	890	989	1172	1309	1010	1109
MT, Great Falls	Hor	508	843	1333	1579	1929	2176	2338	1947	1487	964	567	412
7,828 HDD	30	1007	1384	1801	1751	1916	2061	2266	2074	1855	1473	1056	859
288 CDD	60	1273	1610	1869	1576	1570	1617	1804	1794	1820	1652	1304	1107
	Vert	1236	1463	1523	1104	985	960	1074	1187	1395	1453	1244	1091
NC, Greensboro	Hor	754	1001	1303	1727	1962	2069	1992	1749	1517	1211	894	684
3,848 HDD	30	1147	1344	1524	1777	1834	1853	1818	1724	1692	1580	1345	1080
1,332 CDD	60	1291	1403	1435	1483	1391	1344	1347	1382	1522	1610	1499	1240
	Vert	1149	1164	1062	931	773	710	729	827	1056	1296	1318	1122
ND, Bismarck	Hor	581	924	1292	1653	2029	2161	2253	1907	1406	1005	592	456
8,802 HDD	30	1160	1519	1714	1829	2008	2039	2173	2016	1722	1521	1083	943
471 CDD	60	1467	1765	1760	1639	1635	1591	1723	1734	1672	1696	1327	1210
	Vert	1421	1599	1422	1138	1011	938	1023	1139	1272	1484	1258	1188
NY, Ithaca	Hor	449	747	1038	1281	1727	1984	1970	1693	1310	913	460	364
7,182 HDD	30	699	1054	1257	1347	1667	1836	1858	1731	1522	1245	673	573
312 CDD	60	803	1141	1224	1168	1327	1400	1440	1447	1424	1315	751	664
	Vert	735	985	951	794	807	802	838	923	1046	1105	673	614
NY, New York	Hor	537	773	1148	1392	1675	1936	1907	1811	1329	964	589	471
4,754 HDD	30	837	1061	1383	1456	1602	1777	1783	1836	1520	1290	885	761
1,151 CDD	60	959	1129	1337	1249	1263	1340	1367	1575	1404	1345	995	888
	Vert	873	962	1025	833	759	758	786	943	1016	1115	891	821
NM, Albuquerque	Hor	1134	1436	1885	2319	2533	2721	2540	2342	2084	1646	1244	1034
4,281 HDD	30	1872	2041	2295	2411	2346	2390	2289	2312	2387	2251	1994	1780
1,290 CDD	60	2169	2179	2189	1990	1724	1651	1635	1817	2155	2334	2274	2106
	Vert	1950	1815	1599	1182	868	754	795	1011	1455	1878	2011	1927
NV, Las Vegas	Hor	1027	1421	1859	2290	2585	2747	2489	2308	2051	1579	1170	957
2,239 HDD	30	1691	2055	2287	2398	2410	2428	2259	2294	2369	2175	1889	1657
3,214 CDD	60	1962	2214	2198	1996	1783	1692	1634	1820	2155	2268	2164	1968
	Vert	1772	1861	1622	1205	904	784	817	1031	1473	1839	1926	1811
OH, Cleveland	Hor	456	662	1148	1388	1925	2058	2029	1815	1384	968	519	423
6,121 HDD	30	690	889	1395	1459	1851	1894	1903	1849	1602	1313	767	677
712 CDD	60	783	938	1357	1258	1458	1429	1462	1534	1491	1379	857	789
	Vert	710	798	1047	844	861	803	836	962	1085	1151	767	729

Average Daily Solar Radiation on South-Facing Surfaces, Btu per sq. ft.

State, City	Slope	Jan	Feb	Mar	Apr	May	Jun	Jul	Aug	Sep	Oct	Nov	Dec
OR, Medford	Hor	434	780	1222	1782	2168	2404	2573	2216	1653	1023	559	338
4,539 HDD	30	667	1112	1516	1920	2099	2218	2425	2297	1975	1428	870	516
711 CDD	60	763	1208	1493	1672	1656	1665	1845	1916	1870	1522	996	590
	Vert	696	1045	1162	1112	967	909	1003	1183	1369	1284	904	542
PA, Philadelphia	Hor	645	892	1279	1566	1817	2042	1983	1714	1430	1080	704	560
4,759 HDD	30	1031	1241	1547	1641	1731	1863	1844	1724	1635	1454	1084	926
1,235 CDD	60	1191	1327	1495	1402	1351	1390	1402	1415	1504	1516	1229	1089
	Vert	1085	1129	1139	918	793	768	790	879	1078	1252	1101	1008
SC, Charleston	Hor	931	1115	1443	1896	2025	2062	1925	1826	1502	1263	1049	795
1,755 HDD	30	1376	1449	1652	1915	1855	1811	1726	1765	1628	1583	1520	1194
2,486 CDD	60	1519	1477	1522	1557	1366	1277	1249	1379	1428	1570	1656	1335
	Vert	1325	1196	1093	929	721	647	656	787	960	1229	1423	1181
TN, Nashville	Hor	600	883	1211	1657	1903	2087	2036	1819	1576	1204	799	592
3,677 HDD	30	858	1157	1404	1702	1780	1869	1858	1795	1764	1569	1170	898
1,652 CDD	60	941	1195	1316	1421	1353	1355	1374	1438	1589	1599	1290	1015
	Vert	827	987	975	896	757	714	739	854	1101	1287	1128	912
TX, Dallas	Hor	851	1131	1452	1673	1920	2193	2167	1983	1688	1338	962	814
2,370 HDD	30	1231	1473	1663	1681	1761	1920	1934	1918	1846	1692	1368	1230
2,571 CDD	60	1347	1503	1533	1371	1303	1342	1380	1492	1623	1684	1478	1377
	Vert	1170	1217	1099	834	698	663	694	836	1083	1319	1265	1219
UT, Salt Lake City	Hor	648	964	1347	1826	2191	2540	2342	2084	1671	1233	780	567
5,631 HDD	30	1066	1390	1660	1945	2099	2317	2185	2125	1963	1732	1265	971
1,066 CDD	60	1248	1512	1621	1674	1634	1705	1652	1750	1833	1843	1466	1159
	Vert	1147	1300	1245	1092	932	890	902	1069	1320	1542	1332	1083
WA, Seattle	Hor	287	500	972	1458	1844	1918	2087	1749	1207	696	390	235
4,615 HDD	30	457	711	1240	1605	1829	1817	2020	1848	1461	983	641	386
173 CDD	60	535	779	1254	1440	1500	1433	1615	1597	1414	1067	756	459
	Vert	500	688	1013	1012	946	869	980	1064	1082	925	706	435
WI, Madison	Hor	564	812	1232	1455	1745	2031	2046	1740	1443	993	555	495
7,493 HDD	30	973	1189	1546	1553	1692	1886	1938	1789	1710	1398	885	899
582 CDD	60	1165	1309	1534	1356	1353	1444	1507	1503	1617	1499	1024	1101
	Vert	1090	1143	1203	921	827	830	878	964	1195	1273	937	1048
WY, Laramie	Hor	824	1097	1561	1833	2018	2308	2183	1936	1546	1174	835	673
9,640 HDD	30	1489	1652	1986	1964	1940	2119	2047	1978	1812	1653	1409	1247
22 CDD	60	1805	1833	1972	1699	1524	1583	1564	1639	1694	1765	1659	1531
	Vert	1689	1595	1526	1116	892	863	879	1019	1230	1483	1522	1452

First and Last Frost Dates

Gardeners need to know when they can plant seeds safely and the length of the growing (frost-free) season. Even if you are not a gardener, the arrivals of spring and fall are important climatic considerations.

Seed packets generally display maps of the dates of last frost and specify the minimum length of growing season for the seed. Due to the small size of the package, however, these maps are necessarily crude. As these maps of New York State show, the dates of last spring frost and first fall frost vary by 70 to 80 days across the state. The length of the growing season varies even more—an incredible 120 days!

Detailed downloadable maps of last frost, first frost, and length of frost-free season are available on the website of the National Climate Data Center: *www.ncdc.noaa.gov/oa/climate/freezefrost/frost-freemaps.html.*

Even more detailed downloadable maps are available from many state agricultural extension services, such as the ones displayed here. The ones from Cornell University are:

www.gardening.cornell.edu/weather/frezfree.html

www.gardening.cornell.edu/weather/sprfrost.html

www.gardening.cornell.edu/weather/falfrost.html

Be aware that topography and sizable water bodies can result in local microclimates with altered temperatures and frost dates. Study, for example, the illustrations: *Cold Ponding in a "Flat" Field* and *Valley Temperature Diurnal Swings* on p. 46.

New York State Average Length of Frost-Free Season

Frost-Free Days

> 203 days

183–203 days

163–183 days

143–163 days

123–143 days

103–123 days

<103 days

New York State Average Dates of Last Frost

Last Frost Date

- Before April 10
- April 10–20
- April 20–30
- April 30–May 10
- May 10–20
- May 20–30
- After May 30

New York State Average Dates of First Frost

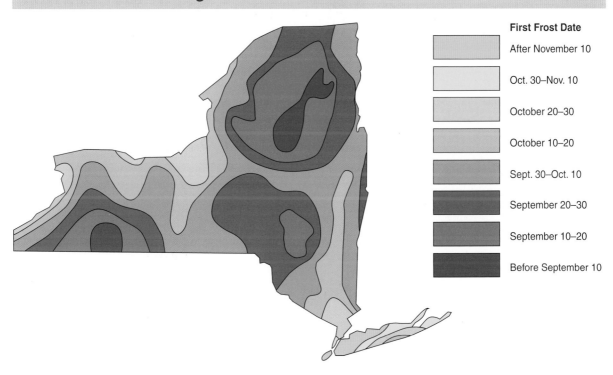

First Frost Date

- After November 10
- Oct. 30–Nov. 10
- October 20–30
- October 10–20
- Sept. 30–Oct. 10
- September 20–30
- September 10–20
- Before September 10

Trees for Shade and Shelter

Trees for Shade and Shelter

Common Name	Hardiness Zones	Type[1]	Height, feet	Width, feet	Spacing, feet	Features
1. Quaking aspen	2–5	D	35	5	7	Excellent visual screen
2. Paper birch	2-5	D	45	20	15	White bark, very hardy
3. White spruce	2-5	E	45	20	10	Good for windbreak
4. Bur oak	2-5	D	45	20	15	Requires good soil for full size
5. Eastern red cedar	2-8	E	50	10	7	Good screen, tolerates dry soil
6. Norway maple	3-6	D	50	30	25	Grows in city, grows fast
7. Sugar maple	3-6	D	80	50	40	Beautiful foliage, sugar sap
8. Norway spruce	3-5	E	60	25	14	Grows fast, prefers sun
9. Red maple	3-6	D	40	30	25	Brilliant foliage, grows fast
10. Green ash	3-6	D	50	30	25	Grows fast in most soils
11. Eastern white pine	3-6	E	70	40	12	Grows very fast in most soils
12. Eastern hemlock	3-7	E	60	30	8	Good screen, grows in shade
13. White poplar	3-5	D	50	12	10	Grows very fast, short life
14. Pin oak	4-7	D	80	50	30	Keeps leaves in winter
15. Japanese cryptomeria	6-8	E	70	20	10	Good screen, grows fast
16. Oriental arborvitae	7–9	E	16	6	3	Grows fast in most soils
17. Rocky Mountain juniper	4-7	E	25	10	6	In West only, dry soils
18. Black haw	4-7	D	15	15	5	White flowers, red berries
19. American holly	6-9	E	20	8	8	Spined leaves, red berries
20. Lombardy poplar	6.8	D	40	6	4	Grows fast, all soils
21. Weeping willow	6-8	D	30	30	30	Drooping branches, wet soils
22. Sea grape	10	E	20	8	4	Very decorative
23. Northern white cedar	3-6	E	30	12	8	Good screen, loamy soil
24. Southern magnolia	8-9	E	30	10	5	Large white flowers
25. Douglas fir	4-6	E	60	25	12	Grows fast, up to 200 ft.

Source: W. R. Nelson, Jr., *Landscaping Your Home* (Urbana-Champaign: University of Illinois, 1975).

[1] D = deciduous, E = evergreen.

Shelterbelt Design

Effect of Shelterbelt on Wind Speed

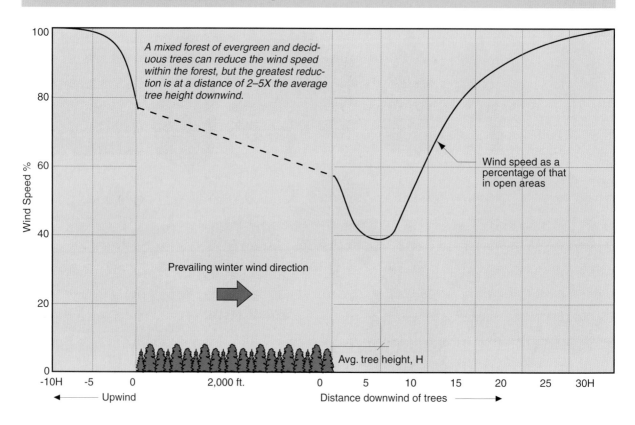

A mixed forest of evergreen and deciduous trees can reduce the wind speed within the forest, but the greatest reduction is at a distance of 2–5X the average tree height downwind.

Wind speed as a percentage of that in open areas

Prevailing winter wind direction

Avg. tree height, H

Wind Speed %

Upwind

Distance downwind of trees

Effect of Shelterbelt on Snow Accumulation

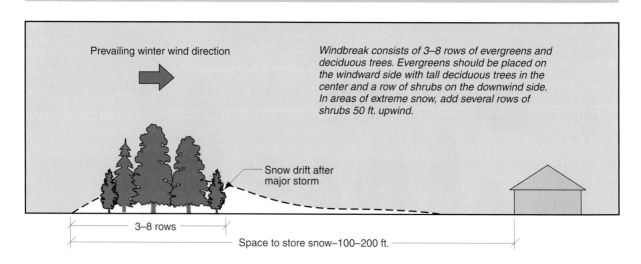

Prevailing winter wind direction

Windbreak consists of 3–8 rows of evergreens and deciduous trees. Evergreens should be placed on the windward side with tall deciduous trees in the center and a row of shrubs on the downwind side. In areas of extreme snow, add several rows of shrubs 50 ft. upwind.

Snow drift after major storm

3–8 rows

Space to store snow–100–200 ft.

Landscaping Strategies for Winter and Summer

LANDSCAPING FOR WINTER WIND ONLY

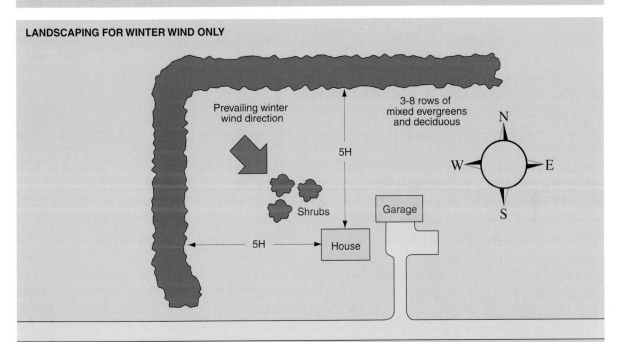

LANDSCAPING FOR WINTER AND SUMMER WIND AND SUN

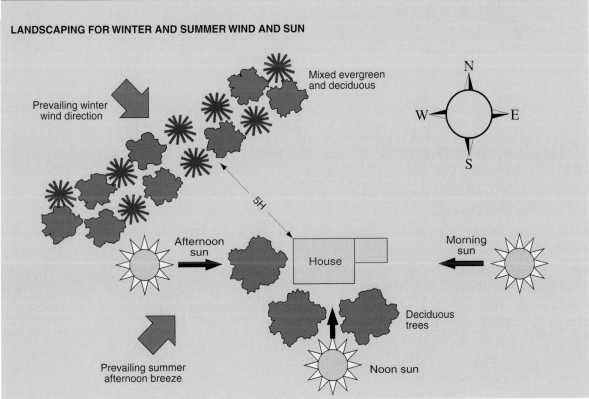

Microclimates

Cold Ponding

If you live in the northern half of the United States, you have heard the weatherman say, "There will be frost, particularly in low-lying areas." The illustration at right shows why. The density of air increases as its temperature decreases. On a clear night, with the ground surface radiating heat to the night sky, the air in contact with the ground cools. With no wind, the cool, dense air flows downhill into any depression, no matter how shallow. With an average air temperature of 35°F, you can still have frost (<32°F air) in low-lying depressions.

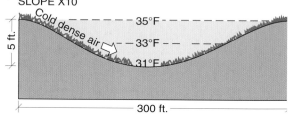

Cold Ponding in a "Flat" Field

Extreme Cold Ponding

Sinkholes occur where limestone caves collapse. These holes have steep sides and can be extremely deep, as shown in the illustration. On a clear night, the bottom of the hole "looks at" (and radiates heat to) outer space, which is at a temperature near Absolute Zero (–273°C or –459°F). Since the cool air generated by contact with the earth is dense and stable, it remains at the bottom where it continues to cool overnight. In the example shown, the temperature of the air at the bottom is an incredible 49F° cooler than that at the top.

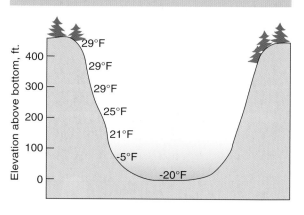

Extreme Ponding in Sinkhole

Valley Temperatures

Did you ever wonder why fruit trees are usually planted on sloping ground? Aside from pests, the biggest problem fruit growers face is frost. Cold air is dense and slides downhill so the bottoms of valleys and hollows receive frost before other areas. Because the air on slopes is nearly always flowing either uphill or downhill, it tends to mix and stay at more average temperatures. The graph of temperatures recorded over 24 hours at the top, bottom, and sloping side of a valley demonstrates the effect. Note that the temperature on the slope is both cooler during the day and warmer at night than at the peak or the bottom.

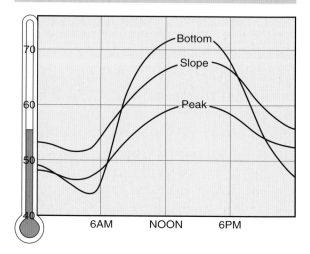

Valley Temperature Diurnal Swings

North and South Slopes

The intensity of direct solar radiation on a clear day is approximately 284 Btu/sq. ft.-hr. The intensity of the radiation striking the surface, however, is a function of the angle of the surface relative to the direct rays and the resulting larger area receiving the radiation. The illustration shows sunlight striking three slopes: 20° to the south, 0° (level), and 20° to the north. In this typical winter case, the intensities—and warming effects—have been reduced to 244, 182, and 99 Btu/sq. ft.-hr. So, on which slope would you build your house?

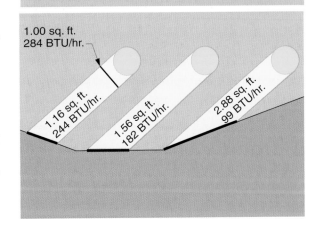

Effect of Slope on Solar Intensity

Reflection of Solar Radiation

Skiers know it; boaters know it: Reflection of the direct rays of the sun from water, snow, or ice is powerful. Of course, the percentage of direct rays reflected (the reflectivity) varies somewhat with the medium, the angle, and the surface roughness, but the 65% shown in the illustration is a fair average. That means the windows of a house facing south over a water body or snow-covered field receive 165% of the normal direct radiation. Such a location would work well for a passive solar or solar-tempered house.

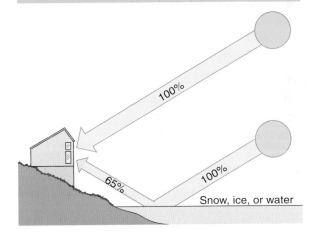

Solar Gain from Water Bodies

Heat Gains in Earth Mounds

Why is corn sometimes planted in rounded mounds or hills? Why do farmers purposely plant in and maintain mounded furrows? Because plants grow earlier and faster in such earthworks. The illustration shows the measured increase in solar heat gain (°F × hours) in three types of mounds.

How can this be? The answer lies in potential theory, a subject familiar to students of physics and applied mathematics. To oversimplify, the ratio of incoming radiant energy to the mass storing the energy is greater in the mounds than in the valleys.

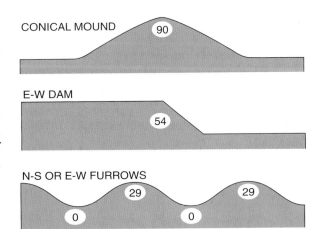

Solar Heat Gain of Earth Mounds

Heating

4

The place to start when designing a heating system is with the *building heat load*: the maximum required number of Btus of delivered heat per hour. Assuming the heating system is properly sized and tuned to its maximum efficiency, the wise homeowner will focus his attention on the *thermostats and setback savings*.

The subjects above are general and apply to all types of heating systems. To achieve further savings, we need to understand how each type of heating system works: *gas furnaces, gas boilers, oil furnaces, oil boilers*, both *air-source* and *ground-source heat pumps*, freestanding *gas stoves, wood stoves*, and *pellet stoves*.

Finally, for even greater savings, we need to understand how the heat is distributed throughout the house. We consider *warm air distribution*, *hydronic distribution*, *radiant heating*, and *free convection heating*.

Building Heat Loads

In selecting a new or replacement heating system for a building, we need to determine two types of heat load (rates of heat loss):

Design Heat Load is the rate at which heat is lost from the building in Btus per hour on that coldest night when the outside temperature is at the design minimum temperature (DMT) for the location. This number is used to size the heating system.

Annual Heat Load is the total heat loss in Btu over the entire heating season. The quantity is used to estimate the annual heating bill in dollars.

Use the work sheet on the facing page to estimate both of these loads for your home. A completed example work sheet follows on pp. 52–53.

Alternatively, you can perform the same analysis interactively on the web. A site using algorithms similar to the method presented here is the "Home Heat Loss Calculator" at *www.builditsolar.com/References/ Calculators/HeatLoss/HeatLoss.htm*. A more sophisticated analysis, accounting for solar gains, thermal mass, and hour-by-hour temperatures, is Home Energy Efficient Design (HEED), available on the web at *www.energy-design-tools.aud.ucla.edu/heed/*.

Work Sheet Instructions

Line 1. Use line 1 if you have an unheated attic. Find the R-value in Chapter 7, or use a value of 3.0 if the attic is totally uninsulated.

Line 2. Use line 2 if the ceiling is also the underside of the roof (a cathedral ceiling). Get the R-value from Chapter 7, or use 3.0 if the roof is uninsulated.

Line 3. Get the wall R-values from Chapter 7, or use 4.0 if the wall is uninsulated. If there are different wall constructions, use a different line for each type. Subtract window and door areas from each wall section.

Line 4. The area of most exterior doors is 20 sq. ft. Use an R-value of 2.0 for solid wood doors, 3.0 for a wood door plus storm door, and 6.0 for an insulated door.

Line 5. Window area is the area of the sash, not just the glazing. A window's R-value is simply 1/U, where U is the window's U-value. Find your windows' U-values from the very complete table of tested U-values on p. 235.

Line 6. Use this line if your home, or a portion of it, sits on piers or over a ventilated crawl space. Get the floor R-values from Chapter 7, or use 5.0 if the floor is uninsulated.

Line 7. Use this line if your home sits on a concrete slab. Use an R-value of 20 if the slab is uninsulated. Add the insulation R-value shown on p. 167 if it is insulated.

Line 8. Use this line if your home has a basement. Use an R-value of 5.0 if the foundation is uninsulated. Add the insulation R-value (from Chapter 7) if the walls are insulated.

Line 9. For air changes per hour, use 1.5 for an older drafty house, 0.75 for a typical 10- to 30-year-old house, 0.50 for an average new house, and 0.25 for a new "green" or "energy-efficient" house. Heated volume is 8× the heated floor area.

Line 10. Add up all of the numbers appearing in the right-hand column above this line.

Line 11. First enter the sum from line 10. Next enter 65 minus the design minimum temperature (DMT) from the table on p. 28. Multiply the entries and enter the result in the right column. Your heating contractor can use this result to properly size your heating system.

Line 12. Enter the sum from line 10. Next find heating degree days, base 65°F (HDD$_{65}$), from the table of climate data on p. 24. Multiply the entries. The result is the total annual heat loss in Btu/year.

To estimate the amount of fuel used, divide this number by 100,000 for gallons of oil; 70,000 per hundred cubic feet of gas; 3,410 for kilowatt-hours (kWh) of electric-resistance heat; and 6,830 for an electric heat pump. (You can see how to adjust for other heating system efficiencies on p. 18.)

Work Sheet for Heat Loads

Surface	Area, sq. ft.	÷	R-value	=	Result
1. Ceiling under attic #1	_____	÷	_____	=	_____
Ceiling under attic #2	_____	÷	_____	=	_____
2. Cathedral ceiling or roof #1	_____	÷	_____	=	_____
Cathedral ceiling or roof #2	_____	÷	_____	=	_____
3. Exterior wall #1	_____	÷	_____	=	_____
Exterior wall #2	_____	÷	_____	=	_____
Exterior wall #3	_____	÷	_____	=	_____
Exterior wall #4	_____	÷	_____	=	_____
Exterior wall #5	_____	÷	_____	=	_____
Exterior wall #6	_____	÷	_____	=	_____
4. Exterior door #1	_____	÷	_____	=	_____
Exterior door #2	_____	÷	_____	=	_____
Exterior door #3	_____	÷	_____	=	_____
5. Window type #1	_____	÷	_____	=	_____
Window type #2	_____	÷	_____	=	_____
Window type #3	_____	÷	_____	=	_____
Window type #4	_____	÷	_____	=	_____
6. Floor over crawl space	_____	÷	_____	=	_____
7. Slab on-grade	_____	÷	_____	=	_____
8. Foundation wall	_____	÷	_____	=	_____
9. Air changes per hour _____	x 0.018 x heated volume in cu. ft. _____			=	_____
10. Sum of results of all lines above				=	_____
11. **Design heat load**: Line 10 _____	X	_____	(65°F - DMT)	=	_____ Btu/hour
12. **Annual heat load**: Line 10 _____	X 24 X	_____	HDD_{65}	=	_____ Btu/year

The facing page contains a sample work sheet showing the calculations for design heat load and annual heat load for a small house located in Boston, Massachusetts, and shown in the illustration below.

The house is kept simple in order to clarify the calculations. Many homes will have more than one type of exterior wall, foundation, or window, and will require multiple entries for these items.

Line 1. The ceiling measures 30 ft. × 40 ft., so its area is 1,200 sq. ft. Chapter 7 lists an R-value of 41.5 for its two R-19 batts.

Line 3. After deducting the areas of windows and doors, the remaining area of exterior wall is 996 sq. ft. The 2×6 wall with R-19 batts has an R-value of 17.3.

Line 4. The first exterior door is solid wood plus a storm door and has a combined R-value of 3.0. The second has an insulated core and R-value of 6.0.

Line 5. All of the windows are double glazed without storm windows (R-values of 2.0). The total area of window sash is 84 sq. ft.

Line 6. The house sits on a crawl space that is ventilated in winter and is insulated with R-19 batts between the joists. This type of floor has a calculated R-value of 20.9.

Line 9. The house is a recently built tract home, so its air change rate is estimated to be 0.50 changes per hour. The heated volume is the floor area times the ceiling height, 8 ft.

Line 10. The sum of all of the results in the right column is 282.3.

Line 11. From the table on pp. 28–29, Boston's DMT is 0°F. The result for this line is a design heat load at 0°F of 18,349 Btu/hr.

Line 12. From the table on pp. 24–25, for Boston the HDD_{65} = 5,630. The result of multiplying the three numbers on line 12 is the annual heat load: 38,144,000 Btu.

If the house were heated with oil, the approximate winter fuel consumption would be the annual heat load divided by 100,000, or 381 gallons of oil.

Example House

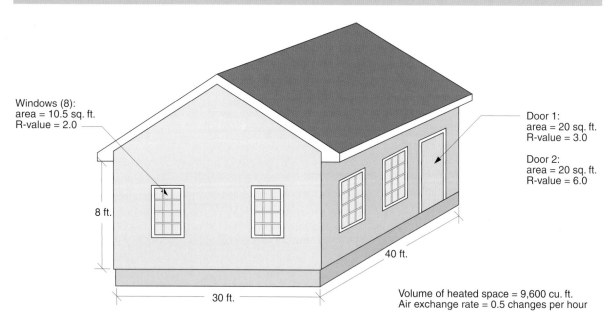

Windows (8):
area = 10.5 sq. ft.
R-value = 2.0

Door 1:
area = 20 sq. ft.
R-value = 3.0

Door 2:
area = 20 sq. ft.
R-value = 6.0

8 ft.

40 ft.

30 ft.

Volume of heated space = 9,600 cu. ft.
Air exchange rate = 0.5 changes per hour

Work Sheet for Heat Loads

Surface	Area, sq. ft.	÷	R-value	=	Result
1. Ceiling under attic #1	1,200	÷	41.5	=	28.9
Ceiling under attic #2		÷		=	
2. Cathedral ceiling or roof #1		÷		=	
Cathedral ceiling or roof #2		÷		=	
3. Exterior wall #1	996	÷	17.3	=	57.6
Exterior wall #2		÷		=	
Exterior wall #3		÷		=	
Exterior wall #4		÷		=	
Exterior wall #5		÷		=	
Exterior wall #6		÷		=	
4. Exterior door #1	20	÷	3.0	=	6.7
Exterior door #2	20	÷	6.0	=	3.3
Exterior door #3		÷		=	
5. Window type #1	84	÷	2.0	=	42.0
Window type #2		÷		=	
Window type #3		÷		=	
Window type #4		÷		=	
6. Floor over crawl space	1,200	÷	20.9	=	57.4
7. Slab on-grade		÷		=	
8. Foundation wall		÷		=	

9. Air changes per hr 0.50 x 0.018 x heated volume in cu. ft. 9,600 = 86.4

10. Sum of results of all lines above = 282.3

11. **Design heat load**: Line 10 282.3 x 65 (65°F - DMT) = 18,349 Btu/hour

12. **Annual heat load**: Line 10 282.3 X 24 X 5,630 HDD$_{65}$ = 38,144,000 Btu/year

Thermostats and Setback Savings

The rate at which your house loses heat in winter (or gains heat in summer) is proportional to the difference in indoor and outdoor temperatures. When it is 30°F outside, the heat loss with the thermostat set at 50°F would be half as great as the heat loss with the thermostat set at 70°F. Were the outdoor temperature to remain at 30°F all heating season, the savings would amount to 2½% per °F of permanent setback.

But outdoor temperatures don't remain constant. To predict the actual savings from a particular setback, Energy Star has provided a Setback Thermostat Calculator on its website: *www.energystar.gov.* Results for various setbacks in seven regions of the country are shown in the tables at right. The annual heating cost figures depend on building size, fuel type, and fuel price, so are unimportant. What are important are the percentage savings applying to any home, including yours: an even more remarkable 3% per °F.

You have already turned down your thermostat to the point of discomfort, however, so what good is this information? Here is where the clock thermostat comes in. Why heat your house while not at home or while sleeping? Your furniture doesn't care, and doctors advise us sleeping in lower temperatures is better for our health. The bottom table shows the savings from clock thermostat setbacks to 55°F during the eight-hour workday and eight sleeping hours—an incredible 34%!

"But you'll burn more fuel heating the house back up than you will save by the setback," doubters say. This is not true! During the time it takes the house to cool from 70°F to 55°F, it is running down its thermal mass battery, and the heating system remains totally idle. During the subsequent warmup from 55°F to 70°F, the "extra" fuel burned is only that required to recharge the thermal mass battery.

The graph on the facing page shows the dynamics. The diurnal outdoor temperature cycle is shown in blue. The heat supplied by the heating system is proportional to the area in red. The heat saved by setting the thermostat back is proportional to the areas in green.

Savings of a Constant 70–69°F Setback

City	Cost @ 70°F	Cost @ 69°F	Saving
Boston, MA	$747	$724	3.1%
Washington, DC	$550	$534	2.9%
Orlando, FL	$88	$85	3.4%
Kansas City, MO	$705	$684	3.0%
Houston, TX	$209	$201	2.9%
Albuquerque, NM	$589	$572	2.9%
Sacramento, CA	$370	$359	3.0%
Seattle, WA	$625	$606	3.0%

Savings of a Constant 70–65°F Setback

City	Cost @ 70°F	Cost @ 65°F	Saving
Boston, MA	$747	$635	15.0%
Washington, DC	$550	$468	14.9%
Orlando, FL	$88	$74	15.9%
Kansas City, MO	$705	$599	15.0%
Houston, TX	$209	$176	15.0%
Albuquerque, NM	$589	$501	14.9%
Sacramento, CA	$370	$315	14.9%
Seattle, WA	$625	$531	15.0%

Savings of a 70–55°F Setback*

City	Cost @ 70°F	Cost @ 55°F	Saving
Boston, MA	$747	$495	33.7%
Washington, DC	$550	$365	33.6%
Orlando, FL	$88	$58	34.1%
Kansas City, MO	$705	$467	33.8%
Houston, TX	$209	$137	33.8%
Albuquerque, NM	$589	$390	33.8%
Sacramento, CA	$370	$245	33.8%
Seattle, WA	$625	$414	33.8%

*This is not a constant setback. Rather, it is an 8-hour setback during the workday plus an 8-hour setback during sleeping hours.

Clock Thermostat

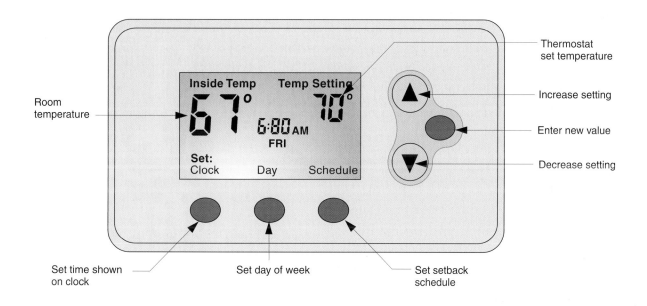

Room temperature

Inside Temp
67°

Temp Setting
70°

6:80 AM
FRI

Set:
Clock   Day   Schedule

Thermostat set temperature

Increase setting

Enter new value

Decrease setting

Set time shown on clock

Set day of week

Set setback schedule

Day and Night Temperature Setback Savings

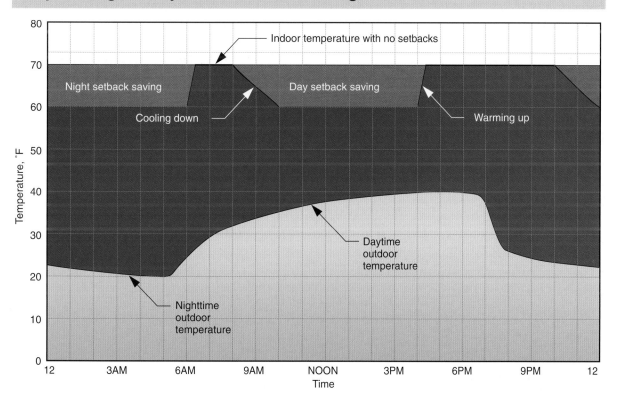

Indoor temperature with no setbacks

Night setback saving

Day setback saving

Cooling down

Warming up

Daytime outdoor temperature

Nighttime outdoor temperature

Temperature, °F

Time

Gas Furnaces

The first furnaces distributed heat by the natural convection of buoyant heated air through large ducts. The modern warm-air gas furnace is a great improvement. Heat is produced by clean and efficient combustion of natural gas or propane, and the warm air is distributed evenly throughout the building by a blower, supply and return ducts, and registers.

Pros include circulation and filtration of air, humidification and dehumidification, possible integration with heat exchangers, and ductwork that can be shared with air-conditioning. Cons include bulky, hard-to-conceal ducts, noise at high air velocity, and sound transmission between rooms.

Here is how the typical gas furnace works:

1. A wall-mounted thermostat in the living space signals the *gas control* for heat.

2. The *gas control* sends gas to the *burner assembly*, where it is ignited by the pilot flame.

3. The hot *flue gases* rise through the thin-walled *heat exchanger* and exit through the *exhaust stack*.

4. The furnace air reaches a low-limit temperature, causing the *fan-and-limit switch* to supply power to the *blower*. If the air reaches the high-limit temperature, the limit switch signals the gas control to turn off.

5. The *blower* draws *return air* in through the return duct and *furnace filter*.

6. The cool return air flows up through the hot *heat exchanger*, where it is reheated.

7. The *heated supply air* flows out from the supply plenum through supply ducts to heat the house.

8. After the thermostat signals the *gas control* to stop heating, the *blower* continues until the furnace air cools to the low temperature limit, and the *limit switch* cuts the blower power.

Inside a Gas Furnace

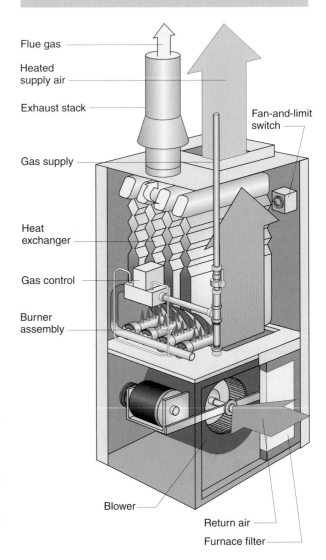

Flue gas

Heated supply air

Exhaust stack

Gas supply

Heat exchanger

Gas control

Burner assembly

Fan-and-limit switch

Blower

Return air

Furnace filter

Efficiencies

Annual fuel utilization efficiencies (AFUE) of pre-1970 gas furnaces average 60%. Newer, conventional gas furnaces average 78%, while new Energy Star furnaces must rate at least 85%.

Gas Boilers

The first boilers were fueled by wood or coal and distributed their heat by the natural expansion and contraction of steam. The modern hydronic boiler is a great improvement. Heat is produced by clean and efficient combustion of natural gas or propane, and the heated supply water is distributed throughout the building by a system of circulator pumps, supply piping, and return piping.

Pros include ease of distribution system installation, silent operation, and longevity. Cons include greater (than the equivalent furnace) cost and susceptibility to freeze damage.

Here is how the typical gas boiler works:

1. A thermostat signals the *gas control* for heat.

2. The *gas control* sends gas to the *burner assembly*, where it is ignited by the *pilot* flame.

3. Hot *flue gases* rise through the water-filled, honeycombed *heat exchanger*, where they are cooled as they heat the boiler water.

4. The cooled *flue gases* are collected and discharged through the *exhaust stack*.

5. When the water in the boiler reaches a low-limit temperature, the *aquastat* signals a circulator pump control that the water is hot enough to circulate. When the boiler water reaches the high-limit temperature, the *aquastat* signals the *gas control* to turn off.

6. Circulator pumps (see p. 69) force the cooled *return water* through the *heat exchanger*, where it is reheated before being sent through the hydronic distribution system.

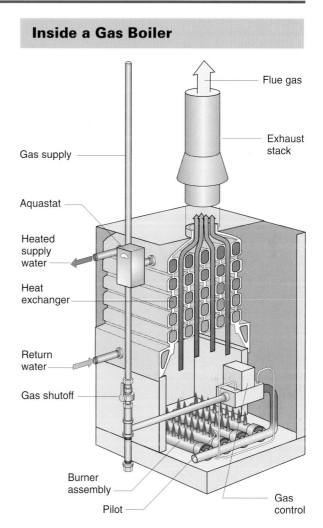

Inside a Gas Boiler

Flue gas

Exhaust stack

Gas supply

Aquastat

Heated supply water

Heat exchanger

Return water

Gas shutoff

Burner assembly

Pilot

Gas control

Efficiencies

The AFUE of a pre-1970 gas boiler averages about 60%. A newer, conventional gas boiler averages 80%, while a new Energy Star-rated boiler must rate at least 85%.

Oil Furnaces

Oil furnaces are similar to gas furnaces, except that heat is provided by the combustion of vaporized heating oil.

Here is how the typical modern oil furnace works:

1. A thermostat in the area to be heated signals the oil *burner* for heat. (See pp. 54 and 68.)

2. The *burner* sprays atomized oil and air into the *combustion chamber*. The burner's high-voltage electrodes ignite the mixture. If the burner's photoelectric cell fails to detect flame within a few seconds, the burner is shut down.

3. The hot *flue gas* flows through the thin-walled *heat exchanger* and exits through the exhaust stack.

4. When the furnace air reaches the low-limit temperature, the *fan limit switch* supplies power to the *blower*. When the air reaches the high temperature limit, the *limit switch* turns the *burner* off.

5. The *blower* draws *cool return air* in through the return duct (p. 68) and through the *heat exchanger*, where it is warmed.

6. The *heated supply air* flows out from the supply plenum through supply ductwork to heat the house.

7. After the thermostat signals the oil *burner* to stop heating, the *blower* continues until the furnace air cools to the low limit, and the *fan limit switch* cuts the *blower* power.

Efficiencies

The AFUEs of a pre-1970 oil furnaces average 65%. New conventional oil furnaces average 80%, while a new Energy Star-rated furnace must rate at least 85%.

Inside an Oil Furnace

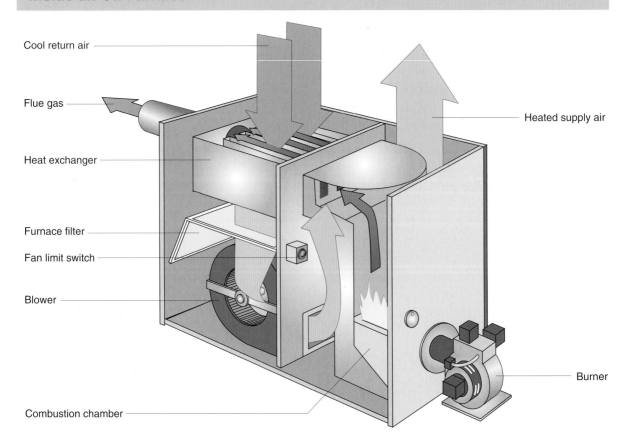

Cool return air

Flue gas

Heat exchanger

Furnace filter

Fan limit switch

Blower

Combustion chamber

Heated supply air

Burner

Oil Boilers

The hydronic, or forced-hot-water, system heats water in a boiler and circulates it through loops of pipe to distribute heat to separate heating zones.

Pros include even heating, ease of zoning with separate thermostats, and small, easily concealed pipes. Cons include no air cleaning or humidification and no sharing of ducts with central air-conditioning.

Here is how the typical modern oil furnace works:

1. A thermostat in the area to be heated signals the *oil burner* for heat. (See pp. 54 and 69.)

2. The burner sprays atomized oil and air into the *combustion chamber*. The burner's high-voltage electrodes ignite the mixture. If the burner's photo-electric cell fails to detect flame within a few seconds, the burner is shut down.

3. The hot *flue gas* rises through passages in the *heat exchanger*, where it is cooled as it heats the boiler water.

4. The cooled flue gas is collected and discharged through the exhaust stack.

5. When the water in the boiler reaches the low-limit temperature, the *aquastat* signals the *zone controller* (p. 69) that the water is hot enough to circulate. If the boiler water reaches the high-limit temperature, the *aquastat* signals the *oil burner* to turn off.

6. Circulator pumps force the *cool return water* through the *heat exchanger*, where it is reheated before being sent through the hydronic distribution system.

Inside an Oil Boiler

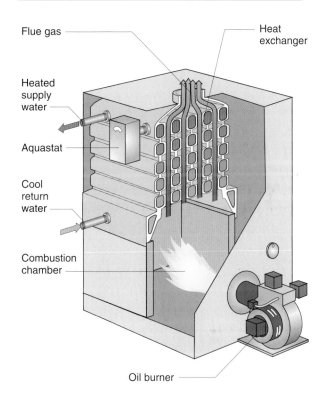

Flue gas

Heat exchanger

Heated supply water

Aquastat

Cool return water

Combustion chamber

Oil burner

Efficiencies

The AFUE of a pre-1970 oil boiler averages about 65%. A newer, conventional oil boiler averages 83%, while a new Energy Star-rated boiler must rate at least 85%.

Air-Source Heat Pumps

If you know that water at atmospheric pressure boils at 212°F, but that its boiling temperature rises at higher pressures (such as in a pressure cooker), and that evaporating water absorbs a lot of heat (think of emerging from the water on a windy day), then you can understand how air conditioners and heat pumps work.

As shown in the graph below, R-410A refrigerant evaporates at -20°F at a pressure of 42 psi, or 27 psig. If we compress it to a pressure of 420 psig, however, its boiling (evaporating) temperature rises to about 120°F.

In the heat pump on the facing page, top, the refrigerant is sucked into a compressor, where it is compressed to at least 420 psig, raising its temperature to 120°F. The hot, compressed vapor then flows through a heat exchanger inside the house. The fan blows air through the coils, cooling it to below its condensation point and changing it back to a liquid.

The hot liquid flows from the heat exchanger to an expansion valve, then to a second heat exchanger and fan located outdoors. The expansion valve drops the pressure to 30 psig, causing the liquid to boil (evaporate) at temperatures above -20°F. Heat is absorbed from the outdoor air through the heat exchanger and is pumped from outside. From the outdoor heat exchanger, the now cool vapor is again sucked into the compressor, and the cycle is repeated.

Efficiencies

A heat pump's efficiency is specified as its Heating Seasonal Performance Factor (HSPF). This is the total Btu output during the heating season divided by the total electric input in watt-hours. The average new heat pump rates 7.7. To qualify as Energy Star-rated, a single unit air-source heat pump must have a HSPF of at least 8.0. Split-system heat pumps must rate at least 8.2.

R-410A Refrigerant

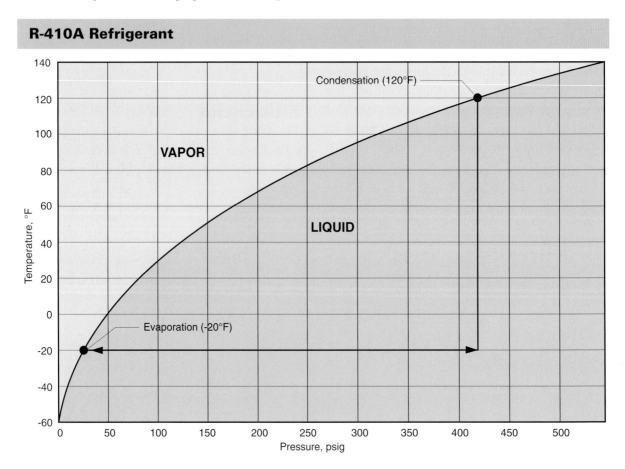

Air-Source Heat Pump in Winter Heating Mode

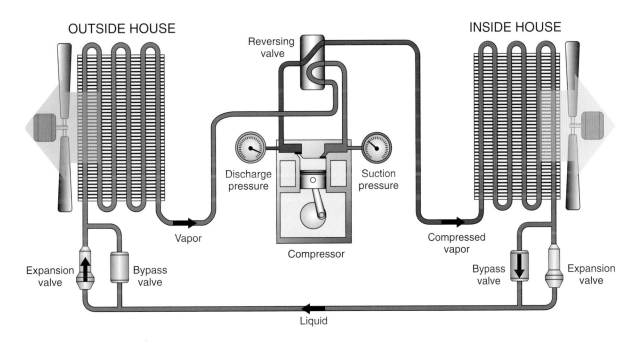

OUTSIDE HOUSE

INSIDE HOUSE

Reversing valve

Discharge pressure

Suction pressure

Vapor

Compressed vapor

Compressor

Expansion valve

Bypass valve

Bypass valve

Expansion valve

Liquid

Air-Source Heat Pump in Summer Cooling Mode

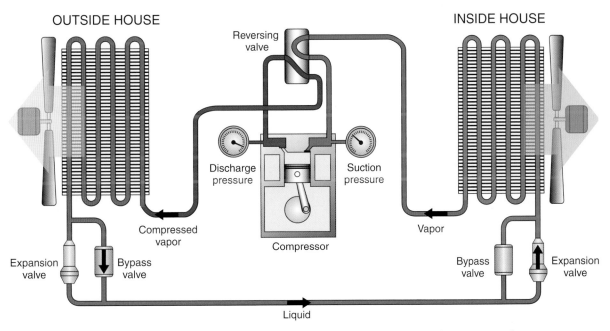

OUTSIDE HOUSE

INSIDE HOUSE

Reversing valve

Discharge pressure

Suction pressure

Compressed vapor

Vapor

Compressor

Expansion valve

Bypass valve

Bypass valve

Expansion valve

Liquid

Simply switching the reversing valve converts the heat pump to an air conditioner for summer cooling.

Ground-Source Heat Pumps

Air-source heat pumps were described on the previous pages. Ground-source heat pumps differ only in that they exchange heat with the ground instead of with outdoor air.

Due to the immense thermal capacity of the earth, while the temperature of outdoor air ranges from over 100°F down to -30°F, the temperature of the earth at depths of 20 ft. or more is essentially the annual average air temperature for the location. Except for the most southern states, this temperature ranges between 45°F and 60°F. Heat pump efficiency is strongly dependent on source temperature, so in the coldest months, ground-source heat pump efficiencies are much greater than those of air-source heat pumps.

To qualify for an Energy Star rating, the minimum Coefficient of Performance (COP, the ratio of total heating capacity to electrical energy input) varies from 3.6 to 4.1 for water-to-air systems. Excepting areas that have very low gas costs or very high electricity costs, the ground-source heat pump is the most economical HVAC system to operate.

High thermal efficiency comes at a cost, however. Installation costs are up to five times those of gas or oil furnaces and boilers. Most of the difference is due to the added cost of the underground piping (ground loop). The three most common loops are shown at right. The "slinky" is lowest in cost and lowest in efficiency. The horizontal loop is the most efficient where there is sufficient land available. Vertical loops are used where lot size prohibits the other two.

Efficiencies

A ground-source, or geothermal, heat pump's efficiency is specified as its Coefficient of Performance (COP). This is the ratio of system heat output to total electric input. To qualify for an Energy Star rating, ground-source heat pumps must have COPs of at least

- 3.1 for a closed-loop water-to-water system
- 3.5 for an open-loop water-to-water system
- 3.6 for a closed-loop water-to-air system
- 4.1 for an open-loop water-to-air system.

"Slinky" Coiled Loops

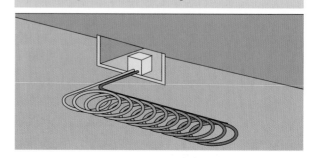

Horizontal Loops

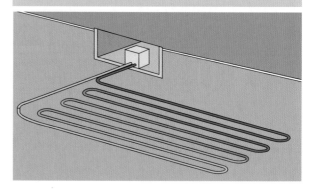

Vertical Loops

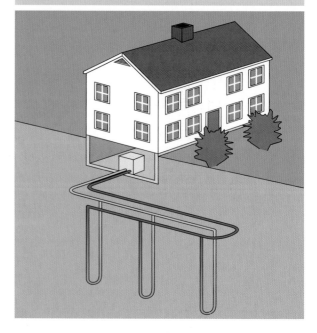

Ground-Source Heat Pump in Winter Heating Mode

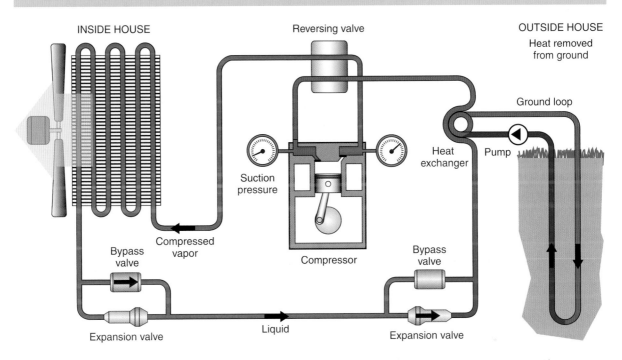

INSIDE HOUSE

Reversing valve

OUTSIDE HOUSE
Heat removed
from ground

Suction
pressure

Heat
exchanger

Ground loop

Pump

Compressed
vapor

Bypass
valve

Compressor

Bypass
valve

Expansion valve

Liquid

Expansion valve

Ground-Source Heat Pump in Summer Cooling Mode

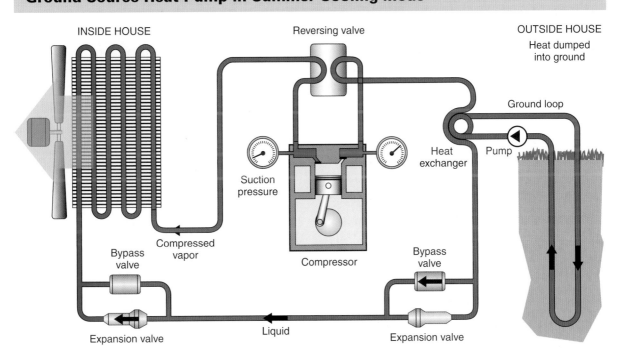

INSIDE HOUSE

Reversing valve

OUTSIDE HOUSE
Heat dumped
into ground

Suction
pressure

Heat
exchanger

Ground loop

Pump

Compressed
vapor

Bypass
valve

Compressor

Bypass
valve

Expansion valve

Liquid

Expansion valve

Gas Stoves

The difference between ventless gas heaters and direct-vent gas heaters (facing page) is that the latter exchange air and combustion gases with the outdoors, while the former exhaust the products of combustion into the building. Complete combustion produces two gases: carbon dioxide (CO_2) and water vapor (H_2O). Incomplete combustion, resulting from a shortage of oxygen, results in carbon monoxide (CO) as well. The ventless heater thus raises two concerns:

- excess water vapor leading to the growth of mold
- dangerous levels of poisonous carbon monoxide.

In fact, ventless heaters commonly raise relative humidity by only 10% to 15%. Most older homes are too dry in winter, so this poses a problem only in tight new homes.

Modern ventless gas heaters prevent excess carbon monoxide by monitoring the percentage of oxygen in the air and shutting off the gas supply before it becomes dangerously low. The illustration below shows the operation of the oxygen depletion sensor, which sends a cutoff signal to the stove's gas control.

Oxygen Depletion Sensor
Here is how the depletion sensor works:

1. Natural gas or propane gas enters the sensor at a constant controlled pressure from a pressure regulator.

2. The piezoelectric igniter produces an electric arc that ignites the gas.

3. The thermocouple, heated by the flame, produces a voltage which opens the main gas supply valve.

4. The pilot flame is precisely tuned to the gas pressure and the normal percentage oxygen in air (21%). Even a 1% decrease in oxygen causes the flame to ignite farther away from the orifice.

5. When oxygen depletion becomes critical, the flame misses the thermocouple completely, reducing its voltage, so the main gas valve shuts off the gas supply.

Efficiency
Assuming complete combustion, a ventless gas stove is, by definition, 100% efficient.

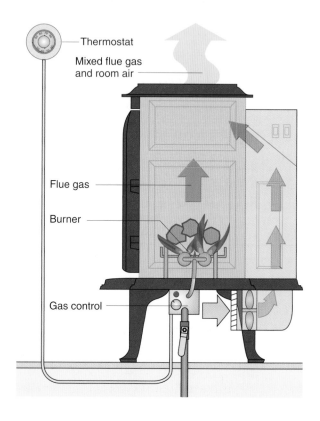

Ventless Gas Stove

- Thermostat
- Mixed flue gas and room air
- Flue gas
- Burner
- Gas control

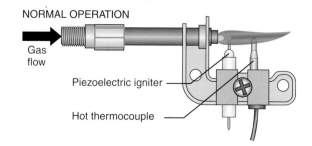

Oxygen Depletion Sensor

NORMAL OPERATION

- Gas flow
- Piezoelectric igniter
- Hot thermocouple

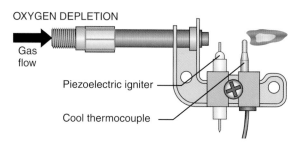

OXYGEN DEPLETION

- Gas flow
- Piezoelectric igniter
- Cool thermocouple

Direct-vent heaters require no chimney flue. Instead, the hot combustion gas exhausts through an inner pipe which is cooled by outside supply air entering through a concentric outer shell. The supply air is warmed, while the combustion gas is cooled.

Here is how a direct-vent gas stove works:

1. The pilot flame is first ignited by clicking a spark generator. This pilot flame remains lit throughout the heating season.

2. The fire can be turned on and off either manually or by a thermostat. The thermostat sends a voltage to the gas control to supply gas and light the fire.

3. Hot flue gases rise and exit through the inner cylinder of the double-wall pipe.

4. Combustion air is drawn in through the outer cylinder, cooling the double-wall pipe and becoming preheated.

5. A second thermostat senses the temperature rise in the enclosing chamber and activates a fan to circulate the warm air to the room.

6. The double-wall pipe is so well insulated and cooled by the inflow of outside combustion air that it can be placed in direct contact with construction materials, eliminating the need for a chimney through the roof.

7. Room air is warmed either through natural convection or by a small fan, as shown in the illustration.

Efficiencies

Because the products of combustion are lost to the outdoors, the latent heat of the water vapor in the flue gas is lost, as well as a portion of the sensible heat in the gases. Efficiencies in most direct-vent stoves run between 80% and 85%.

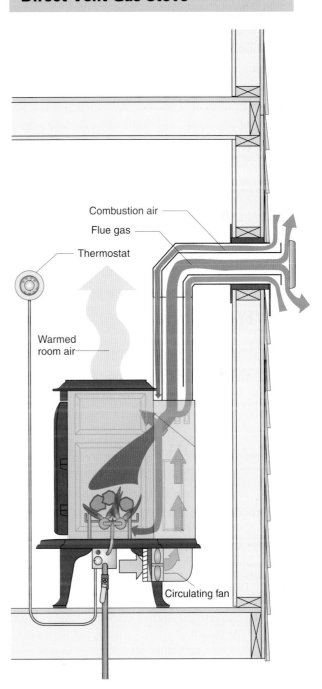

Combustion air

Flue gas

Thermostat

Warmed room air

Circulating fan

Wood Stoves

Nothing warms the soul like an open fireplace with a roaring fire. No method of heating your home is less efficient, either. Even the Rumford fireplace achieves a combustion efficiency of no more than 25%. Having to leave the chimney damper open until all embers are consumed subsequently wastes so much warm air up the chimney that the net efficiency is often less than zero!

Box Stove

A box stove increases efficiency in two ways: 1) Enclosing the fire in a steel or cast-iron box allows control of both the geometry and combustion air; 2) Bringing the fire out of the fireplace and into the room results in greater heat transfer by both radiation and convection. The box stove has an efficiency of 40% to 50%.

Air-Tight Stove

Air-tight joints and a gasketed door give complete control over the amount and location of combustion air. To start the fire, the air intake is opened fully. After the fuel is fully engaged, the air intake is reduced to control the burn rate.

Momentum carries the flue gases to the rear, but a horizontal baffle forces the gases to follow a long "S" path before exiting, transferring much of the gases' heat to the stove's cast-iron surfaces. High-quality air-tight stoves achieve an efficiency of up to 75%.

Catalytic Stove

Again, air-tight joints and a gasketed door give complete control over the amount and location of combustion air. To start a fire, the air intake is opened wide. To increase the draft, a damper in the baffle is opened, allowing flue gas an unrestricted path to the chimney.

After the fire is well established, the damper is closed, forcing flue gas to pass through the catalytic converter, lowering the temperature required for combustion, and resulting in a secondary burn of volatile gases and efficiencies of 70% to 80%.

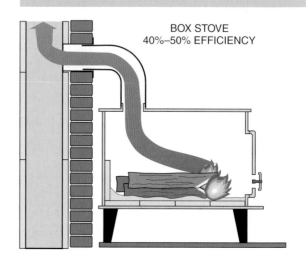

Three Wood Stoves & Efficiencies

BOX STOVE
40%–50% EFFICIENCY

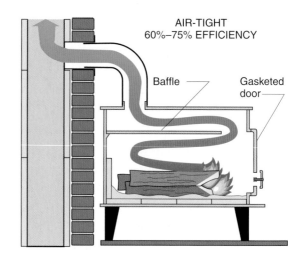

AIR-TIGHT
60%–75% EFFICIENCY

Baffle

Gasketed door

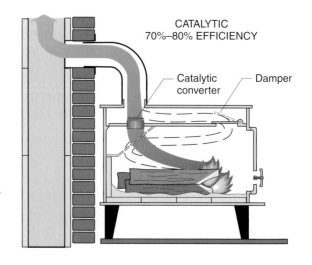

CATALYTIC
70%–80% EFFICIENCY

Catalytic converter

Damper

Pellet Stoves

The pellet stove emulates liquid fuel burners in that the fuel (small compressed pellets of wood fiber) is fed into a small combustion chamber where it is met by just the right amount of combustion air. The result is near perfect combustion. In fact, combustion is so complete and particulate emission so small that the pellet stove is exempt from EPA approval. Due to the complete combustion, efficiencies range from 78% to 85%.

Here is how the pellet stove works:

1. A *pellet hopper* at the top of the stove holds one or more 40-lb. bags of wood pellets.

2. Controlled by a thermostat, a motor-driven *feed auger* forces pellets into the *burn pot.*

3. The fire in the *burn pot* may be ignited manually or by an automatic electric lighter.

4. Combustion air is forced up through the burn pot grate by a thermostat-controlled fan to burn the pellets.

5. *Exhaust* gases flow around heat exchange tubes, then out to a chimney or stove pipe.

6. A separate fan blows room air through the heat exchanger tubes back into the room.

7. Ashes fall through the burn pot grate into an *ash pan* below. With complete combustion, the ash pan requires emptying only after about 50 bags (equivalent to approximately one cord of wood) have been consumed.

Inside a Pellet Stove

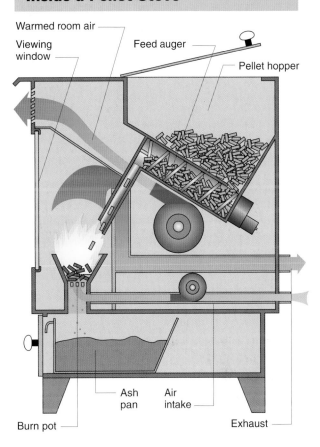

Warmed room air

Viewing window

Feed auger

Pellet hopper

Ash pan

Air intake

Burn pot

Exhaust

Direct Venting a Pellet Stove

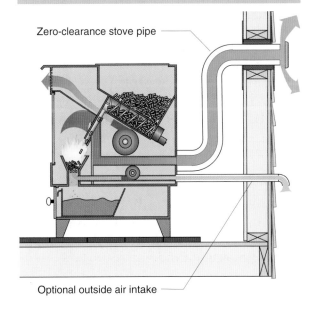

Zero-clearance stove pipe

Optional outside air intake

Warm Air Distribution

Here is how a typical warm air system works:

1. A thermostat (T2) in *zone 2* calls for heat by sending a low-voltage signal to the *zone control panel* (the green box).

2. The zone control opens the motorized *damper* for that zone and signals the furnace to produce heat.

3. When the furnace reaches its low-temperature limit, the *limit switch* turns on the furnace *blower*, which sends warm air through the duct to the zone.

4. The cooler, displaced air in the zone is drawn into the zone's *return duct*, then back into the furnace *return plenum* to be reheated.

The pros include circulation and filtration of air, humidification and dehumidification, possible integration with heat exchangers, and ductwork which can be shared with air-conditioning. Cons include bulky, hard-to-conceal ducts, noise at high air velocity, and sound transmission between rooms.

Multiple-Zone Warm Air System

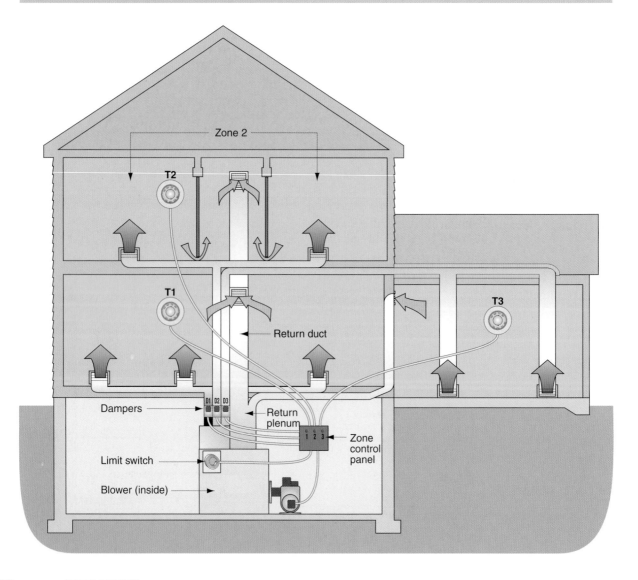

Hydronic Distribution

Here is how a typical hydronic system works:

1. A thermostat (T2) calls for heat by sending a low-voltage signal to the *zone control panel*.

2. The zone controller signals the boiler's oil or gas burner to produce heat.

3. When the boiler reaches its low-temperature limit, the aquastat signals the zone controller.

4. The zone controller turns on zone 2's *circulator pump*.

5. Hot water flows through zone 2's supply pipe to the baseboard heaters.

6. The baseboard heater warms the air in the zone.

7. The cooled water returns through the zone *return pipe* to be heated again.

A *BoilerMate™ water heater* (see p. 104) can be installed as shown as a separate heating zone, or the boiler may be tankless, having a domestic water heating coil within the boiler itself.

Multiple-Zone Hydronic System with BoilerMate

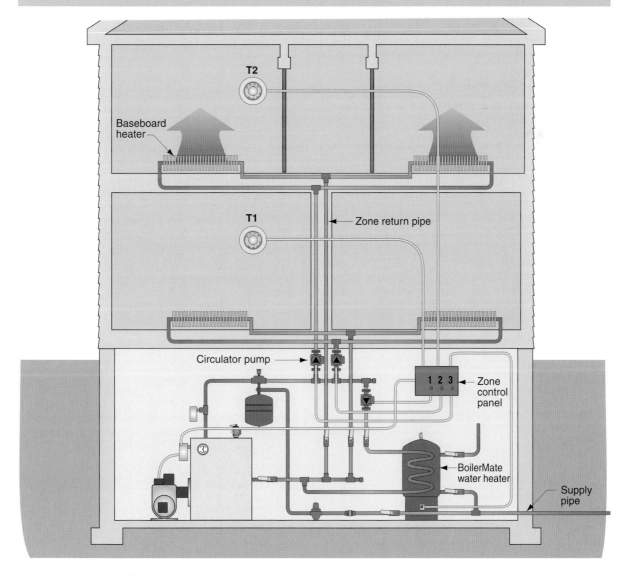

Radiant Heating

Here is how a typical radiant floor heating system works:

1. The thermostat in zone 2 (T2) calls for heat by sending a signal to the *zone control panel*.

2. The control panel signals the boiler's oil or gas burner to produce heat.

3. When the boiler reaches its low-temperature limit, an *aquastat* signals the zone control panel that heat is available.

4. The control panel turns on the *circulator pump* and the *control valve* for zone 2. Note that instead of zone control valves, a separate circulator pump may be provided for each zone.

5. Hot water flows through the serpentine tubing to heat the floor uniformly. Here, the tubing shown has two parallel branches.

6. The cooled water is collected and returns through the *zone return pipe* to be heated again.

Multiple-Zone Radiant Heating System

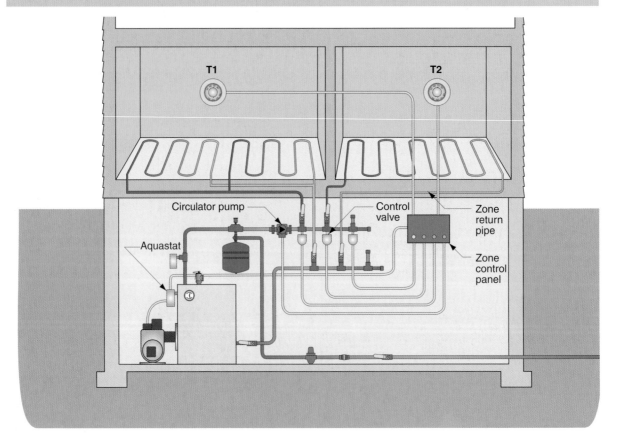

Free Convection

In the era of wood and coal stoves—even in the first wood and coal furnaces—heat was distributed by natural convection: simply warm air rising and cooler air falling. The advent of controlled distribution, made possible by forced warm air and forced hot water (hydronic) systems, made temperature control much more precise.

Two developments are bringing natural convection back, however:

1. Increased insulation and air-tightness, resulting in smaller temperature differences throughout the house.

2. Highly efficient wood and wood pellet direct-vent heaters with built-in air circulation.

The illustrations below show the right and wrong placements of freestanding heaters with the goal of uniformity of temperature. In deciding where to locate a heater, just remember, "Hot air rises; cold air falls."

Free Convection Geometries

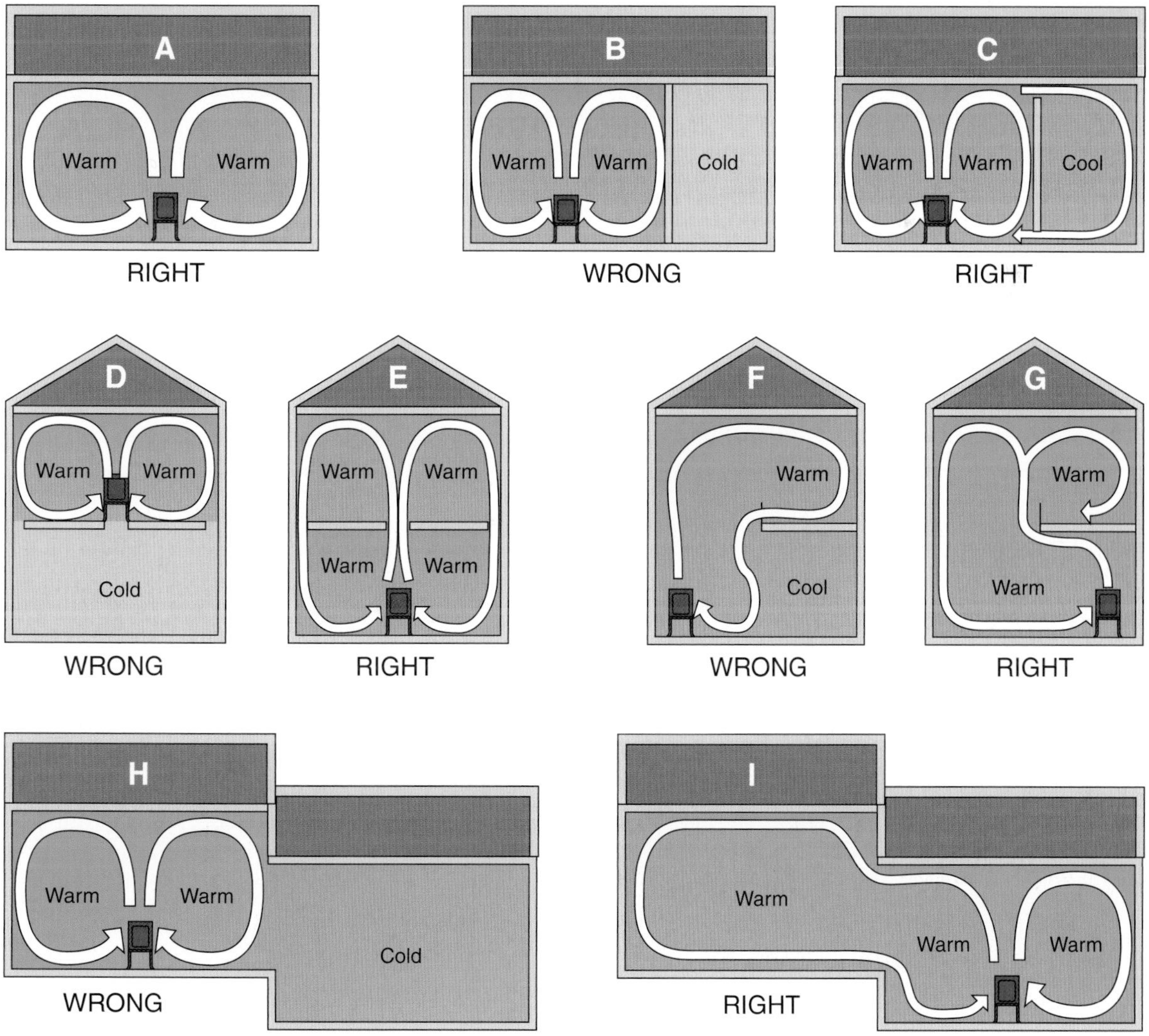

A — RIGHT

B — WRONG

C — RIGHT

D — WRONG

E — RIGHT

F — WRONG

G — RIGHT

H — WRONG

I — RIGHT

Cooling

5

The whole reason for cooling is *comfort*. But, of course, we are interested in staying cool at the least cost. We begin, therefore, by considering three methods utilized by past generations prior to the availability of mechanical cooling: *capturing natural breezes*, *using the stack effect* to vent hot air, and *utilizing a building's thermal mass* to moderate temperature swings.

After exhausting the free methods, we turn to the lowest-cost mechanical means: *creating a breeze with a box (window) fan*, *cooling with a ceiling fan*, and for those living in hot, dry climates, *evaporative cooling*.

If all else fails, or if we simply don't care about the cost, we turn to window and central *air-conditioning*. If cost is an issue, however, *clock thermostat savings* are simple to effect and of significant size.

Comfort

We heat and cool our homes at significant expense in order to be comfortable, so it is worthwhile considering exactly what determines comfort.

All of the environmental variables that determine whether we feel comfortable are embodied in what is called the "human comfort zone" (illustration on the facing page). The variables are:

- air temperature, the vertical location on the chart as shown by the thermometer scale along the left edge
- relative humidity (ratio of the amount of water vapor in the air to the amount possible before saturation and condensation), the horizontal location on the chart
- radiation on our bodies, in Btus per sq. ft.-hr., shown by the horizontal curves below the central comfort zone
- air movement across our bodies, in miles per hour (mph), shown as the horizontal curves above the comfort zone.

The comfort zone, in the absence of radiation or moving air, is shown by the tinted zone containing two seated people. The significance of the comfort zone is that most lightly clothed people—as you normally would be in your home—feel neither too cool nor too warm within the temperature and humidity boundaries of the zone. These limits are roughly 70°F to 82°F and 20% to 70% relative humidity. Ordinarily, below 70°F one would turn on the heating system, and above 82°F one would turn on the air conditioner.

Of course, turning on either the heating system or the air conditioner increases your energy bill. The reason we are exploring the comfort zone here is the possibility of achieving comfort for less money. As you may suspect, radiation and moving air offer those possibilities.

Effect of Radiation

Below the comfort zone are a series of horizontal curves labeled from 0 to 300 Btus per sq. ft.-hr. These curves show how the comfort zone can be depressed as much as 24°F by radiation in the absence of moving air. For perspective, 300 Btus per sq. ft.-hr. is the approximate intensity of the sun's radiation at noon on a clear day.

For example, were you sitting in your normal clothing in the full noon sun with no air movement, you would feel as comfortable at 50°F in the sun as you would at 74°F out of the sun.

Effect of Air Movement

Our skin is normally about 98°F, so air moving across it convects heat away, giving us the feeling that the air is cool. Above the comfort zone are a series of horizontal curves labeled from 0 to 8 mph. These curves show how far the top of the comfort zone can be raised by moving air in the absence of radiation.

For example, were you sitting in the shade in your normal clothing and an 8-mph breeze were blowing across your body, you would feel as comfortable at 94°F as you would at 82°F with no breeze.

Note how the upper edge of the comfort zone bends down as relative humidity increases. This explains why we feel high humidity to be oppressive. Some of the cooling effect of moving air is due to the evaporation of moisture from our skin. The higher the relative humidity, the less the ability of the air to evaporate surface moisture and cool our skin.

In the following pages we will see a number of ways one can take advantage of moving air, both natural and man-made, to achieve cooling without the expense of mechanical air-conditioning.

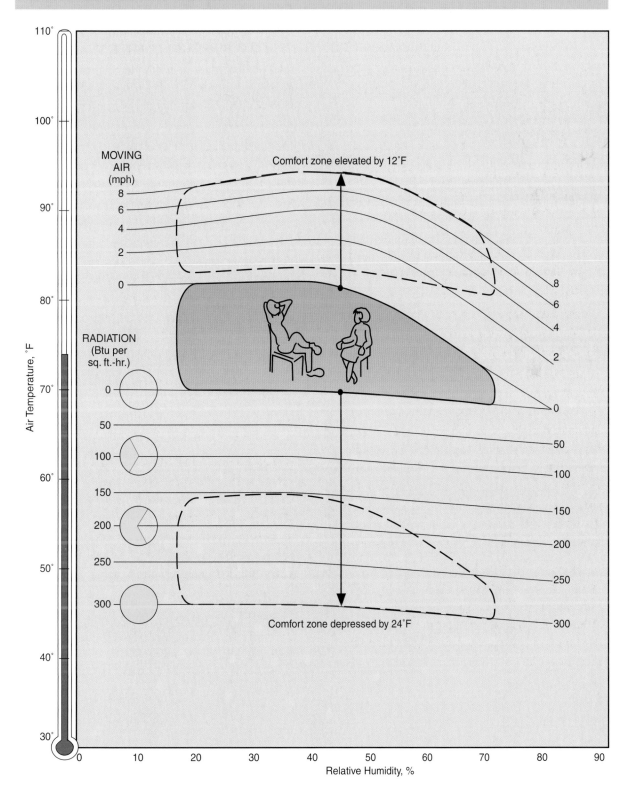

Capturing Natural Breezes

As we saw in the comfort zone diagram on the previous page, air movement across our bodies has the potential to raise our upper comfort limit from about 82°F to about 94°F in an 8-mph breeze. In fact, a breeze of only 2 mph makes us feel 4°F cooler. If you are fortunate (or smart) enough to have openable windows facing into the prevailing summer breeze, you can capture and funnel some of it through your sitting and sleeping areas.

The illustration on the facing page shows the pressure distribution around a house in a breeze. The side of the house facing the wind acts as an obstruction, so the momentum of the wind piling up causes a local increase in pressure. The effect is the opposite on the downwind side. Here, the shortage of air results in an area of lower pressure. Naturally, air will flow from an area of high pressure to an area of low pressure. That is, after all, what causes wind.

By operating windows strategically, one can control the air flow within the house. In the illustration, opening all of the upwind and downwind windows overnight results in a rather uniform cooling of the house. Suppose you wished, however, to maximize the cooling breeze over your bed at location A. By closing the patio door at B, the air entering at the windows, C, would be redirected to the remaining open downwind windows, increasing the flow over your bed.

Note that an additional effect of the breeze is to flush the heat accumulated during the day out of the house. For that reason, you might choose to leave the patio door at B open.

Prevailing Wind Directions in Summer

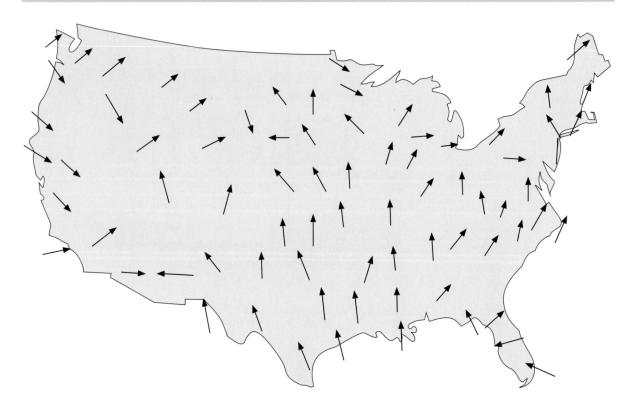

Capturing and Funneling Natural Breezes

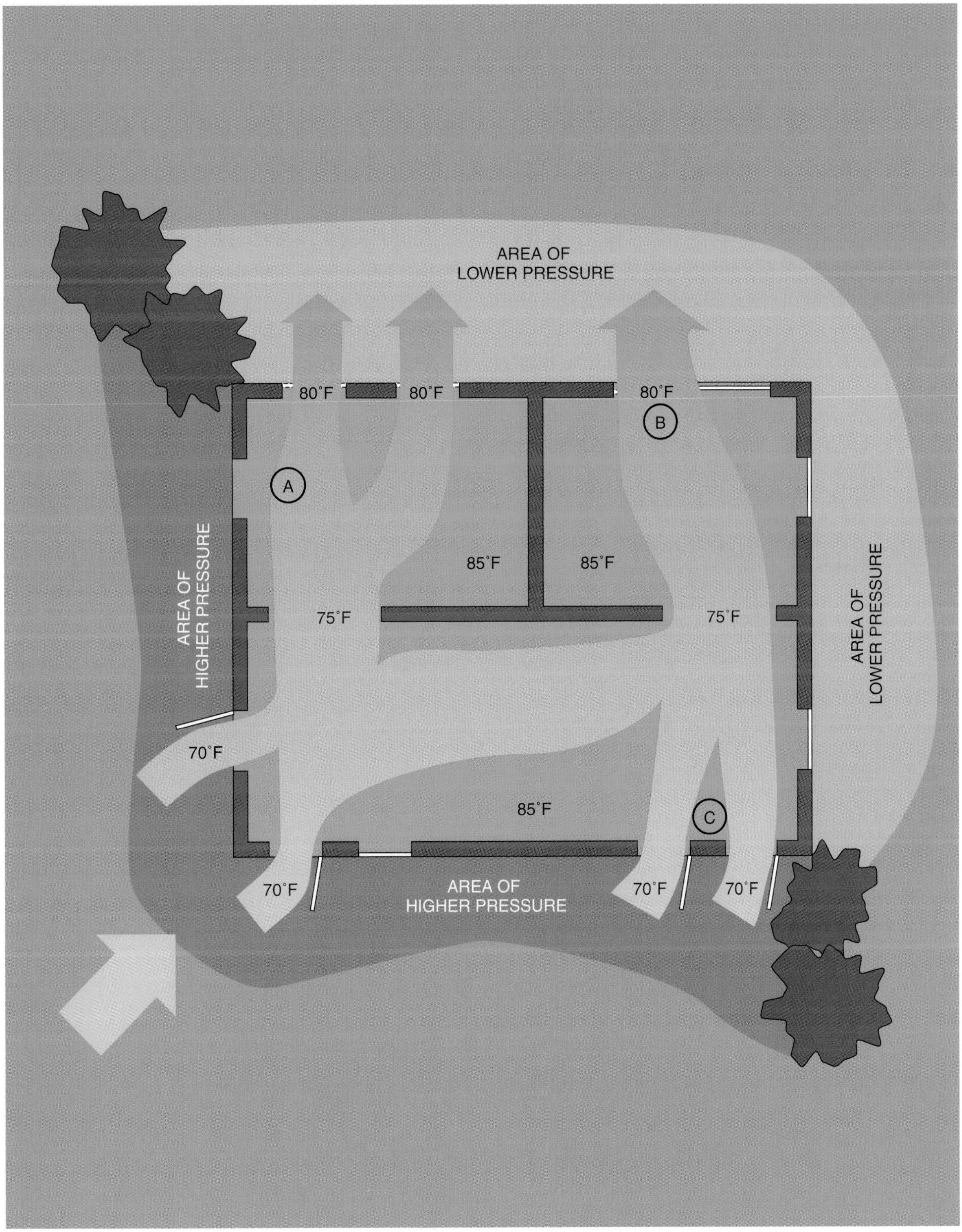

AREA OF
LOWER PRESSURE
80°F
80°F
80°F
B
A
85°F
85°F
75°F
75°F
AREA OF
HIGHER PRESSURE
AREA OF
LOWER PRESSURE
70°F
85°F
C
70°F
AREA OF
HIGHER PRESSURE
70°F
70°F

Using the Stack Effect

The "stack effect" gets its name from the behavior of smoke stacks. If the gas inside the stack is warmer than the surrounding air, the gas is less dense and acts like a giant warm air balloon. The upward flow in the stack depends on the cross-sectional area and height of the stack and the temperature difference between the inside and outside air.

The actual formula uses absolute temperatures (where zero on the scale is -459°F) and the acceleration of gravity. However, over the limited range of temperatures involving houses in summer, we can approximate the formula as:

Air flow, cfm = $13.3A \sqrt{H\Delta T}$

where:
A = area of equal-sized openings in sq. ft.
H = height difference between openings in ft.
ΔT = temperature difference, inside – outside, °F

Example 1: In the tall house in the illustration on the facing page, the effective areas of inlet and outlet are each 10 sq. ft. The difference in height between the patio door at ground level and the skylight and roof window at roof level is three stories, or 26 ft. The difference in temperature is 85°F inside minus 70°F outside, or 15F°. Running the numbers (which will require a calculator with the square root function), the result is an air flow of about 2,530 cu. ft. per min. With an interior volume of 30,000 cu. ft., the entire volume of building air is exchanged every 12 minutes or 5.1 times per hour.

Example 2: The typical house at the bottom of the illustration has the same footprint (24 ft. × 40 ft.), but only two floors instead of four. The average height difference is a lot less: 10 ft. All other factors remain the same. The resulting air flow is 1,570 cu. ft. per min. The 16,000-cu. ft. interior volume of the house is now exchanged in 10 minutes, or 5.9 times per hour.

Dual Cooling Effects

The stack effect cools in two ways:

1. It flushes out the accumulated heat from the day and replaces it with cooler nighttime air.

2. For anyone within the moving column of air, the upper limit of the comfort zone is lowered by the cooling effect of moving air.

As heat is removed from the house, the temperature difference between inside and outside diminishes, so the air flow diminishes accordingly. However, because night ambient temperatures tend to drop from sunset to sunrise, the stack effect remains in operation to some degree all night long.

To maximize the cooling effect on your body:

1. Sleep inside the inlet stream of air where the air temperature is lowest.

2. Make the inlet area smaller than the sum of the outlet areas, forcing the volume of air through a smaller orifice, which results in a greater velocity.

Cooling with the Stack Effect

TALL HOUSE
Air flow = 2,530 cu. ft. per min.
Air changes per hr. = 5

Screened roof & windows.
Effective area = 10 sq. ft.

Interior volume 30,000 cu. ft.

Screened patio door.
Effective area = 10 sq. ft.

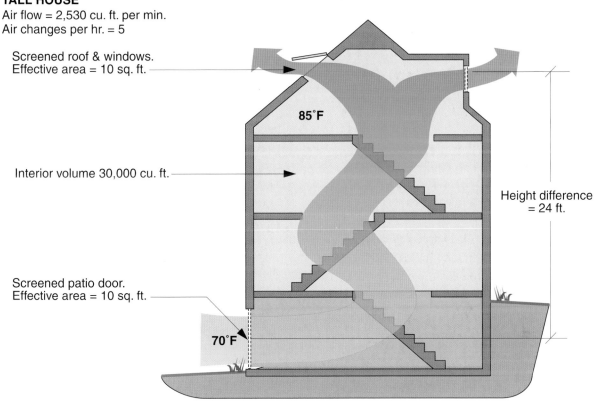

85°F

70°F

Height difference
= 24 ft.

TYPICAL HOUSE
Air flow = 1.570 cu. ft. per min.
Air changes per hr. = 6

Screened double-hung window.
Effective area = 2.5 sq. ft.
Four windows = 10 sq. ft.

Interior volume 16,000 cu. ft.

Screened patio door.
Effective area = 10 sq. ft.

85°F

70°F

Height difference
= 10 ft.

Utilizing a Building's Thermal Mass

Mass is a measure of inertia of rest—the difficulty of getting an object to move. "Thermal mass" is a concept used by building designers and engineers to describe the difficulty of getting a building's temperature to change. Given two otherwise identical buildings, the one with twice the thermal mass of the other would change in temperature only half as much.

Long before scientists defined and quantified heat, the Pueblo Indians of the Southwest United States were using thermal mass to great effect. There, the air temperature swings wildly from over 100°F during the day to 50°F overnight. Like the ocean, the massive mud walls of the pueblos required so much heat to change in temperature that the interior never reached the daily high air temperature. In fact, daytime heat gain was delayed about 12 hours in moving through the mud walls, so the walls actually acted as a heat source for the home during the cold night.

Insulation works to the same end. By reducing the amount of heat flowing through a building's walls, floor, and ceiling, it retards and diminishes the temperature swings due to changes in outdoor temperature. Put the two together—mass plus insulation—and you have the best of all possible worlds.

Your home was probably not built to maximize either mass or insulation. However, it has some amount of thermal mass, so let's consider how you might use it to your advantage.

The Effect of Thermal Mass

The top graph on the facing page shows how the interior temperatures of two houses respond to a cycling outdoor air temperature without intervention on the part of the homeowner. Note that these are idealized sinusoidal temperature swings. Real diurnal temperature swings are less symmetric, depending on length of day vs. night, percentage cloudiness, and effects of wind. However, the sinusoidal internal temperature swings accurately reflect the responses to a sinusoidal outdoor temperature swing.

The red curve is the outdoor temperature cycling through a 20°F range, from a low of 69°F at sunrise, to a high of 89°F at around 4 PM, and back to 69°F at sunrise.

The orange curve shows the temperature response of a typical insulated house having the low thermal mass typical of wood frame construction. Its temperature swing of 17°F is just a little less than that of the outside, and its peak temperature of 88°F occurs right at the family's evening social hours.

The blue curve shows the effect of adding thermal mass to the same house. Now the swing is reduced to 8°F, and the peak temperature is reduced to 83°F.

Thermal Pumping

So far we have played the role of passive occupants, just letting the building's thermal mass respond to the swings in outdoor temperature. But what if we were to open the house to the outside whenever the outdoor temperature fell below the inside temperature?

The bottom graph shows what would happen were we to open all of the windows at the point in the evening when the indoor and outdoor temperatures crossed paths and then closed them as soon as the outdoor temperature began to rise again in the morning.

The low-mass house (orange curve) runs only about 1F° cooler than before. This is because the low mass of the building causes it to respond rapidly to the outdoor temperature anyway, without having to open the windows.

The high-mass house, however, behaves quite differently. With the windows shut from 6AM to 10PM, the thermal mass acts to soak up the heat and hold the temperature down. But with the windows open, the thermal mass is short-circuited, and the building tracks the outdoor temperature much more closely. The result is that the building cycles between only 70°F and 80°F—well within our comfort zone.

The Moderating Effect of Thermal Mass

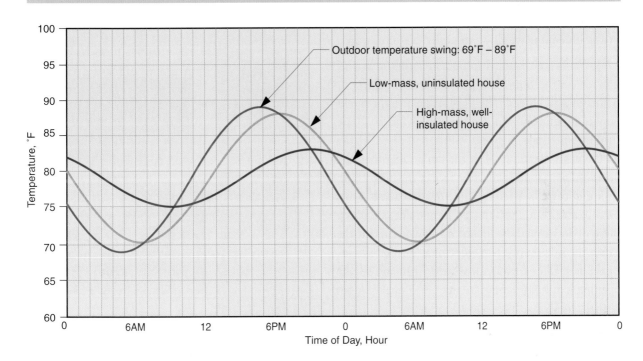

Outdoor temperature swing: 69°F – 89°F

Low-mass, uninsulated house

High-mass, well-insulated house

Temperature, °F

Time of Day, Hour

Cooling a Building by Thermal Pumping

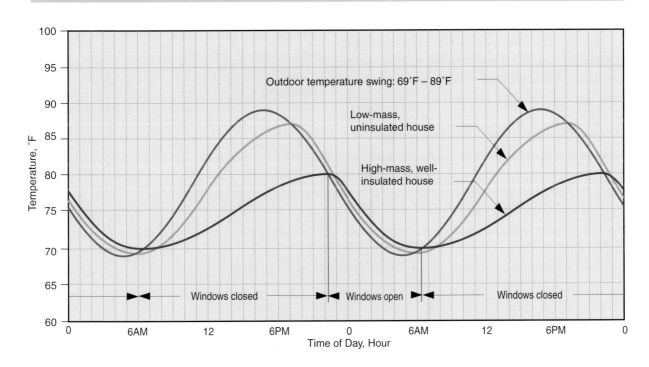

Outdoor temperature swing: 69°F – 89°F

Low-mass, uninsulated house

High-mass, well-insulated house

Temperature, °F

Windows closed

Windows open

Windows closed

Time of Day, Hour

Creating a Breeze with a Box Fan

When the heat in your bedroom is oppressive, and there is not a breath of air outdoors, generate your own breeze. An inexpensive 20-in. box fan mounted in a double-hung window is a pretty fair substitute.

Box fans are designed to operate either in a window or on the floor, but they have no brackets or points of attachment. The illustration at right shows how to mount one in a double-hung window. Raise the bottom sash as high as possible, and place the fan on the inside window sill. If the fan is taller than the opening, push it up against the face of the raised sash. If shorter than the opening, close the raised sash down on top of the fan. Push the fan to one side, and cut a piece of corrugated cardboard or plywood to fill the gap at the side. Apply 2-in.-wide blue "painter's tape" to the fan, filler strip, and window trim to seal the opening and hold the fan in place. Do not use duct tape as it will leave a residue when removed.

Most box fans offer three speeds and move in the neighborhood of 2,000 cfm of air on their high setting. At the fan outlet, that number converts into a breeze of 8 mph. How much of that no-resistance speed is realized depends on the number and size of other open windows.

Another interesting number is the rate of flushing of stale, overheated air from the house. As an example, assume the house shown on the facing page has a floor area of 1,000 sq. ft. and a volume of 8,000 cu. ft. At 2,000 cfm, a single fan could exchange the entire volume of interior air fifteen times every hour!

Assuming the outdoor air is cooler than the indoor air, the box fan can thus cool you in two ways:

- by replacing warm inside air with cooler outside air
- by raising your personal comfort zone with a breeze.

Box Fan Installation

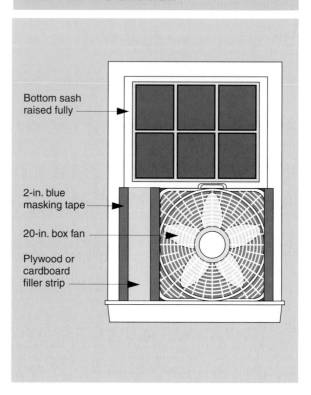

Bottom sash raised fully

2-in. blue masking tape

20-in. box fan

Plywood or cardboard filler strip

Emulating Natural Breezes

One of the only complaints about box fans is that they are noisy. Some people have difficulty sleeping with the fan on high. The illustration on the facing page shows the solution: locate the fan not in the room where you are sleeping, but in a room as far away as possible. The fan noise will be so slight you will go to sleep thinking the breeze is natural.

Note that this technique requires that the fan now blow out of the house. If the fan isn't reversible (most aren't), just reinstall it to blow in the opposite direction.

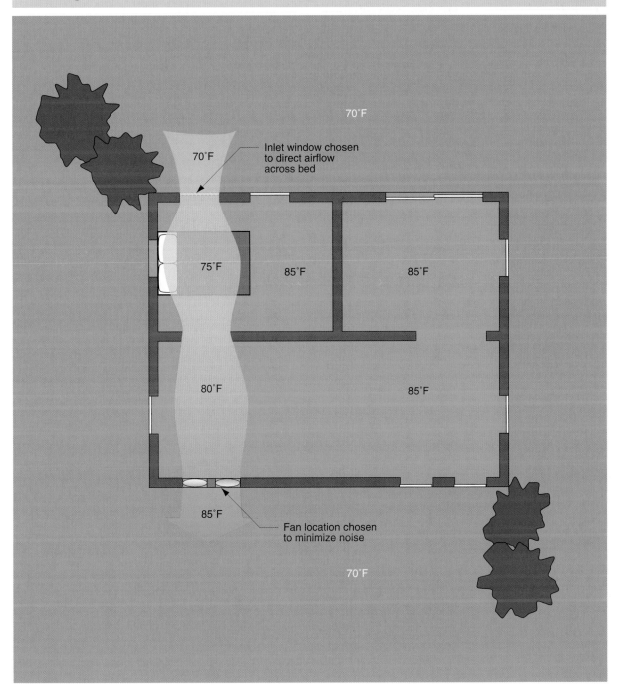

70°F

70°F

Inlet window chosen
to direct airflow
across bed

75°F

85°F

85°F

80°F

85°F

85°F

Fan location chosen
to minimize noise

70°F

Cooling with a Ceiling Fan

Ceiling fans don't lower air temperature. Like box fans, they produce a cooling effect on people by raising the upper limit of the human comfort zone. Before the widespread adoption of air-conditioning, ceiling fans were the predominant means of cooling, particularly in southern states. They nearly disappeared from 1930 until the early 1970s but came back into favor because of their much higher efficiencies compared to those of air conditioners. With further improvements in efficiency, noise level, lighting options, and the addition of remote controls, they have become a common design element in new homes.

Cooling Effect

The illustrations on the facing page show the two primary uses of ceiling fans:

- creating a breeze onto a favorite sitting place
- creating a dream-inducing zephyr over your bed.

A quality fan of 48-in. blade diameter will move at least 5,500 cu. ft. of air per minute (cfm) directly below the blades. This translates into a downward velocity (breeze) of 5 miles per hour. Consulting "The Human Comfort Zone" on p. 75, we see the cooling effect is about 7°F. If the room air were actually 85°F, directly under the fan it would feel as if the air were 78°F.

Efficiency

To lower the temperature of the room air to 78°F would require a medium-size room air conditioner consuming about 600 watts of electricity. The most efficient 48-in. ceiling fan, by contrast, would consume only 60 watts in cooling the occupants—an energy and dollar savings of 90%!

Summer/Winter Operation

The primary purpose of a ceiling fan is to generate moving air that acts as a breeze to cool its subjects, not to homogenize the air in a room. Summertime operation, therefore, requires that the fan blow in a downward direction.

Much is made of the possibility of reversing the fan's direction in winter, the reason being that room air in winter is stratified, with the air close to the ceiling much warmer than the air at floor level. In an uninsulated room heated by a point source such as a wood stove, that is true, but in a well-insulated room heated by a modern distribution system, it is not. However, if you do use a ceiling fan in winter, reverse its direction so that it blows upward. Otherwise, the direct breeze will cool you just as it does in summer, defeating your purpose.

Sizing the Fan

Picking the best size for a ceiling fan depends on two factors: the floor area in sq. ft., and the shape of the room. The chart below shows both the recommended air flow at high speed and the blade span versus the floor area. Note that at over 300 sq. ft., an oblong room would benefit from a pair of smaller fans rather than a single fan. Two fans would result in two separate sitting areas being cooled.

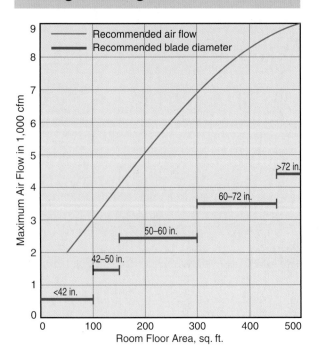

Sizing a Ceiling Fan

Cooling a Sitting Room with a Ceiling Fan

Cooling a Bedroom with a Ceiling Fan

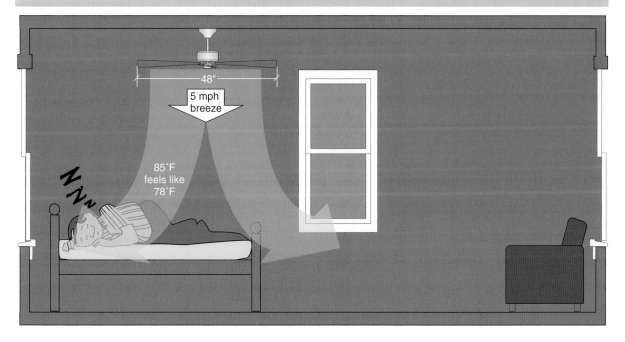

Evaporative Cooling

In the process of evaporating, water absorbs heat, which is why you feel so cool when you emerge from swimming on a dry, breezy day. Evaporative coolers (also known as swamp coolers) utilize this phenomenon to lower air temperature. As the illustration on the facing page shows, hot dry air blown through a water-soaked pad emerges as humid, but much cooler, air. The temperature drop can be predicted from the equation:

$$\text{Temperature drop} = E \times (DB - WB)$$

where: E = cooler efficiency, percent
DB = intake air dry bulb temperature
WB = intake air wet bulb temperature

Evaporative coolers are recommended wherever the temperature drop exceeds 20°F and the cooled air would be below 79°F. The table below lists these criteria for selected cities. Cities that meet both criteria appear in italics. To size an evaporative cooler:

1. Compute the volume of house air in cu. ft.

2. Find the recommended minutes per air change for your location in the table.

3. Divide the house volume by minutes to find the recommended cooler capacity in cfm.

4. If your home is very energy efficient, divide cfm by 2; if not insulated, multiply by 2.

Potential for Evaporative Cooling

Location	DB °F	WB °F	Temp Drop °F	Cooled Temp °F	Minutes per Air Change
AL, Birmingham	96	74	18	78	NR[1]
AZ, Phoenix	109	71	30	79	2
AR, Little Rock	99	76	18	81	NR
CA, Los Angeles	93	70	18	75	2
CO, Denver	93	59	27	66	4
CT, Hartford	91	74	14	77	NR
DE, Wilmington	92	74	14	78	NR
DC, Washington	93	75	14	79	NR
FL, Orlando	94	76	14	80	NR
GA, Atlanta	94	74	16	78	NR
ID, Boise	96	65	25	71	4
IL, Chicago	94	75	15	79	NR
IN, Indianapolis	92	74	14	78	NR
IA, Des Moines	94	75	15	79	NR
KS, Topeka	99	75	20	79	2
KY, Louisville	95	74	17	78	NR
LA, Baton Rouge	95	77	14	81	NR
MA, Boston	91	73	14	77	NR
MI, Detroit	91	73	14	77	NR
MS, Jackson	97	76	17	80	NR
MO, St. Louis	98	75	18	80	NR

Potential for Evaporative Cooling

Location	DB °F	WB °F	Temp Drop °F	Cooled Temp °F	Minutes per Air Change
MT, Great Falls	91	60	25	66	3
NE, North Platte	97	69	22	75	3
NV, Las Vegas	108	66	34	74	3
NH, Concord	90	72	14	76	NR
NJ, Newark	94	74	16	78	NR
NM, Albuquerque	96	61	28	68	3
NY, Syracuse	90	73	14	76	NR
NC, Greensboro	93	74	15	78	NR
ND, Bismarck	95	68	22	73	3
OH, Columbus	92	73	15	77	NR
OK, Tulsa	101	74	22	79	1
OR, Portland	89	68	17	72	NR
PA, Pittsburgh	91	72	15	76	NR
RI, Providence	89	73	13	76	NR
SC, Columbia	97	76	17	80	NR
SD, Rapid City	95	66	23	72	3
TN, Nashville	97	75	18	79	NR
TX, Dallas	102	75	22	80	2
UT, Salt Lake City	97	62	28	69	4
VA, Richmond	95	76	15	80	NR
WY, Casper	92	58	27	65	4

[1] NR = Not Recommended

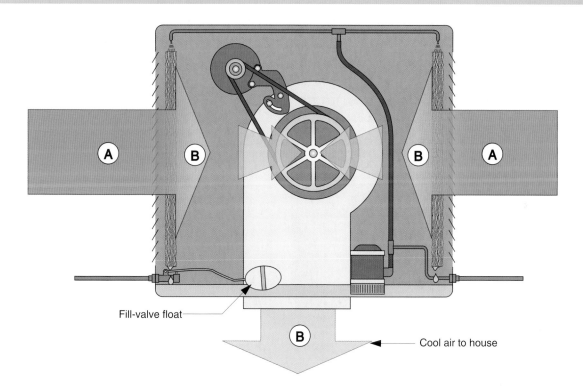

Fill-valve float

Cool air to house

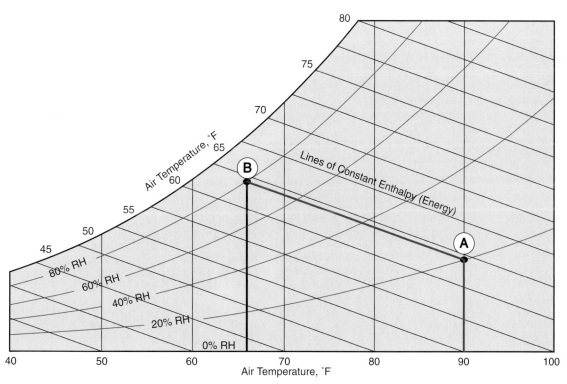

Air Temperature, °F

Lines of Constant Enthalpy (Energy)

80% RH

60% RH

40% RH

20% RH

0% RH

Air Temperature, °F

Air-Conditioning

Window and Central Air Conditioners

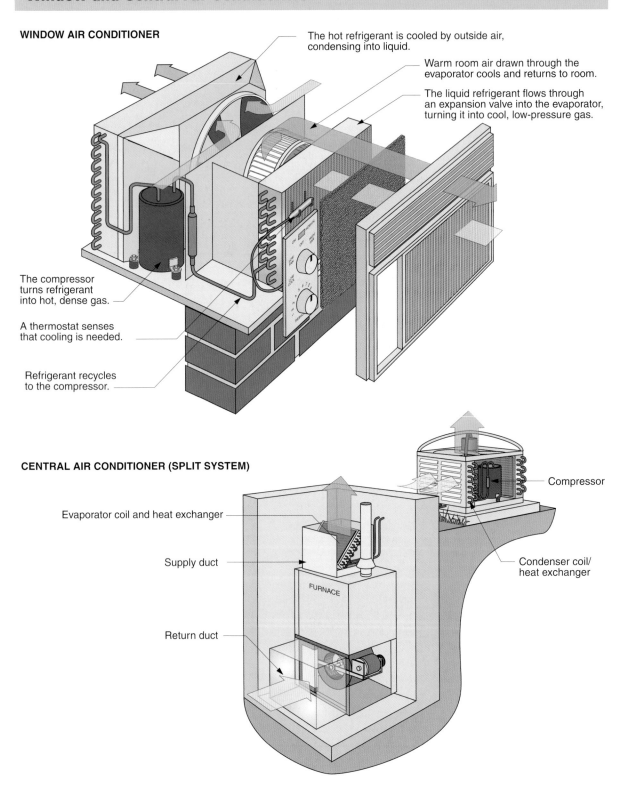

WINDOW AIR CONDITIONER

The hot refrigerant is cooled by outside air, condensing into liquid.

Warm room air drawn through the evaporator cools and returns to room.

The liquid refrigerant flows through an expansion valve into the evaporator, turning it into cool, low-pressure gas.

The compressor turns refrigerant into hot, dense gas.

A thermostat senses that cooling is needed.

Refrigerant recycles to the compressor.

CENTRAL AIR CONDITIONER (SPLIT SYSTEM)

Evaporator coil and heat exchanger

Supply duct

FURNACE

Return duct

Compressor

Condenser coil/ heat exchanger

If all else fails to cool you into the comfort zone, your next option is to air-condition. Air conditioners, powerful but expensive tools, lower both humidity and temperature.

The first thing you will require is an estimate of your peak cooling load, the number of Btu/hr. that need to be removed under the worst conditions of the cooling season. The work sheet and tables on the following pages allow you to find that load, whether you are cooling just a bedroom or your entire house, no matter where you live in the United States.

You may wish to photocopy the work sheet so that you will be able to calculate the peak cooling load for additional rooms.

Read the instructions carefully for each line before entering any numbers. An example calculation follows the work sheet.

When you are finished, go to the Energy Star site at *www.energystar.gov*. There you will find an up-to-date list of all air conditioners, with their *rated cooling capacities* and *energy efficiency ratings (EER)*. Look for models with the highest EER (the ratio of Btus removed to watts of electricity consumed) that also closely match your load. The most efficient air conditioner for your purpose will be one that is just capable of supplying your calculated load.

Cooling Factors for Air Conditioner Work Sheet, Line 9

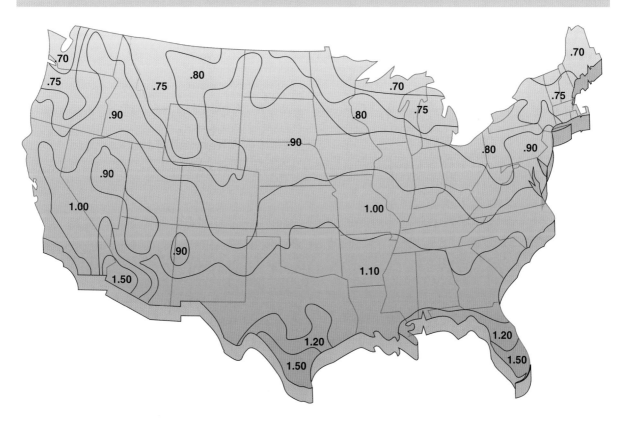

Cooling Work Sheet Instructions

Lines 1 and 2. Use line 1 if your house has a well-ventilated attic; otherwise use line 2. Find the shading factor in column 1 of Table 1. The insulation factor is 0.8 times the nominal R-value of the attic insulation. (See Chapter 7 for insulation R-values.) Use the value 2.4 if there is no insulation present.

Line 3. Follow the same instructions as for lines 1 and 2. Exterior walls are those facing the outdoors. Enter doors as exterior walls. Do not include windows, as they will be entered below.

Line 4. Interior walls are those that separate the cooled space from unconditioned spaces. If you are cooling the entire house, there will be no interior walls. The insulation factor is 0.8 times the nominal R-value of the wall insulation (see Chapter 7 for insulation R-values), or 2.4 if there is none.

Line 5. Get the floor factor from Table 2; the insulation factor is as in line 4.

Line 6. Enter the total floor area of the cooled space. Estimate air changes per hour as 0.4 for the tightest possible house to 1.3 for a drafty one.

Line 7. Calculate window areas as height × width of the sash (the frames holding the glass). Get the glazing factors from Table 3.

Line 8. Get the shading factors from Table 1 and the glazing factors from Table 3.

Line 9. Add the results from lines 1 through 8 and multiply by the cooling factor for your geographic area shown on the map on p. 89.

Line 10. Multiply your average monthly spring or fall kilowatt-hours (get these from your utility bills or by calling your electric utility) by 1.4. For the average home the result should be about 600 kWh/month.

Line 11. Enter the average number of people occupying the cooled space during the hot months.

Line 12. Add lines 9, 10, and 11, then multiply the result by the mass factor from Table 4.

Table 1. Shading Factors

Degree of Shading	Roof, Wall, Ceiling	Windows
Unshaded areas	1.00	1.00
Fully shaded areas	0.70	0.20
Partially shaded by awning, overhang, or small trees	0.90	0.65
Shaded inside by window shades, drapes, or films		0.45

Table 2. Floor Factors

Floor Above	Factor
Open crawl space	1.0
Closed crawl space	0.0
Full basement	0.0
Unconditioned room	0.9
Ground (slab-on-grade)	0.1

Table 3. Glazing Factors

Type of Glazing	Line 7	Line 8
Single-glazed window	1.0	1.0
Double-glazed window	0.5	0.8
Triple-glazed window	0.33	0.65

Table 4. Thermal Mass Factors

Building Construction	Factor
Light wood frame	1.00
Solid masonry or wood frame with exterior masonry veneer	0.90
Wood frame with masonry interior walls, floors, or other mass	0.80
Earth-sheltered (underground) walls and roof	0.50

Work Sheet for Sizing Air Conditioners

Source of Heat Gain	Calculations	Results
1. Roof over ventilated attic	_____ sq. ft. x 44 x _____ shading factor /_____ insulation factor =	_____
2. Cathedral ceiling or roof over unventilated attic	_____ sq. ft. x 48 x _____ shading factor /_____ insulation factor =	_____
3. Exterior wall facing:		
North	_____ sq. ft. x 18 x _____ shading factor / _____ insulation factor =	_____
East	_____ sq. ft. x 28 x _____ shading factor / _____ insulation factor =	_____
South	_____ sq. ft. x 24 x _____ shading factor / _____ insulation factor =	_____
West	_____ sq. ft. x 28 x _____ shading factor / _____ insulation factor =	_____
4. Interior walls facing unconditioned rooms	_____ sq. ft. x 12 / _____ insulation factor =	_____
5. Floors over unconditioned spaces	_____ sq. ft. x 20 x _____ floor factor / _____ insulation factor =	_____
6. Infiltration: area of living space	_____ sq. ft. x _____ air changes/hour x 1.6 =	_____
7. Window conduction	_____ sq. ft. x 16 x _____ glazing factor =	_____
8. Window solar gain:		
North	_____ sq. ft. x 16 x _____ shading factor /_____ glazing factor =	_____
East, South, Southeast	_____ sq. ft. x 80 x _____ shading factor /_____ glazing factor =	_____
West, Southwest, Northwest	_____ sq. ft. x 140 x _____ shading factor /_____ glazing factor =	_____
Northeast	_____ sq. ft. x 50 x _____ shading factor /_____ glazing factor =	_____
9. Sum of lines 1 – 8	_____ x _____ cooling factor from map on p. 89 =	_____
10. Utility gain	_____ watts being consumed in space x 3.4 =	_____
11. People gain	_____ number of people in space x 600 =	_____
12. Peak cooling load, Btu/hour: sum of lines 9 – 11 x _____ thermal mass factor =		_____

Cooling Load Example

The facing page contains a completed form showing the calculations for the required capacity of a central air conditioner for a small house in Boston, MA, shown at right.

The house is deliberately kept simple in order to clarify the calculations. Many homes will have more than one type of exterior wall, foundation, or window, and will require multiple entries for these line items.

Line 1. The ceiling measures 30 ft. × 40 ft., so its area is 1,200 sq. ft. The roof, however, is pitched 30°, so its area is 1,386 sq. ft. The unshaded roof has a shading factor of 1.00, from column 1 of Table 1. The insulation factor is 0.8 × the nominal R-value of 38.

Line 3. The north and south wall areas are each 320 sq. ft., less the window area of 21 sq. ft., or 299 sq. ft. The east and west walls measure 219 sq. ft. by the same process. The west wall is fully shaded, so its shading factor (Table 1) is 0.70. The rest are unshaded, so their shading factors are 1.00. The nominal R-values of 19 are multiplied by 0.8 to get insulation factors of 15.2.

Line 4. The entire house is air-conditioned, so the interior walls have no effect and are left blank.

Line 5. The house sits on a vented (open) crawl space, so the floor factor is 1.0.

Line 6. The house is quite air-tight, so there are estimated to be 0.50 air changes per hour.

Line 7. The glazing factor, from column 1 of Table 3, for double-glazed windows is 0.5.

Line 8. Both east and south windows are entered on a single line. The shading factors are the same as for the walls in line 3. The glazing factor of 0.8 is found in column 2 of Table 3.

Line 9. The sum of the results column for all of the lines above is 13,921. Boston's cooling factor of 0.75 is found from the map on p. 89.

Example House for Cooling Load

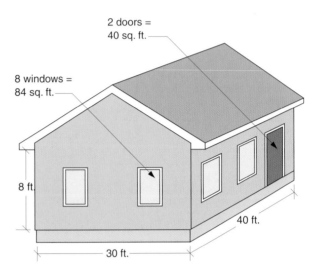

Air exchange rate = 0.5 changes per hour

Ceiling R-38, walls R-19, floor R-19 over vented crawlspace

Windows 21 sq. ft. each facing N, S, E, and W

West wall fully shaded; other walls and roof unshaded

Spring and fall utility bills average 350 kWh/month

Three occupants in summer months

Line 10. The electric utility bills for the spring and fall months show an average consumption of 350 kWh per month.

Line 11. There are three occupants of the home during the cooling season.

Line 12. The thermal mass factor for a light wood frame house (1.00) is found in Table 4. The sum of lines 9 through 11 is 13,906, so the peak cooling load is 13,906 Btu/hr. This is a small cooling load for a house and could be satisfied easily by two 7,000 Btu/hr. window air conditioners.

Work Sheet for Sizing Air Conditioners

Source of Heat Gain	Calculations	Results
1. Roof over ventilated attic	_1,386_ sq. ft. x 44 x _1.00_ shading factor / _30.4_ insulation factor =	2,006
2. Cathedral ceiling or roof over unventilated attic	_____ sq. ft. x 48 x _____ shading factor / _____ insulation factor =	
3. Exterior wall facing: North	_299_ sq. ft. x 18 x _1.00_ shading factor / _15.2_ insulation factor =	354
East	_219_ sq. ft. x 28 x _1.00_ shading factor / _15.2_ insulation factor =	403
South	_299_ sq. ft. x 24 x _1.00_ shading factor / _15.2_ insulation factor =	472
West	_219_ sq. ft. x 28 x _0.70_ shading factor / _15.2_ insulation factor =	282
4. Interior walls facing unconditioned rooms	_____ sq. ft. x 12 / _____ insulation factor =	
5. Floors over unconditioned spaces	_1,200_ sq. ft. x 20 x _1.0_ floor factor / _15.2_ insulation factor =	1,579
6. Infiltration: area of living space	_1,200_ sq. ft. x _0.5_ air changes/hour x 1.6 =	960
7. Window conduction	_84_ sq. ft. x 16 x _0.5_ glazing factor =	672
8. Window solar gain: North	_21_ sq. ft. x 16 x _1.00_ shading factor / _0.8_ glazing factor =	420
East, South, Southeast	_42_ sq. ft. x 80 x _1.00_ shading factor / _0.8_ glazing factor =	4,200
West, Southwest, Northwest	_21_ sq. ft. x 140 x _0.70_ shading factor / _0.8_ glazing factor =	2,573
Northeast	_____ sq. ft. x 50 x _____ shading factor / _____ glazing factor =	
9. Sum of lines 1 – 8	_13,921_ x _0.75_ cooling factor from map on p. 89 =	10,440
10. Utility gain	_350 x 1.4 = 490_ watts being consumed in space x 3.4 =	1,666
11. People gain	_3_ number of people in space x 600 =	1,800
12. Peak cooling load, Btu/hour: sum of lines 9 – 11 x _1.00_ thermal mass factor =		13,906

Clock Thermostat Savings

On p. 54 we saw how using a clock thermostat would save a third of our heating bills by automatically setting back to 55°F when we were not home and when we were sleeping. If your home has central air-conditioning, a similar heating/cooling clock thermostat could save money on your cooling bills, as well.

Again, we can use the Energy Star Setback Thermostat Calculator (*www.energystar.gov*) to compute the savings to be realized by various setups (raising cooling temperatures) in different regions of the country. As you can see from the tables at right, cooling cost savings are uniformly about 6% per °F, regardless of where you live. As noted previously, the dollar figures in the second and third columns can be ignored, as they reflect the specific size of the home and efficiency of the cooling system used to generate the tables. The percentage savings, however, apply to all homes, including yours.

You may already have raised your air-conditioning temperature as high as you are willing in order to lower your cooling bills, but the bottom table shows how the clock thermostat can still save you an additional 25% by raising the temperature by 4°F and 7°F while you are sleeping and while you are at work.

The illustration at the top of the facing page shows a typical combination heating/cooling clock thermostat. This single, easily installed and easily set up unit can save both 34% of your heating dollars and 25% of your cooling dollars.

Like the heating load graph on p. 55, the cooling load graph on the facing page demonstrates how the clock thermostat takes a bite (green area) out of the home's cooling load (red area) as the outdoor temperature follows its typical 20°F to 30°F diurnal swing.

Savings of a 78°F–79°F Setup

City	Cost @ 78°F	Cost @ 79°F	Saving
Boston, MA	$125	$118	5.6%
Washington, DC	$256	$240	6.3%
Orlando, FL	$608	$572	5.9%
Kansas City, MO	$238	$224	5.9%
Houston, TX	$494	$464	6.1%
Albuquerque, NM	$589	$572	5.8%
Sacramento, CA	$214	$201	6.1%
Seattle, WA	$36	$34	5.6%

Savings of a 78°F–83°F Setup

City	Cost @ 78°F	Cost @ 83°F	Saving
Boston, MA	$125	$88	29.6%
Washington, DC	$256	$179	30.0%
Orlando, FL	$608	$426	30.0%
Kansas City, MO	$238	$167	30.0%
Houston, TX	$494	$346	30.0%
Albuquerque, NM	$589	$572	29.9%
Sacramento, CA	$214	$150	30.0%
Seattle, WA	$36	$25	30.6%

Savings of a 78°F/82°F/85°F Setup

City	Cost @ 78°F	Cost @ 82°/85°F	Saving
Boston, MA	$125	$93	25.6%
Washington, DC	$256	$191	25.4%
Orlando, FL	$608	$453	25.5%
Kansas City, MO	$238	$178	25.2%
Houston, TX	$494	$368	25.5%
Albuquerque, NM	$589	$572	25.4%
Sacramento, CA	$214	$160	25.2%
Seattle, WA	$36	$27	25.0%

Typical Heating and Cooling Thermostat

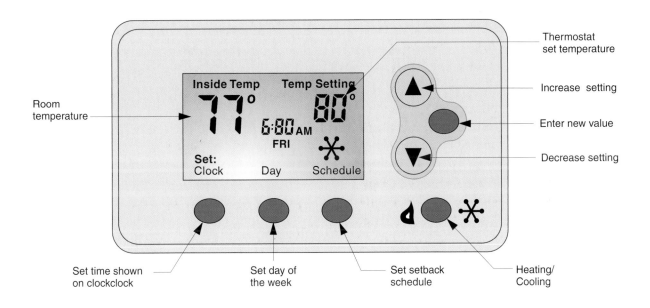

Room temperature

Inside Temp
77°

Temp Setting
80°
6:80 AM
FRI

Set:
Clock   Day   Schedule

Thermostat set temperature

Increase setting

Enter new value

Decrease setting

Set time shown on clockclock

Set day of the week

Set setback schedule

Heating/ Cooling

How a Clock Thermostat Saves Cooling Energy

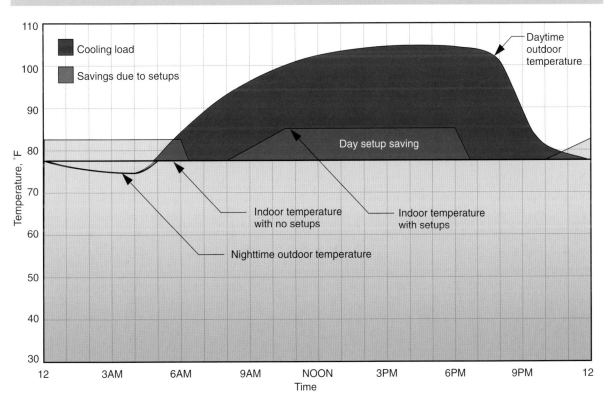

Hot Water

6

Are you overwhelmed by your hot water bill? If yes, this chapter is for you. Of course, your first energy conservation step is simply *using less hot water*.

Many of the following steps require you to understand how your water is presently heated, so we illustrate and explain the workings of the two most common systems: the *gas storage water heater* and the *electric storage water heater*.

Depending on your hot water consumption and the layout of your plumbing system, a possible (but not probable) improvement might be replacing your present heater with a *gas tankless water heater* or an *electric tankless water heater*.

If your space heating system is hydronic (forced hot water), you may save by installing a *BoilerMate indirect water heater* as a separate heating zone off the hydronic boiler.

Particularly if you live in the sunny South, you should consider getting most, if not all, of your hot water from a *solar water heater*.

No matter what type of water heater you have, there are numerous low-cost, no-cost steps you can take to reduce losses in the system. The easiest is simply *lowering the water heater thermostat*. *Low-flow showerheads and aerators* reduce the amount of hot water you consume. If you shower a lot, a *drainwater heat recovery* unit can lower your cost per shower by up to 60%. *Pipe insulation* reduces both heat loss from hot water pipes and destructive summer condensation on your cold water pipes. And if your storage-tank water heater isn't already equipped with them, have your plumber add a pair of *heat traps* to the cold and hot supply pipes.

Finally, do you really know how to boil water? This is no joke! We show you five cooking rules for *cooking with less energy* that can save 92% of the energy required to simply boil water.

Using Less Hot Water

Bring a pot of tap water to a boil on the stove, and you will see that it takes a lot of energy to make hot water. Of all natural substances, water has the highest specific heat: the heat energy required to raise the temperature of the unit mass of a substance by 1 degree.

The specific heat of water in the English system is 1.0 Btu/lb.-°F. In the more universal metric system it is 4.184 Joule/gram-°C. To gauge this quantity, a wooden match releases about 1 Btu in burning completely, and it requires 100 Btu to heat a pint (1 lb.) of tea from 50°F to 150°F.

The pie chart at right shows that heating water consumes the second largest amount of energy (after space heating) in our homes. Adding up the amounts in column three in the table below, the average daily volume of hot water used in a home is seen to be about 65 gal. At 8 lb. per gal., the weight of the water is 520 lb. Assuming the water is heated from a groundwater temperature, 50°F, to 120°F, this requires a daily expenditure of 36,400 Btu.

Fortunately, there are numerous ways you can reduce your hot water bill. These include replacing your heating equipment and/or fuel, reducing flow rates, reducing standby and conductive heat losses from piping, and adopting more efficient practices. Altogether, you should be able to reduce your water heating bill by at least 50%.

The following page lists sixteen ways to save on hot water. Begin with the no-cost and low-cost items, and work your way up to the more expensive options.

Residential Energy Use

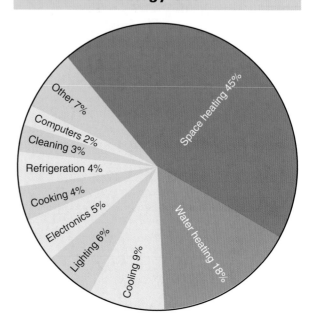

Amounts of Hot Water Consumed

Activity	Gallons per Use
Bath in tub	10–15
5-minute shower, regular head	24
10-minute shower, regular head	48
5-minute shower, low-flow head	12
10-minute shower, low-flow head	24
Hot clothes wash/warm rinse	30
Hot clothes wash/cold rinse	19
Warm clothes wash/cold rinse	10
Dishwasher load or hand dishwashing	8–10

Measured Use of Hot Water in Single-Family Homes[1]

Plumbing Fixture	Gallons per Person per Day	Gallons per Home per Day	Percent of Total Hot Water Used	Percent of Water Use That Is Hot
Faucets	8.6	22.4	34.2	72.7
Dishwasher	0.9	2.3	3.6	100.0
Clothes washer	3.9	10.1	15.5	27.8
Bathtub	4.2	10.9	16.7	78.2
Shower	6.3	16.4	25.1	73.1
Leaks	1.2	3.1	4.8	26.8

[1]Based on measurements in ten single-family homes in Seattle, WA. Average occupants per home: 2.6.

Sixteen Ways to Save Hot Water

Hot water is one of those things we take for granted. If it comes from our space heating boiler, we tend to lump its cost into our heating bill. If it comes from a stand-alone electric water heater, we may consider the cost part of our lighting bill.

Below is a list of sixteen different ways in which you might either reduce your use of hot water or increase the efficiency with which it is generated. Consider each carefully.

1. Lower your water heater thermostat to 120°F (p. 106). A 10°F reduction will save 3% to 5% on your water heating costs.

2. Fix leaking faucets immediately. One drip per second wastes 8.6 gal. per day, or 3,150 gal. per yr.

3. Turn off the faucet when you are not actually using the water, such as while you are brushing your teeth or loading the dishwasher.

4. Install low-flow showerheads and faucet aerators (p. 108). These will reduce flow rates by 25% to 60% and still perform the same tasks.

5. Take short showers with a low-flow shower head (p. 108). If you are really into saving energy, try the "Navy shower" by turning the water off while lathering up.

6. If you or your family insists on lots of long showers, consider installing a drainwater heat recovery unit. This device preheats the cold water flowing into your water heater with heat from the water draining from your tub or shower and reduces the heating cost by half.

7. Run your dishwasher only with full loads, choose shorter wash cycles, and activate the booster heater if your dishwasher has one.

8. If your hot water heater tank is not Energy Star-rated, install a water heater insulation kit. Most utility companies offer them free. It's a simple project, but make sure you follow the manufacturer's instructions.

9. Insulate the hot and cold water pipes connected to your water heater (p. 110). The hot pipe insulation will save hot water and money. The cold pipe insulation will prevent damaging summertime condensation.

10. Install heat traps on the inlet and outlet pipes of your water heater tank (p. 111). These simple devices will reduce your hot water bill by $15 to $30 per year.

11. Ask your electric utility about time-of-day rates and timers. It makes sense to turn off the heater when no one is home and to heat water only when the rate is possibly lower.

12. Use the cold/cold setting in your clothes washer. Your clothes will get just as clean, and they will last longer.

13. Consider upgrading your clothes washer to an Energy Star-rated model. Replacing a 10-year-old washer can save over $135 per year.

14. Consider upgrading your dishwasher to an Energy Star-rated model that uses a third less energy and a third less water.

15. If your water heater is of the conventional storage type and is over 10 years old, consider all of your options, including tankless and solar water heaters.

16. If your present water heater is electric and you have natural gas service, replace the water heater with a gas-fired unit.

Gas Storage Water Heater

Think of the gas storage water heater as a very large tea kettle sitting on top of a gas stove. The chief differences are that water is piped into and out of the kettle, and the flue gases rise through a concentric flue pipe inside the kettle. Heat is transferred, not only through the bottom of the kettle but also through the wall of the flue pipe.

Here is how the typical gas water heater works:

1. Cold water enters through the dip tube, filling the tank from the bottom.

2. The thermostat/gas control maintains a small pilot flame, which ignites the main burner when the water temperature drops below the thermostat set point.

3. The flue pipe runs up the middle of the tank, transferring the heat from the flue gas to the water.

4. The draft hood admits air to the flue in order to maintain a constant, optimum draft at the burner.

5. Hot water is drawn from the top of the tank.

6. A pressure-relief valve prevents excessive pressure in the tank in case the temperature rises to the boiling point.

7. Connecting a garden hose to the tank's drain cock allows draining or flushing of the tank without a mess. This should be done several times each year because sediment on the bottom of the tank hinders the transfer of heat through the bottom of the tank.

8. A replaceable anode helps to prevent corrosion, extending tank life.

Gas Storage Water Heater

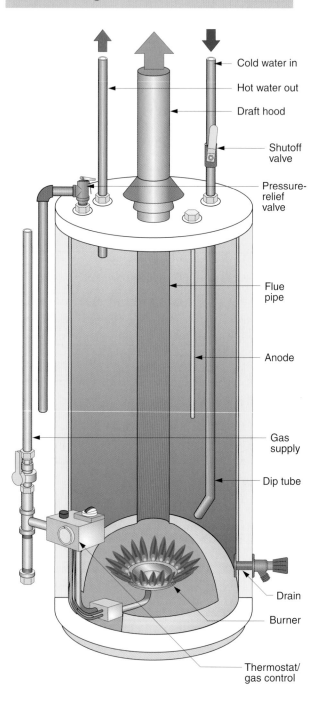

- Cold water in
- Hot water out
- Draft hood
- Shutoff valve
- Pressure-relief valve
- Flue pipe
- Anode
- Gas supply
- Dip tube
- Drain
- Burner
- Thermostat/gas control

Electric Storage Water Heater

The electric storage water heater is similar to the gas version on the facing page, except now the water in the "kettle" is heated by two electric heater elements inside the tank. Since no fuel is burned, there are no flue gases to be vented.

Here's how the typical electric water heater works:

1. Cold water enters through the dip tube, which fills the tank from the bottom up.

2. The upper thermostat, pressed against the side of the tank, switches on the upper element to heat the water.

3. When the water in the top of the tank reaches the set temperature, the upper thermostat switches power to the lower thermostat.

4. The lower thermostat applies power to the lower element until it, too, reaches the set temperature.

5. If the water in the top of the tank becomes too hot, the high-limit switch (red button) will trip, cutting power to both elements.

6. Hot water is drawn from the top of the tank.

7. The pressure-relief valve prevents excessive pressure in the tank in case the temperature rises to the boiling point.

8. Connecting a garden hose to the tank's drain cock allows draining or flushing of the tank without a mess.

9. A replaceable sacrificial zinc anode prevents corrosion in the tank, extending its life.

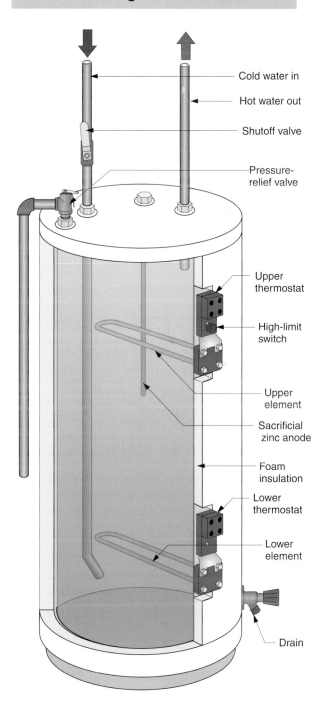

Electric Storage Water Heater

- Cold water in
- Hot water out
- Shutoff valve
- Pressure-relief valve
- Upper thermostat
- High-limit switch
- Upper element
- Sacrificial zinc anode
- Foam insulation
- Lower thermostat
- Lower element
- Drain

Gas Tankless Water Heater

Tankless water heaters have a single advantage over storage-tank heaters: There is no standby heat loss from keeping a tank full of hot water when not needed. With zero standby loss, the gas tankless heater is about 20% more efficient than its conventional counterpart. However, with an average annual gas water heating bill of about $400, that 20% translates into an annual saving of only $80. With an average installed cost of $2,700, compared to $1,100 for a conventional tank, it would take the tankless heater 20 years to pay for itself. You will find plenty of more cost-effective energy conservation options throughout this chapter.

But, just so you know, here is how the typical gas tankless water heater works:

1. Hot water is drawn by showers, tubs, or sinks, and cold water flows in, replacing it.

2. A flow detector senses the inflow and signals the gas control for heat.

3. The gas control turns on the gas and ignites the burner.

4. The heat exchanger transfers most of the heat of the flue gas to the water.

5. An outflow temperature monitor reports the hot water temperature to the computer, allowing it to regulate the gas flow.

6. A small, computer-controlled fan provides a forced draft for optimum combustion and efficiency.

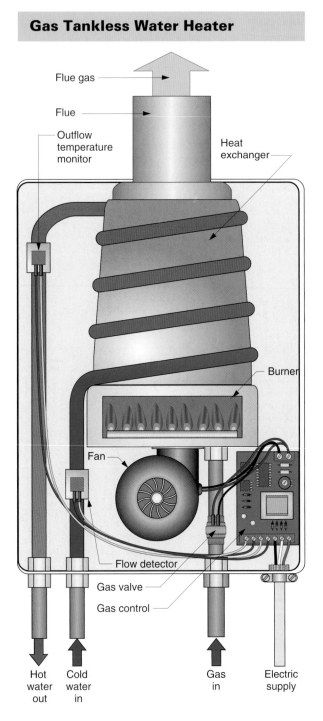

Gas Tankless Water Heater

Flue gas

Flue

Outflow temperature monitor

Heat exchanger

Burner

Fan

Flow detector

Gas valve

Gas control

Hot water out

Cold water in

Gas in

Electric supply

Electric Tankless Water Heater

The electric tankless water heater is similar in cost and percentage savings to the gas-fired version on the facing page. While it doesn't require a flue, it does require very heavy electrical wiring.

An additional disadvantage is its inability to supply more than a single hot water fixture simultaneously. Clothes washing and showering have to be scheduled separately.

With similar costs and savings, the electric tankless water heater has the same long payback period as the gas version. Again, implement your more cost-effective energy conservation measures first.

Here is how the electric tankless heater works:

1. Hot water is drawn by plumbing fixtures, and cold water flows in to replace it.

2. Temperature and flow sensors feed information to the control computer.

3. The control computer regulates the power to the heating elements to maintain a constant set temperature.

4. Electrically resistive elements heat the water flowing through the tubes.

5. Thermal circuit breakers mounted on each of the tubes open the circuits in case of overheating.

6. Three separate 240-VAC circuits provide up to 27,000 watts (92,000 Btu/h) of heat.

Electric Tankless Water Heater

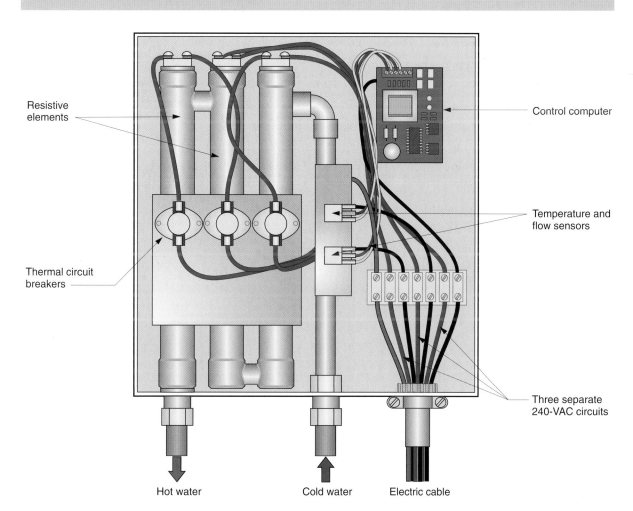

Resistive elements

Control computer

Temperature and flow sensors

Thermal circuit breakers

Three separate 240-VAC circuits

Hot water   Cold water   Electric cable

BoilerMate Indirect Water Heater

If your hot water comes from a hydronic boiler, the boiler has to maintain a temperature of about 150°F throughout the year in order to be able to supply hot water on demand. This results in large standby heat losses and fuel consumption during the summer.

An elegant solution is connecting a BoilerMate as a separate heating zone. The large, well-insulated tank holds about a half day's supply of hot water, so the boiler fires up only a few times a day. Here is how it works:

1. Water fills the tank from the cold water supply.

2. The BoilerMate thermostat signals the zone controller for heat.

3. The zone controller signals the boiler's oil or gas burner to produce heat.

4. When the boiler reaches its low-limit temperature, the aquastat signals the zone controller.

5. The zone controller turns on the BoilerMate circulator pump.

6. Hot water flows through the heat exchanger, heating the water in the tank.

7. Hot water for the home is drawn through a heat trap from the top of the BoilerMate tank.

BoilerMate Hookup

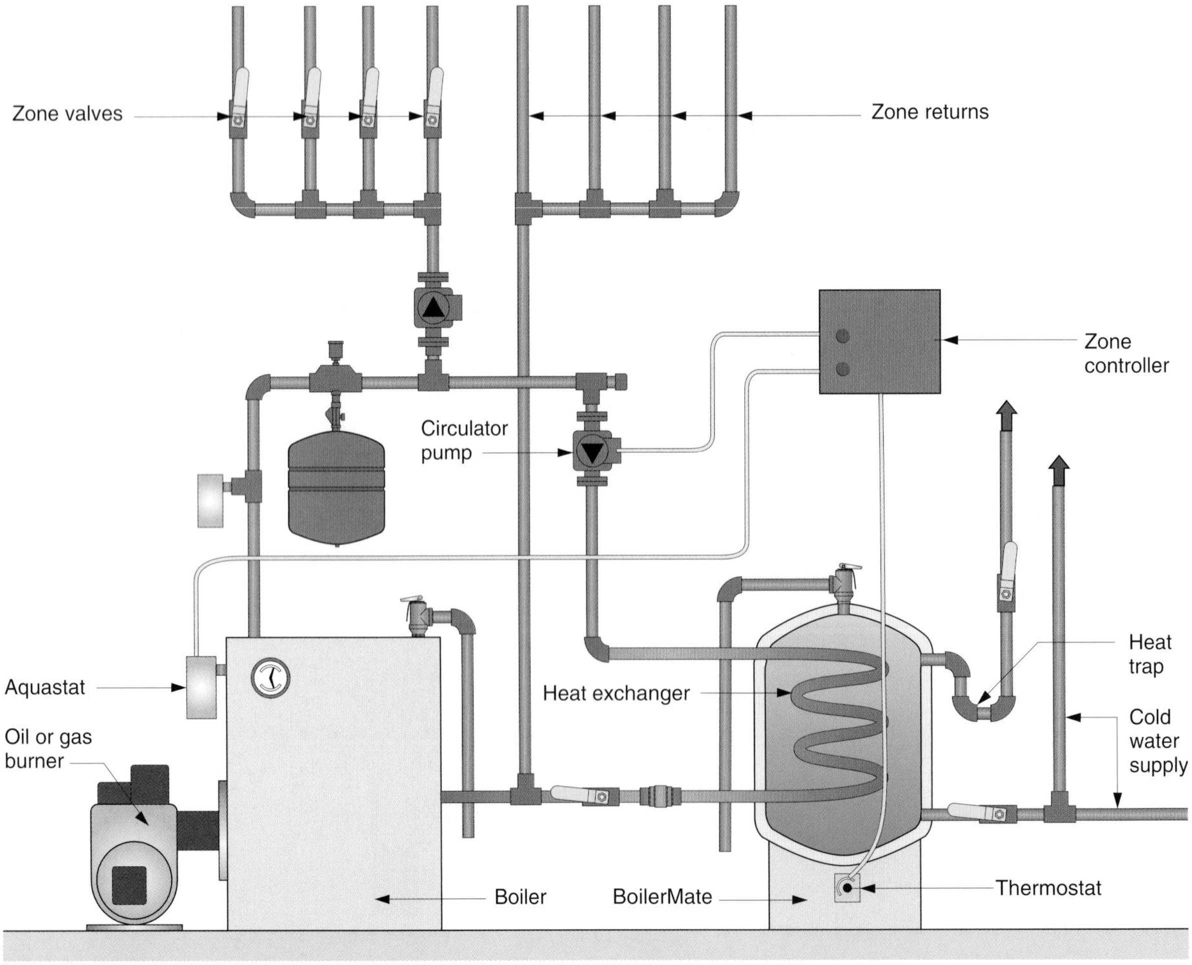

Zone valves

Zone returns

Circulator pump

Zone controller

Aquastat

Heat exchanger

Heat trap

Oil or gas burner

Cold water supply

Boiler

BoilerMate

Thermostat

Solar Water Heater

How about a water heater whose fuel is free? That's the idea behind all of the many solar water heater designs available.

Integral collector-storage passive systems—simply black-painted water tanks in glass-covered boxes—work well in the south where it is both warm and sunny.

In the north, where it is less sunny and often below freezing, a more sophisticated closed-loop, active system is required. In these, a nonfreezing fluid circulates between tubes in the solar collector and a heat exchanger inside a large electric storage water heater. The solar collector supplies a portion of the heat, while the rest is made up by electric heating elements inside the tank.

Solar water heating pays back in every area of the country. Solicit estimates from solar contractors in your area. And don't overlook solar tax credits.

Here is how the closed-loop solar water heater works:

1. Cold water enters through the dip tube, which fills the tank from the bottom up.

2. The control module compares collector and tank temperatures. When the temperature difference reaches a preset level, the module turns on the circulator.

3. A header manifold distributes the circulating water to an array of parallel tubes. In areas subject to freezing, the water must contain propylene glycol ("RV antifreeze") or drain back to prevent freezing.

4. A glass cover plate traps the heat from the sun in the collector.

5. The heated water is collected by the upper manifold and returned to the heat exchanger in or surrounding the bottom of the tank.

6. The water in the tubes absorbs heat as it rises through the collector.

7. Heat is transferred from the heat exchanger to the water in the storage tank.

8. When there is insufficient solar energy, an auxiliary electric heating element in the storage tank makes up the difference.

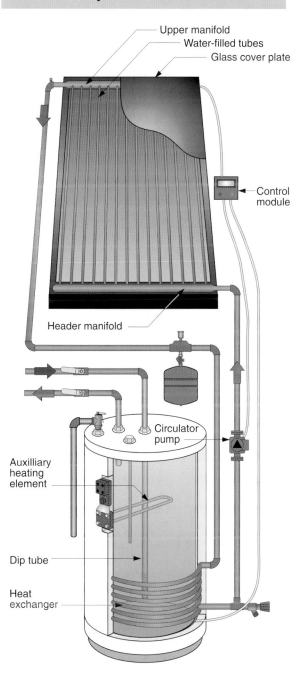

Closed-Loop Solar Water Heater

Upper manifold
Water-filled tubes
Glass cover plate
Control module
Header manifold
Circulator pump
Auxilliary heating element
Dip tube
Heat exchanger

Lowering the Water Heater Thermostat

Electric Water Heater

Water over 120°F can scald and is dangerous when bathing children. Most outdoor thermometers register to over 120°F and can be used to measure the temperature of the water from your kitchen and bathroom spouts. In any case, if you can't keep your hand in the water indefinitely, it is too hot. By the way, if you are going on vacation, turn off the circuit breaker. That will eliminate all heat loss.

To lower the thermostat temperature setting(s):

1. Turn off the circuit breaker serving the heater.

2. Remove the panel(s) covering the thermostats. (Some smaller tanks have a single thermostat.)

3. With a flat screwdriver, turn the thermostat pointer(s) one-eighth of a turn in the appropriate direction.

4. Restore the circuit breaker.

5. After an hour, test the temperature again.

6. Repeat steps 1 through 5 until you reach 120°F.

Electric Water Heater Thermostat

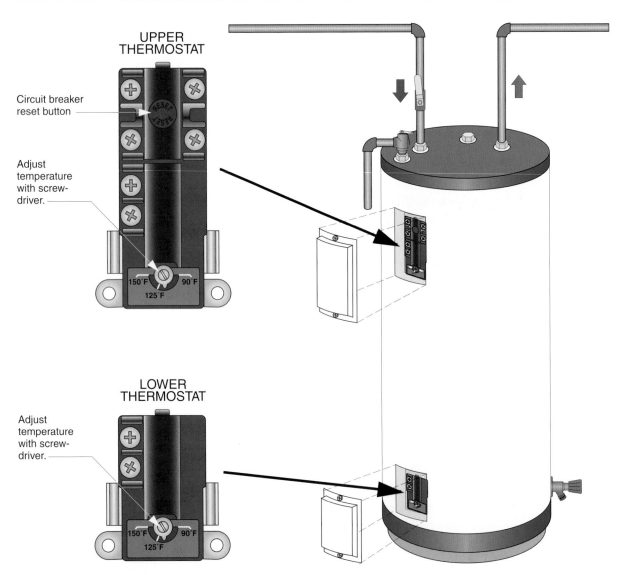

UPPER
THERMOSTAT

Circuit breaker
reset button

Adjust
temperature
with screwdriver.

150°F   90°F
125°F

LOWER
THERMOSTAT

Adjust
temperature
with screwdriver.

150°F   90°F
125°F

Gas Water Heater

Lowering the thermostat on a gas water heater is far simpler than on an electric water heater. First, there is no electricity, so there is no circuit breaker to locate and turn off. Second, there is only a single thermostat. Third, the thermostat is generally exposed, so you don't have to remove a cover panel to access it.

As with an electric water heater, it is the temperature at the spout that counts, not the temperature of the tank. Measure the temperature of water flowing from a kitchen or bath faucet with a thermometer.

If you don't have a suitable thermometer, adjust the temperature until it is as hot as you can stand, holding your hand in it indefinitely.

Most gas thermostats are labeled in relative terms such as "hot," "warm," and "cool" or "vacation." For that reason, make each of your adjustments small and wait at least an hour after adjusting before checking the temperature.

Gas Water Heater Thermostat

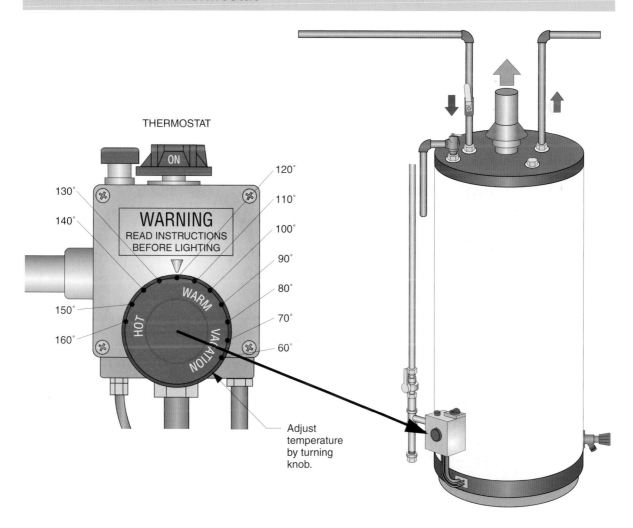

THERMOSTAT

ON

WARNING
READ INSTRUCTIONS
BEFORE LIGHTING

HOT WARM VACATION

130° 140° 150° 160°
120° 110° 100° 90° 80° 70° 60°

Adjust temperature by turning knob.

Low-Flow Showerheads and Aerators

Low-Flow Showerheads

The federal government requires that new shower-heads consume no more than 2.5 gal. per min. at 80 psi water pressure, yet an estimated 30% to 40% of all homes retain the older 5- to 7-gal.-per-min. "flood heads." It is understandable that you might be reluctant to give up the sensation of standing under a Hawaiian waterfall, but the price is high. Low-flow showerheads have been engineered to achieve nearly the same feeling while saving up to 60% on your hot water bill.

Models with an on/off button or knob allow turning the shower on and off without having to adjust the flow and water temperature each time. They also allow the "navy shower"—on, wet head, off, lather head, on, rinse head, off, lather body, on, rinse body, off.

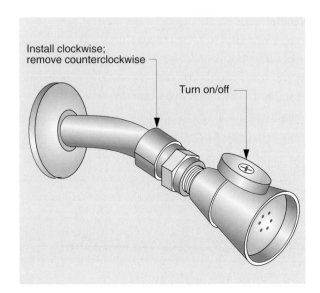

Install clockwise; remove counterclockwise

Turn on/off

Faucet Aerators

Aerators introduce air into a stream of water, thereby reducing the amount of water while seeming to maintain full flow. They are particularly useful if you like to wash dishes with the faucet running continuously.

Both kitchen and bathroom faucets now come with aerators preinstalled that limit the water flow to 2.2 and 1.5 gal./min. Typical realized savings in hot water are 20% and 40% respectively.

Most aerators contain a fine screen. Water from wells sometimes picks up sediment, and hard water can build up lime deposits, both of which will plug screens. Sediment can be removed by unthreading the aerator and blowing through it backward. Lime deposits are easily dissolved by soaking the aerator overnight in vinegar.

Faucet Aerator

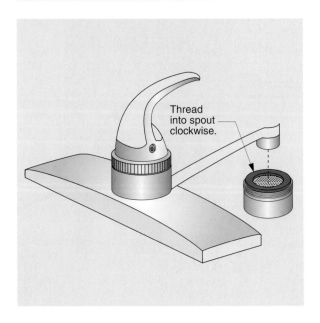

Thread into spout clockwise.

Drainwater Heat Recovery

The principle of drainwater heat recovery is so simple and practical that it is amazing it hasn't become standard practice in all homes. Water entering your home ranges from about 40°F in northern states to 70°F across the south. That is because the thermal mass of the earth evens out seasonal temperature extremes and holds deep earth temperatures to the average annual air temperature. Regardless of the incoming temperature of the water, your water heater must heat it further to 120°F. Doing so accounts for 15% to 20% of your energy bill.

A drainwater heat recovery module is just a heat exchanger—a vertical section of 3-in. or 4-in. copper drainpipe wrapped in a coil of ½-in. copper tubing. Cold supply water enters at the bottom, extracts heat from the outgoing drainwater, then feeds into the water heater. Typical heat recovery efficiency is 50% to 60% with a temperature boost of 25°F.

The most cost-effective application is on a drainpipe that serves a fixture or appliance drawing hot water continuously for an extended time, such as a shower, dishwasher, or clothes washer (all three, if possible).

The cost for new construction is about $600. Retrofits add $200 to $300. Payback is typically 2 to 6 years.

Drainwater Heat Recovery from a Shower

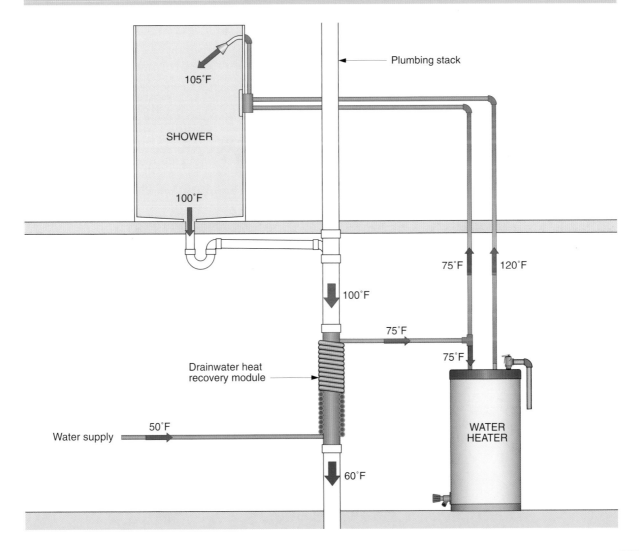

Plumbing stack

105°F

SHOWER

100°F

100°F

75°F

Drainwater heat recovery module

75°F

75°F

75°F

120°F

Water supply

50°F

60°F

WATER HEATER

Pipe Insulation

Copper is a great heat conductor. If you doubt this, touch the pipe at the top of your water heater that leads to the kitchen sink. Insulating that pipe will save money in three ways:

1. Insulating the first 3 ft. to 4 ft. will prevent the pipe from acting as a heat drain from the tank itself.

2. Insulating all pipes from the tank to fixtures (bathtubs, showers, lavatories, sinks) reduces heat loss and temperature drops to the fixtures, allowing you to lower the water heater thermostat by 2°F to 4°F.

3. The volume of water stored in 100 ft. of ¾-in. pipe is 2.3 gal. Insulating the pipe that leads to heavily used sinks and lavatories will save the 2.3 gal. of water that otherwise has to be replaced at every use.

Use polyethylene or neoprene foam pipe insulation that matches the pipe size snugly. Tape the insulation every few feet to keep it closed and in place.

Insulation for Water Heaters

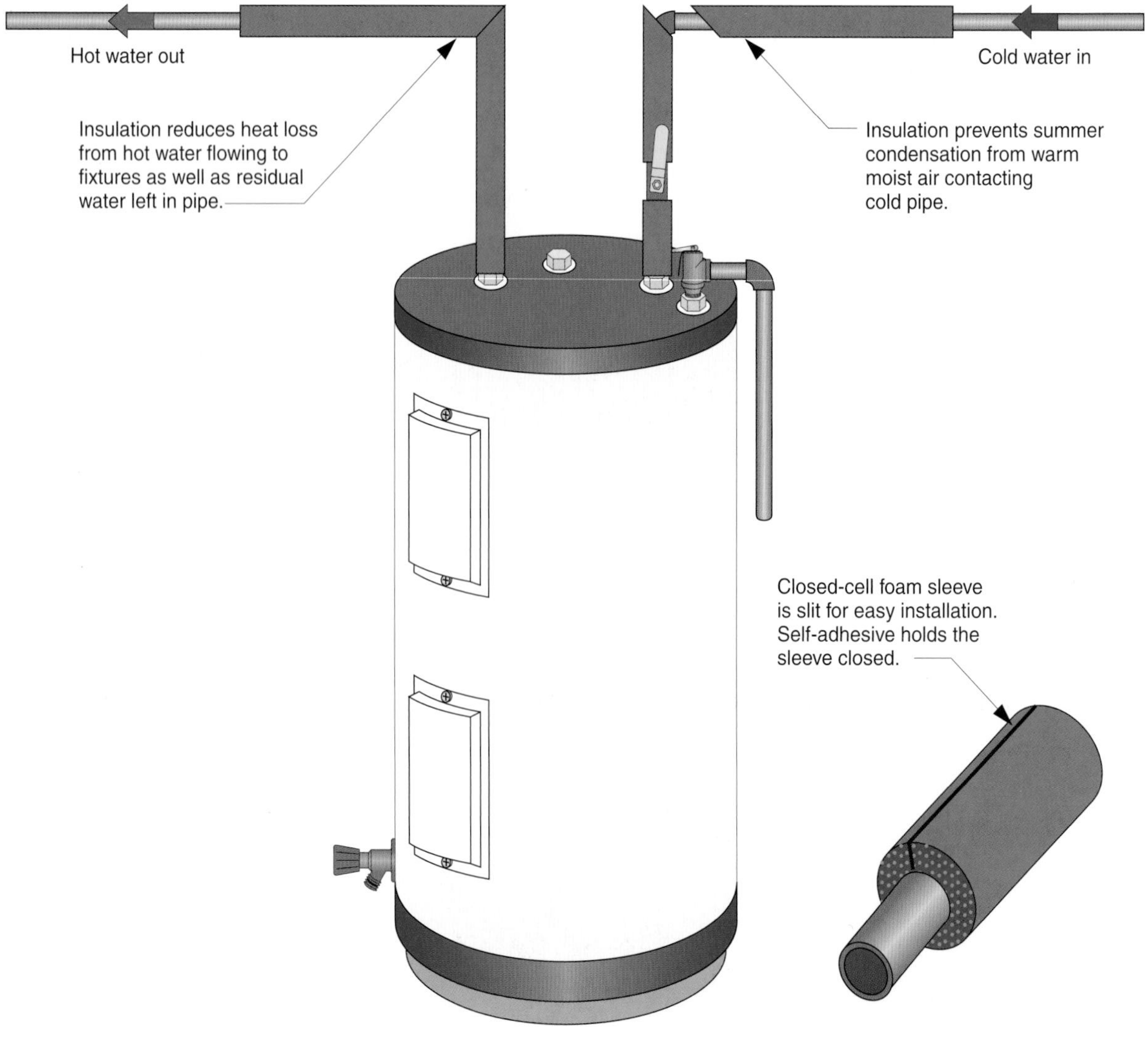

Hot water out

Insulation reduces heat loss from hot water flowing to fixtures as well as residual water left in pipe.

Cold water in

Insulation prevents summer condensation from warm moist air contacting cold pipe.

Closed-cell foam sleeve is slit for easy installation. Self-adhesive holds the sleeve closed.

Heat Traps

Heat traps are one-way valves that allow cold water to flow into a water heater and hot water to flow out but prevent convection of hot water within the pipes when water is not being drawn.

The valves come in pairs, one for the hot water side and one for the cold inlet side. The cost of a pair is about $30, but the savings are $15 to $30 per year.

Installation requires soldering of copper pipe, a skill acquired only through practice, so unless you have plumbing experience, hire a plumber to do the job. Note that many water heaters purchased today contain factory-installed heat traps.

Also note that the presence of heat traps does not negate the need for the pipe insulation shown on the facing page.

Water Heater Heat Traps

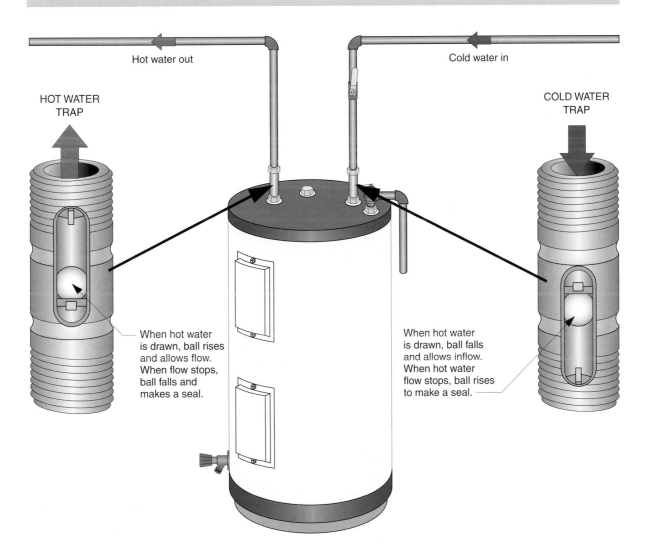

Hot water out

Cold water in

HOT WATER TRAP

COLD WATER TRAP

When hot water is drawn, ball rises and allows flow. When flow stops, ball falls and makes a seal.

When hot water is drawn, ball falls and allows inflow. When hot water flow stops, ball rises to make a seal.

Cooking with Less Energy

Harry Truman once famously said, "If you can't stand the heat, get out of the kitchen." Of course he was referring to political pressure, not heat. But the saying reminds us that much of the heat energy in the kitchen goes to heating the kitchen as well as the food.

How Efficient Is Your Stovetop?

The Electric Power Research Institute (EPRI) tested the efficiency of cooktop burners in heating water from room temperature to boiling. Let's see how your stovetop measures up. By "efficiency" they meant the ratio of Btus that ended up in the water to the Btus consumed by the burner, expressed as a percentage.

The burners tested were the four basic types illustrated at right:

Gas Burner—concentric burner ring with orifices arranged radially around both inside and outside of the ring. Residential burners usually have a pan under the burner to catch spills and to reflect radiant heat back up to the pan. Pros include infinite control, and instant heatup and cooldown. One con is keeping the reflective pan clean.

Electric Coil Element—a set of three or four concentric, flattened tubes that contain electric resistance wire. They usually have reflective (when kept clean) metal pans under the coils. Pros include fairly rapid heatup and simple repair. Cons include lack of continuous control, slow cooldown, and the need to clean the reflective pan.

Radiant Ribbon under Glass—basically the same as the electric coil element, except placed in close contact under a smooth glass or ceramic cooktop. Pros include ease of cleanup and modern look. Cons include slow heatup and cooldown and (in some models) hot surfaces that are not obvious. A variation of this type of burner uses halogen lamps instead of a resistive element to generate the heat. In this case, the intensity of the halogen light indicates the degree of heating.

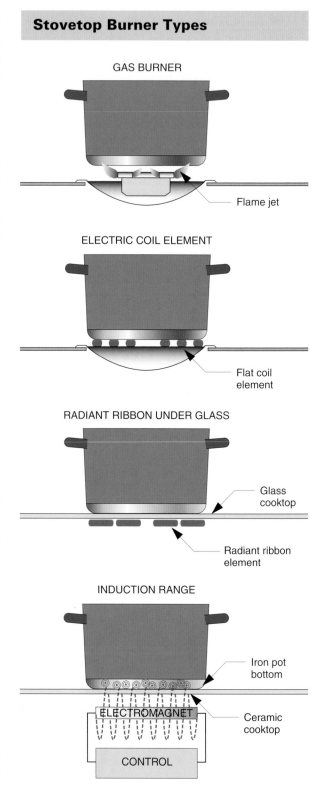

Stovetop Burner Types

GAS BURNER

Flame jet

ELECTRIC COIL ELEMENT

Flat coil element

RADIANT RIBBON UNDER GLASS

Glass cooktop

Radiant ribbon element

INDUCTION RANGE

Iron pot bottom

ELECTROMAGNET

Ceramic cooktop

CONTROL

Induction Range—a completely different principle. Here an electronic unit controls the strength of an electromagnetic field that induces electric currents in the base of an iron or steel pot placed over the unit. Since the current is generated only in the pot, the ceramic surface remains relatively cool. Pros include continuous control, instant heating and cooling, and high efficiency. Cons are high cost and the requirement to use ferrous cooking pots (the unit won't work with pyrex, ceramic, copper, or aluminum pots).

The graph below compares the tested efficiencies. From the graph, several things are apparent:

1. Induction ranges are by far the most efficient.

2. The old-fashioned electric coil and the more modern looking radiant coil under glass have essentially the same efficiencies.

3. Electric ranges are about twice as efficient as gas, but because Btu-to-Btu electricity is twice as expensive as gas, their operating costs are about the same.

4. Commercial gas ranges are extremely inefficient, putting only 30% of the heat into the pot but 70% into the kitchen.

Energy Efficiency of Stovetop Types

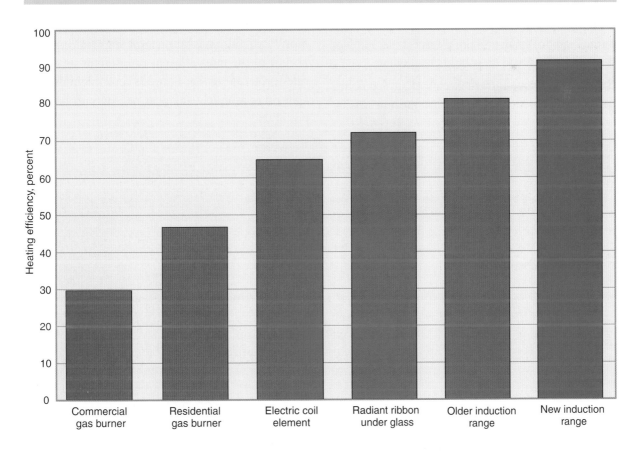

Five Rules for Cooking Efficiently

The illustration on the facing page demonstrates five rules for using your cooktop most efficiently:

Rule 1. Match the burner to the pot. Half of the heating element is in the outer 30% of the disk; for example, in a 10-in. burner, 50% of the heat is within 1½ in. of the outer edge. All of the heat of the uncovered portion of the burner goes into heating the kitchen, not the pot.

Rule 2. Use the lowest heat that will accomplish the task. You may use maximum heat to reach the boiling point, but reduce the heat to minimum to hold the pot at a simmer. Once water reaches its boiling point of 212°F you cannot raise it above 212°F, no matter how much heat you apply!

Rule 3. Adjust gas flames to all blue. A yellow flame consists of incandescent, unburned carbon. The unburned carbon represents both a waste of fuel and soot that will be deposited on your kitchen ceiling.

Rule 4. Keep your burner reflectors clean. A polished chrome surface reflects about 90% of the heat striking it. Much of the heat from either an electric element or a gas flame is in the form of infrared energy that is radiated both upward and downward. Reflecting the downward component back to the pot may increase burner efficiency by 10% or more.

Rule 5. Cook with lids on your pots. Raising the temperature of a pound of water 1°F takes 1 Btu. Turning that same pound of water from water to steam soaks up the "heat of vaporization," 970 Btu. In our 1-qt. (2-lb.) example, bringing the water up to a boil takes 280 Btu, but boiling the water away would take an additional 1,940 Btu. The pot lid causes the steam to return to water, thereby returning the heat of vaporization that would have escaped to the air with the steam.

The graph below shows the amount of waste resulting from flaunting the rules. Comparing the most wasteful case (burner on high setting with no lid) to the most efficient case (following all five rules), you can see that a careless cook might use thirteen times as much energy as necessary to boil that pot of tea.

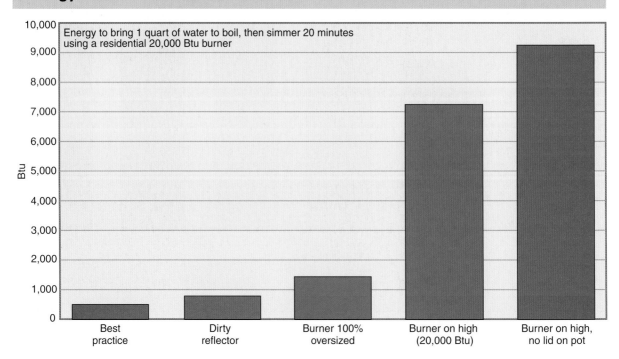

Energy Waste from Bad Practices

Energy to bring 1 quart of water to boil, then simmer 20 minutes using a residential 20,000 Btu burner

The Five Rules for Cooking Efficiently

	RIGHT	WRONG
Rule 1: Match the burner to the pot.		
Rule 2: Use the minimum heat required for the task.		
Rule 3: Adjust the burner flame to all blue.		
Rule 4: Keep the burner reflectors clean.		
Rule 5: Always cook with a lid on the pot.		

Insulation
and R-Value

All insulation products are labeled with an R-value. *Heat transfer and R-value* explains the significance of this number in reducing your home's heat loss or gain. As an aid to both planning and shopping, we offer a comprehensive listing of the *R-values of insulation products* as well as their performance characteristics.

Insulation is just one component of a floor, wall, or ceiling. To compute the total thermal resistance of a construction we need to include the *R-values of surfaces and air spaces*, as well as the *R-values of building materials*.

Unfortunately, the total R-value of a floor, wall, or ceiling is not the simple sum of component R-values, so we explain (and give examples of) the methods for *calculating effective R-values*.

And because this is a handbook, we offer an extensive catalog of the *effective R-values of typical constructions*.

Heat Transfer and R-Value

If heat were immovable, it would simply remain in the furnace, boiler, woodstove, or air conditioner and do nothing to keep us warm in winter or cool in summer. But heat obeys the Second Law of Thermodynamics, which, in layman's terms, says energy flows from higher concentrations toward areas of lower concentrations. Since heat energy concentration is what we call "temperature," heat always flows from hot to cold.

As we saw in Chapter 1, there are three natural heat flow mechanisms, all of which obey the "hot to cold" principle: radiation, convection, and conduction.

Radiation

Radiation is the transfer of energy through space. Radio waves, cellphone signals, warming rays from the sun, and heat felt from a fire—all are examples of the very same thing: electromagnetic radiation. The only difference is the wavelengths of the radiation.

While not intuitive to anyone but a physicist, all matter in the universe continually and simultaneously emits and absorbs radiation. The intensity of emitted radiation is proportional to the matter's absolute temperature raised to the fourth power. Putting this into perspective, matter having twice the surface temperature emits sixteen times as much radiation.

The woodstove in the top illustration on the facing page is warmer than the surrounding room surfaces, so there is a net transfer of heat by radiation from the stove to the room.

Convection

Convection is the mass movement of atoms and molecules in a liquid or a gas. Wind, the uprush of a thunderhead, the circulation of tea leaves in a cup of tea, and the warm air rising from a woodstove are examples of convection. In moving from a warmer area to a cooler area, the molecules comprising the mass transfer heat energy in the direction of the motion.

The middle illustration on the facing page shows a wood- or coal stove in a room in winter. The room is heated to an average air temperature of 70°F, while the outdoor temperature is 0°F. Room air in contact with

the stove is heated and expands. As the room air is less dense than the surrounding air, it rises like a hot air balloon to the ceiling. At the same time, room air in contact with the cold window gives up some of its heat, contracts, and falls to the floor. The convection loop is continuous, resulting in a net transfer of heat from the stove to the window.

Conduction

Conduction is the transfer of heat through solids. The frying pan handle in the bottom illustration on the facing page provides a familiar example. The handle is not in the flame, yet it becomes warm. The molecules of the metal pan and handle are jostling each other and passing vibrational energy down the line to their cooler neighbors. Since the intensity of vibration is greatest in the area heated by the flame, the net transfer of energy is from that area toward the handle.

Materials that transfer heat readily are known as conductors; materials that resist the transfer of heat are insulators. The insulation products sold at home centers and lumberyards, such as fiberglass, cellulose, and the various types of foam, are especially good at resisting heat flow by conduction.

Heat transfer by conduction through homogeneous solid materials is simple to calculate, as shown in the illustration below. In the thermal conductance equation, R is the measure of the material's thermal resistance.

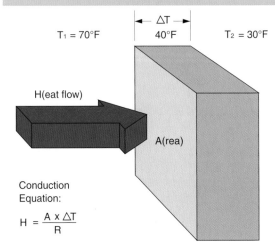

The Conduction Equation and R

$T_1 = 70°F$ ΔT $40°F$ $T_2 = 30°F$

H(eat flow)

A(rea)

Conduction Equation:

$$H = \frac{A \times \Delta T}{R}$$

Three Heat Transfer Mechanisms

RADIATION

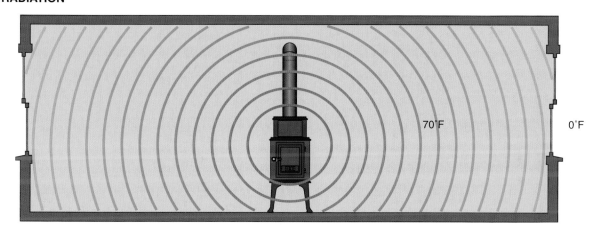

70°F   0°F

CONVECTION

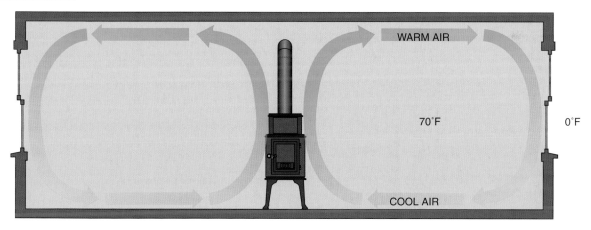

WARM AIR

70°F   0°F

COOL AIR

CONDUCTION

R-Values of Insulation Products

Characteristics of Insulation Materials

Type of Insulation	Rated R/in.	Max. Temp., °F	Vapor Barrier	Resistance to			
				Water Absorption	Moisture Damage	Direct Sunlight	Fire
Roll, Blanket, or Batt							
Fiberglass	3.2 (2.9–3.8)	180	unfaced: P	G	E	E	G
Fiberglass, high-density	4.0 (3.8–4.2)	180	unfaced: P	G	E	E	G
Rock wool	3.2 (2.9–3.8)	>500	unfaced: P	G	E	E	E
Loose Fill							
Cellulose	3.5 (3.2–3.8)	180	P	P	P	G	F
Fiberglass	2.5 (2.2–2.7)	180	P	G	E	E	G
Perlite	2.4	200	P	F	G	E	G
Polystyrene beads	2.3	165	P	P	G	P	P
Rock wool	3.1 (3.0–3.3)	>500	P	G	E	G	G
Vermiculite	2.4	>500	P	G	E	E	G
Rigid Board							
Expanded polystyrene	3.8 (3.6–4.0)	165	P	P	G	P	P
Extruded polystyrene	4.8 (4.5–5.0)	165	G	E	E	P	P
Polyurethane	6.2 (5.5–6.5)	165	G	E	E	P	P
Polyisocyanurate, foil-faced	7.0	180	F	G	E	E	G
Polyisocyanurate, unfaced	5.6	200	G	G	E	P	P
Sprayed or Foamed in Place							
Cellulose	3.5 (3.0–3.7)	165	P	P	F	G	F
Fiberglass, high-density	4.2	180	P	G	E	E	G
Phenolic	4.8	300	G	G	E	E	P
Polyurethane, closed cell	6	165	G	E	E	P	P
Polyurethane, open cell	3.6	165	P	P	E	P	P

Note: E = excellent; G = good; F = fair; P = poor

R-Values of Surfaces and Air Spaces

R-Values of Building Surfaces

Surface	Heat Flow Direction	Type of Surface	
		Nonreflective	Foil-Faced
Still Air			
Horizontal	Upward	0.61	1.32
Sloped 45°	Upward	0.62	1.37
Vertical	Horizontal	0.68	1.70
Sloped 45°	Downward	0.76	2.22
Horizontal	Downward	0.92	4.55
Moving Air, Any Orientation			
7.5 mph wind	Any	0.25	—
15 mph wind	Any	0.17	—

Source: *Handbook of Fundamentals* (Atlanta: American Society of Heating, Refrigeration, and Air-Conditioning Engineers, 1989).

R-Values of Trapped Air Spaces

Thickness, in.	Heat Flow	Season	Type of Surface	
			Nonreflective	One Foil-Faced
Horizontal				
¾	Upward	Winter	0.87	2.21
¾	Downward	Summer	0.85	3.29
3½	Upward	Winter	0.93	2.66
3½	Downward	Summer	1.24	9.27
Sloped 45°				
¾	Upward	Winter	0.94	2.75
¾	Downward	Summer	1.02	3.57
3½	Upward	Winter	0.96	2.95
3½	Downward	Summer	1.08	4.36
Horizontal				
¾	Outward	Winter	1.01	3.46
¾	Inward	Summer	0.84	3.24
3½	Outward	Winter	1.01	3.40
3½	Inward	Summer	0.85	3.40

Source: *Handbook of Fundamentals* (Atlanta: American Society of Heating, Refrigeration, and Air-Conditioning Engineers, 1989).

R-Values of Building Materials

Building Material R-Values

Material	R/in.	R-value	Material	R/in.	R-value
Boards and Panels			**Framing Lumber**		
Gypsum drywall, 1/2 in.		0.45	2 in. nominal (11/2 in.)		1.88
3/8 in.		0.34	4 in. nominal (31/2 in.)		4.38
1/2 in.		0.45	6 in. nominal (51/2 in.)		6.88
5/8 in.		0.56	8 in. nominal (71/4 in.)		9.06
Hardboard			10 in. nominal (91/4 in.)		11.56
Medium density	1.37		12 in. nominal (111/4 in.)		14.06
High-density underlay	1.22		**Masonry**		
High-density tempered	1.00		Cement mortar	0.20	
Laminated paperboard	2.00		Gypsum fiber concrete	0.60	
Particleboard			Sand and gravel aggregate	0.09	
Low density	1.41		Lightweight aggregate		
Medium density	1.06		120 lb./cu. ft.	0.09–0.18	
High density	0.85		80 lb./cu. ft.	0.29–0.40	
Underlayment	1.31		40 lb./cu. ft.	0.90–1.08	
Plywood, fir	1.25		20 lb./cu. ft.	1.43	
Fiberboard	2.64		Perlite, expanded	1.08	
Wood			Stucco	0.20	
Hardwood	0.90		**Masonry Units**		
Softwood	1.25		Brick		
Doors			90 lb./cu. ft.	0.20	
Hollow-core flush lauan, 13/4 in.		1.80	120 lb./cu. ft.	0.11	
Solid-core flush, 13/4 in.		2.17	Clay tile, hollow		
Urethane-filled, steel or fiberglass		5.30	One-cell, 3 in.		0.80
Storm door			One-cell, 4 in.		1.11
Aluminum, 50% glazed		1.00	Two-cell, 6 in.		1.52
Wood, 50% glazed		1.25	Two-cell, 8 in.		1.85
Flooring			Two-cell, 10 in.		2.22
Carpet with fibrous pad		2.08	Three-cell, 12 in.		2.50
Carpet with foam rubber pad		1.23	Concrete block, normal weight		
Cork tile, 1/8 in.		0.28	8 in. empty cores		0.97–1.11
Terrazzo	0.08		8 in. perlite cores		2.00
Tile, linoleum or vinyl, 1/8 in.		0.05	8 in. vermiculite cores		1.37–1.92
Wood			12 in. empty cores		1.23
Hardwood	0.90				
Softwood	1.25				

Building Material R-Values *(continued)*

Material	R/in.	R-value
Concrete block, medium weight		
8 in. empty cores		1.28–1.71
8 in. perlite cores		2.3–3.7
8 in. vermiculite cores		3.3
8 in. expanded polystyrene beads		3.2
Concrete block, medium weight		
6 in. empty cores		1.65–1.93
6 in. perlite cores		4.2
6 in. vermiculite cores		3.0
8 in. empty cores		1.9–3.2
8 in. perlite cores		4.4–6.8
8 in. vermiculite cores		3.9–5.3
8 in. expanded polystyrene beads		4.8
12 in. empty cores		2.3–2.6
12 in. perlite cores		6.3–9.2
12 in. vermiculite cores		5.8
Stone	0.08	
Plasters		
Cement, sand aggregate	0.64	
Gypsum		
Lightweight aggregate	0.20	
Perlite aggregate	0.67	
Sand aggregate	0.18	
Vermiculite aggregate	0.59	
Roofing		
Asbestos-cement shingle		0.21
Asphalt roll (90 lb.)		0.15
Asphalt shingle		0.44
Built-up asphalt, 3/8 in.		0.33
Slate, 1/2 in.		0.05
Wood shingles (not furred)		0.94

Material	R/in.	R-value
Sheathing, Plywood or OSB		
1/4 in. panel		0.31
3/8 in. panel		0.47
1/2 in. panel		0.63
5/8 in. panel		0.77
3/4 in. panel		0.94
Siding		
Shingles		
Asbestos-cement		0.21
Wood, 16 in. (7 in. exposure)		0.87
Wood		
Drop, 1 in. x 8 in.		0.79
Bevel, 1/2 in. x 8 in.		0.81
Bevel, 3/4 in. x 10 in.		1.05
Aluminum or steel		
Hollow		0.61
With 3/8 in. backer		1.82
With 3/8 in. backer and foil		2.96
Windows (use window ratings values if available)		
Single glazing		0.91
Single glazing plus storm panel		2.00
Double-glazed		
3/16 in. air space		1.61
1/4 in. air space		1.69
1/2 in. air space		2.04
3/4 in. air space		2.38
1/2 in. Low-E		3.13
Suspended film plus Low-E		4.05
Triple-glazed		
1/4 in. air spaces		2.56
1/2 in. air spaces		3.23

Calculating Effective R-Values

Uniform Materials

The thermal conduction equation, shown on p. 118, is marvelous in its simplicity. Nothing could be more intuitive than a rate of heat transfer:

- proportional to the area through which it flows
- proportional to the temperature difference
- inversely proportional to R, resistance to flow

Equally marvelous, the total R-value of a layered assembly of uniform materials is simply the sum of the R-values of the component layers.

$$R_{total} = T_1 + T_2 + T_3 + \ldots$$

When applied to constructions faced with air, the appropriate surface or trapped-air-space R-values must be included in the calculation.

The illustration below demonstrates the calculation of total R-value through a section of wall cavity filled with fiberglass insulation.

Non-Uniform Parallel Paths

Few building assemblies consist of a simple layering of uniform materials as in the example below. Structural Insulating Panels (SIPs) are the only ones that come to mind. Most floors, walls, and roofs contain framing. In calculating building heat loads, what we need is the average, or effective, R-value for the entire floor, wall, or roof.

Fortunately, the effective R-value of the combined parallel heat paths is fairly simple to calculate. The process, shown in the illustrations on the facing page, consists of:

1. Calculating the fractions of wall area occupied by framing, F_f, and by insulation, F_i.

2. Calculating the total R- and U-values ($U = 1/R$) through the framing and through the insulation.

3. Multiplying each U-value by its corresponding area fraction and summing the products to get U_{eff}. R_{eff} is simply $1/U_{eff}$.

Calculating the Total R-Value through Uniform Materials

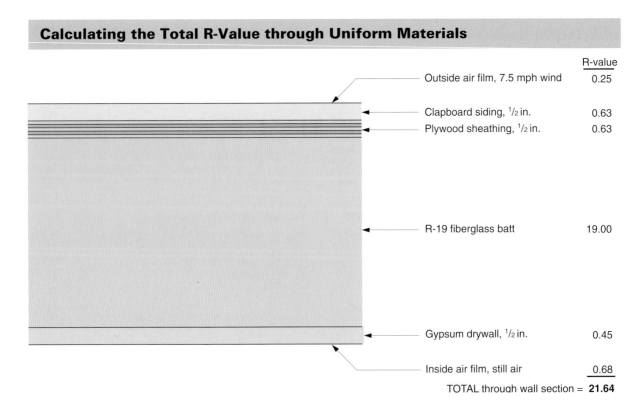

	R-value
Outside air film, 7.5 mph wind	0.25
Clapboard siding, 1/2 in.	0.63
Plywood sheathing, 1/2 in.	0.63
R-19 fiberglass batt	19.00
Gypsum drywall, 1/2 in.	0.45
Inside air film, still air	0.68
TOTAL through wall section =	**21.64**

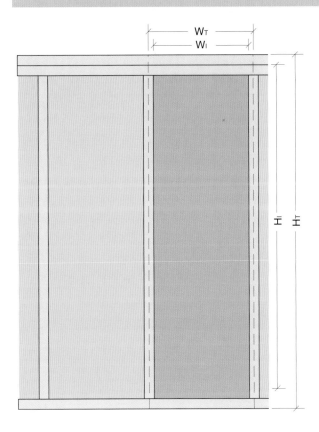

FRAMING 16 IN. ON-CENTER

Total Area, $A_T = W_T \bullet H_T$
  $= 16 \text{ in.} \bullet 96 \text{ in.} = 1{,}536 \text{ in.}^2$

Insulation Area, $A_I = W_I \bullet H_I$
  $= 14.5 \text{ in.} \bullet 91.5 \text{ in.} = 1{,}327 \text{ in.}^2$

Framing Area, $A_F = A_T - A_I$
  $= 1{,}536 \text{ in.}^2 - 1{,}327 \text{ in.}^2 = 209 \text{ in.}^2$

Insulation Fraction, $F_I = A_I/A_T$
  $= 1{,}327 \text{ in.}^2 / 1{,}536 \text{ in.}^2 = 0.864$

Framing Fraction, $F_F = A_F/A_T$
  $= 209 \text{ in.}^2 / 1{,}536 \text{ in.}^2 = 0.136$

OVE FRAMING 24 IN. ON-CENTER
(single top plate)

$A_T = W_T \bullet H_T$
  $= 24 \text{ in.} \bullet 96 \text{ in.} = 2{,}304 \text{ in.}^2$

$A_I = W_I \bullet H_I$
  $= 22.5 \text{ in.} \bullet 93 \text{ in.} = 2{,}093 \text{ in.}^2$

$A_F = A_T - A_I$
  $= 2{,}304 \text{ in.}^2 - 2{,}093 \text{ in.}^2 = 211 \text{ in.}^2$

Insulation Fraction, $F_I = A_I/A_T$
  $= 2{,}093 \text{ in.}^2 / 2{,}304 \text{ in.}^2 = 0.908$

Framing Fraction, $F_F = A_F/A_T$
  $= 211 \text{ in.}^2 / 2{,}304 \text{ in.}^2 = 0.092$

	Section A - A	Section B - B
Outdoor surface, e = .90	0.17	0.17
Clapboard siding, $\frac{1}{2}$ in.	0.63	0.63
Plywood sheathing, $\frac{1}{2}$ in.	0.63	0.63
2x4 stud, 16 in. o.c.	4.38	—
R-11 fiberglass batt	—	11.00
Gypsum drywall, $\frac{1}{2}$ in.	0.45	0.45
Indoor surface, e = .90	0.68	0.68
Section R-value	6.94	13.56
Section U (1/R)	0.1441	0.0737
Area fraction: F_i, F_f	0.136	0.864
U contribution	0.0196	0.0637
U (Total U)	0.0833	
R_{eff} (1/U_{eff})	12.0	

Metal Framing

The parallel-path method works well for ordinary wood-frame construction because the framing member cross sections are simple rectangles and because the wood framing and cavity insulation R-values are not too dissimilar.

Floors, walls, and ceilings framed with steel are a different matter, however. The thermal conductivity of steel is much greater than that of framing lumber and insulation. In fact, the conductivity of carbon steel is about 350 times that of softwoods and 1,300 times that of extruded polystyrene. Compounding the calculation, the cross section of a steel stud is that of a thin C, with 16- or 18-gauge webs and 1½-in. flanges.

Oak Ridge National Laboratory (ORNL) offers an online calculator for determining R_{eff} and U_{eff} for steel-framed walls using the "modified zone method," *www.ornl.gov/sci/roofs+walls/calculators/modzone/index.html*.

An alternate method is to use the correction factors published in *ASHRAE Standard 90.1* and listed in the table below. The illustration at the bottom of the page provides an example calculation.

Steel Wall Framing Correction Factors

Stud Size	Stud Spacing	Cavity Insulation	Correction Factor	Effective R-value
2 × 4	16 in. o.c.	R-11	0.50	R-5.5
		R-13	0.46	R-6.0
		R-15	0.43	R-6.4
2 × 4	24 in. o.c.	R-11	0.60	R-6.6
		R-13	0.55	R-7.2
		R-15	0.52	R-7.8
2 × 6	16 in. o.c.	R-19	0.37	R-7.1
		R-21	0.35	R-7.4
2 × 6	24 in. o.c.	R-19	0.45	R-8.6
		R-21	0.43	R-9.0
2 × 8	16 in. o.c.	R-11	0.31	R-7.8
2 × 8	24 in. o.c.	R-11	0.38	R-9.6

Calculating the Effective R-Value for Steel Framing

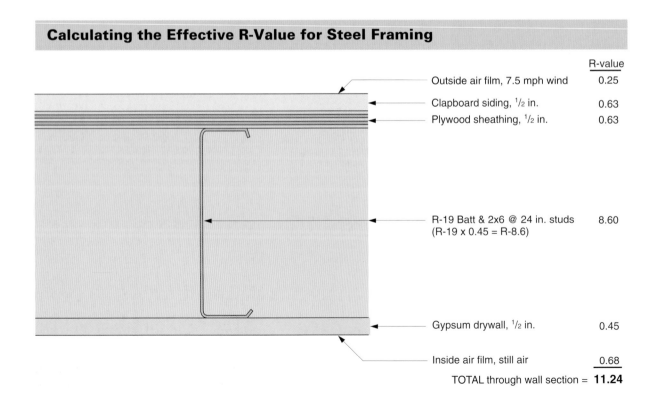

	R-value
Outside air film, 7.5 mph wind	0.25
Clapboard siding, ½ in.	0.63
Plywood sheathing, ½ in.	0.63
R-19 Batt & 2x6 @ 24 in. studs (R-19 x 0.45 = R-8.6)	8.60
Gypsum drywall, ½ in.	0.45
Inside air film, still air	0.68
TOTAL through wall section =	**11.24**

Effective R-Values of Typical Constructions

Oak Ridge National Laboratory maintains an interactive website, the ZIP-Code Insulation Program *(www.ornl.gov/~roofs/Zip/ZipHome.html)* for calculating economic optimum levels of insulation (see Chapter 8, *Recommended R-Values*), taking account of climate, heating and cooling system efficiencies, fuel type and price, and building construction. The ZIP software draws upon a database of calculated effective R- and U-values of standard insulation options for roofs, attics, walls, and floors. These options and their R- and U-values are illustrated in the following illustrated table.

The table also contains effective R- and U-values for concrete masonry wall assemblies from the National Concrete Masonry Association.

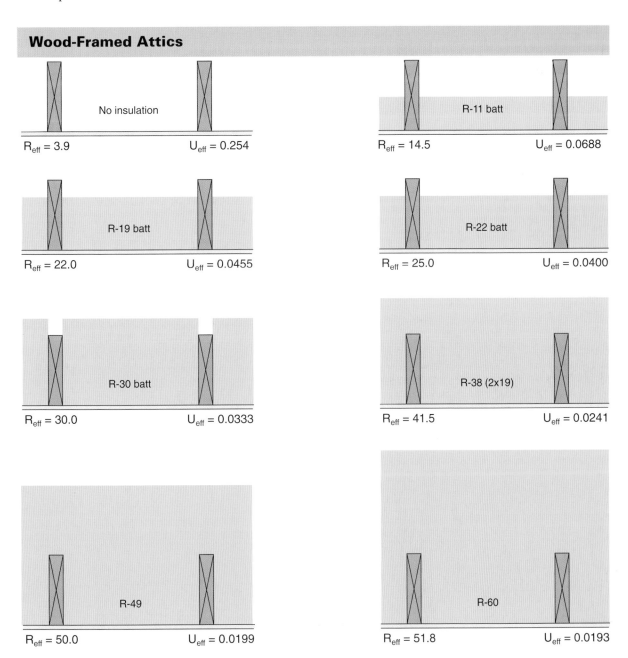

Wood-Framed Attics

No insulation
$R_{eff} = 3.9$ $U_{eff} = 0.254$

R-11 batt
$R_{eff} = 14.5$ $U_{eff} = 0.0688$

R-19 batt
$R_{eff} = 22.0$ $U_{eff} = 0.0455$

R-22 batt
$R_{eff} = 25.0$ $U_{eff} = 0.0400$

R-30 batt
$R_{eff} = 30.0$ $U_{eff} = 0.0333$

R-38 (2x19)
$R_{eff} = 41.5$ $U_{eff} = 0.0241$

R-49
$R_{eff} = 50.0$ $U_{eff} = 0.0199$

R-60
$R_{eff} = 51.8$ $U_{eff} = 0.0193$

Metal-Framed Attics

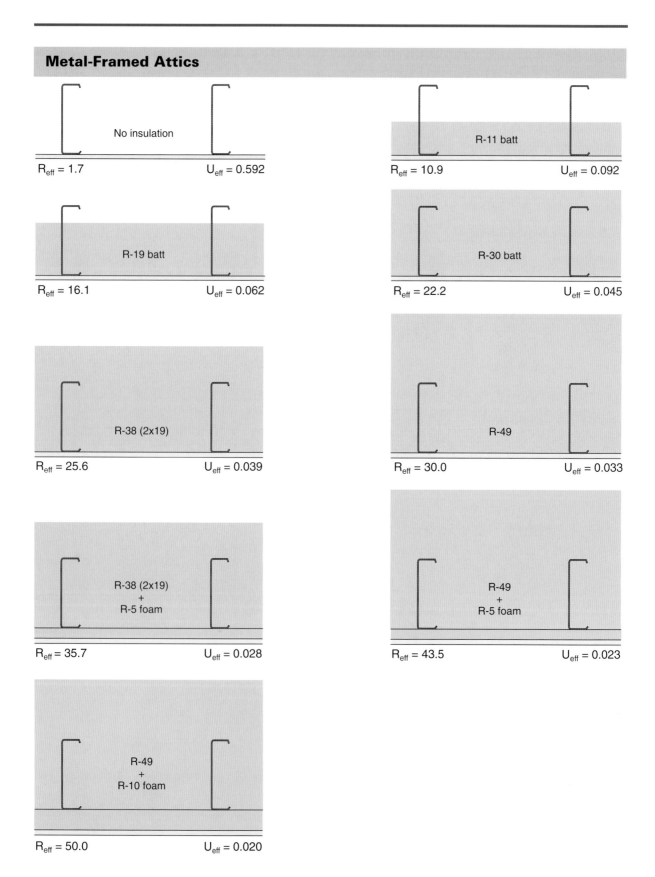

No insulation
$R_{eff} = 1.7$ $U_{eff} = 0.592$

R-11 batt
$R_{eff} = 10.9$ $U_{eff} = 0.092$

R-19 batt
$R_{eff} = 16.1$ $U_{eff} = 0.062$

R-30 batt
$R_{eff} = 22.2$ $U_{eff} = 0.045$

R-38 (2x19)
$R_{eff} = 25.6$ $U_{eff} = 0.039$

R-49
$R_{eff} = 30.0$ $U_{eff} = 0.033$

R-38 (2x19)
+
R-5 foam
$R_{eff} = 35.7$ $U_{eff} = 0.028$

R-49
+
R-5 foam
$R_{eff} = 43.5$ $U_{eff} = 0.023$

R-49
+
R-10 foam
$R_{eff} = 50.0$ $U_{eff} = 0.020$

Cathedral Ceilings

No insulation

$R_{eff} = 3.8$ $U_{eff} = 0.2616$

FG batt

Batt = R-11	$R_{eff} = 13.5$	$U_{eff} = 0.0742$
Batt = R-13	$R_{eff} = 15.0$	$U_{eff} = 0.0666$
Batt = R-15	$R_{eff} = 16.5$	$U_{eff} = 0.0607$

FG batt

Batt = R-19	$R_{eff} = 20.3$	$U_{eff} = 0.0493$
Batt = R-21	$R_{eff} = 21.7$	$U_{eff} = 0.0460$
Batt = R-22	$R_{eff} = 23.0$	$U_{eff} = 0.0434$

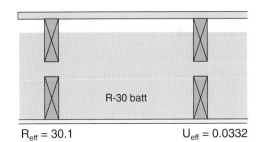

R-30 batt

$R_{eff} = 30.1$ $U_{eff} = 0.0332$

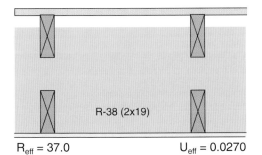

R-38 (2x19)

$R_{eff} = 37.0$ $U_{eff} = 0.0270$

R-49

$R_{eff} = 46.3$ $U_{eff} = 0.0216$

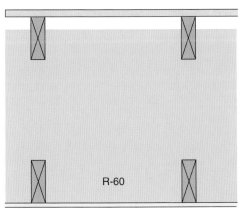

R-60

$R_{eff} = 56.2$ $U_{eff} = 0.0178$

Wood-Framed Walls

2 x 4, 16 in. o.c. WOOD-FRAMED WALL, $^1/_2$ in. WOOD SHEATHING, SIDING, $^1/_2$ in. DRYWALL FINISH

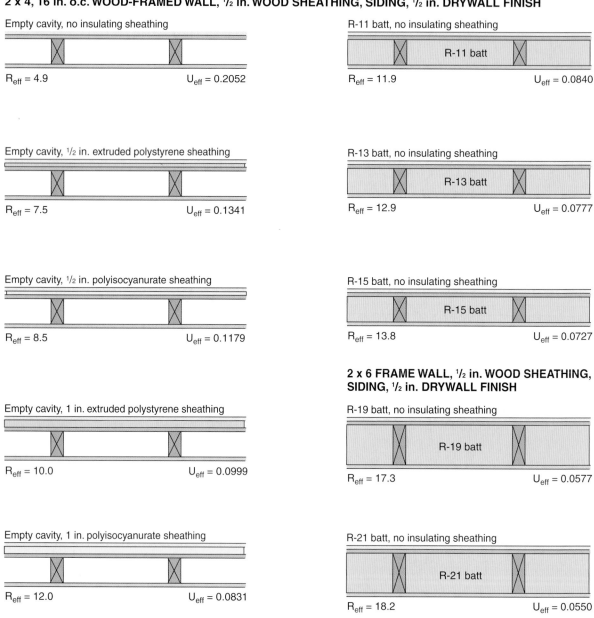

Empty cavity, no insulating sheathing

R_{eff} = 4.9 U_{eff} = 0.2052

Empty cavity, $^1/_2$ in. extruded polystyrene sheathing

R_{eff} = 7.5 U_{eff} = 0.1341

Empty cavity, $^1/_2$ in. polyisocyanurate sheathing

R_{eff} = 8.5 U_{eff} = 0.1179

Empty cavity, 1 in. extruded polystyrene sheathing

R_{eff} = 10.0 U_{eff} = 0.0999

Empty cavity, 1 in. polyisocyanurate sheathing

R_{eff} = 12.0 U_{eff} = 0.0831

R-11 batt, no insulating sheathing

R-11 batt

R_{eff} = 11.9 U_{eff} = 0.0840

R-13 batt, no insulating sheathing

R-13 batt

R_{eff} = 12.9 U_{eff} = 0.0777

R-15 batt, no insulating sheathing

R-15 batt

R_{eff} = 13.8 U_{eff} = 0.0727

2 x 6 FRAME WALL, $^1/_2$ in. WOOD SHEATHING, SIDING, $^1/_2$ in. DRYWALL FINISH

R-19 batt, no insulating sheathing

R-19 batt

R_{eff} = 17.3 U_{eff} = 0.0577

R-21 batt, no insulating sheathing

R-21 batt

R_{eff} = 18.2 U_{eff} = 0.0550

2 x 4, 16 in. o.c. WOOD-FRAMED WALL, ½ in. WOOD SHEATHING, SIDING, ½ in. DRYWALL FINISH

R-11 batt, ½ in. extruded polystyrene sheathing

R_{eff} = 14.6 U_{eff} = 0.0686

R-11 batt, 1 in. extruded polystyrene sheathing

R_{eff} = 17.2 U_{eff} = 0.0581

R-11 batt, ½ in. polyisocyanurate sheathing

R_{eff} = 15.6 U_{eff} = 0.0639

R-11 batt, 1 in. polyisocyanurate sheathing

R_{eff} = 19.3 U_{eff} = 0.0519

R-13 batt, ½ in. extruded polystyrene sheathing

R_{eff} = 15.6 U_{eff} = 0.0639

R-13 batt, 1 in. extruded polystyrene sheathing

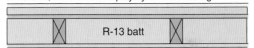

R_{eff} = 18.3 U_{eff} = 0.0545

R-13 batt, ½ in. polyisocyanurate sheathing

R_{eff} = 16.8 U_{eff} = 0.0597

R-13 batt, 1 in. polyisocyanurate sheathing

R_{eff} = 20.4 U_{eff} = 0.0489

R-15 batt, ½ in. extruded polystyrene sheathing

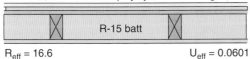

R_{eff} = 16.6 U_{eff} = 0.0601

R-15 batt, 1 in. extruded polystyrene sheathing

R_{eff} = 19.4 U_{eff} = 0.0515

R-15 batt, ½ in. polyisocyanurate sheathing

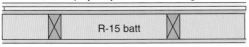

R_{eff} = 17.8 U_{eff} = 0.0563

R-15 batt, 1 in. polyisocyanurate sheathing

R_{eff} = 21.6 U_{eff} = 0.0464

Metal-Framed Walls

2 x 4, 16 in. o.c. METAL-FRAMED WALL, ½ in. WOOD SHEATHING, SIDING, ½ in. DRYWALL FINISH

Empty cavity, no insulating sheathing

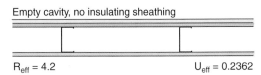

R_{eff} = 4.2 U_{eff} = 0.2362

R-11 batt, no insulating sheathing

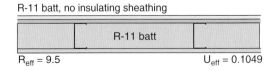

R_{eff} = 9.5 U_{eff} = 0.1049

Empty cavity, ½ in. extruded polystyrene sheathing

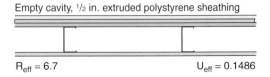

R_{eff} = 6.7 U_{eff} = 0.1486

R-13 batt, no insulating sheathing

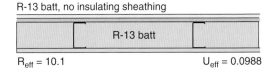

R_{eff} = 10.1 U_{eff} = 0.0988

Empty cavity, ½ in. polyisocyanurate sheathing

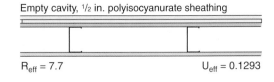

R_{eff} = 7.7 U_{eff} = 0.1293

R-15 batt, no insulating sheathing

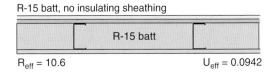

R_{eff} = 10.6 U_{eff} = 0.0942

Empty cavity, 1 in. extruded polystyrene sheathing

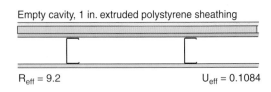

R_{eff} = 9.2 U_{eff} = 0.1084

2 x 6 METAL-FRAMED WALL, ½ in. WOOD SHEATHING, SIDING, ½ in. DRYWALL

R-19 batt, no insulating sheathing

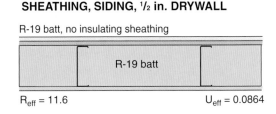

R_{eff} = 11.6 U_{eff} = 0.0864

Empty cavity, 1 in. polyisocyanurate sheathing

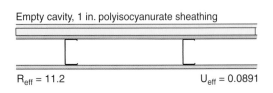

R_{eff} = 11.2 U_{eff} = 0.0891

R-21 batt, no insulating sheathing

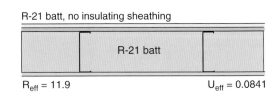

R_{eff} = 11.9 U_{eff} = 0.0841

2 x 4, 16 in. o.c. METAL-FRAMED WALL, ¹/₂ in. WOOD SHEATHING, SIDING, ¹/₂ in. DRYWALL FINISH

R-11 batt, ¹/₂ in. extruded polystyrene sheathing

R_{eff} = 12.4 U_{eff} = 0.0808

R-11 batt, 1 in. extruded polystyrene sheathing

R_{eff} = 14.9 U_{eff} = 0.0672

R-11 batt, ¹/₂ in. polyisocyanurate sheathing

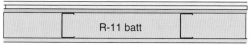

R_{eff} = 13.7 U_{eff} = 0.0731

R-11 batt, 1 in. polyisocyanurate sheathing

R_{eff} = 17.2 U_{eff} = 0.0580

R-13 batt, ¹/₂ in. extruded polystyrene sheathing

R_{eff} = 13.1 U_{eff} = 0.0766

R-13 batt, 1 in. extruded polystyrene sheathing

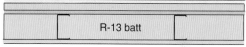

R_{eff} = 15.6 U_{eff} = 0.0642

R-13 batt, ¹/₂ in. polyisocyanurate sheathing

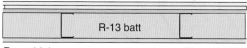

R_{eff} = 14.4 U_{eff} = 0.0693

R-13 batt, 1 in. polyisocyanurate sheathing

R_{eff} = 18.1 U_{eff} = 0.0554

R-15 batt, ¹/₂ in. extruded polystyrene sheathing

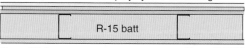

R_{eff} = 13.6 U_{eff} = 0.0733

R-15 batt, 1 in. extruded polystyrene sheathing

R_{eff} = 16.2 U_{eff} = 0.0618

R-15 batt, ¹/₂ in. polyisocyanurate sheathing

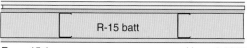

R_{eff} = 15.1 U_{eff} = 0.0662

R-15 batt, 1 in. polyisocyanurate sheathing

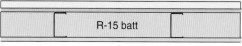

R_{eff} = 18.8 U_{eff} = 0.0533

Optimum Value Engineered (OVE) Wood-Framed Walls

2 x 6, 24 in. o.c. WOOD-FRAMED OVE WALL, $\frac{1}{2}$ in. WOOD SHEATHING, SIDING, $\frac{1}{2}$ in. DRYWALL FINISH

R-19 batt, no insulating sheathing

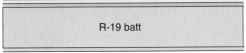

$R_{eff} = 17.9$ $U_{eff} = 0.056$

R-21 batt, no insulating sheathing

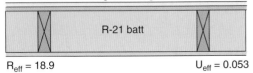

$R_{eff} = 18.9$ $U_{eff} = 0.053$

R-19 batt, $\frac{1}{2}$ in. extruded polystyrene sheathing

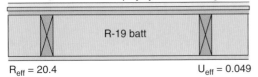

$R_{eff} = 20.4$ $U_{eff} = 0.049$

R-21 batt, $\frac{1}{2}$ in. extruded polystyrene sheathing

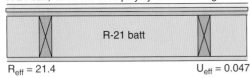

$R_{eff} = 21.4$ $U_{eff} = 0.047$

R-19 batt, $\frac{1}{2}$ in. polyisocyanurate sheathing

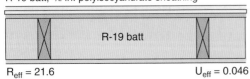

$R_{eff} = 21.6$ $U_{eff} = 0.046$

R-21 batt, $\frac{1}{2}$ in. polyisocyanurate sheathing

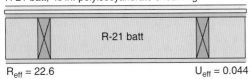

$R_{eff} = 22.6$ $U_{eff} = 0.044$

R-19 batt, 1 in. extruded polystyrene sheathing

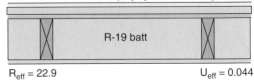

$R_{eff} = 22.9$ $U_{eff} = 0.044$

R-21 batt, 1 in. extruded polystyrene sheathing

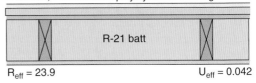

$R_{eff} = 23.9$ $U_{eff} = 0.042$

R-19 batt, 1 in. polyisocyanurate sheathing

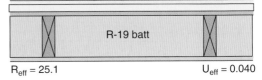

$R_{eff} = 25.1$ $U_{eff} = 0.040$

R-21 batt, 1 in. polyisocyanurate sheathing

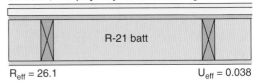

$R_{eff} = 26.1$ $U_{eff} = 0.038$

Single Wythe Concrete Masonry Walls

8 x 16 BLOCK, 135 PCF (pounds per. cu. ft.)

Empty cores

$R_{eff} = 1.9$ $U_{eff} = 0.537$

Empty cores, drywall on metal furring

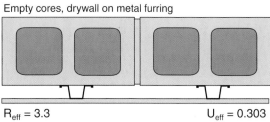

$R_{eff} = 3.3$ $U_{eff} = 0.303$

Solid grouted cores

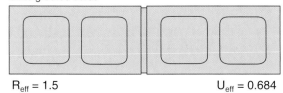

$R_{eff} = 1.5$ $U_{eff} = 0.684$

Solid grouted cores, drywall on metal furring

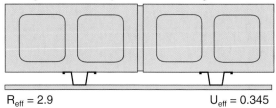

$R_{eff} = 2.9$ $U_{eff} = 0.345$

Perlite-filled cores

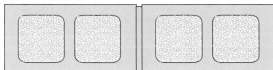

$R_{eff} = 3.2$ $U_{eff} = 0.309$

Perlite-filled cores, drywall on metal furring

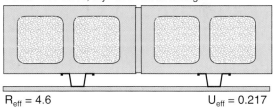

$R_{eff} = 4.6$ $U_{eff} = 0.217$

Vermiculite-filled cores

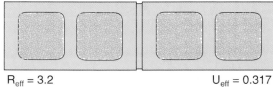

$R_{eff} = 3.2$ $U_{eff} = 0.317$

Vermiculite-filled cores, drywall on metal furring

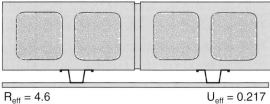

$R_{eff} = 4.6$ $U_{eff} = 0.217$

Polyurethane-filled cores

$R_{eff} = 3.4$ $U_{eff} = 0.298$

Polyurethane-filled cores, drywall on metal furring

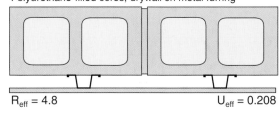

$R_{eff} = 4.8$ $U_{eff} = 0.208$

8 x 16 BLOCK, 135 PCF

Empty cores, foil-faced drywall on metal furring

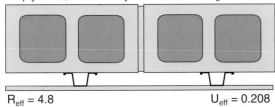

$R_{eff} = 4.8$ $U_{eff} = 0.208$

Solid grouted cores, foil-faced drywall on metal furring

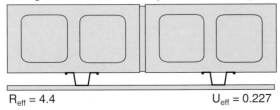

$R_{eff} = 4.4$ $U_{eff} = 0.227$

Perlite cores, foil-faced drywall on metal furring

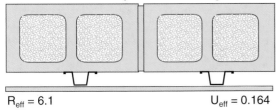

$R_{eff} = 6.1$ $U_{eff} = 0.164$

Vermiculite cores, foil-faced drywall on metal furring

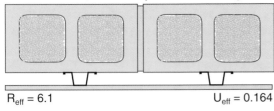

$R_{eff} = 6.1$ $U_{eff} = 0.164$

Polyurethane cores, foil-faced drywall on metal furring

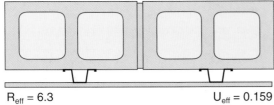

$R_{eff} = 6.3$ $U_{eff} = 0.159$

Empty cores, 1 in. extruded polystyrene, drywall on metal furring

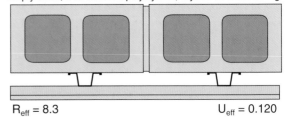

$R_{eff} = 8.3$ $U_{eff} = 0.120$

Concrete cores, 1 in. extruded polystyrene,
drywall on metal furring

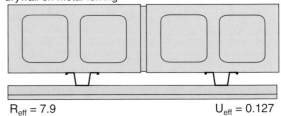

$R_{eff} = 7.9$ $U_{eff} = 0.127$

Perlite cores, 1 in. extruded polystyrene,
drywall on metal furring

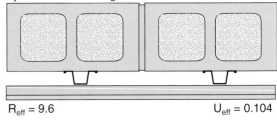

$R_{eff} = 9.6$ $U_{eff} = 0.104$

Vermiculite cores, 1 in. extruded polystyrene,
drywall on metal furring

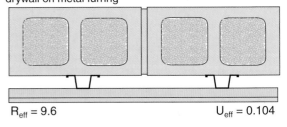

$R_{eff} = 9.6$ $U_{eff} = 0.104$

Polyurethane cores, 1 in. extruded polystyrene,
drywall on metal furring

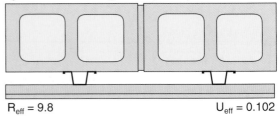

$R_{eff} = 9.8$ $U_{eff} = 0.102$

8 x 16 BLOCK, 135 PCF

Empty cores, 1 in. polyisocyanurate, drywall on metal furring

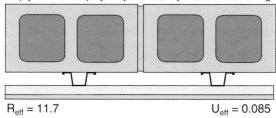

R_eff = 11.7   U_eff = 0.085

Concrete cores, 1 in. polyisocyanurate, drywall on metal furring

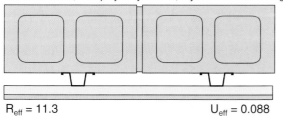

R_eff = 11.3   U_eff = 0.088

Perlite cores, 1 in. polyisocyanurate, drywall on metal furring

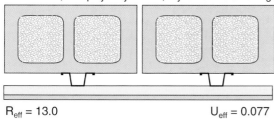

R_eff = 13.0   U_eff = 0.077

Vermiculite cores, 1 in. polyisocyanurate, drywall on metal furring

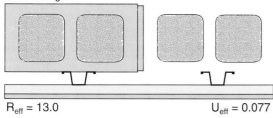

R_eff = 13.0   U_eff = 0.077

Polyurethane cores, 1 in. polyisocyanurate, drywall on metal furring

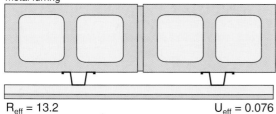

R_eff = 13.2   U_eff = 0.076

Empty cores, 2 in. extruded polystyrene, drywall on metal furring

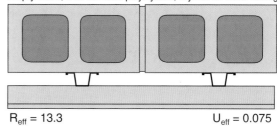

R_eff = 13.3   U_eff = 0.075

Solid cores, 2 in. extruded polystyrene, drywall on metal furring

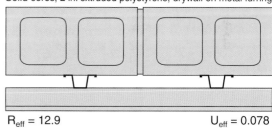

R_eff = 12.9   U_eff = 0.078

Perlite cores, 2 in. extruded polystyrene, drywall on metal furring

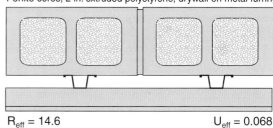

R_eff = 14.6   U_eff = 0.068

Vermiculite cores, 2 in. extruded polystyrene, drywall on metal furring

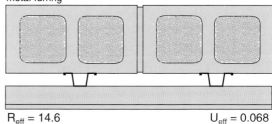

R_eff = 14.6   U_eff = 0.068

Polyurethane cores, 2 in. extruded polystyrene, drywall on metal furring

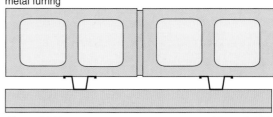

R_eff = 14.8   U_eff = 0.068

8 x 16 BLOCK, 135 PCF

Empty cores, R-11 batt, 2 x 4 studs 24 in. o.c., drywall

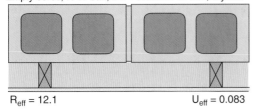

R_{eff} = 12.1   U_{eff} = 0.083

R_{eff} = 12.1 U_{eff} = 0.083

Concrete cores, R-11 batt, 2 x 4 studs 24 in. o.c., drywall

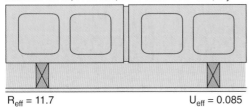

R_{eff} = 11.7 U_{eff} = 0.085

Perlite cores, R-11 batt, 2 x 4 studs 24 in. o.c., drywall

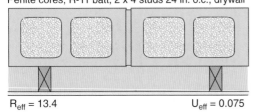

R_{eff} = 13.4 U_{eff} = 0.075

Vermiculite cores, R-11 batt, 2 x 4 studs 24 in. o.c., drywall

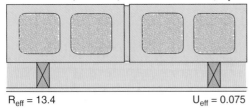

R_{eff} = 13.4 U_{eff} = 0.075

Polyurethane cores, R-11 batt, 2 x 4 studs 24 in. o.c., drywall

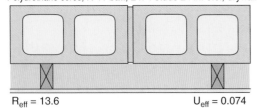

R_{eff} = 13.6 U_{eff} = 0.074

Empty cores, R-19 batt, 2 x 6 studs 24 in. o.c., drywall

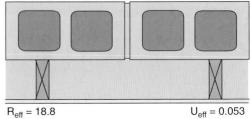

R_{eff} = 18.8 U_{eff} = 0.053

Concrete cores, R-19 batt, 2 x 6 studs 24 in. o.c., drywall

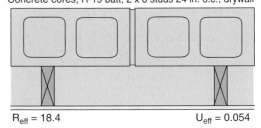

R_{eff} = 18.4 U_{eff} = 0.054

Perlite cores, R-19 batt, 2 x 6 studs 24 in. o.c., drywall

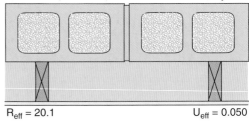

R_{eff} = 20.1 U_{eff} = 0.050

Vermiculite cores, R-19 batt, 2 x 6 studs 24 in. o.c., drywall

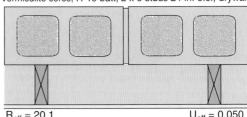

R_{eff} = 20.1 U_{eff} = 0.050

Polyurethane cores, R-19 batt, 2 x 6 studs 24 in. o.c., drywall

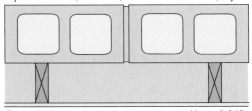

R_{eff} = 20.3 U_{eff} = 0.049

8 x 16 BLOCK, 135 PCF

Empty cores, 2 in. polyisocyanurate, drywall on metal furring

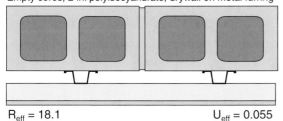

$R_{eff} = 18.1$ $U_{eff} = 0.055$

Solid cores, 2 in. polyisocyanurate, drywall on metal furring

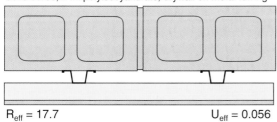

$R_{eff} = 17.7$ $U_{eff} = 0.056$

Perlite cores, 2 in. polyisocyanurate, drywall on metal furring

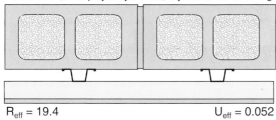

$R_{eff} = 19.4$ $U_{eff} = 0.052$

Vermiculite cores, 2 in. polyisocyanurate, drywall on metal furring

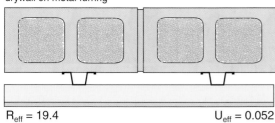

$R_{eff} = 19.4$ $U_{eff} = 0.052$

Polyurethane cores, 2 in. polyisocyanurate, drywall on metal furring

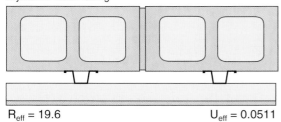

$R_{eff} = 19.6$ $U_{eff} = 0.0511$

Empty cores, exterior 3 in. polyisocyanurate, synthetic stucco

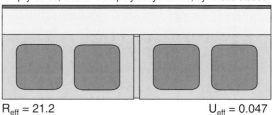

$R_{eff} = 21.2$ $U_{eff} = 0.047$

Solid cores, exterior 3 in. polyisocyanurate, synthetic stucco

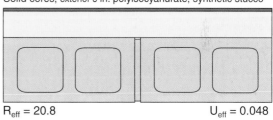

$R_{eff} = 20.8$ $U_{eff} = 0.048$

Perlite cores, exterior 3 in. polyisocyanurate, synthetic stucco

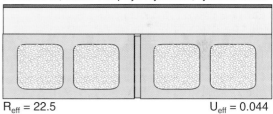

$R_{eff} = 22.5$ $U_{eff} = 0.044$

Vermiculite cores, exterior 3 in. polyisocyanurate, synthetic stucco

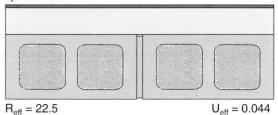

$R_{eff} = 22.5$ $U_{eff} = 0.044$

Polyurethane cores, exterior 3 in. polyisocyanurate, synthetic stucco

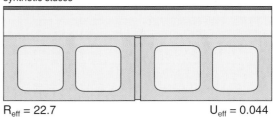

$R_{eff} = 22.7$ $U_{eff} = 0.044$

Concrete Masonry Cavity Assemblies

8 x 16 BLOCK + 4 x 16 VENEER, NO FINISH, 135 PCF

Empty cores, 1 in. extruded polystyrene

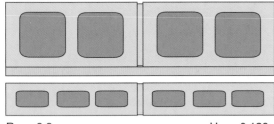

$R_{eff} = 8.3$ $U_{eff} = 0.120$

Empty cores, 1 in. foil-faced polyisocyanurate

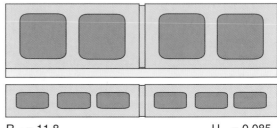

$R_{eff} = 11.8$ $U_{eff} = 0.085$

Empty cores, 1½ in. extruded polystyrene

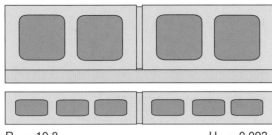

$R_{eff} = 10.8$ $U_{eff} = 0.093$

Empty cores, 1½ in. foil-faced polyisocyanurate

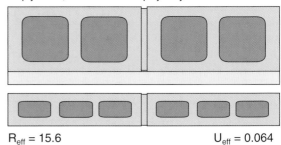

$R_{eff} = 15.6$ $U_{eff} = 0.064$

Empty cores, 2 in. extruded polystyrene

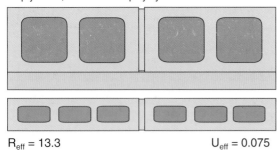

$R_{eff} = 13.3$ $U_{eff} = 0.075$

Empty cores, 2 in. foil-faced polyisocyanurate

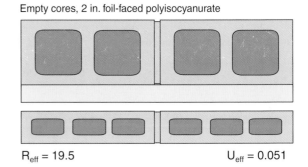

$R_{eff} = 19.5$ $U_{eff} = 0.051$

Empty cores, 3 in. extruded polystyrene

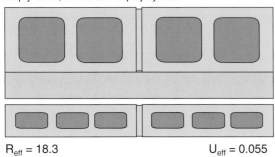

$R_{eff} = 18.3$ $U_{eff} = 0.055$

Empty cores, 3 in. foil-faced polyisocyanurate

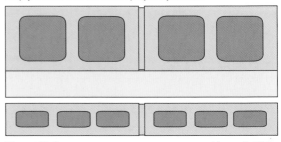

$R_{eff} = 26.3$ $U_{eff} = 0.038$

8 x 16 BLOCK, 4 x 16 VENEER, $1/2$ in. DRYWALL ON METAL FURRING, 135 PCF

Empty cores, 1 in. extruded polystyrene

Empty cores, 1 in. foil-faced polyisocyanurate

Empty cores, $1^1/2$ in. extruded polystyrene

Empty cores, $1^1/2$ in. foil-faced polyisocyanurate

Empty cores, 2 in. extruded polystyrene

Empty cores, 2 in. foil-faced polyisocyanurate

Empty cores, 3 in. extruded polystyrene

Empty cores, 3 in. foil-faced polyisocyanurate

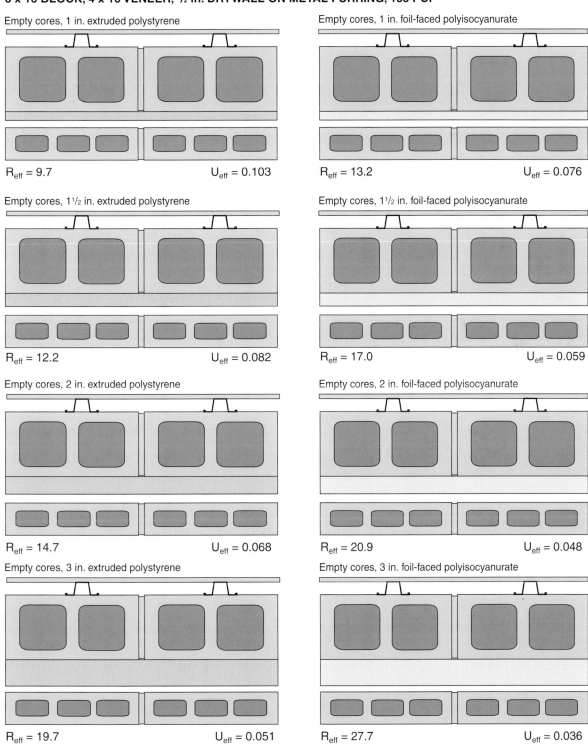

$R_{eff} = 9.7$	$U_{eff} = 0.103$
$R_{eff} = 12.2$	$U_{eff} = 0.082$
$R_{eff} = 14.7$	$U_{eff} = 0.068$
$R_{eff} = 19.7$	$U_{eff} = 0.051$
$R_{eff} = 13.2$	$U_{eff} = 0.076$
$R_{eff} = 17.0$	$U_{eff} = 0.059$
$R_{eff} = 20.9$	$U_{eff} = 0.048$
$R_{eff} = 27.7$	$U_{eff} = 0.036$

Concrete Masonry and Brick Assemblies

8 x 16 BLOCK + 4 x 16 BRICK VENEER, NO FINISH, 135 PCF

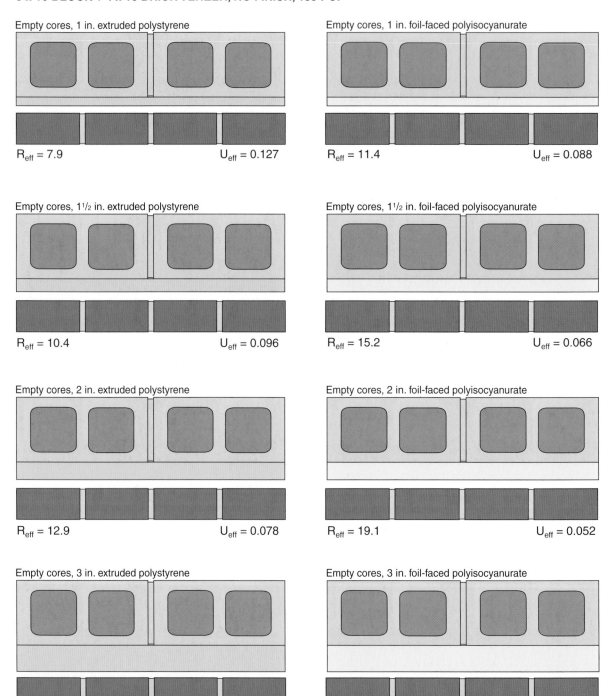

Empty cores, 1 in. extruded polystyrene

$R_{eff} = 7.9$ $U_{eff} = 0.127$

Empty cores, 1 in. foil-faced polyisocyanurate

$R_{eff} = 11.4$ $U_{eff} = 0.088$

Empty cores, 1½ in. extruded polystyrene

$R_{eff} = 10.4$ $U_{eff} = 0.096$

Empty cores, 1½ in. foil-faced polyisocyanurate

$R_{eff} = 15.2$ $U_{eff} = 0.066$

Empty cores, 2 in. extruded polystyrene

$R_{eff} = 12.9$ $U_{eff} = 0.078$

Empty cores, 2 in. foil-faced polyisocyanurate

$R_{eff} = 19.1$ $U_{eff} = 0.052$

Empty cores, 3 in. extruded polystyrene

$R_{eff} = 17.9$ $U_{eff} = 0.056$

Empty cores, 3 in. foil-faced polyisocyanurate

$R_{eff} = 25.9$ $U_{eff} = 0.039$

8 x 16 BLOCK, 4 x 16 BRICK VENEER, $\frac{1}{2}$ in. DRYWALL ON METAL FURRING, 135 PCF

Empty cores, 1 in. extruded polystyrene

Empty cores, 1 in. foil-faced polyisocyanurate

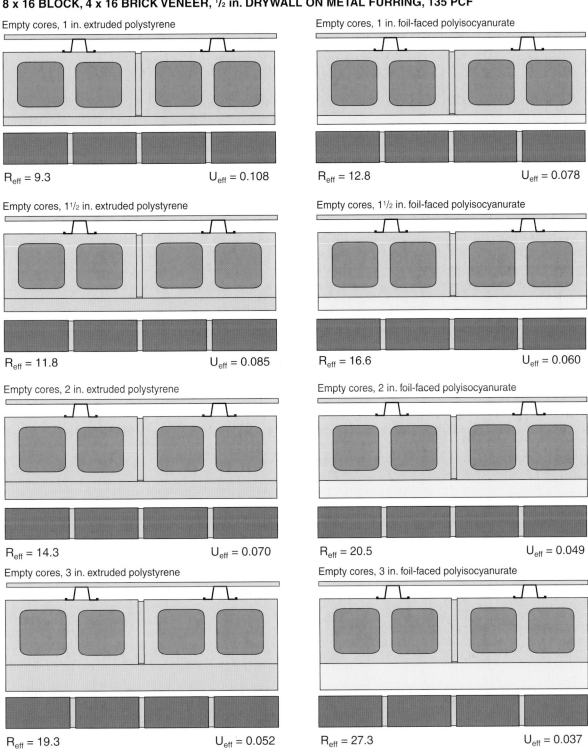

$R_{eff} = 9.3$ $U_{eff} = 0.108$

$R_{eff} = 12.8$ $U_{eff} = 0.078$

Empty cores, 1$\frac{1}{2}$ in. extruded polystyrene

Empty cores, 1$\frac{1}{2}$ in. foil-faced polyisocyanurate

$R_{eff} = 11.8$ $U_{eff} = 0.085$

$R_{eff} = 16.6$ $U_{eff} = 0.060$

Empty cores, 2 in. extruded polystyrene

Empty cores, 2 in. foil-faced polyisocyanurate

$R_{eff} = 14.3$ $U_{eff} = 0.070$

$R_{eff} = 20.5$ $U_{eff} = 0.049$

Empty cores, 3 in. extruded polystyrene

Empty cores, 3 in. foil-faced polyisocyanurate

$R_{eff} = 19.3$ $U_{eff} = 0.052$

$R_{eff} = 27.3$ $U_{eff} = 0.037$

Recommended R-Values

8

How much insulation do I need? That is the number one question homeowners ask when considering investments to lower their heating and cooling bills. And that is the subject of this chapter.

To answer the question, we need to begin at the beginning—*where to insulate: the thermal envelope.* After identifying the component pieces of the thermal envelope (floors, walls, ceilings, windows, and doors), we describe the analytical tool developed by the Oak Ridge National Laboratory (ORNL) for the *determination of recommended R-values.*

If you are mathematically challenged, you may decide to skip the details —gory to some, beautiful to others—and go directly to the *recommended R-values for new construction.*

You may choose to adopt ORNL's R-value recommendations, or you may be forced to comply with your state's energy code. Fortunately, nearly all states have adopted the *International Energy Conservation Code (IECC),* so we have included the *IECC R-values for new construction,* which are based on eight different US climate zones.

An existing home presents a more complex and expensive problem. Because the building is finished, some of the building cavities are no longer open. Filling the cavities requires extra work and expense, making paybacks longer. For your guidance we include Energy Star's *recommended R-values for existing houses,* based on the same eight US climate zones.

Where to Insulate: The Thermal Envelope

In dealing with a building's heat loss and heat gain, building scientists employ a useful concept: the building's thermal envelope. The thermal envelope is the set of contiguous surfaces separating the conditioned (heated and/or cooled) interior of a building from the outdoors and the earth. Included surfaces are roofs, ceilings, exterior walls, foundation walls, floors, windows, and doors.

A useful analogy can be made between a cold-climate thermal envelope in winter and a hot air balloon. As shown in the illustration below, both contain a volume of warm air. Just as conduction through the fabric and air flow through the vent at the top of the balloon will allow hot air to escape, so will gaps in the thermal envelope.

To be maximally effective, every surface comprising the thermal envelope must be insulated to the R-value appropriate to the climate.

What is the appropriate R-value? The rational answer is the R-value that results in minimum life-cycle cost (LCC)—the sum of the costs of heating and cooling losses through the insulated surface plus the initial cost of installing the insulation.

The Oak Ridge National Lab's ZIP-Code Program, found at *www.ornl.gov/~roofs/Zip/ZipHome.html*, lists the LCC-based recommended insulation levels for new and existing houses. The building surfaces included are identified in the thermal envelope illustration on the facing page.

Thermal Envelopes in Winter Are Like Hot Air Balloons

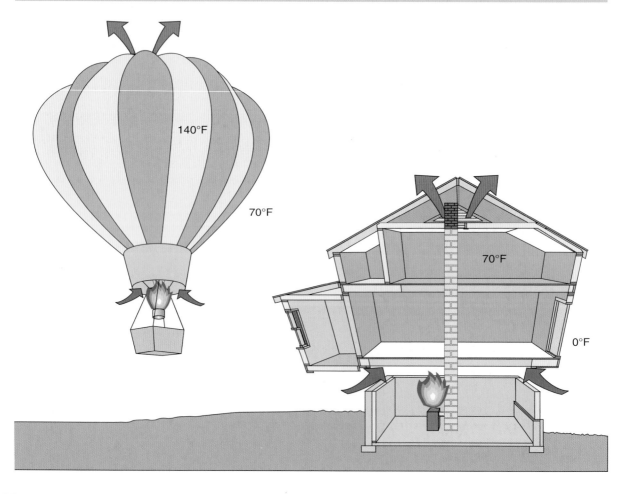

140°F

70°F

70°F

0°F

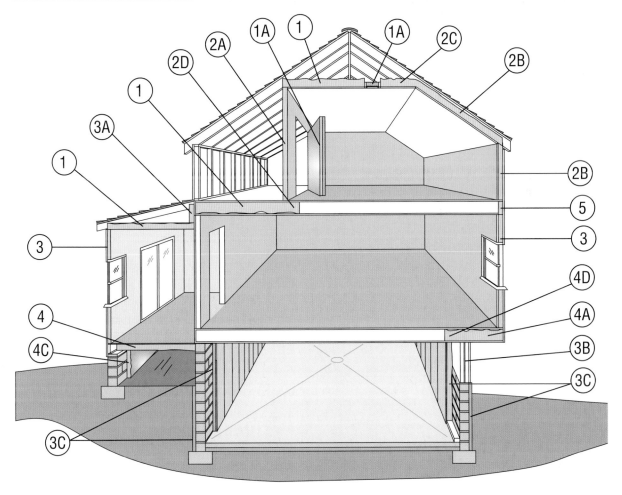

1. In unfinished attic spaces, insulate between and over floor joists to seal off living spaces below.
   1A. attic access door

2. In finished attic rooms with or without dormers, insulate
   2A. between studs of knee walls
   2B. between studs and rafters of exterior walls and roof
   2C. ceilings with cold spaces above
   2D. extend insulation into joist space to reduce air flows

3. All exterior walls, including
   3A. walls between living spaces and unheated garages, shed roofs, or storage areas
   3B. foundation walls above ground level
   3C. foundation walls in heated basements—full wall, either interior or exterior

4. Floors above unconditioned spaces, such as vented crawl spaces and unheated garages. Also insulate
   4A. portion of floor cantilevered beyond exterior wall below
   4B. slab floors at grade level (not shown)
   4C. as an alternative to floor insulation, foundation walls of unvented crawl spaces
   4D. extend insulation into joist space to reduce air flows

5. Band joists.

Determination of Recommended R-Values

From a financial standpoint, the optimum level of insulation is that resulting in the greatest net dollar savings over the life of the building, where net savings equal heating savings plus cooling savings, less cost of the insulation.

The Oak Ridge National Lab's ZIP-Code Program (*www.ornl.gov/-roofs/Zip/ZipHome.html*) uses life-cycle cost analysis to calculate recommended R-values for the building surfaces shown in the illustration on the previous page for any combination of climate, heating/cooling system, and fuel cost. The equations and assumptions used in the analysis are shown below.

Wall and Roof Heating Btu Savings

The equation for heat loss by conduction is:

$$H_h = A \cdot \Delta T \cdot U$$

where:

A = area of surface in sq. ft.
ΔT = temperature difference, °F
U = thermal conductance of material

Note that $U = 1/R\text{-value}$

Per square foot of wall or roof:

$$H_{sqft,h} = \Delta T \cdot U$$

Total annual heat loss per square foot, assuming a balance point temperature of 65°F, is:

$$Q_h = HDD_{65} \cdot 24 \cdot U/1{,}000{,}000$$

where:

Q_h = heat loss in 10^6 Btu/sq. ft. year
HDD_{65} = Heating Degree Days, base 65°F
24 = days to hours conversion

The above equation assumes zero thermal mass (ability of materials to store heat). Computer modeling, using hourly calculations and accounting for thermal mass, results in mass modification factors. For convenience, these factors replace the 24 in the equation, resulting in a more accurate equation for annual heat loss:

$$Q_h = HDD_{65} \cdot M_h \cdot U/1{,}000{,}000$$

where:

Q_h = heat loss in 10^6 Btu/sq. ft. year
HDD_{65} = Heating Degree Days, base 65°F

M_h = heating mass factor:
25.91 for attics and ceilings
21.19 for frame walls
20.02 for masonry walls

Note that heat losses for different U-values are directly proportional to the U-values:

$$Q_{h1} = \text{Constant} \cdot U_1$$
$$Q_{h2} = \text{Constant} \cdot U_2$$

Heating energy saved annually by decreasing U-value is therefore:

$$\Delta Q_h = Q_{h1} - Q_{h2}$$
$$= \text{Constant} \cdot U - \text{Constant} \cdot U_2$$
$$= \text{Constant} \cdot (U - U_2)$$
$$= \text{Constant} \cdot \Delta U$$

Thus, $\Delta Q_h = HDD_{65} \cdot M_h \cdot \Delta U/1{,}000{,}000$
where:

ΔQ_h = saving in 10^6 Btu/sq. ft. year
HDD_{65} = Heating Degree Days, base 65°F
ΔU = change in U-factor from base value
M_h = heating mass factor

Wall and Roof Cooling Btu Savings

Similarly, annual cooling energy saved is:

$$\Delta Q_c = CDH_{74} \cdot M_c \cdot \Delta U / 1{,}000{,}000$$

where:

ΔQ_c = saving in 10^6 Btu/sq. ft. year
CDH_7 = Cooling Degree Hours, base 74°F
ΔU = change in U-value from base value
M_c = cooling mass factor:
1.978 for attics and ceilings
1.005 for frame walls and band joists
0.739 for masonry walls

Floor and Foundation Btu Savings

Reductions in heating and cooling losses per HDD and CDH for added R are interpolated from results of several studies of basement and slab heat loss.

The equations for heating and cooling savings from insulation added to floors, foundations, and slabs use the equations and factors β_h and β_c shown in the illustration on the facing page.

Heating Btu Savings

$$\Delta Q_h = HDD_{65} \cdot \text{ß}_h / 1{,}000{,}000$$

where:

ΔQ_h = saving in 10^6 Btu/sq. ft. year for floors and 108^6 Btu/lin. ft. year for others

HDD_{65} = Heating Degree Days, base 65°F

$\text{ß}_h = Q_h$ reduction per HDD for added R

Cooling Btu Savings

$$\Delta Q_c = CDH_{74} \cdot \text{ß}_c / 1{,}000{,}000$$

where:

ΔQ_c = saving in 10^6 Btu/sq. ft. year for floors and 10^6 Btu/lin. ft. year for others

CDH_{74} = Cooling Degree Hours, base 74°F

$\text{ß}_c = Q_c$ reduction per CDH for added R

ß$_h$ and ß$_c$ Factors for Floors and Foundations

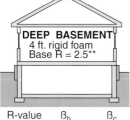

DEEP BASEMENT
4 ft. rigid foam
Base R = 2.5**

R-value	ß_h	ß_c
4	20.69	0.34
5	21.70	0.37
8	23.62	0.44
10	24.48	0.47
12	25.18	0.50
15	26.07	0.54

DEEP BASEMENT
8 ft. rigid foam
Base R = 2.5**

R-value	ß_h	ß_c
4	28.57	0.45
5	30.00	0.47
8	32.75	0.50
10	34.00	0.51
12	35.03	0.52
15	35.35	0.54

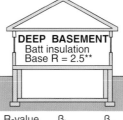

DEEP BASEMENT
Batt insulation
Base R = 2.5**

R-value	ß_h	ß_c
11	34.24	0.51
19	35.20	0.52
30	37.55	0.53

SHALLOW BASEMENT
8 ft. rigid foam
Base R = 2.5**

R-value	ß_h	ß_c
4	44.35	0.95
5	46.38	0.99
8	50.04	1.06
10	51.56	1.08
12	52.75	1.10
15	54.17	1.12

SHALLOW BASEMENT
Batt insulation
Base R = 2.5**

R-value	ß_h	ß_c
11	51.36	1.08
19	52.48	1.10
30	54.98	1.13

CRAWL SPACE
Rigid foam
Base R = 2.5**

R-value	ß_h	ß_c
5	19.51	0.83
7	20.59	0.86
10	21.56	0.88
14	22.37	0.90

CRAWL SPACE
Batt insulation
Base R = 2.5**

R-value	ß_h	ß_c
11	21.80	0.93
13	22.20	0.94

NOTES

** Savings are per linear foot

* Savings are per square foot

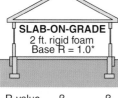

SLAB-ON-GRADE
2 ft. rigid foam
Base R = 1.0*

R-value	ß_h	ß_c
4	2.79	0.23
5	2.94	0.24
8	3.25	0.25
10	3.40	0.25
12	3.53	0.25

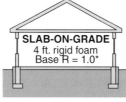

SLAB-ON-GRADE
4 ft. rigid foam
Base R = 1.0*

R-value	ß_h	ß_c
4	3.56	0.23
5	3.78	0.24
8	4.25	0.25
10	4.50	0.25
12	4.72	0.25

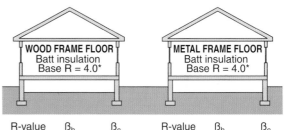

WOOD FRAME FLOOR
Batt insulation
Base R = 4.0*

R-value	ß_h	ß_c
11	1.70	0.12
19	1.96	0.12
30	2.22	0.12

METAL FRAME FLOOR
Batt insulation
Base R = 4.0*

R-value	ß_h	ß_c
11	1.05	0.07
19	1.33	0.09
30	1.52	0.11

Present Worth Factor

In order to compare the performance of insulation R-values based on the value of recurring heating and cooling savings over an n-year lifetime less the initial cost of installing the insulation, we need to know the present value of each year's savings.

Assume we are heating and cooling with electricity at $0.10/kWh. If the price of electricity rises 5% per year, in year two we will pay $0.10 (1.05) = $0.105/kWh. In the third year we will pay $0.10 (1.05)(1.05) = $0.11025/kWh. In year n we will pay $0.10 (1.05)^n$.

But general inflation reduces the value of future dollars. Further, there is a time value of money in that we may have financed our insulation investment, or, if we paid cash, we could have put the money instead into an interest–bearing account. Economists combine these negative factors into a *discount rate*. Assume a discount rate of 3% per year (ORNL assumed a discount rate of 3.4% in their analysis). A dollar one year from today, considering inflation and missed interest, will be worth a discounted $1.00/(1.03) = $0.97. N years from now that same dollar will be worth $1.00/(1.03)^n$.

Combining both fuel price escalation and the discount rate, the present value of the single year n's saving is that year's saving times a present value factor or multiplier:

$$PV_n = EF_n / (1 + discount\ rate)^n$$

where:

PV_n = multiplier for year n saving
EF_n = fuel escalation factor in year n

Adding up all thirty years of present value factors:

$$n = lifetime$$

$$PWF = \sum EF_n / (1 + discount\ rate)^n$$

$$n = 1$$

where:

PWF = present worth factor
$\sum$ = the summation of each year's present value factor from year 1 to year n

Present Value of Fuel Savings

We have both the annual Btu heating and cooling savings from an increased insulation R-value (pp. 148–149) and a present worth factor for converting annual savings to lifetime savings. With these numbers we can calculate the dollar value of an insulation option:

$$Savings = \Delta Q_h \bullet P_h \bullet PWF_h / (e_h \bullet e_d) +$$
$$\Delta Q_c \bullet P_c \bullet PWF_c / (e_c \bullet e_d) - Cost$$

where:

Savings = present value of net savings due to insulation, $/sq. ft. or $/lf
ΔQ_h = heat reduction, 10^6 Btu/sq. ft. or 10^6 Btu/lf
P_h = year-one heating fuel price, $/$10^6$ Btu
PWF_h = present worth factor for heating
e_h = heating system efficiency
e_d = distribution system efficiency
ΔQ_c = saving, 10^6 Btu/sq. ft. or 10^6 Btu/lf
P_c = year-one cooling fuel price, $/$10^6$ Btu
PWF_c = present worth factor for cooling
e_c = cooling system efficiency
Cost = cost of insulation, $/sq. ft. or $/lf

The ORNL savings calculations assume the following heating and cooling efficiencies, e_h, e_c, and e_d:

Furnace or Boiler: gas, propane, or fuel oil:	
existing	67.5%
new	80.0%
Electric Baseboard:	100%
Furnace Ducts:	
in heated space	100%
in unheated space	75%
Heat Pumps:	
$e_h = 1.06 (2.3 - HDD_{65}/1,000) \bullet HSPF/6.7$	
where HSPF, in Btu/Wh:	
existing	100%
new	75%
Air Conditioner SEER, Btu/Wh:	
existing	9.0
new	11.0

Costs of Added Insulation

The cost of insulating is a critical factor in determining optimum R-values. After all, if it cost nothing to insulate, the optimum amount of insulation would be infinite.

To determine costs, ORNL solicited estimates from builders throughout the United States for insulation options. The mean costs reported by the builders are listed below.

Costs of Added Insulation

Added R-Value Sheathing	Cavity	Cost ($/sq. ft.) New Const.	Retrofit
Wood-Framed Attic			
–	11	0.24	0.27
–	19	0.33	0.37
–	22	0.37	–
–	30	0.45	0.49
–	38	0.56	0.60
–	49	0.68	0.77
–	60	0.82	–
Metal-Framed Attic			
–	11	0.24	–
–	19	0.33	–
–	30	0.45	–
–	38	0.56	–
–	49	0.68	–
5	38	1.14	–
5	49	1.26	–
10	49	1.53	–
Cathedral Ceiling			
–	11	0.34	–
–	13	0.46	–
–	15	0.63	–
–	19	0.53	–
–	21	0.62	–
–	22	0.59	–
–	30	0.73	–
–	38	0.87	–
–	49	2.02	–
–	60	2.29	–

Added R-Value Sheathing	Cavity	Cost ($/sq. ft.) New Const.	Retrofit
Wood-Framed Wall			
2.5	–	0.47	–
3.5	–	0.65	–
5	–	0.58	–
7	–	0.87	–
–	11	0.30	–
–	13	0.36	–
–	15	0.56	–
–	19	1.27	–
–	21	1.38	–
2.5	11	0.77	–
3.5	11	0.95	–
2.5	13	0.83	–
3.5	13	1.01	–
2.5	15	1.03	–
3.5	15	1.21	–
2.5	19	1.74	–
3.5	19	1.92	–
2.5	21	1.85	–
3.5	21	2.03	–
5	11	0.88	–
7	11	1.17	–
5	13	0.94	–
7	13	1.23	–
5	15	1.14	–
7	15	1.43	–
5	19	1.85	–
7	19	2.14	–
5	21	1.96	–
7	21	2.25	–

Costs of Added Insulation

Added R-Value Sheathing	Cavity	Cost ($/sq. ft.) New Const.	Retrofit	Added R-Value Sheathing	Cavity	Cost ($/sq. ft.) New Const.	Retrofit
Metal-Framed Wall				**OVE Wood-Framed Wall**			
2.5	–	0.47	–	–	19	0.44	–
3.5	–	0.65	–	–	21	0.55	–
5	–	0.58	–	2.5	19	0.91	–
7	–	0.87	–	2.5	21	1.02	–
–	11	NR[1]	–	3.5	19	1.09	–
–	13	NR[1]	–	3.5	21	1.20	–
–	15	NR[1]	–	5	19	1.02	–
–	19	NR[1]	–	5	21	1.13	–
–	21	NR[1]	–	7	19	1.31	–
2.5	11	0.77	–	7	21	1.42	–
3.5	11	0.95	–	**Masonry Walls**			
2.5	13	0.83	–	3.8		0.22	–
3.5	13	1.01	–	5.7		0.36	–
2.5	15	1.03	–	7.6		0.52	–
3.5	15	1.21	–	9.5		0.67	–
2.5	19	1.74	–	11.4		0.82	–
3.5	19	1.92	–	15.0		1.78	–
2.5	21	1.85	–	21.6		2.20	–
3.5	21	2.03	–	**Add Insulating Sheathing to Empty Wall**			
5	11	0.88	–	2.5		–	0.47
7	11	1.17	–	5		–	0.58
5	13	0.94	–	**Add Insulating Sheathing to R-11 in Cavity Wall**			
7	13	1.23	–	2.5		–	0.47
5	15	1.14	–	5		–	0.58
7	15	1.43	–	**Wood- or Metal-Framed Floor**			
5	19	1.85	–	11		0.37	0.38
7	19	2.14	–	13		0.41	0.46
5	21	1.96	–	19		0.53	0.58
7	21	2.25		25		0.62	0.76

[1] Not recommended without minimum R-2.5 sheathing

Added R-Value	Cost ($/lin. ft.)	
	New Const.	Retrofit
Basement Walls–Exterior Application		
4	6.20	–
5	7.01	–
8	9.30	–
10	10.87	–
12	12.30	–
15	14.55	–
Basement Walls–Including Interior Stud Wall		
11	6.48	6.48
13	7.20	7.20
19	9.30	9.30
Crawl Space Walls–Interior Application		
11	1.47	1.49
13	1.63	1.75
19	2.08	2.19
Slab Edge		
5	1.40	–
10	1.82	–
Band Joist		
11	0.31	–
13	0.36	–
19	0.45	–
30	0.60	–

Recommended R-Values for New Construction

Climate and Fuel Price Assumptions for ORNL–Recommended R-Values

State, City	ZIP CODE	DMT[1]	CDH[2]	HDD[3]	Gas $/1,000 cf	Oil $/gal	Elect ¢/kWh
AL, Birmingham	352XX	21	21,000	2,900	13.21	0.91	6.8
AK, Fairbanks	997XX	-47	0	14,000	4.24	1.27	10.7
AK, Juneau	998XX	1	0	9,000	4.24	1.27	10.7
AZ, Flagstaff	860XX	4	400	7,300	11.89	1.20	7.3
AZ, Phoenix	850XX	34	55,000	1,400	11.89	1.20	7.3
AR, Little Rock	722XX	20	23,800	3,200	9.76	0.91	7.5
CA, Los Angeles	900XX	43	10,600	1,200	9.84	1.20	9.6
CO, Denver	802XX	1	5,900	6,000	9.63	0.99	6.5
CO, Fort Collins	805XX	-4	3,800	6,400	9.63	0.99	6.5
CT, Hartford	061XX	7	4,800	6,200	12.67	1.18	10.3
DE, Wilmington	198XX	14	8,200	5,000	12.03	1.20	8.3
DC, Washington	200XX	17	12,400	4,200	12.73	1.39	7.5
FL, Miami	331XX	47	39,000	200	16.36	1.22	8.2
FL, Orlando	328XX	38	34,000	700	16.36	1.22	8.2
GA, Atlanta	303XX	22	16,800	3,000	10.50	1.22	7.7
ID, Boise	837XX	10	8,000	5,800	8.72	0.96	5.3
IL, Chicago	606XX	0	9,700	6,200	9.05	1.09	8.4
IN, Indianapolis	462XX	2	9,100	5,700	7.64	1.11	6.7
IA, Des Moines	503XX	-5	10,500	6,600	9.64	1.14	8.2
KS, Topeka	666XX	4	16,600	5,300	10.88	1.14	7.5
KY, Louisville	402XX	10	13,300	4,500	11.01	1.13	5.3
LA, Baton Rouge	708XX	29	26,900	1,700	9.97	0.91	7.8
ME, Caribou	047XX	-13	900	9,600	13.33	1.16	10.3
ME, Portland	041XX	-1	1,100	7,500	13.33	1.16	10.3
MD, Baltimore	212XX	13	9,500	4,700	11.52	1.30	7.5
MA, Boston	021XX	9	5,400	5,600	13.53	1.16	11.6
MA, Springfield	011XX	0	5,200	6,000	13.53	1.16	11.6
MI, Detroit	482XX	6	4,900	6,600	6.39	1.22	8.2
MI, Sault Ste. Marie	497XX	-12	2,000	8,000	6.39	1.22	8.2
MN, Duluth	558XX	-16	800	9,900	8.64	1.10	7.3
MN, Int'l Falls	566XX	-25	2,200	10,200	8.64	1.10	7.3
MS, Jackson	392XX	25	25,200	2,400	10.44	0.91	7.2
MO, St. Louis	631XX	6	17,800	4,900	12.27	1.14	6.8
MT, Great Falls	594XX	-15	3,600	7,800	7.33	0.99	6.2
MT, Missoula	598XX	-6	1,100	7,800	7.33	0.99	6.2
NE, North Platte	691XX	-4	8,500	6,900	8.50	1.14	6.4
NV, Las Vegas	891XX	28	43,000	2,500	8.33	1.07	5.8
NV, Reno	895XX	11	2,200	6,000	8.33	1.07	5.8

State, City	ZIP CODE	DMT[1]	CDH[2]	HDD[3]	Gas $/1,000 cf	Oil $/gal	Elect ¢/kWh
NH, Concord	033XX	-3	2,000	7,400	12.80	1.19	11.8
NJ, Newark	071XX	14	9,100	5,000	7.95	1.25	9.7
NM, Albuquerque	871XX	16	11,000	4,400	9.15	0.86	7.7
NM, Santa Fe	875XX	10	1,200	6,400	9.15	0.86	7.7
NY, New York	100XX	15	9,500	4,900	12.26	1.30	13.3
NY, Syracuse	132XX	2	3,500	6,800	12.26	1.30	13.3
NC, Greensboro	274XX	18	11,000	3,900	13.24	1.22	8.0
ND, Bismarck	585XX	-19	4,600	9,100	7.99	1.14	6.5
OH, Columbus	432XX	5	7,500	5,700	10.57	1.14	8.1
OK, Tulsa	741XX	13	26,500	3,700	10.09	1.13	7.0
OR, Bend	977XX	4	600	7,042	9.78	1.12	5.5
OR, Salem	973XX	23	1,000	5,000	9.78	1.12	5.5
PA, Philadelphia	191XX	14	8,900	5,000	12.54	1.10	9.1
PA, Pittsburgh	152XX	5	5,000	6,000	12.54	1.10	9.1
RI, Providence	029XX	9	3,600	5,900	12.53	1.18	11.4
SC, Columbia	292XX	24	22,000	2,600	12.30	1.22	7.4
SD, Rapid City	577XX	-7	8,200	7,300	8.76	1.14	7.5
TN, Nashville	372XX	14	18,500	3,800	10.55	1.13	6.2
TX, Austin	787XX	28	35,200	1,800	9.47	0.91	8.4
TX, Brownsville	785XX	39	42,500	600	9.47	0.91	8.4
TX, Dallas	752XX	22	36,700	2,300	9.47	0.91	8.4
TX, Houston	770XX	33	30,500	1,500	9.47	0.91	8.4
UT, Salt Lake City	841XX	8	9,900	5,800	8.23	0.99	5.9
VT, Burlington	054XX	-7	2,600	8,000	10.87	1.20	11.8
VA, Norfolk	235XX	22	13,700	3,500	14.01	1.17	7.5
VA, Richmond	232XX	17	12,300	4,000	14.01	1.17	7.5
WA, Seattle	981XX	26	1,000	5,100	9.87	1.23	5.0
WV, Charleston	253XX	11	8,800	4,700	8.76	1.11	6.1
WI, Madison	537XX	-7	3,300	7,600	8.49	1.16	7.7
WY, Casper	826XX	-5	4,500	6,900	9.41	0.99	5.9

[1] Design Minimum Temperature

[2] Cooling Degree Hours

[3] Heating Degree Days

ORNL–Recommended R-Values for Natural Gas Heating and Electric Air Conditioning

State, City	Attic Floor	Cathedral Ceiling	Wall[1] Sheath	Wall[1] Cavity	OVE[2] Sheath	OVE[2] Cavity	Masonry Wall[3]	Crawl Ceiling[4]	Slab Edge	Crawl Wall[5]	Basement Exterior[6]	Basement Interior[7]
AL, Birmingham	38	38	0	13	0	19	11.4	25	8	19	8	11
AK, Fairbanks	38	30	0	13	0	19	11.4	25	8	19	5	11
AK, Juneau	38	30	0	13	0	19	11.4	13	4	13	4	11
AZ, Flagstaff	49	38	5	13	5	19	11.4	25	8	19	15	11
AZ, Phoenix	38	30	0	13	0	19	11.4	11	4	13	4	11
AR, Little Rock	38	38	0	13	0	19	11.4	25	8	19	8	11
CA, Los Angeles	22	19	0	11	0	19	5.7	11	0	11	4	11
CO, Denver	49	38	5	13	0	19	11.4	25	8	19	10	11
CO, Fort Collins	49	38	5	13	0	19	11.4	25	8	19	12	11
CT, Hartford	49	38	5	13	0	19	11.4	25	8	19	12	11
DE, Wilmington	49	38	5	13	0	19	11.4	25	8	19	10	11
DC, Washington	49	38	5	13	0	19	11.4	25	8	19	10	11
FL, Miami	38	22	0	11	0	19	5.7	11	4	11	0	0
FL, Orlando	38	30	0	13	0	19	11.4	11	4	13	4	11
GA, Atlanta	38	38	0	13	0	19	11.4	25	8	19	5	11
ID, Boise	49	38	5	13	0	19	11.4	25	8	19	8	11
IL, Chicago	38	38	0	13	0	19	11.4	25	8	19	8	11
IN, Indianapolis	38	38	0	13	0	19	11.4	25	8	19	8	11
IA, Des Moines	49	38	5	13	0	19	11.4	25	8	19	12	11
KS, Topeka	49	38	5	13	0	19	11.4	25	8	19	12	11
KY, Louisville	49	38	5	13	0	19	11.4	25	8	19	10	11
LA, Baton Rouge	38	30	0	13	0	19	11.4	13	4	13	4	11
ME, Caribou	49	38	7	13	5	21	11.4	25	8	19	15	19
ME, Portland	49	38	7	13	5	19	11.4	25	8	19	15	13
MD, Baltimore	49	38	5	13	0	19	11.4	25	8	19	10	11
MA, Boston	49	38	5	13	0	19	11.4	25	8	19	12	11
MA, Springfield	49	38	5	13	0	19	11.4	25	8	19	12	11
MI, Detroit	38	38	0	13	0	19	11.4	25	8	19	8	11
MI, Sault St. Marie	49	38	5	13	0	19	11.4	25	8	19	12	11
MN, Duluth	49	38	5	13	0	19	11.4	25	8	19	15	11
MN, Int'l Falls	49	38	5	13	5	19	11.4	25	8	19	15	11
MS, Jackson	38	38	0	13	0	19	11.4	25	8	19	5	11
MO, St. Louis	49	38	5	13	0	19	11.4	25	8	19	10	11
MT, Great Falls	49	38	5	13	0	19	11.4	25	8	19	12	11
MT, Missoula	49	38	5	13	0	19	11.4	25	8	19	12	11
NE, North Platte	49	38	5	13	0	19	11.4	25	8	19	15	11
NV, Las Vegas	38	30	0	13	0	19	11.4	13	4	13	4	11

State, City	Attic Floor	Cathedral Ceiling	Wall[1] Sheath	Wall[1] Cavity	OVE[2] Sheath	OVE[2] Cavity	Masonry Wall[3]	Crawl Ceiling[4]	Slab Edge	Crawl Wall[5]	Basement Exterior[6]	Basement Interior[7]
NH, Concord	49	38	5	13	5	19	11.4	25	8	19	15	11
NJ, Newark	38	30	0	13	0	19	11.4	25	8	19	5	11
NM, Albuquerque	38	38	0	13	0	19	11.4	25	8	19	8	11
NM, Santa Fe	49	38	5	13	0	19	11.4	25	8	19	12	11
NY, New York	38	38	0	13	0	19	11.4	25	8	19	8	11
NY, Syracuse	49	38	5	13	0	19	11.4	25	8	19	15	11
NC, Greensboro	49	38	5	13	0	19	11.4	25	8	19	12	11
ND, Bismarck	49	38	5	13	5	19	11.4	25	8	19	15	11
OH, Columbus	49	38	5	13	0	19	11.4	25	8	19	10	11
OK, Tulsa	49	38	0	13	0	19	11.4	25	8	19	8	11
OR, Bend	49	38	5	13	0	19	11.4	25	8	19	12	11
OR, Salem	38	38	0	13	0	19	11.4	25	8	19	8	11
PA, Philadelphia	49	38	5	13	0	19	11.4	25	8	19	8	11
PA, Pittsburgh	49	38	5	13	0	19	11.4	25	8	19	12	11
RI, Providence	49	38	5	13	0	19	11.4	25	8	19	12	11
SC, Columbia	49	38	0	13	0	19	11.4	25	8	19	8	11
SD, Rapid City	49	38	5	13	0	21	11.4	25	8	19	15	11
TN, Nashville	49	38	0	13	0	19	11.4	25	8	19	8	11
TX, Austin	38	38	0	13	0	19	11.4	13	4	13	4	11
TX, Brownsville	38	22	0	13	0	19	5.7	11	4	11	4	11
TX, Dallas	38	38	0	13	0	19	11.4	13	8	19	5	11
TX, Houston	38	30	0	13	0	19	11.4	11	4	13	4	11
UT, Salt Lake City	49	38	5	13	0	19	11.4	25	8	19	8	11
VT, Burlington	49	38	5	13	5	19	11.4	25	8	19	15	13
VA, Norfolk	49	38	5	13	0	19	11.4	25	8	19	12	11
VA, Richmond	49	38	5	13	0	19	11.4	25	8	19	12	11
WA, Seattle	38	38	0	13	0	19	11.4	25	8	19	8	11
WV, Charleston	38	38	0	13	0	19	11.4	25	8	19	8	11
WI, Madison	49	38	5	13	0	19	11.4	25	8	19	12	11
WY, Casper	49	38	5	13	0	19	11.4	25	8	19	12	11

[1] It is important to use both the insulative sheathing and cavity insulation recommended. Insulative sheathing may be placed outside of wood sheathing product, or special braces can be used.

[2] This recommendation assumes that a 2x6 wall can be built for the same cost as a 2x4 wall, using a careful design procedure called Optimum Value Engineering (OVE).

[3] Insulation should be placed on the interior side of an above-grade wall.

[4] Over unheated, uninsulated space.

[5] Crawl space walls are insulated only if the crawl space is unvented and the floor above the crawl space is uninsulated.

[6] Exterior insulation on a below-grade wall is used only if you choose not to insulate the interior side of your basement wall.

[7] Interior insulation on a below-grade wall is used only if you choose not to insulate the exterior side of your basement wall.

Recommended R-Values for New Construction   157

ORNL–Recommended R-Values for Heat Pump Heating and Electric Air Conditioning

State, City	Attic Floor	Cathedral Ceiling	Wall[1] Sheath	Wall[1] Cavity	OVE[2] Sheath	OVE[2] Cavity	Masonry Wall[3]	Crawl Ceiling[4]	Slab Edge	Crawl Wall[5]	Basement Exterior[6]	Basement Interior[7]
AL, Birmingham	38	22	0	13	0	19	11.4	11	4	13	4	11
AK, Fairbanks	49	38	7	15	7	21	15	25	8	19	15	19
AK, Juneau	49	38	5	13	0	19	11.4	25	8	19	15	11
AZ, Flagstaff	49	38	5	13	0	19	11.4	25	8	19	12	11
AZ, Phoenix	38	22	0	11	0	19	5.7	11	4	11	4	11
AR, Little Rock	38	30	0	13	0	19	11.4	13	8	19	5	11
CA, Los Angeles	19	11	0	11	0	11	5.7	11	0	11	0	11
CO, Denver	38	38	0	13	0	19	11.4	25	8	19	8	11
CO, Fort Collins	38	38	0	13	0	19	11.4	25	8	19	8	11
CT, Hartford	49	38	5	13	0	19	11.4	25	8	19	12	11
DE, Wilmington	38	38	0	13	0	19	11.4	25	8	19	8	11
DC, Washington	38	30	0	13	0	19	11.4	25	8	19	5	11
FL, Miami	22	22	0	11	0	11	5.7	11	0	11	0	0
FL, Orlando	38	22	0	11	0	19	5.7	11	0	11	0	0
GA, Atlanta	38	30	0	13	0	19	11.4	13	4	13	5	11
ID, Boise	38	30	0	13	0	19	11.4	25	8	19	5	11
IL, Chicago	49	38	5	13	0	19	11.4	25	8	19	8	11
IN, Indianapolis	38	38	0	13	0	19	11.4	25	8	19	8	11
IA, Des Moines	49	38	5	13	0	19	11.4	25	8	19	12	11
KS, Topeka	49	38	5	13	0	19	11.4	25	8	19	8	11
KY, Louisville	38	30	0	13	0	19	11.4	13	4	19	5	11
LA, Baton Rouge	38	22	0	11	0	19	7.6	11	4	11	4	11
ME, Caribou	49	38	7	13	5	21	11.4	25	8	19	15	19
ME, Portland	49	38	7	13	5	19	11.4	25	8	19	15	13
MD, Baltimore	38	38	0	13	0	19	11.4	25	8	19	8	11
MA, Boston	49	38	5	13	0	19	11.4	25	8	19	10	11
MA, Springfield	49	38	5	13	0	19	11.4	25	8	19	15	11
MI, Detroit	49	38	5	13	0	19	11.4	25	8	19	10	11
MI, Sault St. Marie	49	38	5	13	5	19	11.4	25	8	19	15	11
MN, Duluth	49	38	5	13	5	19	11.4	25	8	19	15	11
MN, Int'l Falls	49	38	7	13	5	19	11.4	25	8	19	15	13
MS, Jackson	38	30	0	13	0	19	11.4	13	4	13	4	11
MO, St. Louis	38	30	0	13	0	19	11.4	25	8	19	5	11
MT, Great Falls	49	38	5	13	0	19	11.4	25	8	19	12	11
MT, Missoula	49	38	5	13	0	19	11.4	25	8	19	12	11
NE, North Platte	49	38	5	13	0	19	11.4	25	8	19	12	11
NV, Las Vegas	38	22	0	11	0	19	5.7	11	0	11	4	11

State, City	Attic Floor	Cathedral Ceiling	Wall[1] Sheath	Wall[1] Cavity	OVE[2] Sheath	OVE[2] Cavity	Masonry Wall[3]	Crawl Ceiling[4]	Slab Edge	Crawl Wall[5]	Basement Exterior[6]	Basement Interior[7]
NH, Concord	49	38	5	13	5	19	11.4	25	8	19	15	13
NJ, Newark	38	38	0	13	0	19	11.4	25	8	19	8	11
NM, Albuquerque	38	30	0	13	0	19	11.4	25	8	19	5	11
NM, Santa Fe	49	38	5	13	0	19	11.4	25	8	19	10	11
NY, New York	49	38	5	13	0	19	11.4	25	8	19	8	11
NY, Syracuse	49	38	7	13	5	19	11.4	25	8	19	15	13
NC, Greensboro	38	38	0	13	0	19	11.4	25	8	19	8	11
ND, Bismarck	49	38	5	13	5	19	11.4	25	8	19	15	13
OH, Columbus	49	38	0	13	0	19	11.4	25	8	19	8	11
OK, Tulsa	38	30	0	13	0	19	11.4	25	8	19	5	11
OR, Bend	38	38	0	13	0	19	11.4	25	8	19	8	11
OR, Salem	38	22	0	13	0	19	11.4	13	4	13	5	11
PA, Philadelphia	38	38	0	13	0	19	11.4	25	8	19	8	11
PA, Pittsburgh	49	38	5	13	0	19	11.4	25	8	19	12	11
RI, Providence	49	38	5	13	0	19	11.4	25	8	19	12	11
SC, Columbia	38	30	0	13	0	19	11.4	13	4	13	5	11
SD, Rapid City	49	38	5	13	5	19	11.4	25	8	19	15	11
TN, Nashville	38	30	0	13	0	19	11.4	13	4	19	5	11
TX, Austin	38	30	0	13	0	19	11.4	11	4	13	4	11
TX, Brownsville	38	22	0	11	0	19	5.7	11	4	11	0	11
TX, Dallas	38	30	0	13	0	19	11.4	13	4	13	5	11
TX, Houston	38	22	0	13	0	19	7.6	11	4	11	4	11
UT, Salt Lake City	38	38	0	13	0	19	11.4	25	8	19	8	11
VT, Burlington	49	38	7	13	5	21	11.4	25	8	19	15	19
VA, Norfolk	38	30	0	13	0	19	11.4	25	8	19	5	11
VA, Richmond	38	38	0	13	0	19	11.4	25	8	19	8	11
WA, Seattle	38	22	0	13	0	19	11.4	13	4	13	4	11
WV, Charleston	38	30	0	13	0	19	11.4	25	4	19	5	11
WI, Madison	49	38	5	13	0	19	11.4	25	8	19	12	11
WY, Casper	49	38	5	13	0	19	11.4	25	8	19	8	11

[1] It is important to use both the insulative sheathing and cavity insulation recommended. Insulative sheathing may be placed outside of wood sheathing product, or special braces can be used.

[2] This recommendation assumes that a 2x6 wall can be built for the same cost as a 2x4 wall, using a careful design procedure called Optimum Value Engineering (OVE).

[3] Insulation should be placed on the interior side of an above-grade wall.

[4] Over unheated, uninsulated space.

[5] Crawl space walls are insulated only if the crawl space is unvented and the floor above the crawl space is uninsulated.

[6] Exterior insulation on a below-grade wall is used only if you choose not to insulate the interior side of your basement wall.

[7] Interior insulation on a below-grade wall is used only if you choose not to insulate the exterior side of your basement wall.

ORNL–Recommended R-Values for Fuel Oil Heating and Electric Air Conditioning

State, City	Attic Floor	Cathedral Ceiling	Wall[1] Sheath	Wall[1] Cavity	OVE[2] Sheath	OVE[2] Cavity	Masonry Wall[3]	Crawl Ceiling[4]	Slab Edge	Crawl Wall[5]	Basement Exterior[6]	Basement Interior[7]
AL, Birmingham	38	30	0	13	0	19	11.4	13	4	13	4	11
AK, Fairbanks	49	38	5	13	0	19	11.4	25	8	19	15	11
AK, Juneau	38	38	0	13	0	19	11.4	25	8	19	8	11
AZ, Flagstaff	49	38	5	13	0	19	11.4	25	8	19	12	11
AZ, Phoenix	38	30	0	13	0	19	11.4	11	4	13	4	11
AR, Little Rock	38	38	0	13	0	19	11.4	13	8	19	5	11
CA, Los Angeles	22	19	0	11	0	19	5.7	11	0	11	4	11
CO, Denver	38	38	0	13	0	19	11.4	25	8	19	8	11
CO, Fort Collins	38	38	0	13	0	19	11.4	25	8	19	8	11
CT, Hartford	38	38	5	13	0	19	11.4	25	8	19	8	11
DE, Wilmington	38	38	0	13	0	19	11.4	25	8	19	8	11
DC, Washington	49	38	0	13	0	19	11.4	25	8	19	8	11
FL, Miami	38	22	0	11	0	19	5.7	11	4	11	0	0
FL, Orlando	38	22	0	13	0	19	5.7	11	4	11	4	11
GA, Atlanta	38	38	0	13	0	19	11.4	25	8	19	5	11
ID, Boise	38	38	0	13	0	19	11.4	25	8	19	8	11
IL, Chicago	38	38	0	13	0	19	11.4	25	8	19	8	11
IN, Indianapolis	49	38	5	13	0	19	11.4	25	8	19	8	11
IA, Des Moines	49	38	5	13	0	19	11.4	25	8	19	12	11
KS, Topeka	49	38	5	13	0	19	11.4	25	8	19	8	11
KY, Louisville	38	38	0	13	0	19	11.4	25	8	19	8	11
LA, Baton Rouge	38	22	0	11	0	19	11.4	11	4	11	4	11
ME, Caribou	49	38	5	13	5	19	11.4	25	8	19	15	11
ME, Portland	49	38	5	13	0	19	11.4	25	8	19	12	11
MD, Baltimore	49	38	5	13	0	19	11.4	25	8	19	8	11
MA, Boston	38	38	0	13	0	19	11.4	25	8	19	8	11
MA, Springfield	38	38	0	13	0	19	11.4	25	8	19	8	11
MI, Detroit	49	38	5	13	0	19	11.4	25	8	19	10	11
MI, Sault St. Marie	49	38	5	13	5	19	11.4	25	8	19	15	11
MN, Duluth	49	38	5	13	0	19	11.4	25	8	19	12	11
MN, Int'l Falls	49	38	5	13	5	19	11.4	25	8	19	15	11
MS, Jackson	38	30	0	13	0	19	11.4	13	4	13	4	11
MO, St. Louis	38	38	0	13	0	19	11.4	25	8	19	8	11
MT, Great Falls	49	38	5	13	0	19	11.4	25	8	19	12	11
MT, Missoula	49	38	5	13	0	19	11.4	25	8	19	12	11
NE, North Platte	49	38	5	13	0	19	11.4	25	8	19	15	11
NV, Las Vegas	38	22	0	13	0	19	11.4	13	4	13	4	11

State, City	Attic Floor	Cathedral Ceiling	Wall[1] Sheath	Wall[1] Cavity	OVE[2] Sheath	OVE[2] Cavity	Masonry Wall[3]	Crawl Ceiling[4]	Slab Edge	Crawl Wall[5]	Basement Exterior[6]	Basement Interior[7]
NH, Concord	49	38	5	13	0	19	11.4	25	8	19	12	11
NJ, Newark	38	38	0	13	0	19	11.4	25	8	19	8	11
NM, Albuquerque	38	30	0	13	0	19	11.4	13	4	19	5	11
NM, Santa Fe	38	38	0	13	0	19	11.4	25	8	19	8	11
NY, New York	38	30	0	13	0	19	11.4	25	8	19	5	11
NY, Syracuse	49	38	5	13	0	19	11.4	25	8	19	12	11
NC, Greensboro	49	38	0	13	0	19	11.4	25	8	19	8	11
ND, Bismarck	49	38	5	13	5	19	11.4	25	8	19	15	11
OH, Columbus	49	38	0	13	0	19	11.4	25	8	19	8	11
OK, Tulsa	38	38	0	13	0	19	11.4	25	8	19	8	11
OR, Bend	49	38	5	13	0	19	11.4	25	8	19	8	11
OR, Salem	38	30	0	13	0	19	11.4	25	8	19	8	11
PA, Philadelphia	38	30	0	13	0	19	11.4	25	8	19	5	11
PA, Pittsburgh	49	38	0	13	0	19	11.4	25	8	19	8	11
RI, Providence	38	38	0	13	0	19	11.4	25	8	19	8	11
SC, Columbia	38	38	0	13	0	19	11.4	25	8	19	5	11
SD, Rapid City	49	38	5	13	0	19	11.4	25	8	19	15	11
TN, Nashville	38	38	0	13	0	19	11.4	25	8	19	8	11
TX, Austin	38	30	0	13	0	19	11.4	11	4	13	4	11
TX, Brownsville	38	22	0	13	0	19	5.7	11	4	11	4	11
TX, Dallas	38	30	0	13	0	19	11.4	13	4	13	4	11
TX, Houston	38	22	0	13	0	19	7.6	11	4	11	4	11
UT, Salt Lake City	38	38	0	13	0	19	11.4	25	8	19	8	11
VT, Burlington	49	38	5	13	0	21	11.4	25	8	19	15	11
VA, Norfolk	38	38	0	13	0	19	11.4	25	8	19	8	11
VA, Richmond	49	38	0	13	0	19	11.4	25	8	19	8	11
WA, Seattle	38	38	0	13	0	19	11.4	25	8	19	8	11
WV, Charleston	38	38	0	13	0	19	11.4	25	8	19	8	11
WI, Madison	49	38	5	13	0	19	11.4	25	8	19	12	11
WY, Casper	49	38	5	13	0	19	11.4	25	8	19	10	11

[1] It is important to use both the insulative sheathing and cavity insulation recommended. Insulative sheathing may be placed outside of wood sheathing product, or special braces can be used.

[2] This recommendation assumes that a 2x6 wall can be built for the same cost as a 2x4 wall, using a careful design procedure called Optimum Value Engineering (OVE).

[3] Insulation should be placed on the interior side of an above-grade wall.

[4] Over unheated, uninsulated space.

[5] Crawl space walls are insulated only if the crawl space is unvented and the floor above the crawl space is uninsulated.

[6] Exterior insulation on a below-grade wall is used only if you choose not to insulate the interior side of your basement wall.

[7] Interior insulation on a below-grade wall is used only if you choose not to insulate the exterior side of your basement wall.

ORNL–Recommended R-Values for Natural Gas Heating and No Air Conditioning

State, City	Attic Floor	Cathedral Ceiling	Wall[1] Sheath	Wall[1] Cavity	OVE[2] Sheath	OVE[2] Cavity	Masonry Wall[3]	Crawl Ceiling[4]	Slab Edge	Crawl Wall[5]	Basement Exterior[6]	Basement Interior[7]
AL, Birmingham	38	38	0	13	0	19	11.4	25	8	19	8	11
AK, Fairbanks	38	30	0	13	0	19	11.4	25	8	19	5	11
AK, Juneau	38	22	0	13	0	19	11.4	25	4	13	4	11
AZ, Flagstaff	49	38	5	13	5	19	11.4	25	8	19	15	11
AZ, Phoenix	22	22	0	11	0	19	5.7	11	0	11	4	11
AR, Little Rock	38	30	0	13	0	19	11.4	25	8	19	8	11
CA, Los Angeles	19	11	0	11	0	11	5.7	0	0	11	4	11
CO, Denver	49	38	5	13	0	19	11.4	25	8	19	10	11
CO, Fort Collins	49	38	5	13	0	19	11.4	25	8	19	12	11
CT, Hartford	49	38	5	13	0	19	11.4	25	8	19	12	11
DE, Wilmington	49	38	5	13	0	19	11.4	25	8	19	10	11
DC, Washington	49	38	5	13	0	19	11.4	25	8	19	10	11
FL, Miami	11	11	0	0	0	0	0	0	0	11	0	0
FL, Orlando	19	11	0	11	0	19	5.7	11	0	11	4	11
GA, Atlanta	38	30	0	13	0	19	11.4	25	8	19	5	11
ID, Boise	49	38	5	13	0	19	11.4	25	8	19	8	11
IL, Chicago	38	38	0	13	0	19	11.4	25	8	19	8	11
IN, Indianapolis	38	38	0	13	0	19	11.4	25	8	19	8	11
IA, Des Moines	49	38	5	13	0	19	11.4	25	8	19	12	11
KS, Topeka	49	38	5	13	0	19	11.4	25	8	19	12	11
KY, Louisville	49	38	5	13	0	19	11.4	25	8	19	10	11
LA, Baton Rouge	38	22	0	11	0	19	11.4	13	0	13	4	11
ME, Caribou	49	38	7	13	5	21	11.4	25	8	19	15	19
ME, Portland	49	38	7	13	5	19	11.4	25	8	19	15	13
MD, Baltimore	49	38	5	13	0	19	11.4	25	8	19	10	11
MA, Boston	49	38	5	13	0	19	11.4	25	8	19	10	11
MA, Springfield	49	38	5	13	0	19	11.4	25	8	19	12	11
MI, Detroit	38	30	0	13	0	19	11.4	25	8	19	8	11
MI, Sault St. Marie	49	38	5	13	0	19	11.4	25	8	19	12	11
MN, Duluth	49	38	5	13	0	19	11.4	25	8	19	15	11
MN, Int'l Falls	49	38	5	13	5	19	11.4	25	8	19	15	11
MS, Jackson	38	30	0	13	0	19	11.4	25	4	19	5	11
MO, St. Louis	49	38	5	13	0	19	11.4	25	8	19	10	11
MT, Great Falls	49	38	5	13	0	19	11.4	25	8	19	12	11
MT, Missoula	49	38	5	13	0	19	11.4	25	8	19	12	11
NE, North Platte	49	38	5	13	0	19	11.4	25	8	19	12	11
NV, Las Vegas	22	22	0	11	0	19	7.6	13	0	13	4	11

State, City	Attic Floor	Cathedral Ceiling	Wall[1] Sheath	Wall[1] Cavity	OVE[2] Sheath	OVE[2] Cavity	Masonry Wall[3]	Crawl Ceiling[4]	Slab Edge	Crawl Wall[5]	Basement Exterior[6]	Basement Interior[7]
NH, Concord	49	38	5	13	5	19	11.4	25	8	19	15	11
NJ, Newark	38	30	0	13	0	19	11.4	25	8	19	5	11
NM, Albuquerque	38	38	0	13	0	19	11.4	25	8	19	8	11
NM, Santa Fe	49	38	5	13	0	19	11.4	25	8	19	12	11
NY, New York	38	38	0	13	0	19	11.4	25	8	19	8	11
NY, Syracuse	49	38	5	13	0	19	11.4	25	8	19	15	11
NC, Greensboro	49	38	5	13	0	19	11.4	25	8	19	12	11
ND, Bismarck	49	38	5	13	5	19	11.4	25	8	19	15	11
OH, Columbus	49	38	5	13	0	19	11.4	25	8	19	10	11
OK, Tulsa	38	38	0	13	0	19	11.4	25	8	19	8	11
OR, Bend	49	38	5	13	0	19	11.4	25	8	19	12	11
OR, Salem	38	38	0	13	0	19	11.4	25	8	19	8	11
PA, Philadelphia	49	38	5	13	0	19	11.4	25	8	19	8	11
PA, Pittsburgh	49	38	5	13	0	19	11.4	25	8	19	12	11
RI, Providence	49	38	5	13	0	19	11.4	25	8	19	12	11
SC, Columbia	38	38	0	13	0	19	11.4	25	8	19	8	11
SD, Rapid City	49	38	5	13	0	21	11.4	25	8	19	15	11
TN, Nashville	38	38	0	13	0	19	11.4	25	8	19	8	11
TX, Austin	38	22	0	13	0	19	11.4	13	0	13	4	11
TX, Brownsville	19	11	0	11	0	11	3.8	0	0	11	0	0
TX, Dallas	38	22	0	13	0	19	11.4	13	4	13	5	11
TX, Houston	22	22	0	11	0	19	5.7	11	0	11	4	11
UT, Salt Lake City	38	38	0	13	0	19	11.4	25	8	19	8	11
VT, Burlington	49	38	5	13	5	19	11.4	25	8	19	15	13
VA, Norfolk	49	38	5	13	0	19	11.4	25	8	19	12	11
VA, Richmond	49	38	5	13	0	19	11.4	25	8	19	12	11
WA, Seattle	38	38	0	13	0	19	11.4	25	8	19	8	11
WV, Charleston	38	38	0	13	0	19	11.4	25	8	19	8	11
WI, Madison	49	38	5	13	0	19	11.4	25	8	19	12	11
WY, Casper	49	38	5	13	0	19	11.4	25	8	19	12	11

[1] It is important to use both the insulative sheathing and cavity insulation recommended. Insulative sheathing may be placed outside of wood sheathing product, or special braces can be used.

[2] This recommendation assumes that a 2x6 wall can be built for the same cost as a 2x4 wall, using a careful design procedure called Optimum Value Engineering (OVE).

[3] Insulation should be placed on the interior side of an above-grade wall.

[4] Over unheated, uninsulated space.

[5] Crawl space walls are insulated only if the crawl space is unvented and the floor above the crawl space is uninsulated.

[6] Exterior insulation on a below-grade wall is used only if you choose not to insulate the interior side of your basement wall.

[7] Interior insulation on a below-grade wall is used only if you choose not to insulate the exterior side of your basement wall.

ORNL–Recommended R-Values for Fuel Oil Heating and No Air Conditioning

State, City	Attic Floor	Cathedral Ceiling	Wall[1] Sheath	Wall[1] Cavity	OVE[2] Sheath	OVE[2] Cavity	Masonry Wall[3]	Crawl Ceiling[4]	Slab Edge	Crawl Wall[5]	Basement Exterior[6]	Basement Interior[7]
AL, Birmingham	38	22	0	13	0	19	11.4	13	0	13	4	11
AK, Fairbanks	49	38	5	13	0	19	11.4	25	8	19	15	11
AK, Juneau	38	38	0	13	0	19	11.4	25	8	19	8	11
AZ, Flagstaff	49	38	5	13	0	19	11.4	25	8	19	12	11
AZ, Phoenix	22	11	0	11	0	19	5.7	11	0	11	4	11
AR, Little Rock	38	22	0	13	0	19	11.4	13	4	19	5	11
CA, Los Angeles	19	11	0	11	0	11	5.7	0	0	11	0	11
CO, Denver	38	38	0	13	0	19	11.4	25	8	19	8	11
CO, Fort Collins	38	38	0	13	0	19	11.4	25	8	19	8	11
CT, Hartford	38	38	0	13	0	19	11.4	25	8	19	8	11
DE, Wilmington	38	38	0	13	0	19	11.4	25	8	19	8	11
DC, Washington	38	38	0	13	0	19	11.4	25	8	19	8	11
FL, Miami	0	0	0	0	0	0	0	0	0	0	0	0
FL, Orlando	19	11	0	11	0	11	3.8	0	0	11	0	0
GA, Atlanta	38	30	0	13	0	19	11.4	25	4	19	5	11
ID, Boise	38	38	0	13	0	19	11.4	25	8	19	8	11
IL, Chicago	38	38	0	13	0	19	11.4	25	8	19	8	11
IN, Indianapolis	38	38	0	13	0	19	11.4	25	8	19	8	11
IA, Des Moines	49	38	5	13	0	19	11.4	25	8	19	10	11
KS, Topeka	49	38	5	13	0	19	11.4	25	8	19	8	11
KY, Louisville	38	38	0	13	0	19	11.4	25	8	19	8	11
LA, Baton Rouge	22	19	0	11	0	19	5.7	11	0	11	4	11
ME, Caribou	49	38	5	13	5	21	11.4	25	8	19	15	11
ME, Portland	49	38	5	13	0	19	11.4	25	8	19	12	11
MD, Baltimore	49	38	0	13	0	19	11.4	25	8	19	8	11
MA, Boston	38	30	0	13	0	19	11.4	25	8	19	8	11
MA, Springfield	38	38	0	13	0	19	11.4	25	8	19	8	11
MI, Detroit	49	38	5	13	0	19	11.4	25	8	19	10	11
MI, Sault St. Marie	49	38	5	13	5	19	11.4	25	8	19	15	11
MN, Duluth	49	38	5	13	0	19	11.4	25	8	19	12	11
MN, Int'l Falls	49	38	5	13	5	19	11.4	25	8	19	15	11
MS, Jackson	38	22	0	13	0	19	11.4	13	0	13	4	11
MO, St. Louis	38	38	0	13	0	19	11.4	25	8	19	8	11
MT, Great Falls	49	38	5	13	0	19	11.4	25	8	19	12	11
MT, Missoula	49	38	5	13	0	19	11.4	25	8	19	12	11
NE, North Platte	49	38	5	13	0	19	11.4	25	8	19	15	11
NV, Las Vegas	22	22	0	11	0	19	5.7	13	0	11	4	11

State, City	Attic Floor	Cathedral Ceiling	Wall[1] Sheath	Wall[1] Cavity	OVE[2] Sheath	OVE[2] Cavity	Masonry Wall[3]	Crawl Ceiling[4]	Slab Edge	Crawl Wall[5]	Basement Exterior[6]	Basement Interior[7]
NH, Concord	49	38	5	13	0	19	11.4	25	8	19	12	11
NJ, Newark	38	30	0	13	0	19	11.4	25	8	19	8	11
NM, Albuquerque	38	22	0	13	0	19	11.4	13	4	19	5	11
NM, Santa Fe	38	38	0	13	0	19	11.4	25	8	19	8	11
NY, New York	38	30	0	13	0	19	11.4	25	8	19	5	11
NY, Syracuse	49	38	5	13	0	19	11.4	25	8	19	12	11
NC, Greensboro	38	38	0	13	0	19	11.4	25	8	19	8	11
ND, Bismarck	49	38	5	13	5	19	11.4	25	8	19	15	11
OH, Columbus	38	38	0	13	0	19	11.4	25	8	19	8	11
OK, Tulsa	38	30	0	13	0	19	114	25	8	19	8	11
OR, Bend	49	38	5	13	0	19	11.4	25	8	19	8	11
OR, Salem	38	30	0	13	0	19	11.4	25	8	19	8	11
PA, Philadelphia	38	30	0	13	0	19	11.4	25	8	19	5	11
PA, Pittsburgh	38	38	0	13	0	19	11.4	25	8	19	8	11
RI, Providence	38	38	0	13	0	19	11.4	25	8	19	8	11
SC, Columbia	38	30	0	13	0	19	11.4	25	4	19	5	11
SD, Rapid City	49	38	5	13	0	19	11.4	25	8	19	15	11
TN, Nashville	38	30	0	13	0	19	11.4	25	8	19	8	11
TX, Austin	22	19	0	11	0	19	5.7	11	0	11	4	11
TX, Brownsville	11	11	0	0	0	0	3.8	0	0	11	0	0
TX, Dallas	22	22	0	11	0	19	7.6	13	0	13	4	11
TX, Houston	19	11	0	11	0	19	5.7	11	0	11	4	11
UT, Salt Lake City	38	38	0	13	0	19	11.4	25	8	19	8	11
VT, Burlington	49	38	5	13	0	21	11.4	25	8	19	15	11
VA, Norfolk	38	30	0	13	0	19	11.4	25	8	19	8	11
VA, Richmond	38	38	0	13	0	19	11.4	25	8	19	8	11
WA, Seattle	38	38	0	13	0	19	11.4	25	8	19	8	11
WV, Charleston	38	38	0	13	0	19	11.4	25	8	19	8	11
WI, Madison	49	38	5	13	0	19	11.4	25	8	19	12	11
WY, Casper	49	38	5	13	0	19	11.4	25	8	19	10	11

[1] It is important to use both the insulative sheathing and cavity insulation recommended. Insulative sheathing may be placed outside of wood sheathing product, or special braces can be used.

[2] This recommendation assumes that a 2x6 wall can be built for the same cost as a 2x4 wall, using a careful design procedure called Optimum Value Engineering (OVE).

[3] Insulation should be placed on the interior side of an above-grade wall.

[4] Over unheated, uninsulated space.

[5] Crawl space walls are insulated only if the crawl space is unvented and the floor above the crawl space is uninsulated.

[6] Exterior insulation on a below-grade wall is used only if you choose not to insulate the interior side of your basement wall.

[7] Interior insulation on a below-grade wall is used only if you choose not to insulate the exterior side of your basement wall.

IECC R-Values for New Construction

Prescriptive R-Values and U-Factors

Most states have adopted a version of the *International Energy Conservation Code* (IECC). The Code lists prescriptive (required) R-values for floors, walls, and ceilings comprising the thermal envelope, plus U-factors and Solar Heat Gain Coefficients (SHGC) for fenestration and skylights for each of eight climate zones (see the facing page).

A certificate listing the R-values, U-values, SHGCs of fenestration, and types and efficiencies of heating, cooling, and water heating equipment must be posted on the electrical distribution panel.

To make compliance simple for contractors, the R-values prescribed are the simple sums of the R-values printed on the insulation blankets, batts, and boards. In other words there is no requirement to calculate the effects of framing.

Details and Exceptions

The Code spells out exceptions to the simplistic prescriptive R-values where necessary or practical:

Attics R-30 and R-38 insulations may be substituted for R-38 and R-49 above wall top plates at the eaves, provided the insulation is not compressed.

Cathedral Ceilings R-30 insulation is allowed where the construction doesn't allow higher values, but the exception is limited to an area of 500 sq. ft.

Mass Walls Mass walls are defined as walls of concrete block, solid concrete, insulated concrete form, masonry cavity, brick (except brick veneer), adobe, compressed earth block, rammed earth, and solid timber/logs. The "Mass Wall R-Values" in the table apply when at least 50% of the required R-value is on the exterior of, or integral to, the wall. Otherwise, the wall must be treated as wood frame.

Floors The insulation must be in contact with the underside of the subfloor.

Basement Walls Conditioned basement walls must be insulated full height. Unconditioned basement walls must be similarly insulated unless the floor above is insulated.

Crawl Space Walls Crawl space walls may be insulated, provided the crawl space is not vented. The insulation must extend downward from the floor to grade plus an additional 24 in. either downward or horizontally from the wall. Exposed earth must be covered with a continuous vapor retarder with joints overlapped 6 in. and sealed or taped. Edges of the vapor retarder must be attached to the wall.

Slabs on Grade Slabs less than 12 in. below grade must be insulated. The distance listed in the table is from the top of the slab down, out, or inward by any combination. Insulation extending outward must be protected either by pavement or at least 10 in. of soil. Slab insulation is not required in areas of very heavy termite infestation.

Fenestration Prescriptive U-factors and SHGCs may be satisfied by area-weighted averages. Replacement fenestrations (replacement windows) must meet the prescriptive U-factor and SHGC requirements of new construction.

Thermally Isolated Sunrooms Minimum ceiling insulation R-values are R-19 in Zones 1–4 and R-24 in zones 5–8. The minimum wall R-value is R-13 in all zones. In new construction, walls that separate the sunroom from conditioned space must meet the prescribed wall requirements.

In Zones 4–8, thermally isolated sunroom fenestration must have a maximum U-factor of 0.50. Maximum skylight U-factors must be 0.75.

IECC Climate Zones

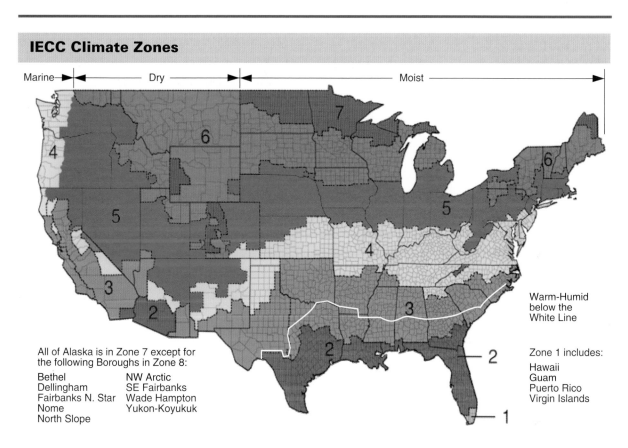

Marine ← | → Dry ← | → Moist →

All of Alaska is in Zone 7 except for the following Boroughs in Zone 8:

Bethel
Dellingham
Fairbanks N. Star
Nome
North Slope

NW Arctic
SE Fairbanks
Wade Hampton
Yukon-Koyukuk

Warm-Humid below the White Line

Zone 1 includes:
Hawaii
Guam
Puerto Rico
Virgin Islands

IECC Residential Insulation and Fenestration Requirements by Component[a]

Climate Zone	Fenestration[b] U-Factor	Skylight U-Factor	Glazed Fenestration SHGC	Ceiling R-Value	Wood Frame Wall R-Value	Mass Wall R-Value	Floor R-Value	Basement[c] Wall R-Value	Slab[d] R-Value & Depth	Crawl Space[c] Wall R-Value
1	1.20	0.75	0.40	30	13	3	13	0	0	0
2	0.75	0.75	0.40	30	13	4	13	0	0	0
3	0.65	0.65	0.40[e]	30	13	5	19	0	0	5/13
4 except Marine	0.40	0.60	NR	38	13	5	19	10/13	10, 2 ft.	10/13
5 and Marine[f]	0.35	0.60	NR	38	19 or 13+5[g]	13	30[f]	10/13	10, 2 ft.	10/13
6	0.35	0.60	NR	49	19 or 13+5[g]	15	30[f]	10/13	10, 4 ft.	10/13
7 & 8	0.35	0.60	NR	49	21	19	30[f]	10/13	10, 4 ft.	10/13

[a] R-values are minimums. U-factors and SHGC are maximums. R-19 shall be permitted to be compressed into a 2×6 cavity.

[b] The fenestration U-factor column excludes skylights. The SHGC column applies to all glazed fenestration.

[c] The first R-value applies to continuous insulation, the second to framing cavity insulation; either insulation meets the requirement.

[d] R-5 shall be added to the required slab edge R-values for heated slabs.

[e] There are no SHGC requirements in the Marine zone.

[f] Or insulation sufficient to fill the framing cavity, R-19 minimum.

[g] "13+5" means R-13 cavity insulation plus R-5 insulated sheathing. If structural sheathing covers 25% or less of the exterior, insulating sheathing is not required where structural sheathing is used. If structural sheathing covers more than 25% of exterior, structural sheathing shall be supplemented with insulated sheathing of at least R-2.

U-Factor Alternative Method

The IECC provides several alternative methods of compliance. The first, called the "U-factor alternative," requires each component assembly of the thermal envelope to have a U-factor less than or equal to the values in the table below. Mass walls are the exception, having less than half of their prescribed R-values exterior to the walls. For such walls the U-factors may be up to:

- 0.17 in Climate Zone 1
- 0.14 in Climate Zone 2
- 0.12 in Climate Zone 3.

Equivalent U-Factors

Climate Zone	Fenestration U-Factor	Skylight U-Factor	Ceiling R-Factor	Wood Frame Wall R-Factor	Mass Wall R-Factor	Floor R-Factor	Basement Wall R-Factor	Crawl Space Wall R-Factor
1	1.20	0.75	30	13	3	13	0	0
2	0.75	0.75	30	13	4	13	0	0
3	0.65	0.65	30	13	5	19	0	5/13
4 except Marine	0.40	0.60	38	13	5	19	10/13	10/13
5 and Marine	0.35	0.60	38	19 or 13+5	13	30	10/13	10/13
6	0.35	0.60	49	19 or 13+5	15	30	10/13	10/13
7 & 8	0.35	0.60	49	21	19	30	10/13	10/13

Total UA Alternative Method

The second alternative method of compliance is the "Total UA alternative." It requires that the total thermal envelope UA (sum of U-factors times component areas) be less than or equal to the total UA when using the U-factors in the table above. The calculation must include the thermal bridging effects of framing materials. The fenestration SHGC requirements remain the same as in the prescriptive method.

Simulated Performance Alternative

Yet a third alternative is compliance based on computer-simulated energy performance. The proposed building design must be calculated to have an annual energy cost less than or equal to the annual energy cost of a standard reference design that has the same geometry and surface areas.

Recommended R-Values for Existing Houses

While energy codes grandfather (exempt) existing homes from required levels of insulation, adding insulation to wood-framed buildings having attics and empty wall cavities is generally cost-effective.

To encourage retrofit, Energy Star has published the recommendations below based on the climate zones referenced by the IECC.

Zone Map for Insulation Recommendations for Existing Wood-Framed Houses

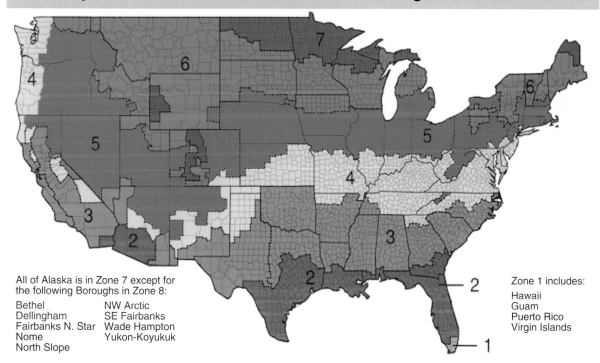

All of Alaska is in Zone 7 except for the following Boroughs in Zone 8:

Bethel	NW Arctic
Dellingham	SE Fairbanks
Fairbanks N. Star	Wade Hampton
Nome	Yukon-Koyukuk
North Slope	

Zone 1 includes:
Hawaii
Guam
Puerto Rico
Virgin Islands

Recommended Insulation R-Values for Existing Wood-Framed Buildings

Zone	Insulation to Add		
	To Uninsulated Attic	To 3 in.–4 in. of Existing Attic Insulation	Under Floor
1	R30 to R49	R25 to R30	R13
2	R30 to R60	R25 to R38	R13 to R19
3	R30 to R60	R25 to R38	R19 to R25
4	R38 to R60	R38	R25 to R30
5–8	R49 to R60	R38 to R49	R25 to R30

In addition, whenever exterior siding is removed from an uninsulated wood-framed wall:

- Drill holes in the sheathing and blow insulation into the cavity before replacing siding.
- In Zones 3–4, add R5 foam sheathing beneath the new siding.
- In Zones 5–8, add R5 to R6 foam sheathing beneath the new siding.

For insulated wood-framed walls in Zones 4–8, add R5 foam sheathing over the existing sheathing before covering with new siding.

Best Insulating Practices

9

Chapter 7 explained how insulation works to retard heat flow, either into or out of a home's thermal envelope. Chapter 8 examined the concept of an optimum insulation R-value for a given location and type of fuel.

Insulating the surfaces of the thermal envelope—floors, walls, and ceilings—involves a lot more than selecting a type of insulation and the optimum R-value. The best insulation, installed improperly and without regard to moisture, will prove a disaster in the long run. As the saying goes, "It's all in the details."

So detail we do. In the following pages, you will find detailed drawings for forty examples of best-practice insulating: six *attics and cathedral ceilings*, twelve *walls*, eight *slab foundations*, four *crawl spaces*, six *full basements*, and four *retrofitted full basements*.

Insulating Attics and Cathedral Ceilings

Four issues must be addressed when insulating attics and cathedral ceilings:

1. The insulation should have the R-value recommended in the tables on the facing page for the building location and energy sources.

2. There should be no air leaks from the conditioned space below.

3. The type(s) of insulation and vapor barriers should be such that condensation does not occur within the attic or cathedral ceiling except in rare instances.

4. In areas of snow buildup (Zones 5 and above), the construction should be such that ice dams do not occur.

The six examples shown below and detailed on pp. 174–179 provide a range of solutions that satisfy all of the criteria.

Attic and Cathedral Ceiling Insulation Configurations

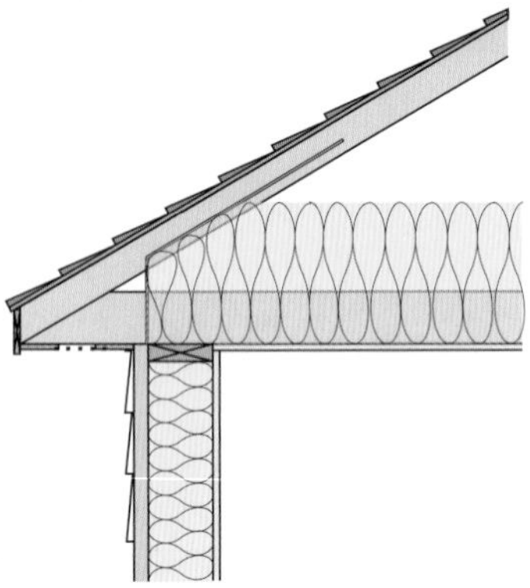

Vented attic with
ceiling insulation

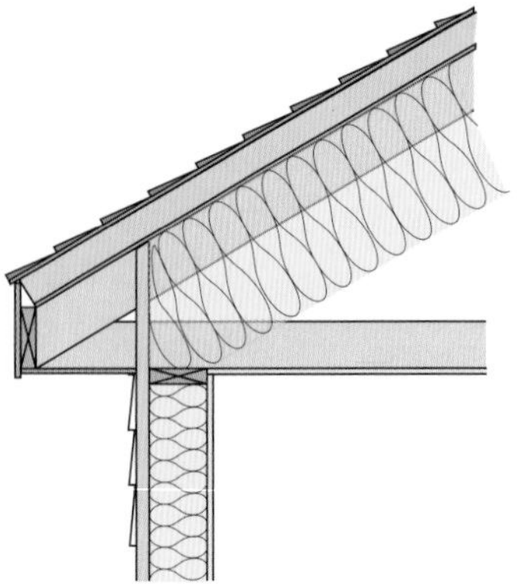

Unvented attic with
roof insulation

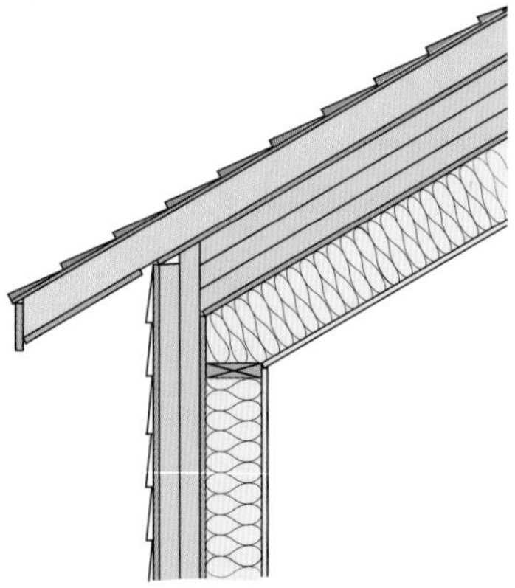

High R-value vented
cathedral ceiling

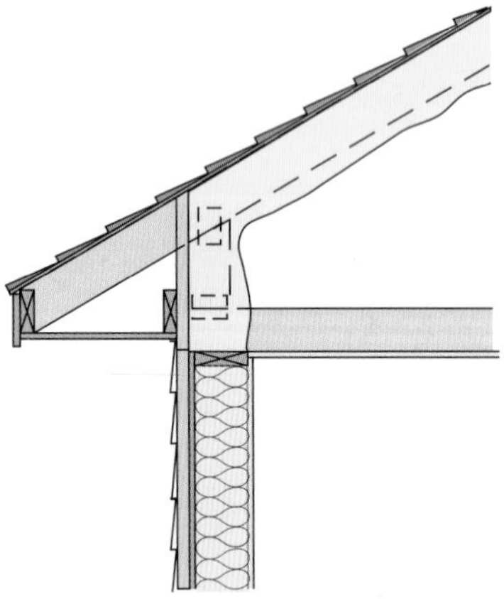

Unvented attic with
spray foam roof insulation

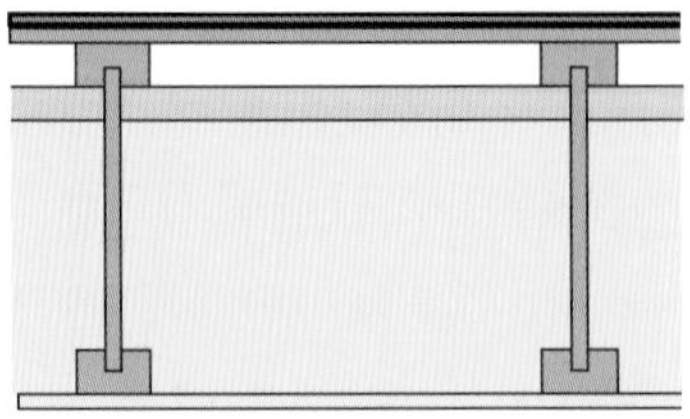

Vented cathedral ceiling
with I-joist rafters

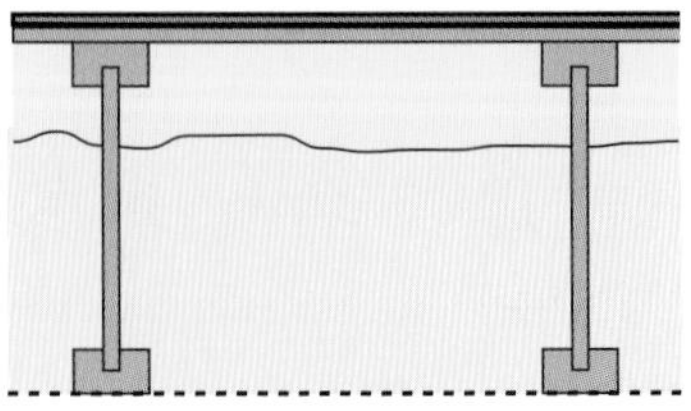

Unvented cathedral ceiling
with I-joist rafters

Recommended R-Values for Attic Floors

Location	Natural Gas Heat Electric AC	Heat Pump Heat Electric AC	Fuel Oil Heat Electric AC	Natural Gas Heat No AC	Fuel Oil Heat No AC
AZ, Phoenix	38	38	38	22	22
CA, Los Angeles	22	19	22	19	19
CO, Denver	49	38	38	49	38
DC, Washington	49	38	49	49	38
FL, Miami	38	22	38	11	0
GA, Atlanta	38	38	38	38	38
IL, Chicago	38	49	38	38	38
LA, Baton Rouge	38	38	38	38	22
MA, Boston	49	49	38	49	38
ME, Portland	49	49	49	49	49
MN, Duluth	49	49	49	49	49
MO, St. Louis	49	38	38	49	38
NY, New York	38	49	38	38	38
TX, Dallas	38	38	38	38	22
VT, Burlington	49	49	49	49	49
WA, Seattle	38	38	38	38	38

Recommended R-Values for Cathedral Ceilings

Location	Natural Gas Heat Electric AC	Heat Pump Heat Electric AC	Fuel Oil Heat Electric AC	Natural Gas Heat No AC	Fuel Oil Heat No AC
AZ, Phoenix	30	22	30	22	11
CA, Los Angeles	19	11	19	11	11
CO, Denver	38	38	38	38	38
DC, Washington	38	30	38	38	38
FL, Miami	22	22	22	11	0
GA, Atlanta	38	30	38	30	30
IL, Chicago	38	38	38	38	38
LA, Baton Rouge	30	22	22	22	19
MA, Boston	38	38	38	38	30
ME, Portland	38	38	38	38	38
MN, Duluth	38	38	38	38	38
MO, St. Louis	38	30	38	38	38
NY, New York	38	38	30	38	30
TX, Dallas	38	30	30	22	22
VT, Burlington	38	38	38	38	38
WA, Seattle	38	22	38	38	38

Vented Attic with Ceiling Insulation

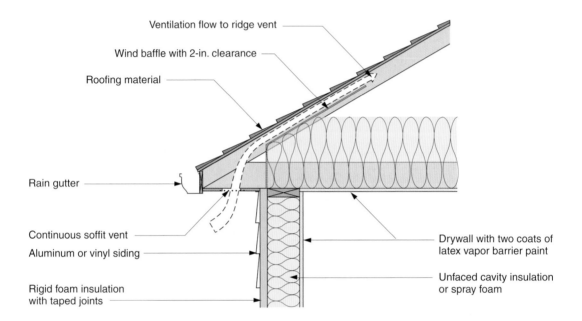

Ventilation flow to ridge vent

Wind baffle with 2-in. clearance

Roofing material

Rain gutter

Continuous soffit vent

Aluminum or vinyl siding

Rigid foam insulation
with taped joints

Drywall with two coats of
latex vapor barrier paint

Unfaced cavity insulation
or spray foam

The ability of air to contain water vapor decreases with decreasing temperature, so the relative humidity of the atmosphere rises overnight. At the same time, due to radiational cooling, the temperature of roofing and the underlying roof sheathing drops by as much as 20°F. This combination very often results in condensation on the underside of the roof sheathing.

During the following day, the roof warms and the moisture is driven from the sheathing. With sufficient ventilation the moist air is flushed out of the attic. Without proper ventilation, however, the high humidity results in mold growing on the surface of the sheathing. In extreme cases the sheathing may rot.

Proper ventilation consists of clear, straight air paths from low vents in the soffits to a continuous ridge vent. As thicker layers of insulation are added to the attic floor, this air path is choked off at the eaves. Two solutions are to: (1) use raised-heel trusses to provide more height (not shown), and (2) install a durable wind baffle (shown) to maintain a 2-in. minimum air path between the insulation and the sheathing.

To prevent transport of moisture from the living space into the attic, two safeguards are required: (1) eliminate unsealed penetrations of the ceiling (such as lighting fixtures), and (2) include a warm-side ceiling vapor barrier, such as two coats of a latex vapor barrier paint or polyethylene sheeting.

Unvented Attic with Roof Insulation

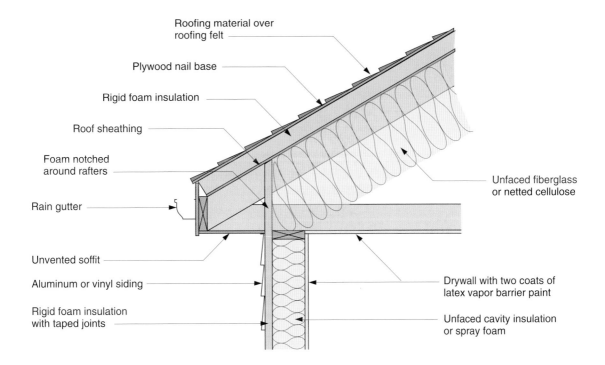

Roofing material over roofing felt

Plywood nail base

Rigid foam insulation

Roof sheathing

Foam notched around rafters

Rain gutter

Unvented soffit

Aluminum or vinyl siding

Rigid foam insulation with taped joints

Unfaced fiberglass or netted cellulose

Drywall with two coats of latex vapor barrier paint

Unfaced cavity insulation or spray foam

An alternative to venting attics to prevent condensation is to install closed-cell foam insulation exterior to (above) the roof sheathing. Provided the R-value of the foam is great enough, the sheathing below will never become cold enough to become a condensing surface. Obviously, the colder the climate, the greater the fraction of total roof R-value the foam must contribute. However, any wood above the foam serving as a nail base for asphalt shingles or selvage or for metal roofing might still incur damage from condensation. To be safe, the roofing itself must be able to breathe. Tile, slate, and wood shingles installed over wood strips would qualify.

In warmer climates, the question is whether the combination of temperature and relative humidity of the interior air might result in condensation at the overnight low temperature of the roof. A rule of thumb is that serious condensation will not occur where the average monthly temperature remains above 45°F and the home's relative humidity in the coldest months remains below 45%. Moisture accumulating in the sheathing during the occasional cold snap is likely to dissipate once temperatures return to normal.

High R-Value Vented Cathedral Ceiling

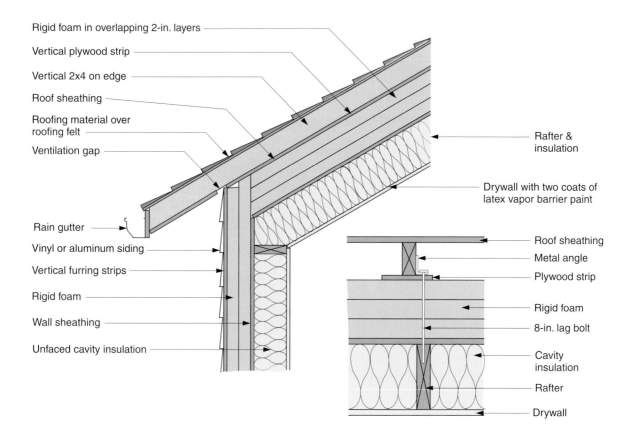

Rigid foam in overlapping 2-in. layers

Vertical plywood strip

Vertical 2x4 on edge

Roof sheathing

Roofing material over roofing felt

Ventilation gap

Rain gutter

Vinyl or aluminum siding

Vertical furring strips

Rigid foam

Wall sheathing

Unfaced cavity insulation

Rafter & insulation

Drywall with two coats of latex vapor barrier paint

Roof sheathing

Metal angle

Plywood strip

Rigid foam

8-in. lag bolt

Cavity insulation

Rafter

Drywall

The unvented cathedral ceiling shown on the previous page works to prevent condensation, but there is another potential moisture problem—ice dams. In areas with heavy snow accumulation, these dams of ice at the eaves can cause melt water to back up, penetrate the roofing material, and flow down onto the ceiling or into the wall cavity.

The R-value of snow is often cited as R-1/in., but it has been measured as high as R-1.8/in. in fluffy, dry snow. A 24-in. accumulation of powdery snow on the roof could have an R-value as high as 43.

The temperature at the snow/roofing interface is determined by the indoor and outdoor temperatures and the R-values of the snow and the insulation. With equal R-values, an indoor temperature of 70°F, and an outdoor temperature of 0°F, the temperature at the surface of the roofing will be 35°F and the snow will melt. As soon as the melt water reaches the 0°F eave, however, it will refreeze, resulting in an ice dam and a backup pool of water.

The solution is to create a ventilation channel between the roof sheathing and the top of the insulation, as shown in the smaller sectional illustration above. A small gap at the top of the wall and a continuous vent at the ridge serve as the vent inlet and outlet.

Unvented Attic with Spray Foam Roof Insulation

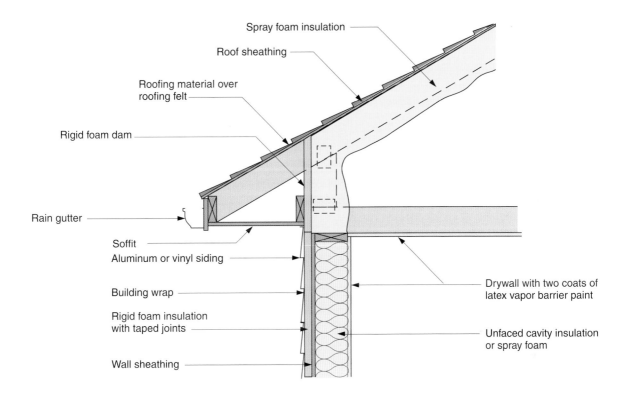

Spray foam insulation

Roof sheathing

Roofing material over roofing felt

Rigid foam dam

Rain gutter

Soffit

Aluminum or vinyl siding

Building wrap

Rigid foam insulation with taped joints

Wall sheathing

Drywall with two coats of latex vapor barrier paint

Unfaced cavity insulation or spray foam

A simpler but no less expensive solution to the attic condensation problem is to spray a layer of closed-cell foam onto the underside of the roof sheathing, thick enough to enclose the framing as well.

In Climate Zones 4 or less, any closed-cell foam will suffice. In Zones 5 and above, either the foam must have a vapor permeance of 1 perm or less, or the interior surface of the foam must be coated with a vapor barrier paint.

Note that the lack of a ventilation channel between the insulation and the roof sheathing makes this roof vulnerable to ice dams in areas of deep snow cover. Although the melt water could not penetrate the attic or wall cavities through the impervious foam, it could saturate the wood sheathing and cause it to rot. In heavy snow areas, a ventilation channel could be created by adding strapping and a second sheathing with an eave slot and ridge vent.

Vented Cathedral Ceiling with I-Joist Rafters

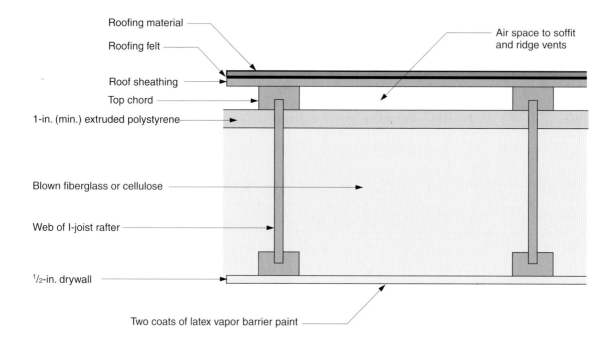

Roofing material

Roofing felt

Roof sheathing

Top chord

1-in. (min.) extruded polystyrene

Blown fiberglass or cellulose

Web of I-joist rafter

$^1/_2$-in. drywall

Air space to soffit and ridge vents

Two coats of latex vapor barrier paint

Achieving a high R-value in conventionally framed cathedral ceilings is expensive. Either very deep rafters, such as 2×12s, must be employed to provide enough depth for the insulation, or expensive closed-cell foam must be sprayed onto the underside of the roof sheathing.

An ingenious alternative is to use I-joist (TJI®) rafters as shown above. After the rafters are fastened in place, 1-in. extruded polystyrene panels are fastened to the bottoms of the TJI top chords between the rafters. The foam panels serve both as the tops of cavities for fibrous insulation and the bottoms of ventilation channels.

The R-value of the roof is limited only by the depth of the TJI rafters and the thickness of the foam. With a thin (less than 2 in.) layer of foam and a thick (greater than 6 in.) layer of fibrous insulation, a ceiling vapor barrier is required in Climate Zones 5 and higher.

To prevent transport of moisture from the living space into the attic, two safeguards are required: (1) zero unsealed penetrations of the ceiling (such as lighting fixtures), and (2) a warm-side ceiling vapor barrier, such as two coats of a latex vapor barrier paint or polyethylene sheeting.

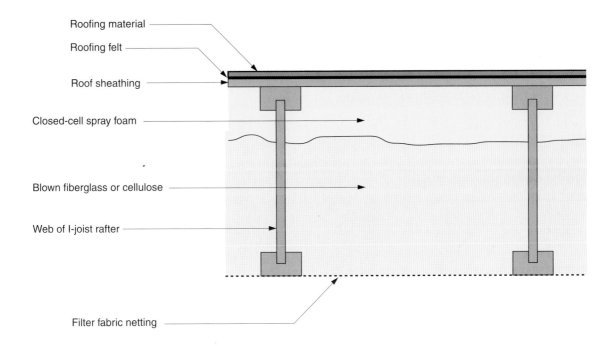

Roofing material

Roofing felt

Roof sheathing

Closed-cell spray foam

Blown fiberglass or cellulose

Web of I-joist rafter

Filter fabric netting

Complex roofs, such as those containing dormers or skylights, are difficult to ventilate. The unvented cathedral ceiling shown above provides a simple solution. The same technique can be used in a flat roof, where ventilation doesn't have the driving force of a height difference between air inlets and outlets.

To avoid condensation, one of two conditions must be met: (1) the fibrous insulation must be sealed off from the warm, moist air of the conditioned space by an air- and water vapor-impermeable membrane, or (2) the closed-cell foam must have a perm rating of 1 or less and sufficient R-value to keep the fiber-filled cavity above the condensation (dew) point.

The vapor-impermeable membrane could be either polyethylene sheeting or two coats of vapor barrier paint on drywall. In either case, care should be taken to eliminate air leaks such as those around and through lighting fixtures. Where the bottom of the fibrous insulation is constrained only by fabric netting, make sure it satisfies the local fire code. In most cases, ½-in. drywall will be required.

Insulating Walls

Three criteria should be satisfied when building or retrofitting walls:

1. The insulation should have the IRC-recommended R-value(s) listed in the tables on the facing page appropriate to the building location and sources of heating and cooling.

2. There should be no through-wall air leaks.

3. The type(s) of insulation and vapor barriers should be such that condensation does not occur anywhere within the wall cavity or materials.

The twelve examples shown below and detailed on pp. 182–193 provide a wide range of possible solutions, from new construction to retrofit.

Wall Insulation Configurations

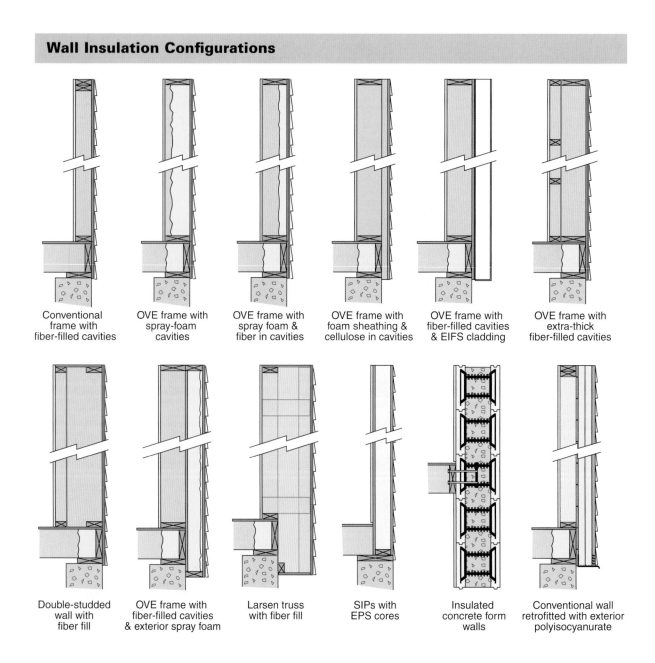

Conventional frame with fiber-filled cavities	OVE frame with spray-foam cavities	OVE frame with spray foam & fiber in cavities
OVE frame with foam sheathing & cellulose in cavities	OVE frame with fiber-filled cavities & EIFS cladding	OVE frame with extra-thick fiber-filled cavities
Double-studded wall with fiber fill	OVE frame with fiber-filled cavities & exterior spray foam	Larsen truss with fiber fill
SIPs with EPS cores	Insulated concrete form walls	Conventional wall retrofitted with exterior polyisocyanurate

Recommended R-Values for Conventional Wall Sheathing/Cavity

Location	Natural Gas Heat Electric AC	Heat Pump Heat Electric AC	Fuel Oil Heat Electric AC	Natural Gas Heat No AC	Fuel Oil Heat No AC
AZ, Phoenix	0/13	0/11	0/13	0/11	0/11
CA, Los Angeles	0/11	0/11	0/11	0/11	0/11
CO, Denver	5/13	0/13	0/13	5/13	0/13
DC, Washington	5/13	0/13	0/13	5/13	0/13
FL, Miami	0/11	0/11	0/11	0/0	0/0
GA, Atlanta	0/13	0/13	0/13	0/13	0/13
IL, Chicago	0/13	5/13	0/13	0/13	0/13
LA, Baton Rouge	0/13	0/11	0/11	0/11	0/11
MA, Boston	5/13	5/13	0/13	5/13	0/13
ME, Portland	7/13	7/13	5/13	7/13	5/13
MN, Duluth	5/13	5/13	5/13	5/13	5/13
MO, St. Louis	5/13	0/13	0/13	5/13	0/13
NY, New York	0/13	5/13	0/13	0/13	0/13
TX, Dallas	0/13	0/13	0/13	0/13	0/11
VT, Burlington	5/13	7/13	5/13	5/13	5/13
WA, Seattle	0/13	0/13	0/13	0/13	0/13

Recommended R-Values for OVE Wall Sheathing/Cavity

Location	Natural Gas Heat Electric AC	Heat Pump Heat Electric AC	Fuel Oil Heat Electric AC	Natural Gas Heat No AC	Fuel Oil Heat No AC
AZ, Phoenix	0/19	0/19	0/19	0/19	0/19
CA, Los Angeles	0/19	0/11	0/19	0/11	0/11
CO, Denver	0/19	0/19	0/19	0/19	0/19
DC, Washington	0/19	0/19	0/19	0/19	0/19
FL, Miami	0/19	0/11	0/19	0/0	0/0
GA, Atlanta	0/19	0/19	0/19	0/19	0/19
IL, Chicago	0/19	0/19	0/19	0/19	0/19
LA, Baton Rouge	0/19	0/19	0/19	0/19	0/19
MA, Boston	0/19	0/19	0/19	0/19	0/19
ME, Portland	5/19	5/19	0/19	5/19	0/19
MN, Duluth	0/19	5/19	0/19	0/19	0/19
MO, St. Louis	0/19	0/19	0/19	0/19	0/19
NY, New York	0/19	0/19	0/19	0/19	0/19
TX, Dallas	0/19	0/19	0/19	0/19	0/19
VT, Burlington	5/19	5/21	0/21	5/19	0/21
WA, Seattle	0/19	0/19	0/19	0/19	0/19

Conventional Frame with Fiber-Filled Cavities

This is the most common wall assembly of all. Unfortunately, it is one of the poorest performers, both in terms of retarding heat loss and in preventing moisture damage. The nominal R-value of the cavity insulation (R-19 or R-21 in the case of fiberglass batts) is reduced by 25% by conduction through the wood framing. In addition, the fibrous insulation is neither air- nor water vapor-tight. As a result, holes (electrical fixtures) and cracks (construction joints) allow the passage of both air and water vapor.

Best practice for this wall requires:

1. Careful fitting of insulation blankets or batts to minimize convective looping.

2. Housewrap over the wall sheathing to minimize air leakage while allowing drying.

3. An effective, continuous vapor barrier on the warm side (interior in heating climates, exterior in cooling climates) of the insulation to prevent penetration of the wall cavities by water vapor.

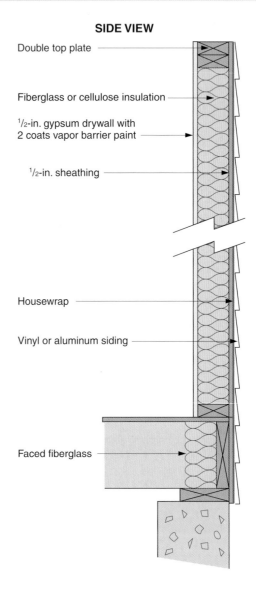

SIDE VIEW

Double top plate

Fiberglass or cellulose insulation

^{1}/₂-in. gypsum drywall with 2 coats vapor barrier paint

^{1}/₂-in. sheathing

Housewrap

Vinyl or aluminum siding

Faced fiberglass

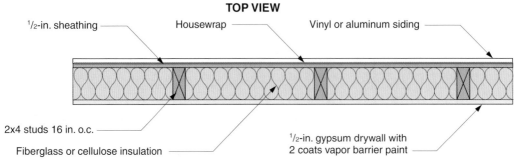

TOP VIEW

^{1}/₂-in. sheathing

Housewrap

Vinyl or aluminum siding

2x4 studs 16 in. o.c.

Fiberglass or cellulose insulation

^{1}/₂-in. gypsum drywall with 2 coats vapor barrier paint

OVE Frame with Spray-Foam Cavities

The OVE frame wall utilizes 2×6 studs spaced 24 in. on-center to improve thermal performance in two ways:

1. With half as much framing, thermal bridging is cut by half.

2. The 2×6 studs provide a wall cavity 2 in. deeper, allowing the use of an R-19 batt vs. an R-11 batt.

The wall shown substitutes sprayed closed-cell foam for fiberglass batt, which results in two further improvements to thermal performance:

1. The foam R-value is 6.0/in. vs. 3.2/in. for fiberglass batt.

2. The sprayed foam adheres to the framing, completely sealing the cavity against both infiltration and convective looping.

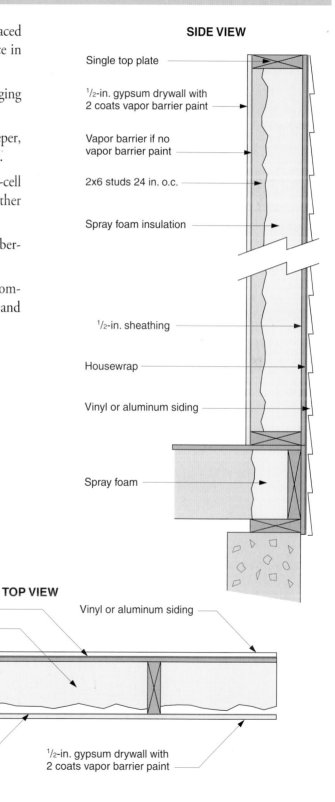

SIDE VIEW

Single top plate

1/2-in. gypsum drywall with 2 coats vapor barrier paint

Vapor barrier if no vapor barrier paint

2x6 studs 24 in. o.c.

Spray foam insulation

1/2-in. sheathing

Housewrap

Vinyl or aluminum siding

Spray foam

TOP VIEW

1/2-in. sheathing

Housewrap

Vinyl or aluminum siding

Spray foam

2x6 studs 24 in. o.c.

Optional polyethylene vapor barrier

1/2-in. gypsum drywall with 2 coats vapor barrier paint

OVE Frame with Spray Foam and Fiber in Cavities

Sprayed closed-cell foam is much more expensive than fiberglass or cellulose. The wall shown here is a cost-effective compromise between the two insulations. A 1-in. to 2-in. layer of foam applied to the inside of the wall sheathing provides an R-value of 5 to 10 and seals the cavities against air infiltration. In Climate Zones 4 and below, the foam also protects against condensation of water vapor in the wall cavities in winter.

The remaining 4 in. of cavity is filled with fiberglass or cellulose, either sprayed or dense-packed, bringing the total wall R-value up to about 25.

While the spray foam equipment is on hand, it is worthwhile spraying the pockets between the rim joists and floor joists, eliminating another major source of air infiltration.

Even with 2 in. of spray foam in the cavities, it is still wise to provide a warm-side vapor barrier in the form of either two coats of vapor barrier paint or polyethylene sheeting.

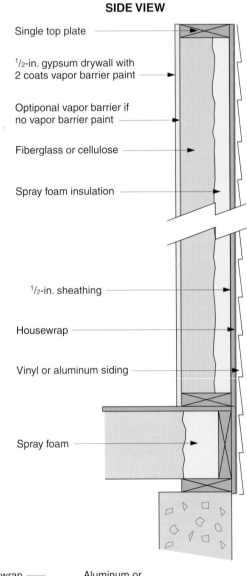

SIDE VIEW

Single top plate

1/2-in. gypsum drywall with 2 coats vapor barrier paint

Optiponal vapor barrier if no vapor barrier paint

Fiberglass or cellulose

Spray foam insulation

1/2-in. sheathing

Housewrap

Vinyl or aluminum siding

Spray foam

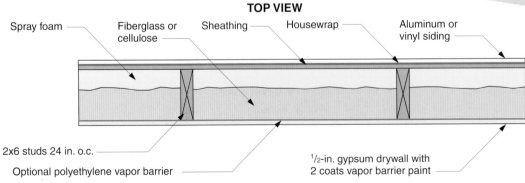

TOP VIEW

Spray foam

Fiberglass or cellulose

Sheathing

Housewrap

Aluminum or vinyl siding

2x6 studs 24 in. o.c.

Optional polyethylene vapor barrier

1/2-in. gypsum drywall with 2 coats vapor barrier paint

OVE Frame with Foam Sheathing and Cellulose in Cavities

Substituting extruded polystyrene sheathing for wood-based sheathing improves performance in three ways:

1. Whole wall R-value is increased at the rate of 5.0/in. of foam.

2. Thermal bridging through the framing is reduced slightly.

3. The wall cavity temperature is increased, reducing the risk of condensation.

The minimum recommended thickness of foam sheathing is 1 in. The maximum practical thickness is 2 in. due to the added complexity of window and door trim.

Vertical furring strips nailed through the foam into the studs provide a drainage plane, preventing entry of rain and allowing siding to dry after it gets wet.

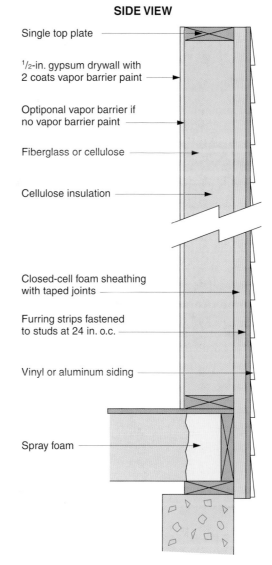

SIDE VIEW

Single top plate

1/2-in. gypsum drywall with 2 coats vapor barrier paint

Optiponal vapor barrier if no vapor barrier paint

Fiberglass or cellulose

Cellulose insulation

Closed-cell foam sheathing with taped joints

Furring strips fastened to studs at 24 in. o.c.

Vinyl or aluminum siding

Spray foam

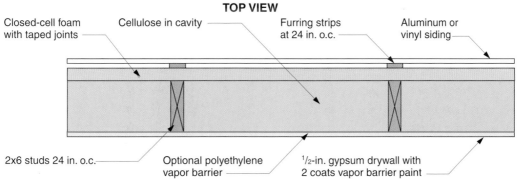

TOP VIEW

Closed-cell foam with taped joints

Cellulose in cavity

Furring strips at 24 in. o.c.

Aluminum or vinyl siding

2x6 studs 24 in. o.c.

Optional polyethylene vapor barrier

1/2-in. gypsum drywall with 2 coats vapor barrier paint

OVE Frame with Fiber-Filled Cavities and EIFS Cladding

The exterior insulation finishing system (EIFS) carries exterior insulation to the limit. Instead of lap siding, 2-ft. by 4-ft. foam panels are fastened to the exterior (OSB sheathing or masonry) of the wall and covered with a synthetic stucco.

The foam most often used is expanded polystyrene ("beadboard") and ranges in thickness from 1 in. to 4 in. At R-4.0/in. the foam increases whole-wall R-value by R-4 to R-16. Installed over an OVE wall with fiberglass insulation, the wall's total effective R-value measures R-22 to R-34.

EIFS systems have been around for fifty years, and some of the earlier installations had mixed success. The earlier problems have been addressed with new materials and techniques, including a liquid-applied moisture/air barrier between the wall sheathing and the foam.

Success depends on a host of details particular to the system. It is recommended that EIFS be installed as a total system.

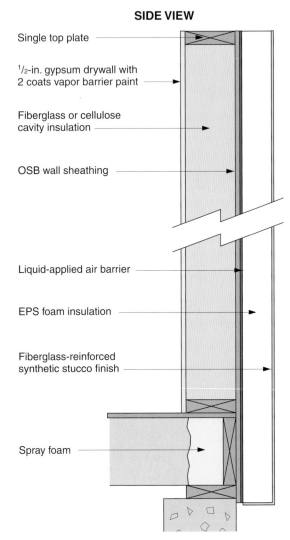

SIDE VIEW

Single top plate

1/2-in. gypsum drywall with 2 coats vapor barrier paint

Fiberglass or cellulose cavity insulation

OSB wall sheathing

Liquid-applied air barrier

EPS foam insulation

Fiberglass-reinforced synthetic stucco finish

Spray foam

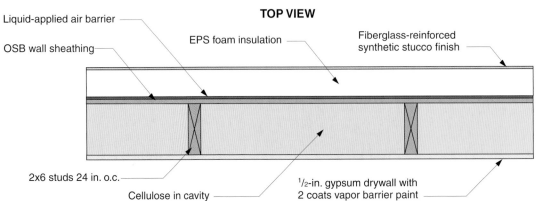

TOP VIEW

Liquid-applied air barrier

OSB wall sheathing

EPS foam insulation

Fiberglass-reinforced synthetic stucco finish

2x6 studs 24 in. o.c.

Cellulose in cavity

1/2-in. gypsum drywall with 2 coats vapor barrier paint

OVE Frame with Extra-Thick Fiber-Filled Cavities

One way of increasing total wall R-value is simply to use wider and wider studs, possibly all the way up to 2 in. by 12 in. The thermal performance of the wall, however, is not a simple linear function of the R-value of the cavity insulation. Two spoilers are as follows:

1. The R-value of the wood framing is only 1.25/in. (about one-third that of the insulation), which reduces incremental gain by 15% to 25%.

2. Penetrations of the interior finish and vapor barrier by electrical switch and receptacle boxes allow air and water vapor leakage.

The wall illustrated here adds 2½ in. of insulation and addresses the two issues above:

1. Running horizontal 2×3 strapping interrupts the thermal short circuits through the studs.

2. Sandwiching a polyethylene vapor barrier between the studs and the strapping allows the wiring to be run entirely on the warm side of the now-unpenetrated barrier.

The integrity of the vapor barrier is heightened due to the extra thickness of the insulation, increasing the potential for condensation toward the outside of the cavity.

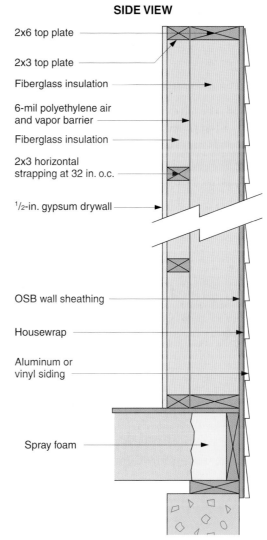

SIDE VIEW

2x6 top plate

2x3 top plate

Fiberglass insulation

6-mil polyethylene air and vapor barrier

Fiberglass insulation

2x3 horizontal strapping at 32 in. o.c.

1/2-in. gypsum drywall

OSB wall sheathing

Housewrap

Aluminum or vinyl siding

Spray foam

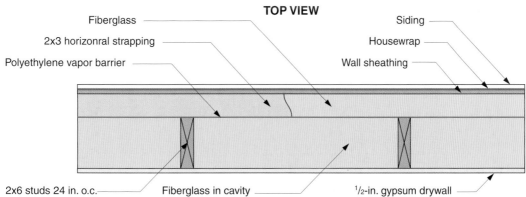

TOP VIEW

Fiberglass

2x3 horizonral strapping

Polyethylene vapor barrier

Siding

Housewrap

Wall sheathing

2x6 studs 24 in. o.c.

Fiberglass in cavity

1/2-in. gypsum drywall

One of the reasons builders turned to OVE framing was the reduction in heat flow through the frame. This was accomplished by using 2×6 studs spaced 24 in. on-center in place of the conventional 2×4s spaced 16 in. on-center. However:

1. The R-value of the wood framing is only 1.25/in. (about one-third that of the insulation), which reduces incremental gain in R by 15% to 25%.

2. Penetrations of the interior finish and vapor barrier by electrical switch and receptacle boxes allow air and water vapor leakage.

The wall illustrated here adds about 8 in. of insulation and addresses the two issues above:

1. Adding a separate 2×3 stud wall on the interior interrupts the thermal short circuits through the studs.

2. Installing the polyethylene vapor barrier on the cavity side of the 2×3 studs allows the wiring to be run entirely on the warm side of the now-unpenetrated barrier.

The integrity of the vapor barrier is heightened due to the extra thickness of the insulation, increasing the potential for condensation toward the outside of the cavity.

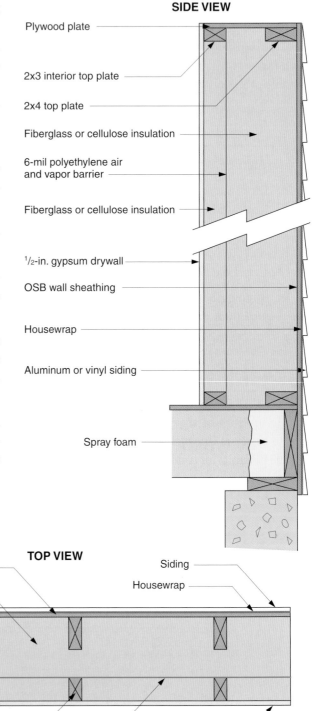

SIDE VIEW

Plywood plate

2x3 interior top plate

2x4 top plate

Fiberglass or cellulose insulation

6-mil polyethylene air and vapor barrier

Fiberglass or cellulose insulation

1/2-in. gypsum drywall

OSB wall sheathing

Housewrap

Aluminum or vinyl siding

Spray foam

TOP VIEW

Wall sheathing

Fiberglass

Siding

Housewrap

2x4 studs at 16 in. o.c.

Fiberglass or cellulose

2x3 studs at 16 in. o.c.

Polyethylene vapor barrier

1/2-in. drywall

OVE Frame with Fiber-Filled Cavities and Exterior Spray Foam

The EIFS cladding system is not the only way to add significant R-value on the outside of a wall. Two possible problems with EIFS are:

1. The exterior finish resembles stucco, which may not seem appropriate in the neighborhood (New England Colonial, for example).

2. EIFS systems are proprietary and may require application by licensed contractors.

Shown here is a stud wall hanging outside a conventional OVE wall. Its advantages include:

1. The sprayed closed-cell foam has an R-value of 6.0/in. vs. 4.0/in. for expanded polystyrene.

2. The exterior wall extends downward to cover the entire rim joist area, a major thermal bypass and source of infiltration.

3. It allows conventional window and door treatments and the attachment of cladding.

4. It would be an excellent retrofit option where the existing cladding requires replacing.

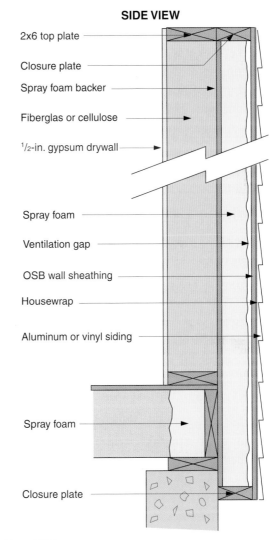

SIDE VIEW

- 2x6 top plate
- Closure plate
- Spray foam backer
- Fiberglas or cellulose
- $1/2$-in. gypsum drywall
- Spray foam
- Ventilation gap
- OSB wall sheathing
- Housewrap
- Aluminum or vinyl siding
- Spray foam
- Closure plate

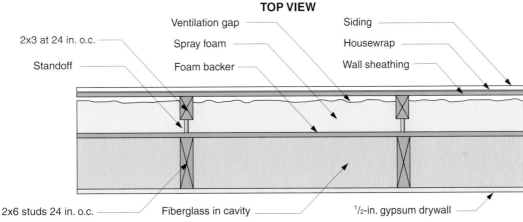

TOP VIEW

- 2x3 at 24 in. o.c.
- Standoff
- Ventilation gap
- Spray foam
- Foam backer
- Siding
- Housewrap
- Wall sheathing
- 2x6 studs 24 in. o.c.
- Fiberglass in cavity
- $1/2$-in. gypsum drywall

Larsen Truss with Fiber Fill

The Larsen truss creates a wall cavity limited in depth only by the width of the plywood gussets connecting the 2× chords. The original Larsen truss, constructed on-site of 2×2 chords and ⅜-in. plywood gussets, hung entirely exterior to a conventional load-bearing wall. Its sole purpose was to house 8 in. to 12 in. of sprayed or blown fiberglass or cellulose.

The version illustrated here is technically a wall truss, where the inner chords form a 2×4 load-bearing wall.

Two advantages of the wall are:

1. The great thickness of insulation gives the wall an R-value of up to 40.

2. Hanging two-thirds of the wall outside the foundation line means the square footage of the conditioned space is not diminished beyond the usual. If, in a 24-ft. by 40-ft. building, the entire 12-in. truss were inside the foundation line, the additional loss of living space would amount to 57 sq. ft. per floor. At $150/sq. ft, the lost space would be worth about $8,500.

As with other extra-thick walls, the high R-value makes a perfect warm-side vapor barrier crucial.

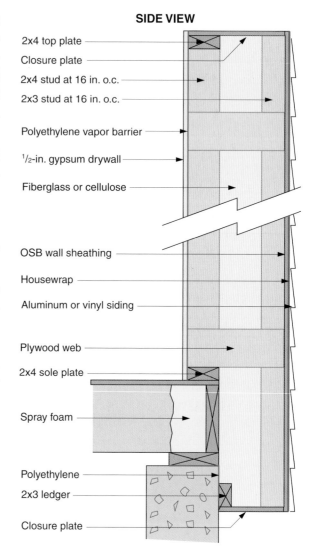

SIDE VIEW

2x4 top plate
Closure plate
2x4 stud at 16 in. o.c.
2x3 stud at 16 in. o.c.
Polyethylene vapor barrier
½-in. gypsum drywall
Fiberglass or cellulose
OSB wall sheathing
Housewrap
Aluminum or vinyl siding
Plywood web
2x4 sole plate
Spray foam
Polyethylene
2x3 ledger
Closure plate

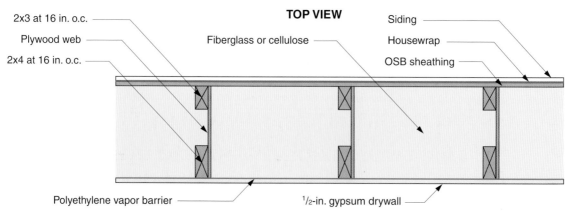

TOP VIEW

2x3 at 16 in. o.c.
Plywood web
2x4 at 16 in. o.c.
Fiberglass or cellulose
Siding
Housewrap
OSB sheathing
Polyethylene vapor barrier
½-in. gypsum drywall

Structural Insulated Panels (SIPs) with EPS Cores

Structural insulated panels (SIPs) consist of expanded polystyrene (EXP), extruded polystyrene (EPS), or polyisocyanurate (PIC) sandwiched between panels. The panels supply both tensile and compressive strength, while the foam serves as a separator or web. Due to their geometry, the panels are structural elements requiring no extra framing.

The combination of OSB panels and EPS foam shown in the illustration are the most cost effective and most commonly used. Although greater thicknesses are available, the majority of SIPs have 3½-in. or 5½-in. cores. Panels with EXP cores have R-values of 14 and 20, while EPS-cored panels rate R-20 and R-30.

Advantages of SIPs include:

1. With less framing, their R-values are 16% to 18% higher than conventionally framed walls.

2. Provided the joints between panels are effectively caulked or gasketed, they are more air tight.

3. Although more expensive, their reduction in on-site labor and heat transfer leads to a lower life-cycle cost.

A single disadvantage is the difficulty of running wiring through the panels after installation.

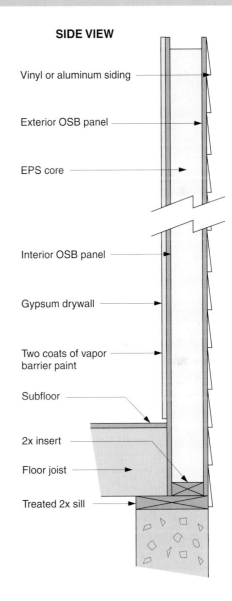

SIDE VIEW

Vinyl or aluminum siding

Exterior OSB panel

EPS core

Interior OSB panel

Gypsum drywall

Two coats of vapor barrier paint

Subfloor

2x insert

Floor joist

Treated 2x sill

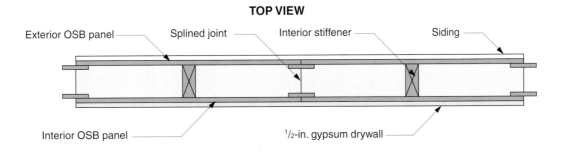

TOP VIEW

Exterior OSB panel — Splined joint — Interior stiffener — Siding

Interior OSB panel — ½-in. gypsum drywall

Insulated Concrete Form (ICF) Wall

Insulated concrete forms (ICFs) are the inverse of structural insulated panels (SIPs). In the ICF, the structural strength lies in the poured concrete core, while the thermal resistance is provided by a form of EPS foam.

The most common ICF in residential construction has a whole-wall R-value of about 20. The R-value alone doesn't convey the entire thermal performance story, however:

1. The monolithic poured concrete core, except for wiring penetrations from the outside, provides a perfectly air-tight skin.

2. The great thermal mass of the concrete attenuates the heat flows from diurnal temperature swings and thus reduces loads on the heating system.

Unlike the usual poured concrete or concrete block wall, an ICF wall has fastening strips embedded in the foam, which simplify the attachment of interior finish and exterior cladding.

SIDE VIEW

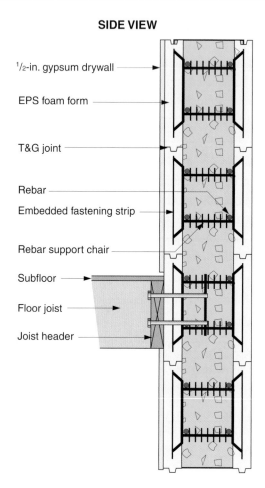

½-in. gypsum drywall

EPS foam form

T&G joint

Rebar

Embedded fastening strip

Rebar support chair

Subfloor

Floor joist

Joist header

TOP VIEW

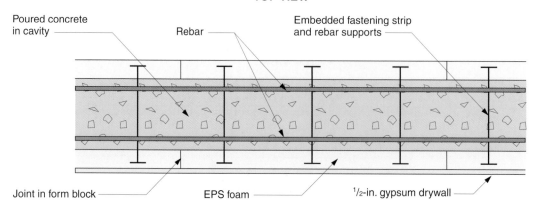

Poured concrete in cavity

Rebar

Embedded fastening strip and rebar supports

Joint in form block

EPS foam

½-in. gypsum drywall

Conventional Wall Retrofitted with Exterior Polyisocyanurate Foam

Re-siding an older home presents a wonderful opportunity to turn an average wall into a super-insulated wall. Vinyl and aluminum siding contractors often apply a thin layer of extruded polystyrene over the old sheathing and under the new cladding. While the foam increases R-value and decreases infiltration a small amount, it is more an advertising gimmick than an effective retrofit. Furthermore, the thin closed-cell foam layer acts as a vapor barrier on the wrong side of the wall.

The illustration shows an expensive, but much better, retrofit solution: two overlapped sheets of 1½-in. foil-faced polyisocyanurate and vertical furring strips fastened through the foam to the studs. Here is what you gain:

1. The combination of 3 in. of R-6/in. foam and the air space between the furring strips adds R-20 to the existing R-11 wall.

2. The condensation plane will now be located within the closed-cell foam, which solves the moisture problem without requiring a vapor barrier.

3. The overlapped and taped sheets of foam comprise an air-tight skin.

4. The furring strips create a drainage plane, allowing any type of siding to dry out.

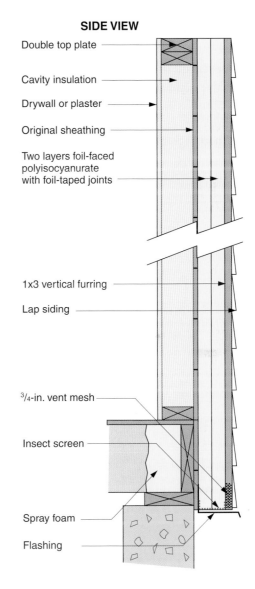

SIDE VIEW

Double top plate
Cavity insulation
Drywall or plaster
Original sheathing
Two layers foil-faced polyisocyanurate with foil-taped joints
1x3 vertical furring
Lap siding
³/₄-in. vent mesh
Insect screen
Spray foam
Flashing

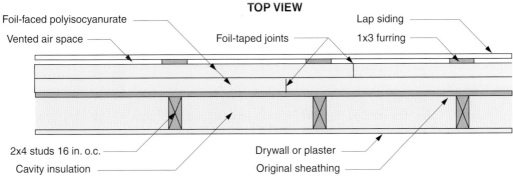

TOP VIEW

Foil-faced polyisocyanurate
Vented air space
Foil-taped joints
Lap siding
1x3 furring
2x4 studs 16 in. o.c.
Cavity insulation
Drywall or plaster
Original sheathing

Insulating Slab Foundations

It was long believed that slabs lost little heat. After all, the earth itself is a source of heat, and the temperature of the soil at depth is roughly the same as the average annual air temperature for the location. Both of these facts are true, but what was overlooked is the short circuit to the outside through the thermally conductive perimeter of the slab.

Below and on the following pages are eight approaches to preventing slab heat loss. All use closed-cell, waterproof extruded polystyrene with an R-value of 5/in. thickness to retard heat flow, plus a continuous vapor retarder (usually polyethylene sheeting) to prevent incursion of radon gas and moisture from the soil below.

Slab-on-Grade Insulation Configurations

Monolithic slab with down & out perimeter insulation
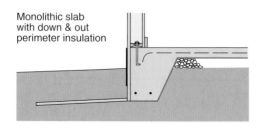

Slab on masonry foundation wall with edge & cavity insulation
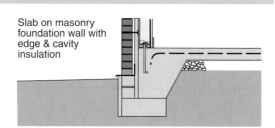

Slab on grade beam with perimeter insulation
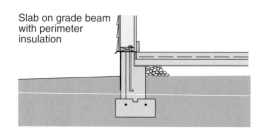

Slab on masonry stem wall with perimeter insulation
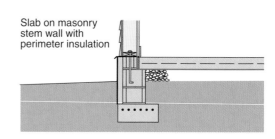

Slab on concrete stem wall with interior edge & slab insulation
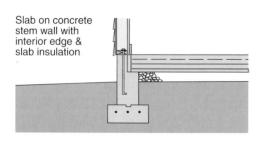

Slab on masonry foundation wall with interior edge & slab insulation
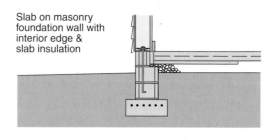

Slab on masonry stem wall with interior edge insulation
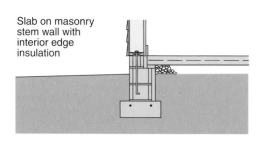

Slab on masonry foundation wall with edge & under-slab insulation
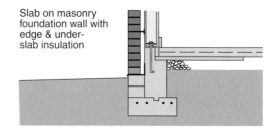

Recommended R-Values for Slab Edge Insulation

Location	Natural Gas Heat Electric AC	Heat Pump Heat Electric AC	Fuel Oil Heat Electric AC	Natural Gas Heat No AC	Fuel Oil Heat No AC
AZ, Phoenix	4	4	4	0	0
CA, Los Angeles	0	0	0	0	0
CO, Denver	8	8	8	8	8
DC, Washington	8	8	8	8	8
FL, Miami	4	0	4	0	0
GA, Atlanta	8	4	8	8	4
IL, Chicago	8	8	8	8	8
LA, Baton Rouge	4	4	4	0	0
MA, Boston	8	8	8	8	8
ME, Portland	8	8	8	8	8
MN, Duluth	8	8	8	8	8
MO, St. Louis	8	8	8	8	8
NY, New York	8	8	8	8	8
TX, Dallas	8	4	4	4	0
VT, Burlington	8	8	8	8	8
WA, Seattle	8	4	8	8	8

Monolithic Slab with Down-and-Out Perimeter Insulation

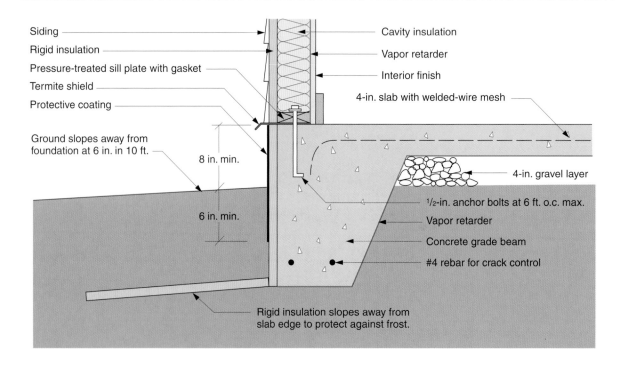

Siding

Rigid insulation

Pressure-treated sill plate with gasket

Termite shield

Protective coating

Ground slopes away from foundation at 6 in. in 10 ft.

8 in. min.

6 in. min.

Cavity insulation

Vapor retarder

Interior finish

4-in. slab with welded-wire mesh

4-in. gravel layer

½-in. anchor bolts at 6 ft. o.c. max.

Vapor retarder

Concrete grade beam

#4 rebar for crack control

Rigid insulation slopes away from slab edge to protect against frost.

Millions of homes have been constructed in Scandinavia and Canada on frost-protected shallow foundations (FPSFs). These were developed not so much for energy savings but to prevent frost heaving in clay soils. Of course, it turns out they do both.

The rule of thumb is that extruded polystyrene foam panels extending down and then out a total distance equal to the local frost depth have the same effect as vertical panels to the frost depth. The obvious advantage is savings in the amounts of excavation, forming, and concrete.

Much of the initial resistance to this innovative technique was due to the 8 in. to 12 in. of extruded polystyrene exposed above ground. Unprotected, EPS degrades when exposed to ultraviolet light. Several products have been developed specifically to solve this problem:

1. Foam panels precoated with either granular or stucco finish are available in thicknesses from 1 in. (R-5) to 3 in. (R-15).

2. Latex-modified (for flexibility and toughness) cementitious coatings can be either brushed or troweled on to give the appearance of concrete.

A second issue is that the foam can provide a hidden termite path from soil to sill. This problem may be overcome by a metal termite shield installed under the sill and extending over the top of the foam and protective coating.

Slab on Masonry Foundation Wall with Edge and Cavity Insulation

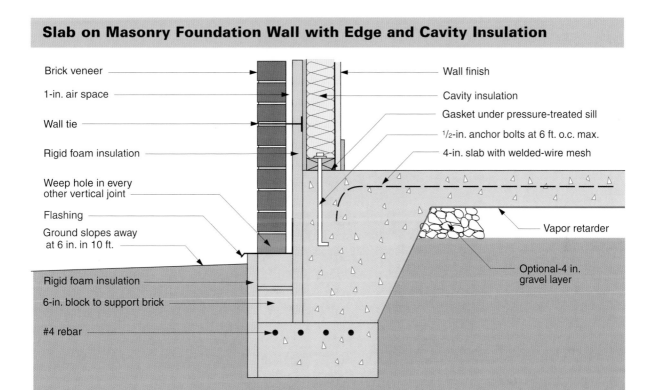

Brick veneer

1-in. air space

Wall tie

Rigid foam insulation

Weep hole in every other vertical joint

Flashing

Ground slopes away at 6 in. in 10 ft.

Rigid foam insulation

6-in. block to support brick

#4 rebar

Wall finish

Cavity insulation

Gasket under pressure-treated sill

$\frac{1}{2}$-in. anchor bolts at 6 ft. o.c. max.

4-in. slab with welded-wire mesh

Vapor retarder

Optional-4 in. gravel layer

Brick veneer, which must be supported by the edge of the foundation, poses the problem of how to prevent (or at least minimize) the thermal short circuit from exposed brick to the slab.

The illustration above shows one possible solution. (Another is detailed on p. 203.) A continuous layer of extruded polystyrene is attached to the sheathing of the stud wall and extends over the slab perimeter to the footing. The brick veneer sits on a base of concrete blocks and is spaced out from the foam to create a 1-in. air space. Then the edges of the perimeter footing and supporting blocks are protected by a second layer of foam. Heat flow from the brick veneer to the slab has to travel a tortuous path through and around the supporting blocks before reaching the slab.

Note that EPS foam panels could also extend outward from the base of the footing to create a frost-protected shallow foundation, as shown on the facing page.

Slab on Grade Beam with Perimeter Insulation

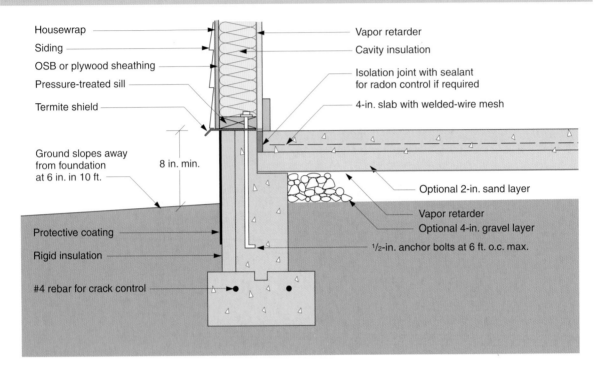

Housewrap
Siding
OSB or plywood sheathing
Pressure-treated sill
Termite shield

Ground slopes away from foundation at 6 in. in 10 ft.

8 in. min.

Protective coating
Rigid insulation

#4 rebar for crack control

Vapor retarder
Cavity insulation
Isolation joint with sealant for radon control if required
4-in. slab with welded-wire mesh

Optional 2-in. sand layer

Vapor retarder
Optional 4-in. gravel layer
1/2-in. anchor bolts at 6 ft. o.c. max.

Where applying a layer of foam sheathing from sill to top plate is not desired, a 2×6 stud wall can be cantilevered over the concrete perimeter wall by the thickness of the foam. For example, the 2×6 sill (actual width 5½ in.) extended 2 in. over a 2-in. foam board will still have 3½ in. bearing on the top of the concrete. This technique offers two advantages:

1. Particularly if the foam is covered with a cementitious coating, the foundation/siding interface will appear as normal concrete.

2. The projecting sill serves to prevent frost from heaving the foam upward, eliminating the need to fasten the foam to the concrete.

Again, the foam could be extended horizontally from the top of the footing to create a frost-protected shallow foundation.

As with all exterior foundation insulation, a metal termite shield should be placed between the top of the perimeter wall and the wood sill and extend over the top of the foam and protective coating.

Note that the forms for the perimeter wall must be shortened by twice the thickness of the foam so that the building frame still measures a multiple of 2 ft. or 4 ft.

Slab on Masonry Stem Wall with Perimeter Insulation

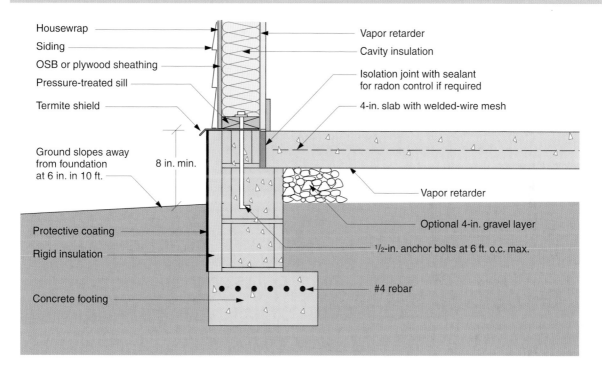

Housewrap

Siding

OSB or plywood sheathing

Pressure-treated sill

Termite shield

Ground slopes away from foundation at 6 in. in 10 ft.

8 in. min.

Protective coating

Rigid insulation

Concrete footing

Vapor retarder

Cavity insulation

Isolation joint with sealant for radon control if required

4-in. slab with welded-wire mesh

Vapor retarder

Optional 4-in. gravel layer

$^1/_2$-in. anchor bolts at 6 ft. o.c. max.

#4 rebar

Here's what would happen, if you'd forgotten to tell the foundation subcontractor to subtract twice the foam thickness from the perimeter dimensions. The only problem is that the 2-in. bulge at the sill would look odd.

Note the difference in footing reinforcement between the designs on this page and the facing page. Because the block stem wall has little or no bending strength, the footing has to be heavily reinforced.

Notice also that water running down the siding and striking the metal termite shield might wick back under the sheathing and sill. It would be wise to make at least the first few feet of sheathing rot-proof pressure-treated plywood.

Slab on Concrete Stem Wall with Interior Edge and Slab Insulation

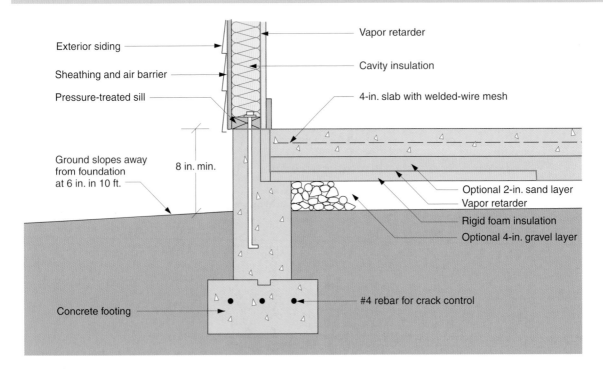

Exterior siding

Sheathing and air barrier

Pressure-treated sill

Ground slopes away from foundation at 6 in. in 10 ft.

8 in. min.

Concrete footing

Vapor retarder

Cavity insulation

4-in. slab with welded-wire mesh

Optional 2-in. sand layer
Vapor retarder
Rigid foam insulation
Optional 4-in. gravel layer

#4 rebar for crack control

If you are fortunate enough to be building on a sandy, well-drained soil, your slab and foundation won't heave regardless of frost depth. It's simple: No water in the soil, no ice and no heaving. If, however, you are building on a wet or clay soil, stick to the foundation shown on p. 196.

Here, we insulate only against heat flow through the slab. Insulating under the entire slab rarely pays back. A good rule of thumb is 4 ft. in from the edges, which is also convenient because that is the width of the largest foam panels. What R-value? Refer to the table on p. 195.

The optional 2-in. layer of sand is a good idea if you are pouring on poorly compacted soil. As the soil settles, traffic on the slab will cause the sand to shift and level itself under the slab. Even with the sand layer however, welded-wire mesh, glass fiber-reinforced concrete, and control joints are recommended.

No metal termite barrier between stem wall and sill is shown because the 8-in. minimum bare concrete exposure makes it easy to spot termite tubes.

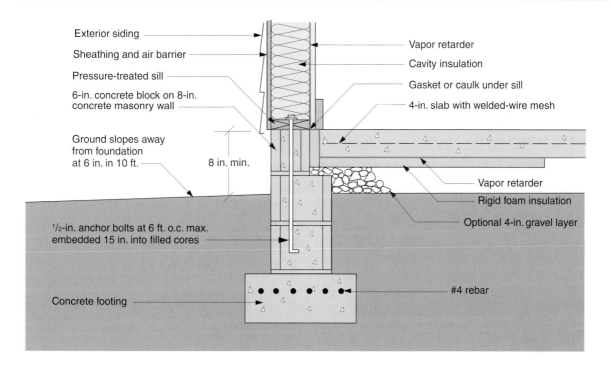

Exterior siding

Sheathing and air barrier

Pressure-treated sill

6-in. concrete block on 8-in. concrete masonry wall

Ground slopes away from foundation at 6 in. in 10 ft.

8 in. min.

¹/₂-in. anchor bolts at 6 ft. o.c. max. embedded 15 in. into filled cores

Concrete footing

Vapor retarder

Cavity insulation

Gasket or caulk under sill

4-in. slab with welded-wire mesh

Vapor retarder

Rigid foam insulation

Optional 4-in. gravel layer

#4 rebar

Where the soil is both well drained and undisturbed or compacted, a layer of sand is not required under the slab because there should be no settling or heaving.

The same foam guidelines apply as in the design on the facing page:

1. Select 1-in.-, 1½-in.-, or 2-in.-thick extruded polystyrene (R-5/in.), consulting the table of recommended R-values on p. 154 and the IECC recommended R-value table on p. 167.

2. Install the width (or depth) listed in the IECC recommended R-value table on p. 167. Or, for comfort or good measure, go with the full 4-ft. width of the panels.

Slab on Masonry Stem Wall with Interior Edge Insulation

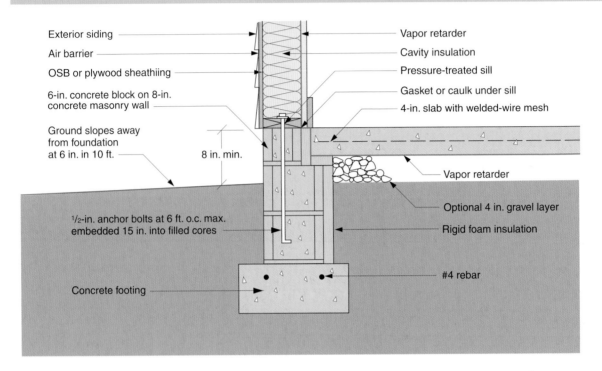

Exterior siding

Air barrier

OSB or plywood sheathiing

6-in. concrete block on 8-in. concrete masonry wall

Ground slopes away from foundation at 6 in. in 10 ft.

8 in. min.

½-in. anchor bolts at 6 ft. o.c. max. embedded 15 in. into filled cores

Concrete footing

Vapor retarder

Cavity insulation

Pressure-treated sill

Gasket or caulk under sill

4-in. slab with welded-wire mesh

Vapor retarder

Optional 4 in. gravel layer

Rigid foam insulation

#4 rebar

This is the same wall as detailed on p. 196, except here the soil is well drained and undisturbed. Because well-drained soil is not subject to frost heaving regardless of the supposed depth of frost, there is no need to keep the stem wall and footing above freezing. The purpose of the foam is to retard heat loss from the perimeter of the slab.

Just because the soil is well drained doesn't mean there isn't a transfer of water vapor upward from the soil. The continuous vapor retarding membrane (4-mil or 6-mil polyethylene sheeting) isolates the conditioned space from this sometimes large source of water vapor. As a bonus, the polyethylene holds the water in the concrete while curing, producing a stronger slab.

Note that, with no frost heaving and no soil settling, little reinforcement is required in the stemwall footing.

For the foam R-value and depth, consult the IECC recommended R-value table on p. 167.

Slab on Masonry Foundation Wall with Edge and Under-Slab Insulation

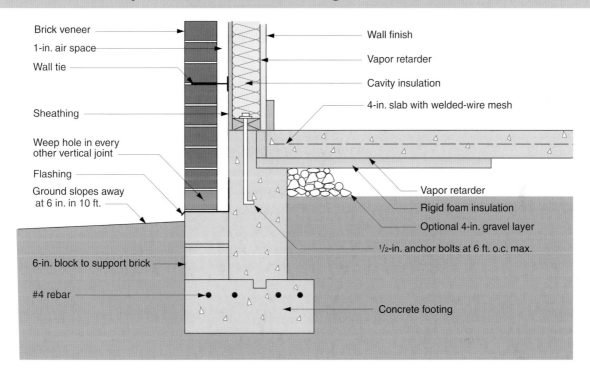

Brick veneer
1-in. air space
Wall tie
Sheathing
Weep hole in every other vertical joint
Flashing
Ground slopes away at 6 in. in 10 ft.
6-in. block to support brick
#4 rebar

Wall finish
Vapor retarder
Cavity insulation
4-in. slab with welded-wire mesh
Vapor retarder
Rigid foam insulation
Optional 4-in. gravel layer
$\frac{1}{2}$-in. anchor bolts at 6 ft. o.c. max.
Concrete footing

This is the same brick veneer design as detailed on p. 197, except that here the soil is well drained and undisturbed. Because well-drained soil is not subject to frost heaving regardless of frost depth (maximum depth to which the soil cools to 32°F in winter), there is no need to keep the stem wall and footing above freezing. The purpose of the foam is simply to retard heat loss from the slab.

This is the simplest and most effective solution for a brick veneer wall.

Why the heavy reinforcement of the stem wall footing? Because, with no control joints, brick walls are very rigid and subject to cracking.

Insulating Crawl Spaces

Many building codes require crawl spaces to be ventilated in order to remove moisture in the summer. Counter to intuition, however, warm humid summer air condenses moisture on the cooler building surfaces in the crawl space, leading to dry rot. It is now considered better to tightly seal the crawl space and install an effective moisture barrier over the soil.

Furthermore, vented crawl spaces must be insulated at the floor above, leaving pipes exposed to freezing. Insulating the walls of an unvented crawl space places pipes and ducts inside the home's thermal envelope.

Crawl Space Insulation Configurations

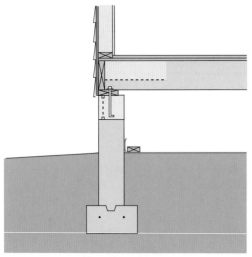

Vented crawl space
with floor insulation

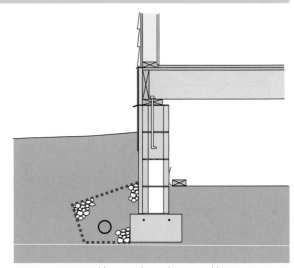

Unvented crawl space with
exterior foam perimeter insulation

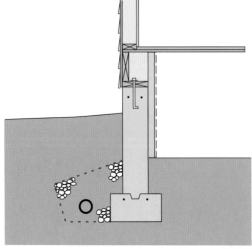

Unvented crawl space with
interior foam perimeter insulation

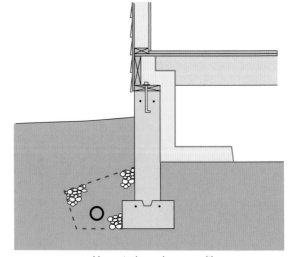

Unvented crawl space with
interior batt perimeter insulation

Recommended R-Values for Crawl Space Ceilings

Location	Natural Gas Heat Electric AC	Heat Pump Heat Electric AC	Fuel Oil Heat Electric AC	Natural Gas Heat No AC	Fuel Oil Heat No AC
AZ, Phoenix	11	11	11	11	11
CA, Los Angeles	11	11	11	0	0
CO, Denver	25	25	25	25	25
DC, Washington	25	25	25	25	25
FL, Miami	11	11	11	0	0
GA, Atlanta	25	13	25	25	25
IL, Chicago	25	25	25	25	25
LA, Baton Rouge	13	11	11	13	11
MA, Boston	25	25	25	25	25
ME, Portland	25	25	25	25	25
MN, Duluth	25	25	25	25	25
MO, St. Louis	25	25	25	25	25
NY, New York	25	25	25	25	25
TX, Dallas	13	13	13	13	13
VT, Burlington	25	25	25	25	25
WA, Seattle	25	13	25	25	25

Recommended R-Values for Crawl Space Walls

Location	Natural Gas Heat Electric AC	Heat Pump Heat Electric AC	Fuel Oil Heat Electric AC	Natural Gas Heat No AC	Fuel Oil Heat No AC
AZ, Phoenix	13	11	13	11	11
CA, Los Angeles	11	11	11	11	11
CO, Denver	19	19	19	19	19
DC, Washington	19	19	19	19	19
FL, Miami	11	11	11	11	0
GA, Atlanta	19	13	19	19	19
IL, Chicago	19	19	19	19	19
LA, Baton Rouge	13	11	11	13	11
MA, Boston	19	19	19	19	19
ME, Portland	19	19	19	19	19
MN, Duluth	19	19	19	19	19
MO, St. Louis	19	19	19	19	19
NY, New York	19	19	19	19	19
TX, Dallas	19	13	13	13	13
VT, Burlington	19	19	19	19	19
WA, Seattle	19	13	19	19	19

Vented Crawl Space with Floor Insulation

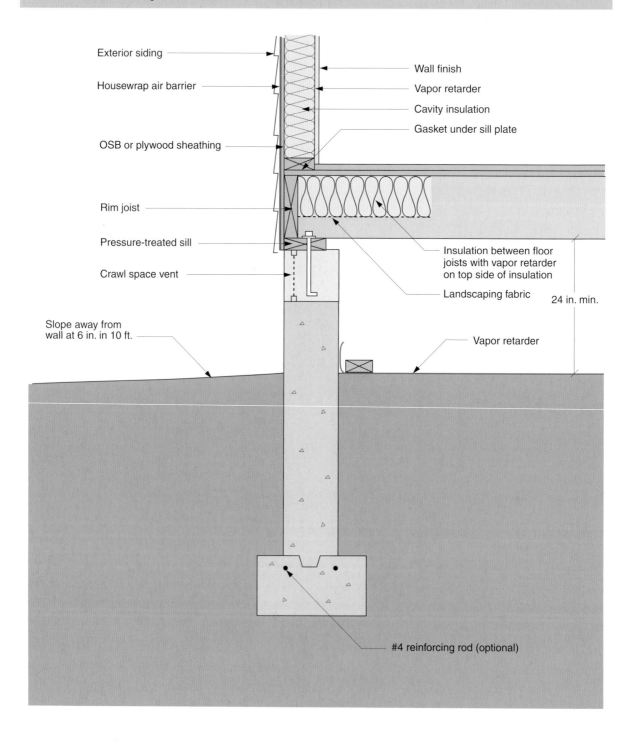

Exterior siding

Housewrap air barrier

OSB or plywood sheathing

Rim joist

Pressure-treated sill

Crawl space vent

Slope away from wall at 6 in. in 10 ft.

Wall finish

Vapor retarder

Cavity insulation

Gasket under sill plate

Insulation between floor joists with vapor retarder on top side of insulation

Landscaping fabric

24 in. min.

Vapor retarder

#4 reinforcing rod (optional)

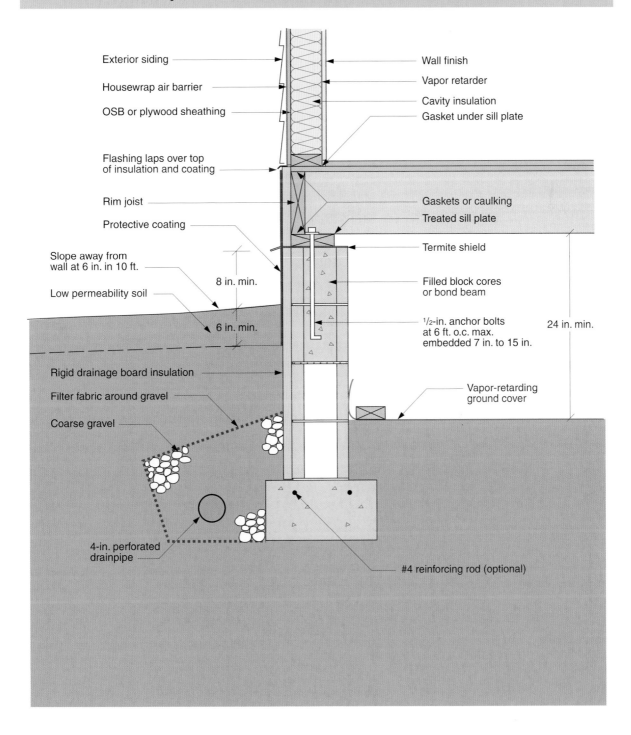

Exterior siding

Housewrap air barrier

OSB or plywood sheathing

Flashing laps over top
of insulation and coating

Rim joist

Protective coating

Slope away from
wall at 6 in. in 10 ft.

Low permeability soil

Rigid drainage board insulation

Filter fabric around gravel

Coarse gravel

4-in. perforated
drainpipe

Wall finish

Vapor retarder

Cavity insulation

Gasket under sill plate

Gaskets or caulking

Treated sill plate

Termite shield

Filled block cores
or bond beam

$1/2$-in. anchor bolts
at 6 ft. o.c. max.
embedded 7 in. to 15 in.

Vapor-retarding
ground cover

#4 reinforcing rod (optional)

8 in. min.

6 in. min.

24 in. min.

Unvented Crawl Space with Interior Foam Perimeter Insulation

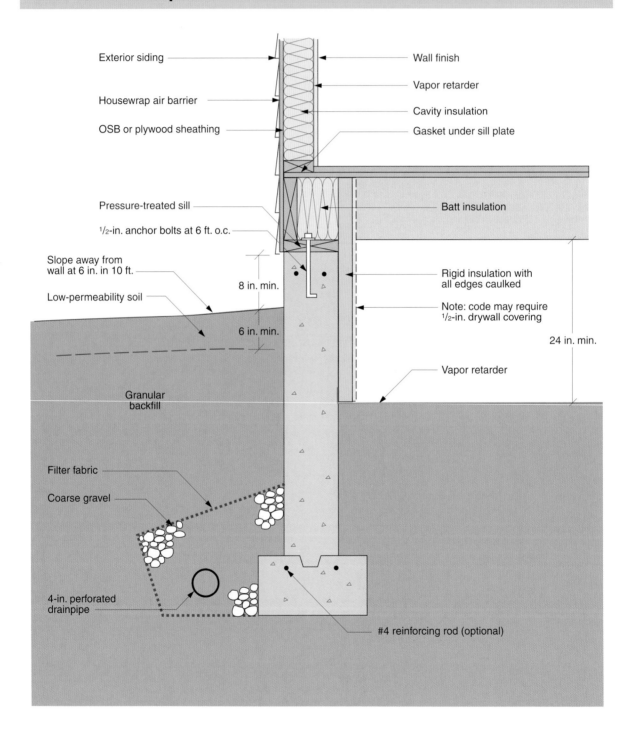

Exterior siding

Housewrap air barrier

OSB or plywood sheathing

Wall finish

Vapor retarder

Cavity insulation

Gasket under sill plate

Pressure-treated sill

1/2-in. anchor bolts at 6 ft. o.c.

Batt insulation

Slope away from
wall at 6 in. in 10 ft.

Low-permeability soil

8 in. min.

Rigid insulation with
all edges caulked

Note: code may require
1/2-in. drywall covering

6 in. min.

24 in. min.

Vapor retarder

Granular
backfill

Filter fabric

Coarse gravel

4-in. perforated
drainpipe

#4 reinforcing rod (optional)

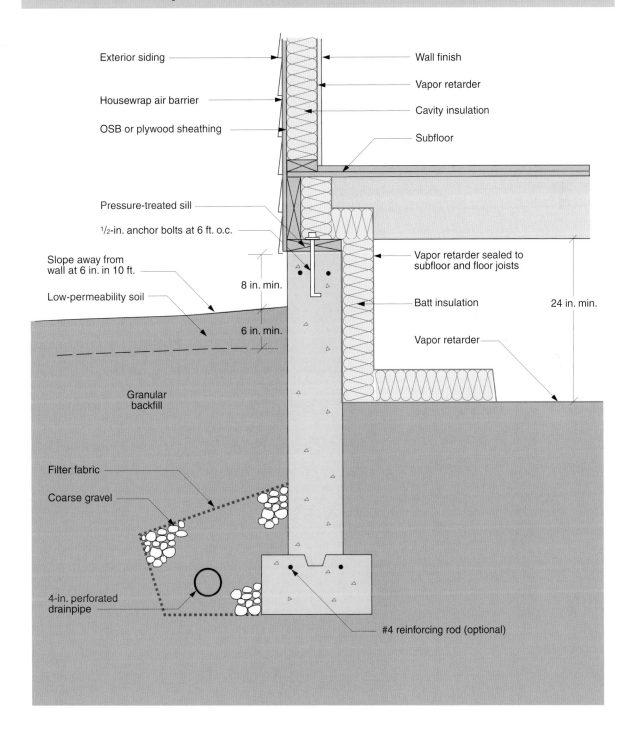

Exterior siding

Housewrap air barrier

OSB or plywood sheathing

Wall finish

Vapor retarder

Cavity insulation

Subfloor

Pressure-treated sill

1/2-in. anchor bolts at 6 ft. o.c.

Slope away from wall at 6 in. in 10 ft.

Low-permeability soil

8 in. min.

6 in. min.

Vapor retarder sealed to subfloor and floor joists

Batt insulation

24 in. min.

Vapor retarder

Granular backfill

Filter fabric

Coarse gravel

4-in. perforated drainpipe

#4 reinforcing rod (optional)

Insulating Full Basements

Full basements are popular in cold climates because they provide spaces for wiring, plumbing, heating equipment, and storage. It is easy to believe they lose little heat because the surrounding earth serves as a thermal mass, while the house above provides a steady source of heat. It is now known that the basement walls of a building, otherwise insulated to current standards, account for up to 25% of total heat loss.

The IRC recommends basement wall (or floor above) insulation in all climate zones, as shown in the tables on the facing page.

The following six pages detail basement wall and floor insulation alternatives for new construction. Following these six, we detail four approaches to retrofitting insulation to existing homes.

Basement Insulation Configurations

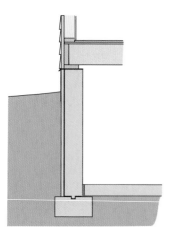

Continuous rigid foam
wall and foundation sheathing

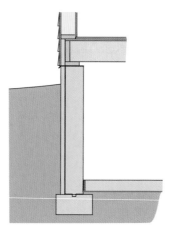

Full-height exterior foam
and cantilevered wall framing

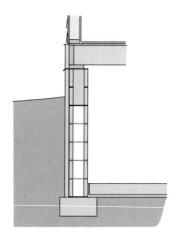

Full-height exterior foam
extended over rim joist

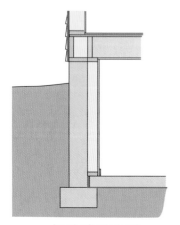

Interior framed wall
with batt insulation

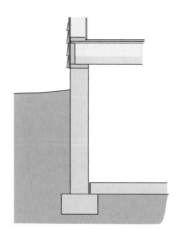

Unconditioned basement
with floor insulation

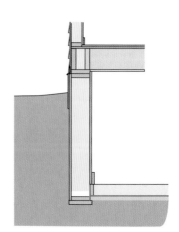

All-weather wood foundation
with batt insulation

Recommended R-Values for Basement Wall Exteriors

Location	Natural Gas Heat Electric AC	Heat Pump Heat Electric AC	Fuel Oil Heat Electric AC	Natural Gas Heat No AC	Fuel Oil Heat No AC
AZ, Phoenix	4	4	4	4	4
CA, Los Angeles	4	0	4	4	0
CO, Denver	10	8	8	10	8
DC, Washington	10	5	8	10	8
FL, Miami	0	0	0	0	0
GA, Atlanta	5	5	5	5	5
IL, Chicago	8	8	8	8	8
LA, Baton Rouge	4	4	4	4	4
MA, Boston	12	10	8	10	8
ME, Portland	15	15	12	15	12
MN, Duluth	15	15	12	15	12
MO, St. Louis	10	5	8	10	8
NY, New York	8	8	5	8	5
TX, Dallas	5	5	4	5	4
VT, Burlington	15	15	15	15	15
WA, Seattle	8	4	8	8	8

Recommended R-Values for Basement Wall Interiors

Location	Natural Gas Heat Electric AC	Heat Pump Heat Electric AC	Fuel Oil Heat Electric AC	Natural Gas Heat No AC	Fuel Oil Heat No AC
AZ, Phoenix	11	11	11	11	11
CA, Los Angeles	11	11	11	11	11
CO, Denver	11	11	11	11	11
DC, Washington	11	11	11	11	11
FL, Miami	0	0	0	0	0
GA, Atlanta	11	11	11	11	11
IL, Chicago	11	11	11	11	11
LA, Baton Rouge	11	11	11	11	11
MA, Boston	11	11	11	11	11
ME, Portland	13	13	11	13	11
MN, Duluth	11	11	11	11	11
MO, St. Louis	11	11	11	11	11
NY, New York	11	11	11	11	11
TX, Dallas	11	11	11	11	11
VT, Burlington	13	19	11	13	11
WA, Seattle	11	11	11	11	11

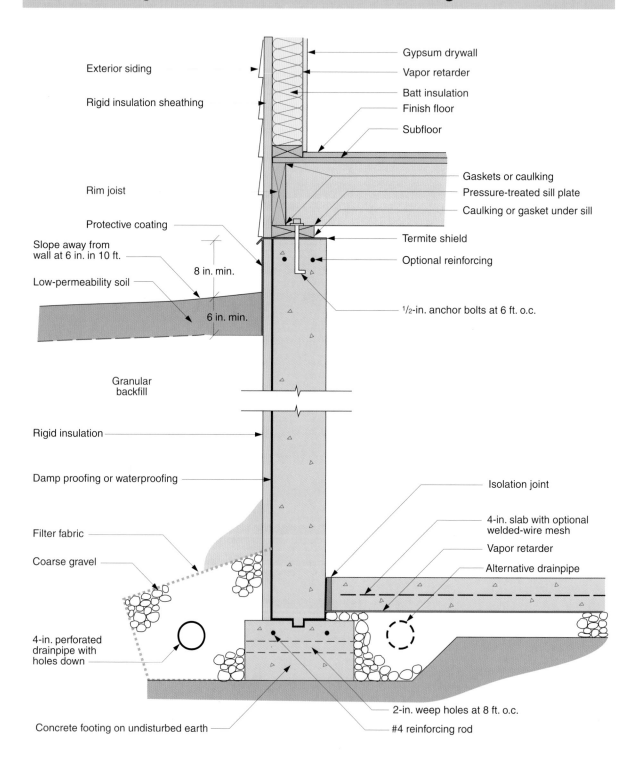

Exterior siding

Rigid insulation sheathing

Rim joist

Protective coating

Slope away from wall at 6 in. in 10 ft.

Low-permeability soil

8 in. min.

6 in. min.

Granular backfill

Rigid insulation

Damp proofing or waterproofing

Filter fabric

Coarse gravel

4-in. perforated drainpipe with holes down

Concrete footing on undisturbed earth

Gypsum drywall

Vapor retarder

Batt insulation

Finish floor

Subfloor

Gaskets or caulking

Pressure-treated sill plate

Caulking or gasket under sill

Termite shield

Optional reinforcing

$1/2$-in. anchor bolts at 6 ft. o.c.

Isolation joint

4-in. slab with optional welded-wire mesh

Vapor retarder

Alternative drainpipe

2-in. weep holes at 8 ft. o.c.

#4 reinforcing rod

Full-Height Exterior Foam and Cantilevered Wall Framing

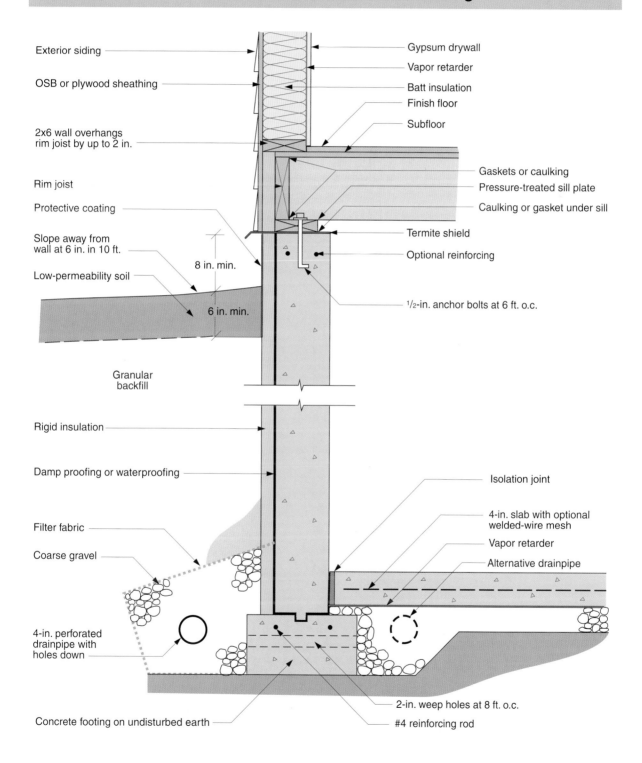

Exterior siding

OSB or plywood sheathing

2x6 wall overhangs rim joist by up to 2 in.

Rim joist

Protective coating

Slope away from wall at 6 in. in 10 ft.

8 in. min.

Low-permeability soil

6 in. min.

Granular backfill

Rigid insulation

Damp proofing or waterproofing

Filter fabric

Coarse gravel

4-in. perforated drainpipe with holes down

Concrete footing on undisturbed earth

Gypsum drywall

Vapor retarder

Batt insulation

Finish floor

Subfloor

Gaskets or caulking

Pressure-treated sill plate

Caulking or gasket under sill

Termite shield

Optional reinforcing

$\frac{1}{2}$-in. anchor bolts at 6 ft. o.c.

Isolation joint

4-in. slab with optional welded-wire mesh

Vapor retarder

Alternative drainpipe

2-in. weep holes at 8 ft. o.c.

#4 reinforcing rod

Full-Height Exterior Foam Extended over Rim Joist

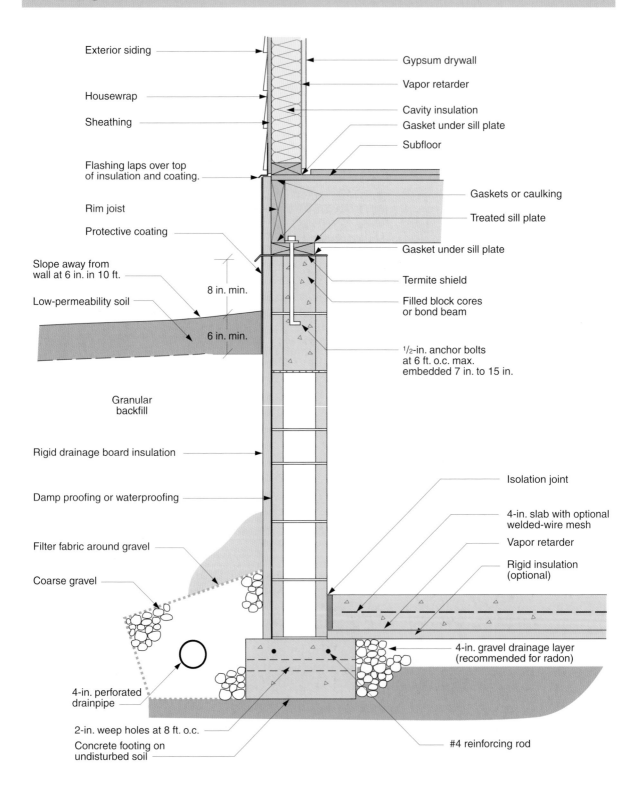

Exterior siding

Housewrap

Sheathing

Flashing laps over top
of insulation and coating.

Rim joist

Protective coating

Slope away from
wall at 6 in. in 10 ft.

Low-permeability soil

8 in. min.

6 in. min.

Granular
backfill

Rigid drainage board insulation

Damp proofing or waterproofing

Filter fabric around gravel

Coarse gravel

4-in. perforated
drainpipe

2-in. weep holes at 8 ft. o.c.

Concrete footing on
undisturbed soil

Gypsum drywall

Vapor retarder

Cavity insulation

Gasket under sill plate

Subfloor

Gaskets or caulking

Treated sill plate

Gasket under sill plate

Termite shield

Filled block cores
or bond beam

$^1/_2$-in. anchor bolts
at 6 ft. o.c. max.
embedded 7 in. to 15 in.

Isolation joint

4-in. slab with optional
welded-wire mesh

Vapor retarder

Rigid insulation
(optional)

4-in. gravel drainage layer
(recommended for radon)

#4 reinforcing rod

Interior Framed Wall with Batt Insulation

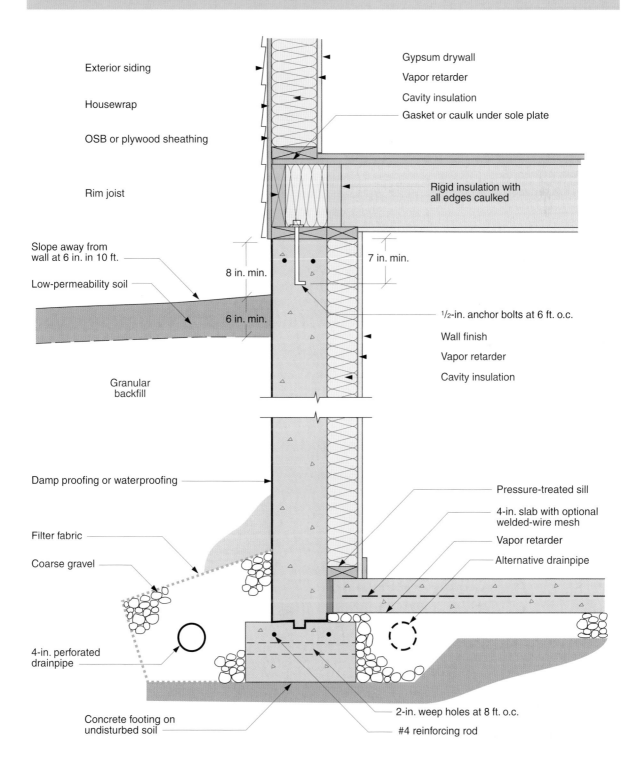

Exterior siding

Housewrap

OSB or plywood sheathing

Rim joist

Slope away from wall at 6 in. in 10 ft.

Low-permeability soil

Granular backfill

Damp proofing or waterproofing

Filter fabric

Coarse gravel

4-in. perforated drainpipe

Concrete footing on undisturbed soil

Gypsum drywall

Vapor retarder

Cavity insulation

Gasket or caulk under sole plate

Rigid insulation with all edges caulked

8 in. min.

7 in. min.

6 in. min.

1/2-in. anchor bolts at 6 ft. o.c.

Wall finish

Vapor retarder

Cavity insulation

Pressure-treated sill

4-in. slab with optional welded-wire mesh

Vapor retarder

Alternative drainpipe

2-in. weep holes at 8 ft. o.c.

#4 reinforcing rod

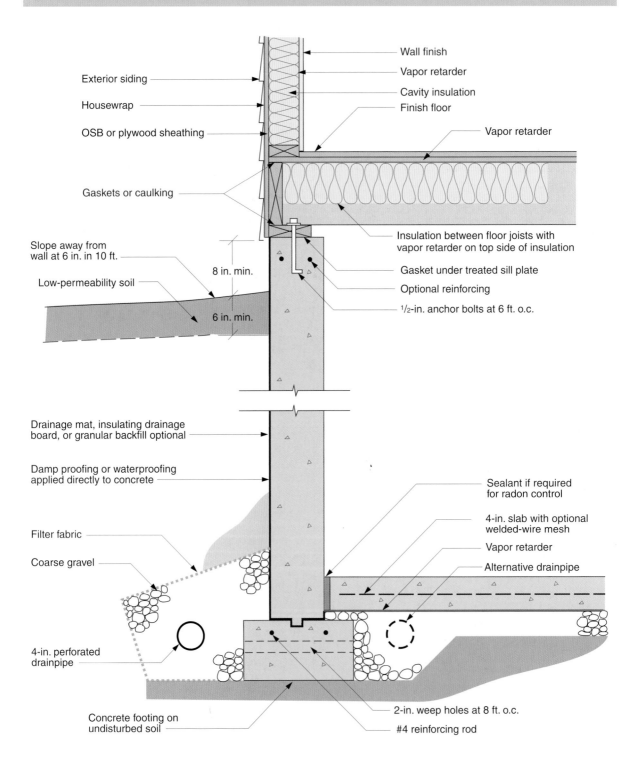

Exterior siding

Housewrap

OSB or plywood sheathing

Gaskets or caulking

Wall finish

Vapor retarder

Cavity insulation

Finish floor

Vapor retarder

Insulation between floor joists with vapor retarder on top side of insulation

Gasket under treated sill plate

Optional reinforcing

$1/2$-in. anchor bolts at 6 ft. o.c.

Slope away from wall at 6 in. in 10 ft.

Low-permeability soil

8 in. min.

6 in. min.

Drainage mat, insulating drainage board, or granular backfill optional

Damp proofing or waterproofing applied directly to concrete

Filter fabric

Coarse gravel

4-in. perforated drainpipe

Sealant if required for radon control

4-in. slab with optional welded-wire mesh

Vapor retarder

Alternative drainpipe

Concrete footing on undisturbed soil

2-in. weep holes at 8 ft. o.c.

#4 reinforcing rod

All-Weather Wood Foundation with Batt Insulation

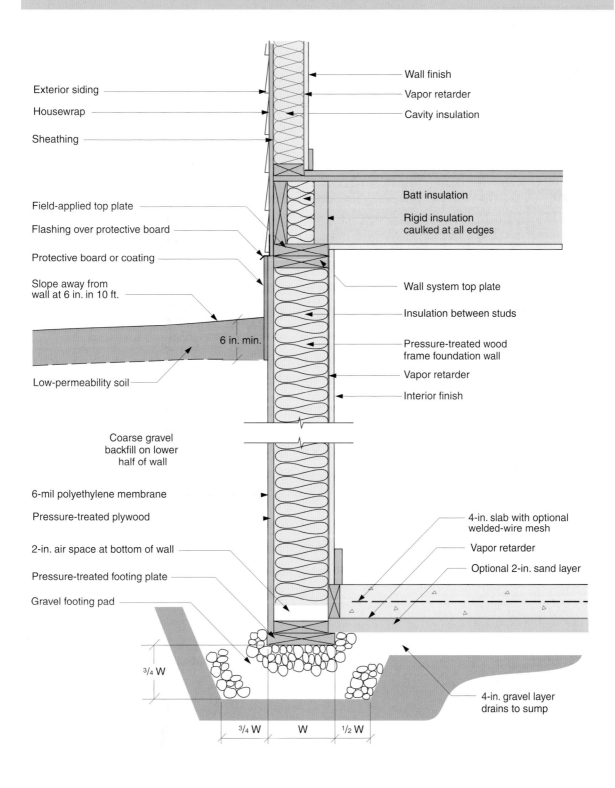

Exterior siding

Housewrap

Sheathing

Wall finish

Vapor retarder

Cavity insulation

Field-applied top plate

Flashing over protective board

Protective board or coating

Slope away from wall at 6 in. in 10 ft.

Low-permeability soil

Coarse gravel backfill on lower half of wall

6-mil polyethylene membrane

Pressure-treated plywood

2-in. air space at bottom of wall

Pressure-treated footing plate

Gravel footing pad

Batt insulation

Rigid insulation caulked at all edges

Wall system top plate

Insulation between studs

Pressure-treated wood frame foundation wall

Vapor retarder

Interior finish

6 in. min.

4-in. slab with optional welded-wire mesh

Vapor retarder

Optional 2-in. sand layer

4-in. gravel layer drains to sump

³/₄ W

³/₄ W   W   ¹/₂ W

Retrofitting Full Basements

If an existing full basement had been constructed correctly, it would have a perimeter drain and be dry. Unfortunately, this is often not the case. Here, we offer four alternatives for both reducing heat loss and creating a drier basement space. The first is appropriate where the existing slab is broken and/or uneven. The second and third solve a flooding problem at the same time as creating a more useful space below ground. The fourth minimizes three problems: air leakage, heat loss, and summer humidity.

Alternatives 2 through 4 also offer the chance to install wiring if you decide to turn the basement into habitable space.

Basement Retrofit Configurations

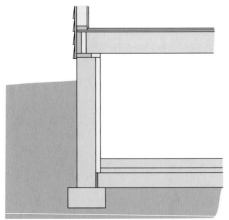

Basement retrofit with
foam wall and floor insulation

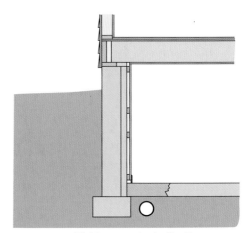

Wet basement retrofit with
foam and interior drainage

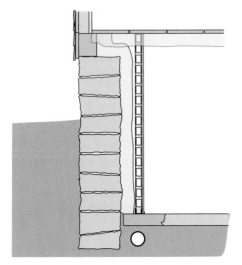

Rubble wall retrofit with spray foam,
finished wall, and interior drainage

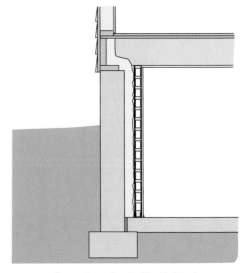

Concrete wall retrofit with interior
spray foam and finished wall

Basement Retrofit with Foam Wall and Floor Insulation

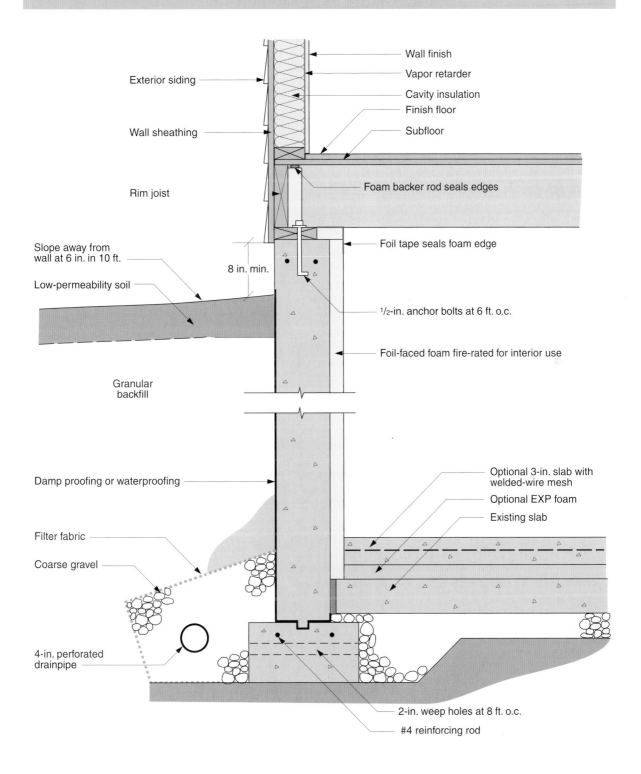

Exterior siding

Wall sheathing

Rim joist

Slope away from wall at 6 in. in 10 ft.

Low-permeability soil

Granular backfill

Damp proofing or waterproofing

Filter fabric

Coarse gravel

4-in. perforated drainpipe

8 in. min.

Wall finish

Vapor retarder

Cavity insulation

Finish floor

Subfloor

Foam backer rod seals edges

Foil tape seals foam edge

$1/2$-in. anchor bolts at 6 ft. o.c.

Foil-faced foam fire-rated for interior use

Optional 3-in. slab with welded-wire mesh

Optional EXP foam

Existing slab

2-in. weep holes at 8 ft. o.c.

#4 reinforcing rod

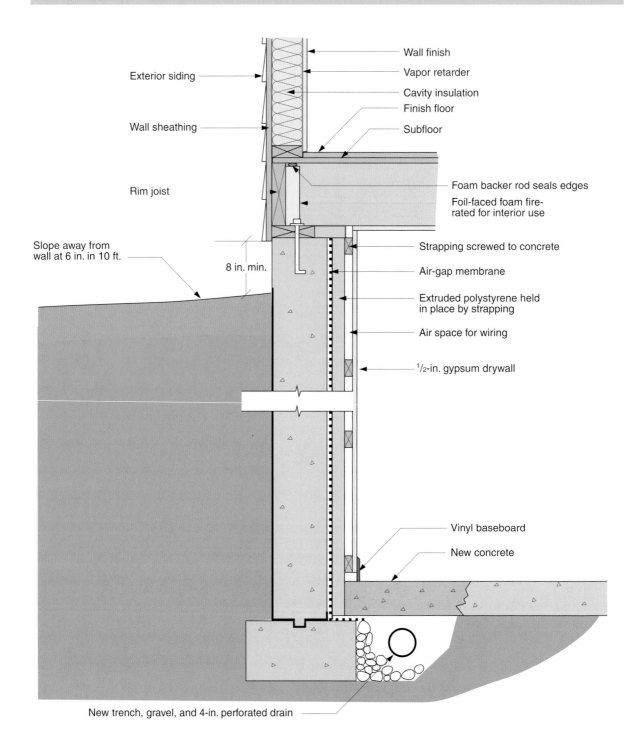

Wall finish

Exterior siding

Vapor retarder

Cavity insulation

Finish floor

Wall sheathing

Subfloor

Rim joist

Foam backer rod seals edges

Foil-faced foam fire-rated for interior use

Slope away from wall at 6 in. in 10 ft.

8 in. min.

Strapping screwed to concrete

Air-gap membrane

Extruded polystyrene held in place by strapping

Air space for wiring

$1/2$-in. gypsum drywall

Vinyl baseboard

New concrete

New trench, gravel, and 4-in. perforated drain

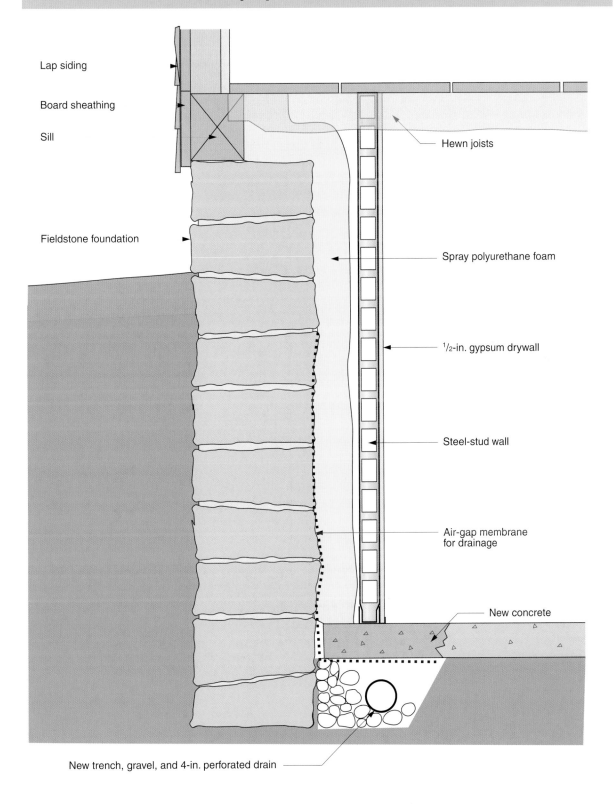

Lap siding

Board sheathing

Sill

Fieldstone foundation

Hewn joists

Spray polyurethane foam

1/2-in. gypsum drywall

Steel-stud wall

Air-gap membrane for drainage

New concrete

New trench, gravel, and 4-in. perforated drain

Concrete Wall Retrofit with Interior Spray Foam and Finished Wall

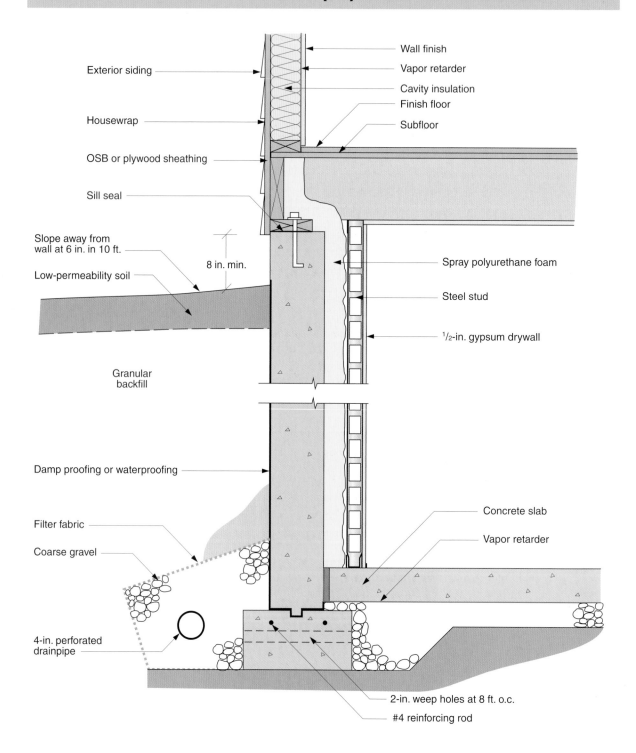

Exterior siding

Housewrap

OSB or plywood sheathing

Sill seal

Slope away from wall at 6 in. in 10 ft.

Low-permeability soil

8 in. min.

Granular backfill

Damp proofing or waterproofing

Filter fabric

Coarse gravel

4-in. perforated drainpipe

Wall finish

Vapor retarder

Cavity insulation

Finish floor

Subfloor

Spray polyurethane foam

Steel stud

$1/2$-in. gypsum drywall

Concrete slab

Vapor retarder

2-in. weep holes at 8 ft. o.c.

#4 reinforcing rod

10

Windows and Exterior Doors

Every year Americans spend roughly 30 billion dollars on windows. That's $30 followed by nine zeros! Of the estimated 46,000,000 windows sold in 2013, 29,000,000 were replacement units. Were those replacements justified? The purpose of this chapter is to explain the new window technologies and to present all of your options so you can make informed decisions.

We begin by examining the old technology—*windows with clear glazings*. The primary performance criteria are: *thermal conductance (U), visible transmittance (VT)*, and *solar heat gain coefficient (SHGC)*. We show how to read *window energy performance labels* to make sure you know what you are getting.

Then we examine the new technologies—*low-E windows*. You will find that it is not simply a question of clear glazing versus low-E. Different versions of low-E are suited to different regions of the country, so we include a section on *matching low-E windows to climate*.

The second half of this chapter considers the second option—*improving existing windows*. You don't hear much about this underappreciated option because it costs so little, and it can be done by the homeowner.

Adding or replacing *weatherstripping* can make your old windows nearly as airtight as new. And instead of buying new triple- or quadruple-glazed replacement windows, you can achieve the same performance by *adding glazings*. We give detailed instructions for making your own *shrink-wrapped insert panels* and *screen-splined insert panels*.

Most of this chapter is spent on windows because there are so many of them. We do cover *exterior doors*, however. Doors rarely require replacing, but *weatherstripping exterior doors* is an extremely cost-effective option.

Windows with Clear Glazings

Window Types

The illustration below shows eight generic types of residential windows. Except for the way they open, all are the same in terms of energy performance.

Double-hung windows contain two sashes, both of which slide up and down. A variation is the single-hung window, in which the top sash is fixed.

Casement windows hinge to one side, which is specified when a unit is ordered. They are very effective at capturing breezes, provided they open toward the prevailing breeze.

Fixed windows are often used in conjunction with operable windows of other styles. Inexpensive "window walls" can be constructed of patio doors and site-built fixed windows utilizing patio door glazing units of the same size.

Awning windows are used for ventilation at low levels, such as in a sun space, or as high windows in bathrooms and kitchens.

Skylights, also known as roof windows, are extremely effective summer exhaust ventilators. They are also more effective in admitting natural daylight than are vertical windows of the same size.

Sliding windows are an inexpensive alternative for high windows in bathrooms and kitchens.

Bay windows add space to rooms (often with window seats) in addition to adding an architectural design feature. They most often are assembled from a center fixed unit and two double-hung or casement flankers.

Bow windows are more elegant expressions of the bay window. They are often assembled from fixed and casement units.

Common Residential Window Types

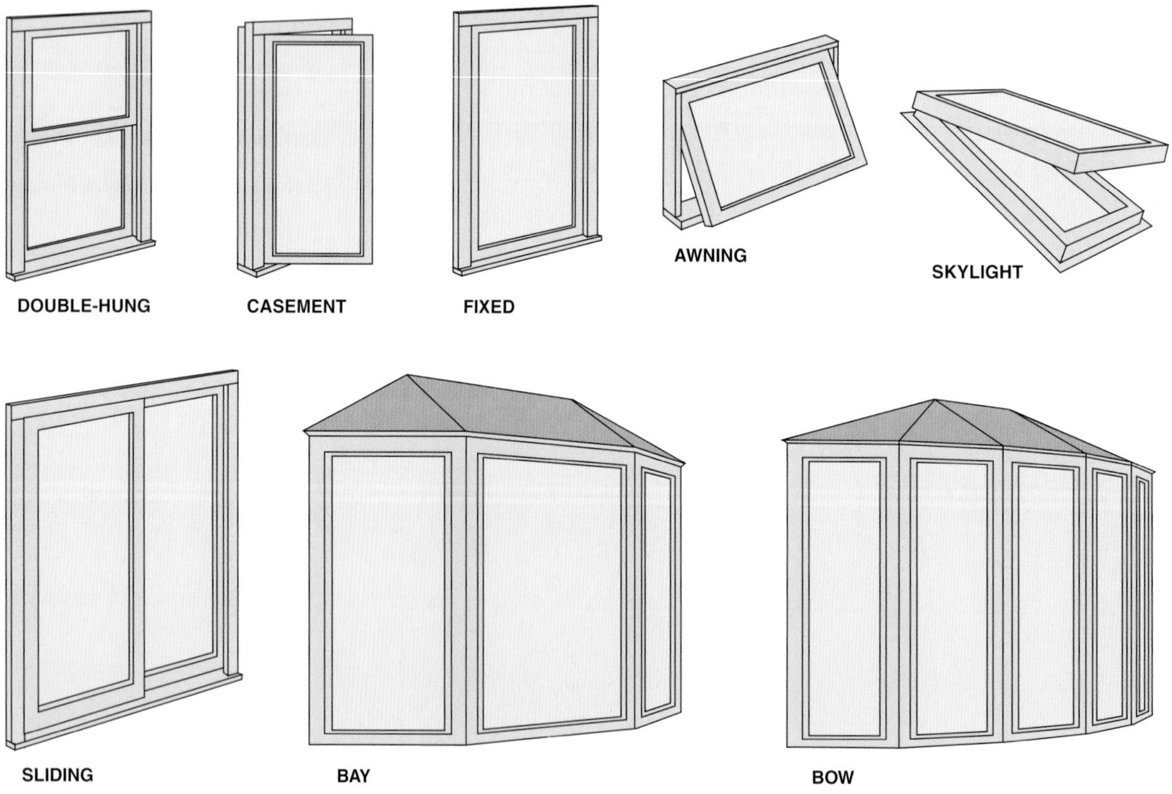

DOUBLE-HUNG   CASEMENT   FIXED   AWNING   SKYLIGHT

SLIDING   BAY   BOW

Anatomy of a Typical Older Double-Hung Window

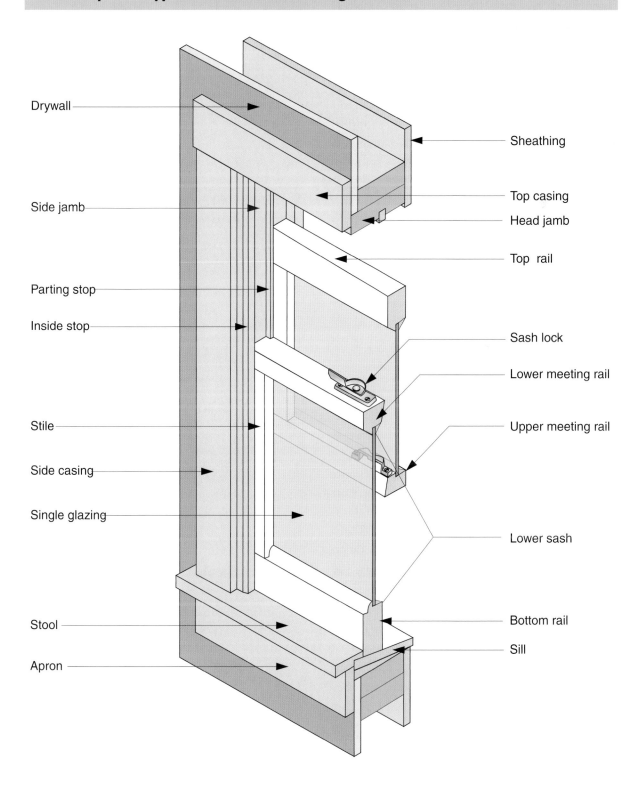

Drywall

Side jamb

Parting stop

Inside stop

Stile

Side casing

Single glazing

Stool

Apron

Sheathing

Top casing

Head jamb

Top rail

Sash lock

Lower meeting rail

Upper meeting rail

Lower sash

Bottom rail

Sill

Thermal Conductance (U)

Engineers and physicists calculate heat transmission through a solid material using the material's thermal conductivity, k, which is independent of the material's thickness. The material's thermal conductance, U, takes into account the material's thickness.

Unless schooled in physics—and perhaps even then—most people find the concept of thermal resistance, R, more intuitive. That is the reason all insulation materials are labeled with their R-values. R is simply 1/U.

Windows = Glass + Air

The total R-value of an assembly of materials is simply the sum of the R-values of the component parts. Therefore, to calculate the total R-value of the glazed portion of a window we need nothing more than the R-values of the glass pane and the various associated layers of air.

Regardless of the number of glazings, we need just four R-values:

- Outside air film, 0.17 in a 15 mph wind
- Trapped air space, 1.07 for a ½-in. space
- Inside, unmoving air film, 0.68
- Glass pane, 0.06 for ¼-in. glass

As the illustration at right demonstrates, most of a window's R-value comes from the thermal resistance of dead (unmoving) air. The glass panes contribute only about 6% to the total. Thus, neither the thickness of the glass, nor whether the glazing is instead a thin clear sheet of plastic, makes a significant difference. For air space thicknesses of ½ in. to 4 in., you would not be far off in assuming:

Total R = 1.0 × number of glazings

Note, however, that while the R-value of a ½-in. air space is 1.07, the R-value of a ¼-in. air space is only 0.72, a difference of 0.35. In a quadruple-glazed window, the difference in total R-value between ¼-in. and ½-in. spacings amounts to R-1.05. Thin may be more attractive, but in the case of windows, it will cost you.

R- and U-Factors for Clear Glazings

SINGLE GLAZING

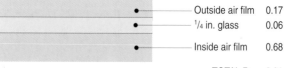

Outside air film	0.17
¼ in. glass	0.06
Inside air film	0.68

TOTAL R = 0.91
U = 1/R = 1.10

DOUBLE GLAZING

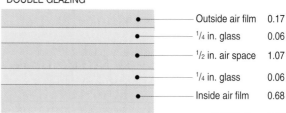

Outside air film	0.17
¼ in. glass	0.06
½ in. air space	1.07
¼ in. glass	0.06
Inside air film	0.68

TOTAL R = 2.04
U = 1/R = 0.49

TRIPLE GLAZING

Outside air film	0.17
¼ in. glass	0.06
½ in. air space	1.07
¼ in. glass	0.06
½ in. air space	1.07
¼ in. glass	0.06
Inside air film	0.68

TOTAL R = 3.17
U = 1/R = 0.32

QUADRUPLE GLAZING

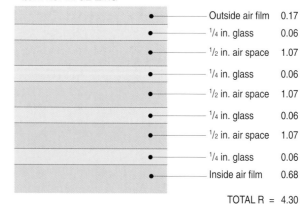

Outside air film	0.17
¼ in. glass	0.06
½ in. air space	1.07
¼ in. glass	0.06
½ in. air space	1.07
¼ in. glass	0.06
½ in. air space	1.07
¼ in. glass	0.06
Inside air film	0.68

TOTAL R = 4.30
U = 1/R = 0.23

Visible Transmittance (VT)

Visible transmittance (VT) is defined as the fraction of energy in the visible portion of the spectrum that passes through an object.

The graph below shows the intensity (vertical scale on left) vs. wavelength (horizontal scale on bottom) of solar radiation received at the earth's surface. The entire spectrum contains three wavelength bands, from left to right:

- Ultraviolet (UV), 10–400 nanometers
- Visible, 400–700 nanometers
- Infrared (IR), 700 nanometers–1 millimeter

Clearly, the human eye has evolved to respond to the visible (daylight) portion of the spectrum.

Superimposed are plots of spectral transmittance (vertical scale on right) of 1, 2, 3, and 4 clear glazings. Visible transmittance is that portion (highlighted in red) of spectral transmittance in the visible range. As the graph shows, the visible transmittance of a single clear glazing averages 0.90. The visible transmittance of multiple glazings is easily calculated as:

$$VT_n = (VT_1)^n$$

where:

VT_1 = visible transmittance of a single glazing
n = number of glazings

Example: What is the VT of a triple glazing where the VT of a single glazing is 0.90? By the formula:

$$VT_3 = (VT_1)^3 = (0.90)^3 = 0.73$$

Note that the VT of windows, as opposed to just the glazings, includes the frames holding the glazings. Thus, the VTs listed on NFRC Energy Performance Labels (see p. 231) range from 0.30 to 0.70.

Visible Transmittances of 1, 2, 3, and 4 Clear Glazings

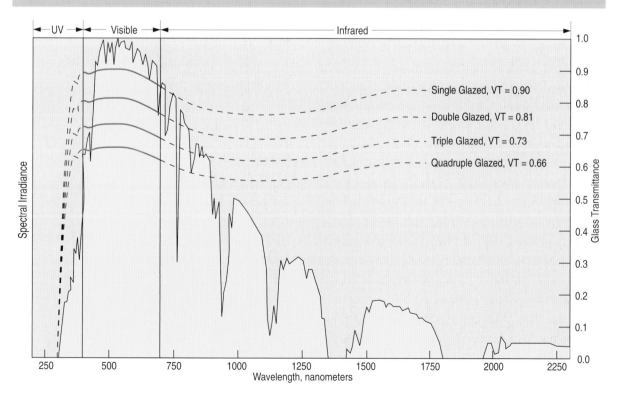

Solar Heat Gain Coefficient (SHGC)

Seasonal Paths of the Sun

No wonder the ancients believed the sun revolved about the earth. Standing facing the sun, there is no evidence that we are, in fact, rotating about the earth's center at nearly 1,000 mph while revolving about the sun at 64,000 mph. What seems "apparent" is the path of the sun through the sky, rising to our east, passing due south at noon, and setting to our west.

Over the course of a year, particularly for those living in northern climates, it is also apparent that the sun climbs to nearly overhead at noon in summer but barely above the horizon in winter. The ancient Greeks and Pueblo Indians utilized this apparent motion of the sun in their architecture, capturing free heat from the sun in winter and rejecting its unwanted heat in summer.

In the following pages, we will show how to manage your home's built-in solar collectors (windows) to lower both your heating and cooling bills.

Clear-Sky Solar Radiation on Windows Facing N, S, E, and W

Solar collectors are designed to collect heat from the sun, but ordinary south-facing windows can collect as much energy during the peak heating season as slanted rooftop collectors.

Unfortunately, the same cannot be said of windows facing north, east, or west. The graph at right shows the solar radiation striking windows on clear days at 40°N latitude. Note that in winter, south-facing windows receive three times as much energy as those facing east or west and ten times as much as those facing north. The reason is in the angles. First, the sun spends most of the day to the south of a house. Second, in winter, the sun is lower in the sky, so its rays strike vertical windows more nearly at a right angle.

Solar radiation received on windows facing N, S, E, and W on December 21 and June 21 at 25°, 30°, 35°, 40°, 45°, and 50° North latitude is shown in the graphs on pp. 34–35.

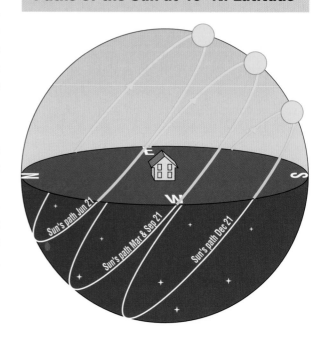

Paths of the Sun at 40° N. Latitude

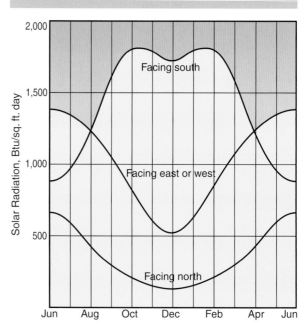

Vertical Surface Radiation at 40° N

Solar Heat Gain Coefficient (SHGC) is defined as the fraction of total solar radiation received at the surface of the earth that passes through an object, in this case a window. As with visible transmittance, VT, the value of SHGC may refer to just that of the glazing, or it may include the entire area of the window unit, including the frame.

The graph below is the same as that on p. 227, except here the four superimposed red curves are for SHGC instead of VT. Note that the whole length of the curves is now highlighted in red because here we are measuring the transmission of energy across the entire solar spectrum, not just the visible portion.

Calculation of SHGC for multiple glazings is not quite as simple as that for VT because it consists of the sum of two parts:

1. The fraction of radiation that directly passes through the glazing, the *primary transmittance*, and

2. The fraction of radiation absorbed in the window, the *secondary transmittance*.

As with the visible transmittance curves on p. 227, the curves and SHGC values shown below for 1, 2, 3, and 4 glazings are for the glazings alone and do not include the frames holding the glazings.

The SHGCs listed on NFRC Energy Performance Labels (see p. 231) are for entire window units, including frames, and range from 0.25 to 0.60.

Solar Heat Gain Coefficients of 1, 2, 3, and 4 Clear Glazings

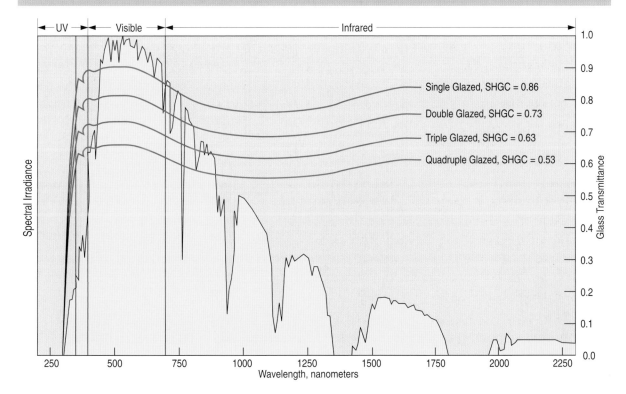

Window Energy Performance Labels

In the previous four pages we have defined and discussed three glazing performance factors: thermal conductance (U), visible transmittance (VT), and solar heat gain coefficient (SHGC). To give you a better feel for how these factors relate to the number of glazings in a window unit, we have illustrated four window types below, all containing clear glass:

- Single glazed
- Double glazed
- Triple glazed
- Quadruple glazed

On the facing page we describe the National Fenestration Research Council (NFRC) Energy Performance Labels found on all Energy Star-listed windows. The Energy Performance Labels list the certified, tested values of U, VT, and SHGC for the window unit as a whole, not just the glazings. In addition, the labels list an air-leakage factor, which indicates the window unit's rate of infiltration under test conditions.

Note that U, VT, and SHGC values for non-clear glass windows (reflective, tinted, and low-E windows) can be quite different (see p. 235).

Three Window Performance Factors for 1, 2, 3, and 4 Clear Glazings

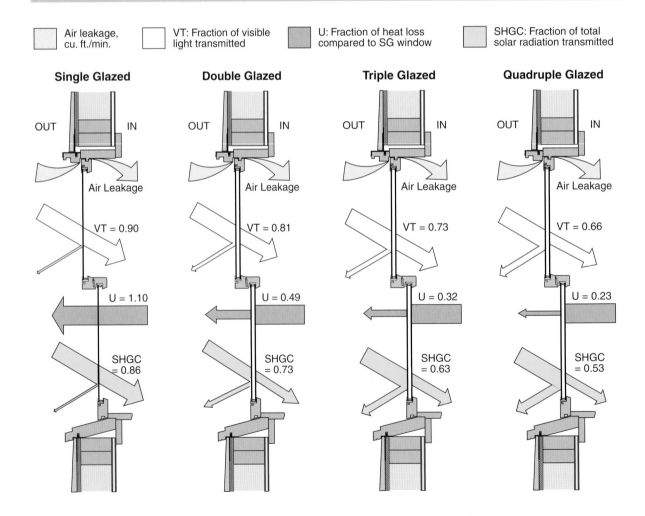

| Air leakage, cu. ft./min. | VT: Fraction of visible light transmitted | U: Fraction of heat loss compared to SG window | SHGC: Fraction of total solar radiation transmitted |

Single Glazed
OUT — IN
Air Leakage
VT = 0.90
U = 1.10
SHGC = 0.86

Double Glazed
OUT — IN
Air Leakage
VT = 0.81
U = 0.49
SHGC = 0.73

Triple Glazed
OUT — IN
Air Leakage
VT = 0.73
U = 0.32
SHGC = 0.63

Quadruple Glazed
OUT — IN
Air Leakage
VT = 0.66
U = 0.23
SHGC = 0.53

The National Fenestration Research Council (NFRC) is a non-profit public/private collaboration of manufacturers, builders, designers, specifiers, code officials, consumers, utilities, and regulators that has established a national energy performance rating system for fenestration products. The NFRC system rates a fenestration product's U-factor, solar heat gain coefficient, visible light transmittance, and air leakage, which can be used to determine whether a product meets an energy code.

NFRC labels can be found on all Energy Star window, door, and skylight products, but Energy Star bases its qualification only on U-factor and SHGC ratings.

Performance Factors

Windows, doors, and skylights gain and lose heat in the following ways:

- Conduction through the glazing and frame
- Radiation from outside (typically from the sun) and from inside from room-temperature objects, such as people, furniture, and interior walls
- Air leakage

These properties are measured and rated in the following energy performance characteristics:

U-Factor The rate at which the unit conducts non-solar heat flow, in Btu/hr.-sq. ft.-°F. For windows, skylights, and glass doors, a U-factor may refer to just the glazing alone. But National Fenestration Rating Council U-factor ratings represent the entire window performance, including frame and spacer material. The lower the U-factor, the more energy-efficient the window, door, or skylights.

Solar Heat Gain Coefficient (SHGC) The fraction of solar radiation admitted through the unit—either directly and/or absorbed, and subsequently released as heat inside a home. The lower the SHGC, the less solar heat it transmits and the greater its shading ability. Units with high SHGC ratings are more efficient at collecting solar heat gain during the

winter. Units with low SHGC ratings are more effective at reducing cooling loads during the summer by blocking heat gained from the sun. The target SHGC should therefore be determined by factors including climate, orientation, and external shading.

Visible Transmittance (VT) The fraction of the visible spectrum of sunlight (380 to 720 nanometers), weighted by the sensitivity of the human eye, transmitted through a unit's glazing. Units with higher VT transmit more visible light. The target VT should be determined by daylighting and interior glare requirements.

Air Leakage The rate of air infiltration around or through a unit subjected to a specific pressure difference, in units of cubic feet per minute per square foot of frame area (cfm/sq. ft.).

Low-E Windows

Emissivity, e, is the relative ability of a surface to emit radiant energy. It is the ratio of energy radiated to the energy radiated by a black body at the same temperature. By definition, the e of a black body is 1. Generally, the duller and darker a material, the closer its emissivity is to 1. The more reflective a material, the closer its emissivity is to 0. Highly polished metals such as gold, silver, and aluminum foil have emissivities of about 0.03. The emissivity of ordinary glass is 0.93.

The opposite of emissivity is reflectivity, the relative ability of a surface to reflect, or reject, radiant energy. It is the ratio of energy reflected to the energy reflected by a black body at the same temperature. By definition, the reflectivity of a black body is 0. The relationship between emissivity and reflectivity is simple: *reflectivity = 1 − emissivity*. Thus, the reflectivity of polished aluminum foil is 0.97, while the reflectivity of ordinary glass is 0.07.

How do emissivity and reflectivity relate to windows? Although our eyes detect the visible portion of solar radiation, a substantial portion of the sun's radiation lies beyond detection in the infrared (see illustrations below and on the facing page). In terms of heat loss in winter, a large portion of the heat flow from inside to outside is in the form of infrared radiation. In fact, most of the heat loss through multilayer windows occurs as infrared radiation from warmer to cooler glass surfaces. If we could lower the emissivity (thus raising the reflectivity) of glass in just the infrared region, we could have a window that still transmits a high percentage of visible radiation but blocks much of the infrared (thermal) radiation. In terms of window performance parameters, we would be retaining a high VT while lowering U and SHGC.

Lowering the emissivity of glass is achieved by depositing on its surface invisible, microscopic layers of certain metals and metal oxides. As graphed in the lower illustration on the facing page, different types of low-E coatings result in high solar gain (orange curve), moderate solar gain (green), and low solar gain (blue).

High-solar gain windows perform better in heating climates, particularly in solar-tempered designs, because the solar gain reduces the heating bill.

Low-solar gain windows perform better in cooling climates because there any solar gain increases cooling bills.

A guide to selecting the appropriate low-E windows for your climate follows on pp. 234–242. All of the data have been derived and adapted from the website of the Efficient Windows Collaborative: *www.efficientwindows.org.*

The Electromagnetic Spectrum

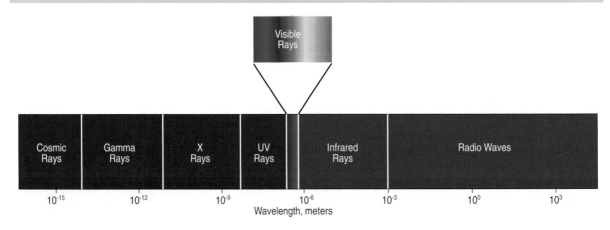

Ideal Spectral Transmittances for Hot and Cold Climate Glazings

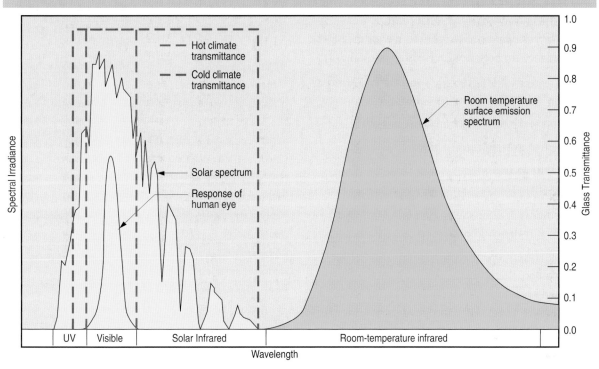

Actual Spectral Transmittances for Low-E Glazings

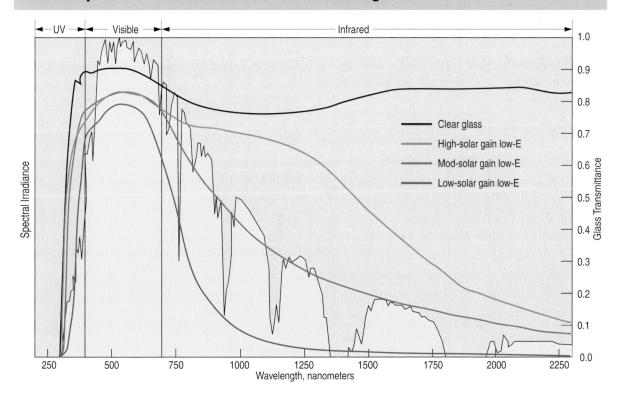

Matching Low-E Windows to Climate

As mentioned on p. 232, different climates (heating, cooling, and mixed) call for different window types. The Efficient Windows Collaborative website—*www.efficientwindows.org*—contains window selection guidance for both new and existing buildings.

Of greatest value is the site's interactive Window Selection Tool. The tool allows you to select:

- One of 219 US and Canadian cities
- New or existing construction
- Windows or skylights
- Type of glass (including all types)
- Window frame (metal or non-metal, with or without thermal breaks)

Using current energy prices from its database, the Selection Tool calculates the estimated annual heating and cooling bills for each window type, assuming either a typical new house (2,250 sq. ft.) or a typical existing house (2,150 sq. ft.), 15% window-to-floor areas equally distributed on all four sides, and typical shading (interior shades, overhangs, trees, and neighboring buildings). The U-factor and SHGC for each window type are for the entire window, including the frame.

For the purpose of this handbook, we present the results obtained by running the Selection Tool for forty cities (see table at right) and eight window types (see the **bold** window numbers in the table on the facing page).

To select windows for a project, find the city in the table at right whose cooling degree hours (CDH) and heating degree days (HDD) most closely match those for your project's location. Then find the bar graph results for that city on pp. 236–242. The heights of the bar graphs show the annual heating bills (red bars) and annual cooling bills (blue bars) for each of the eight bold-numbered window types listed in the table on the facing page. Compare the total heating plus cooling bills of the different window types to find the most efficient type for your climate.

For an even more comprehensive comparison, go to the website and run your own analysis.

Window Cities and Climate

State, City	DMT	CDH	HDD
Alabama, Birmingham	21	21,000	2,900
Alaska, Fairbanks	-47	0	14,000
Arizona, Phoenix	34	55,000	1,400
Arkansas, Little Rock	20	23,800	3,200
California, Los Angeles	43	10,600	1,200
Colorado, Denver	1	5,900	6,000
Connecticut, Hartford	7	4,800	6,200
Delaware, Wilmington	14	8,200	5,000
DC, Washington	17	12,400	4,200
Florida, Miami	47	39,000	200
Georgia, Atlanta	22	16,800	3,000
Idaho, Boise	10	8,000	5,800
Illinois, Chicago	0	9,700	6,200
Indiana, Indianapolis	2	9,100	5,700
Iowa, Des Moines	-5	10,500	6,600
Kentucky, Louisville	10	13,300	4,500
Maine, Portland	-1	1,100	7,500
Maryland, Baltimore	13	9,500	4,700
Massachusetts, Boston	9	5,400	5,600
Michigan, Detroit	6	4,900	6,600
Minnesota, Duluth	-16	800	9,900
Mississippi, Jackson	25	25,200	2,400
Missouri, St. Louis	6	17,800	4,900
Montana, Great Falls	-15	3,600	7,800
Nevada, Las Vegas	28	43,000	2,500
New Hampshire, Concord	-3	2,000	7,400
New Mexico, Albuquerque	16	11,000	4,400
New York, New York	15	9,500	4,900
North Dakota, Bismarck	-19	4,600	9,100
Oklahoma, Tulsa	13	26,500	3,700
Pennsylvania, Pittsburgh	5	5,000	6,000
Rhode Island, Providence	9	3,600	5,900
Tennessee, Nashville	14	18,500	3,800
Texas, Houston	33	30,500	1,500
Utah, Salt Lake City	8	9,900	5,800
Vermont, Burlington	-7	2,600	8,000
Virginia, Richmond	17	12,300	4,000
Washington, Seattle	26	1,000	5,100
West Virginia, Charleston	11	8,800	4,700
Wisconsin, Madison	-7	3,300	7,600

Window Characteristics

Window #	Glazings	Tint	Coating	Ar/Kr Gas?	Frame	U-value	SHGC	VT
1	Single	Clear	None	No	Metal	≥1.00	≥.60	≥.60
2	Single	Tinted	None	No	Metal	≥1.00	≥.60	≥.60
3	Double	Clear	None	No	Metal	.71–.99	≥.60	≥.60
4	Double	Tinted	None	No	Metal	.71–.99	.41–.60	.51–.60
5	Double	Hi-Perf. Tint	None	No	Metal	.71–.99	.41–.60	.51–.60
6	Double	Clear	HSG Low-E	Yes	Metal	.56–.70	≥0.60	≥0.60
7	Double	Clear	MSG Low-E	Yes	Metal	.56-.70	.26-.40	.51-.60
8	Double	Clear	LSG Low-E	Yes	Metal	.56-.70	≤.25	.51-.60
9	Double	Clear	None	No	Metal/TB	.56-.70	>.60	>.60
10	Double	Tinted	None	No	Metal/TB	.56-.70	.41-.60	.41-.50
11	Double	Hi-Perf. Tint	None	No	Metal/TB	.56-.70	.41-.60	.51-.60
12	Double	Clear	HSG Low-E	Yes	Metal/TB	.41-.50	.41-.60	.51-.60
13	Double	Clear	MSG Low-E	Yes	Metal/TB	.41-.55	.26-.40	.51-.60
14	Double	Clear	LSG Low-E	Yes	Metal/TB	.41-.55	≤.25	.51-.60
15	Single	Clear	None	No	Non-metal	.71-.99	≥.61	≥.60
16	Single	Tinted	None	No	Non-metal	.71-.99	.41-.60	.41-.50
17	Double	Clear	None	No	Non-metal	.41-.55	.41-.60	.51-.60
18	Double	Tinted	None	No	Non-metal	.41-.55	.41-.60	≤.40
19	Double	Hi-Perf. Tint	None	No	Non-metal	.41-.50	.26-.40	.41-.50
20	Double	Clear	HSG Low-E	Yes	Non-metal	.31-.40	.41-.60	.51-.60
21	Double	Clear	MSG Low-E	Yes	Non-metal	.31-.40	.26-.40	.51-.60
22	Double	Clear	LSG Low-E	Yes	Non-metal	.31-.40	≤.25	.41-.50
23	Triple	Clear	MSG Low-E	Yes	Non-metal	.21-.25	.26-.40	.41-.50
24	Triple	Clear	LSG Low-E	Yes	Non-metal	.21-.25	≤.25	≤.40
25	Double	Clear	HSG Low-E	Yes	Non-metal, TI	.26-.30	.41-.60	.51-.60
26	Double	Clear	MSG Low-E	Yes	Non-metal, TI	.26-.30	.26-.40	.51-.60
27	Double	Clear	LSG Low-E	Yes	Non-metal, TI	.26-.30	≤.25	.41-.50
28	Triple	Clear	MSG Low-E	Yes	Non-metal, TI	≤.20	.26-.40	.41-.50
29	Triple	Clear	LSG Low-E	Yes	Non-metal, TI	≤.20	≤.25	≤.40

KEY:

Ar/Kr = Argon/Krypton gas fill

HSG = High Solar Gain

LSG = Low Solar Gain

MSG = Medium Solar Gain

TB = Thermal Break

TI = Thermally Improved

The following seven pages show the results of running the Efficient Windows Collaborative Window Selection Tool for forty US cities. The bar heights indicate the annual heating (red) and cooling (blue) bills for typical new 2,250-sq. ft. homes where all of the windows are of one of eight types. The numbered window types are those shown in **bold** numbers in the table on p. 235.

The heating and cooling dollar figures reflect the fuel prices current at the time of the analysis, 2013. The true value of the analysis, however, lies in the relative costs rather than the absolute costs. For the most up-to-date results, go to the website: *www.efficientwindows.org.*

Example: Your site has a climate similar to that of Hartford, CT. According to the bar graph for Hartford, most of the annual heating plus cooling bill is due to heating. Your question is how much you might save by installing triple-glazed with nonmetallic frame, moderate-solar-gain low-E windows (window type 28) versus double-glazed with nonmetallic frame, high-solar-gain low-E windows (window type 20).

The total heating and cooling bills for windows #28 and #20 are $720 and $850, respectively, so the savings would be $130 per year. Without allowing for inflation, the 30-year saving would total approximately $3,900.

Birmingham, Alabama

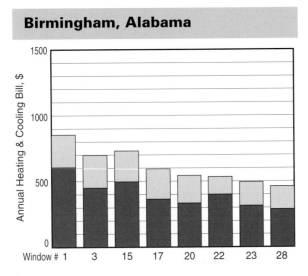

Fairbanks, Alaska

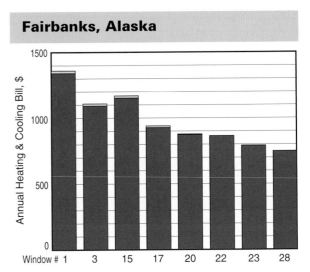

Phoenix, Arizona

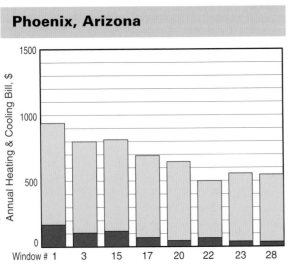

Little Rock, Arkansas

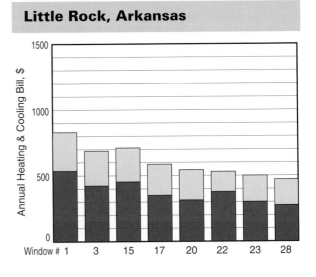

Los Angeles, California

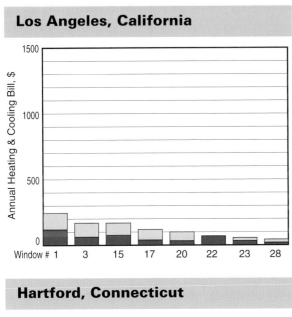

Denver, Colorado

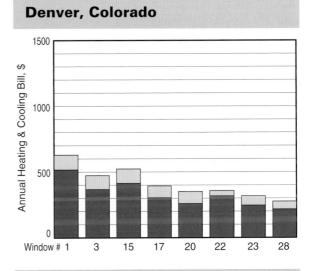

Hartford, Connecticut

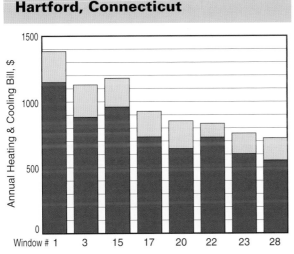

Wilmington, Delaware

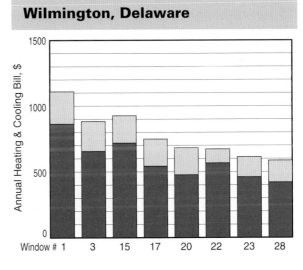

Washington, DC

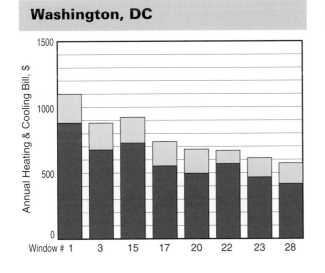

Miami, Florida

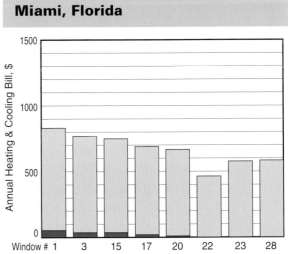

Atlanta, Georgia

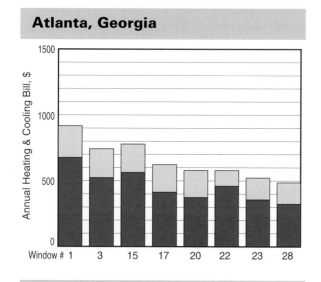

Boise, Idaho

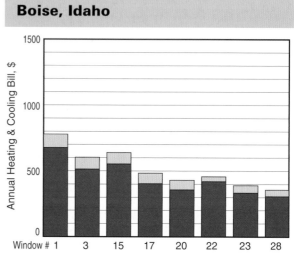

Chicago, Illinois

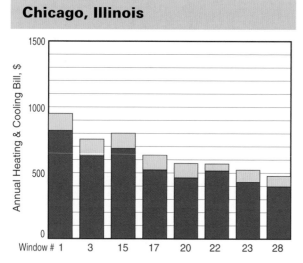

Indianapolis, Indiana

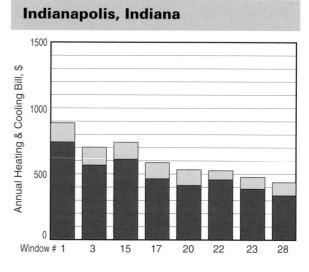

Des Moines, Iowa

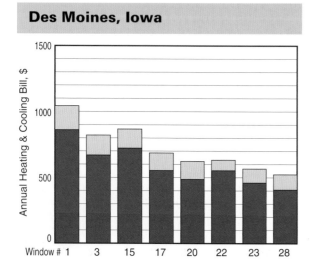

Louisville, Kentucky

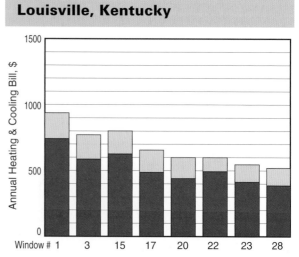

Portland, Maine

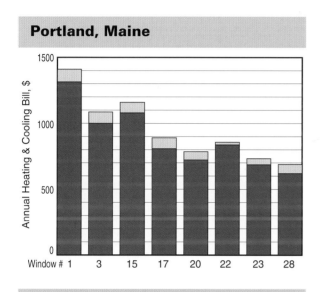

Baltimore, Maryland

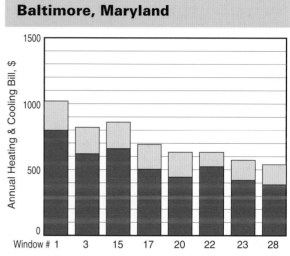

Boston, Massachusetts

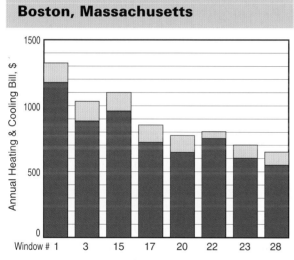

Detroit, Michigan

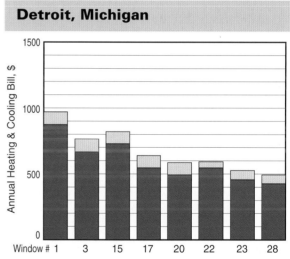

Duluth, Minnesota

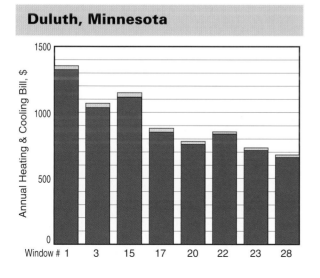

Jackson, Mississippi

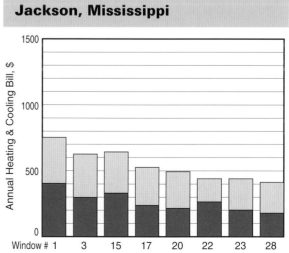

St. Louis, Missouri

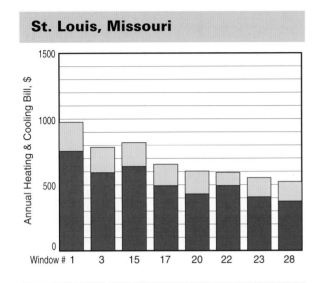

Great Falls, Montana

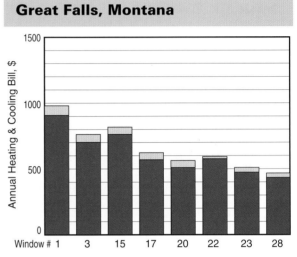

Las Vegas, Nevada

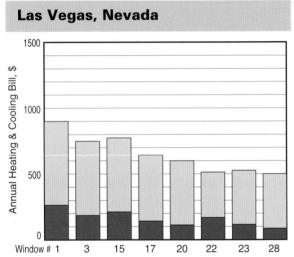

Concord, New Hampshire

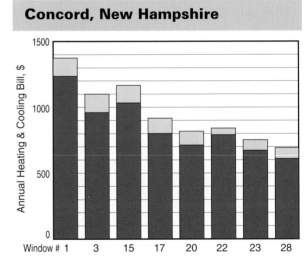

Albuquerque, New Mexico

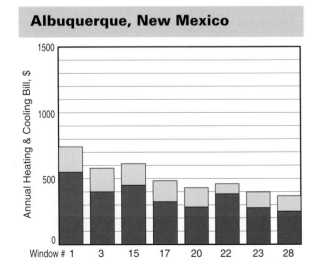

New York, New York

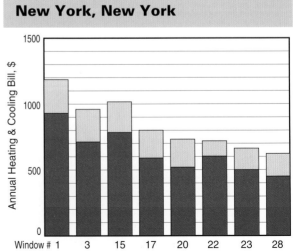

Bismarck, North Dakota

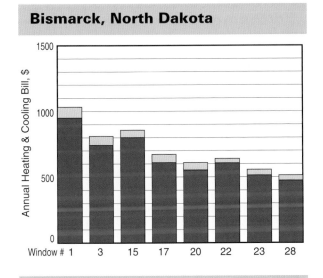

Tulsa, Oklahoma

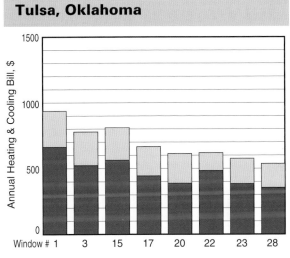

Pittsburgh, Pennsylvania

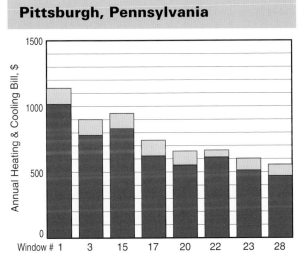

Providence, Rhode Island

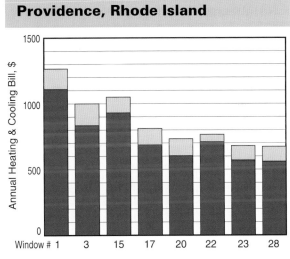

Nashville, Tennessee

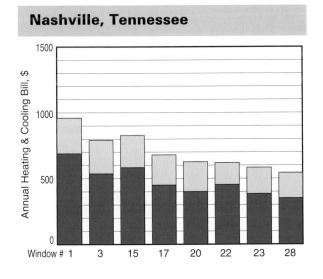

Houston, Texas

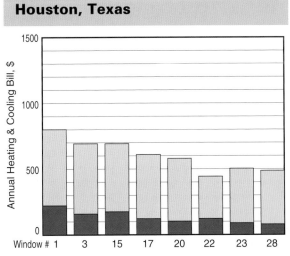

Salt Lake City, Utah

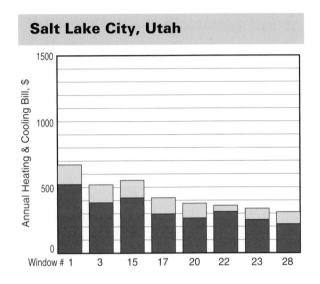

Burlington, Vermont

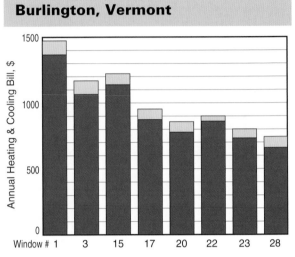

Richmond, Virginia

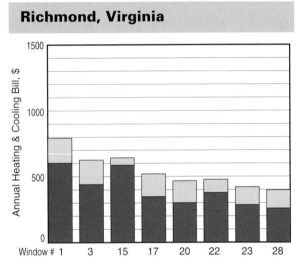

Seattle, Washington

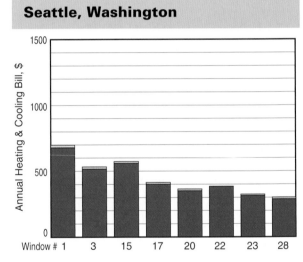

Charleston, West Virginia

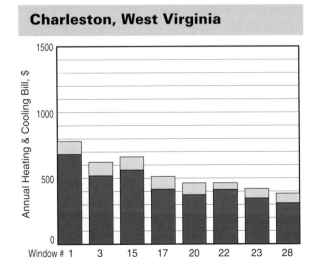

Madison, Wisconsin

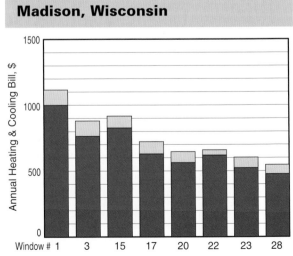

Improving Existing Windows

To listen to the commercials, you might think that replacing all of your existing windows would make your home cozy for the first time and cut your fuel bill in half. That might be true if your windows were missing entire panes or so loose in their frames they rattled in the slightest breeze. The truth, however, is that the typical new vinyl- or wood-framed, double-glazed window is no more energy efficient than a properly maintained, single-glazed wood window with an old-fashioned wood storm window.

Maintaining

The key, of course, is in the meaning of "properly maintained." By that we mean solid wood frames, glass properly sealed in place with glazing compound, functioning sash locks, and air-tight weatherstripping.

Solid Wood Frames are the norm in windows more than 40 years old because the wood used was denser and more weather resistant than the tree-farmed woods used today. If there is minor rot, it can be solidified by injecting it with a marine-grade epoxy such as West System® epoxy.

Glazing Compound is easily removed with a little heat and an inexpensive 5-function painter's tool. Replacing the compound has never been easier with the new latex compounds.

Sash Locks can be found at any home center or hardware store. Chances are good that, even if they no longer lock, they are not broken; they just need adjusting. Remove the mounting screws and insert a wood or cardboard shim of the required thickness under the half of the lock that needs adjusting. Replace the screws, and the lock will cinch the sashes together like new.

Air-Tight Weatherstripping can be installed without even removing sashes. Self-adhesive vinyl V-strip can be applied to all four edges of a window sash, as shown on pp. 244–247, and often makes a window as air-tight as new.

Adding Glazings

One of the reasons you may wish to replace your existing windows is to upgrade from single-glazed to double-glazed, or from double-glazed to triple-glazed. Realize that an existing single-glazed window plus storm window is, in fact, a double glazing. Better yet, an existing double-glazed window plus storm is, in fact, triple glazing.

Regardless of the number of glazings in your present window system, you can add simple, inexpensive, double-glazed window inserts, as illustrated in detail on pp. 248–269. Low-E glazings are not an option, but we present a thorough analysis of the relative costs and savings of upgrading with these low-cost do-it-yourself insert panels. They increase the R-value of your present windows by at least 2.0 and reduce air infiltration at the same time. If you have a handyperson bent and the most basic carpentry tools, give these panels a try. You will be amazed at their performance and cost-effectiveness.

Weatherstripping Windows

There is a simple test to see whether a window sash would benefit from weatherstripping. Open the sash and place a dollar bill between the sash and the frame. Close the sash and tighten the sash lock. If you can pull the dollar bill out easily, the window needs weatherstripping. Perform this test on all four edges of the sash.

Sash Channels

The illustration below shows V-strip weatherstripping in the sash channel. Self-adhesive polypropylene V-strip is perfect for the application because it compresses to $1/16$ in. and is slippery. To apply to the lower sash (the upper sash is analogous):

1. Raise the lower sash and clean the surface where the V-strip will be applied with detergent, followed by a fresh-water rinse. Let dry.

2. Measure the height of the sash and cut the V-strip about 1 in. longer.

3. Close the sash and push the strip down into the channel as far as it will go.

4. Staple the exposed strip top with a T-50 staple.

5. Raise the sash and peel the backing from the exposed length of strip.

6. Lower the sash. The pressure between the sash and frame will now adhere the strip to the channel.

Weatherstripping the Sash Channels

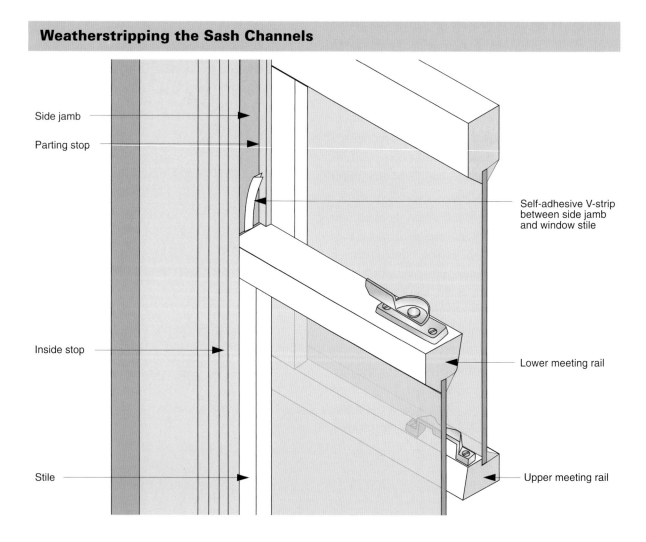

Side jamb

Parting stop

Self-adhesive V-strip between side jamb and window stile

Inside stop

Lower meeting rail

Stile

Upper meeting rail

Sash Top

Because the V-strip has a thickness, however small, it is important to apply the strip to the top and bottom of the window before addressing the middle parting rail. The small added heights may cause a misalignment of the two halves of the sash lock and necessitate shimming. Therefore, install the strips in the order presented here.

The top of the top rail is the simplest installation because it is totally accessible. To apply the strip:

1. Lower the upper sash and clean the top surface where the V-strip will be applied with detergent. Follow with a fresh-water rinse. Let dry.

2. Measure the width of the sash and cut the V-strip about ⅛ in. shorter.

3. Fold the V-strip and remove the self-adhesive protective backing.

4. Orient the strip with the V opening outward and press into place.

5. Raise the sash and engage the sash lock. The pressure from the sash lock will keep the V-strip folded and in place.

Weatherstripping the Top of the Upper Sash

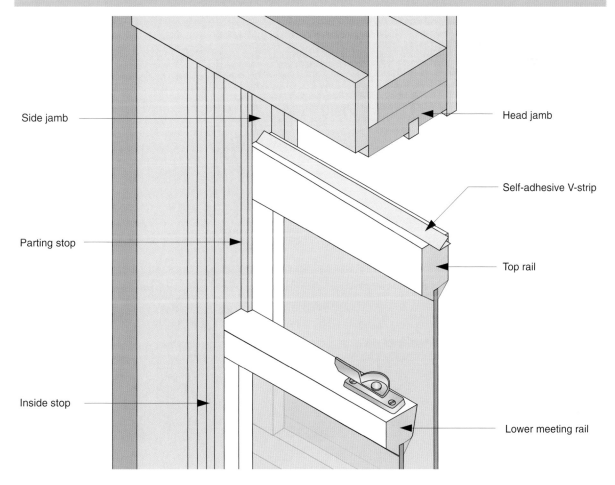

Side jamb

Head jamb

Self-adhesive V-strip

Parting stop

Top rail

Inside stop

Lower meeting rail

Sash Bottom

The bottom of the window where the lower sash meets the window sill is nearly as simple as the top. The only issue is whether to adhere the strip to the sash or to the sill. In the first case, you are fighting gravity, and the strip may eventually fall off unless fastened at each end with a heavy-duty T-50 staple. In the latter case, the strip is subject to more water and physical abuse. Installation on the sill is preferable because it can be seen.

To apply the strip to the sill, as shown:

1. Raise the lower sash and clean the sill with detergent. Follow with a fresh-water rinse. Let dry.

2. Measure the width of the sash and cut the V-strip about ⅛ in. shorter.

3. Fold the V-strip and remove the self-adhesive protective backing.

4. Orient the strip with the V opening outward and press into place. Adhering it close to, or actually touching, the edge of the stool makes it less visible and less susceptible to damage.

Weatherstripping the Lower Sash Bottom

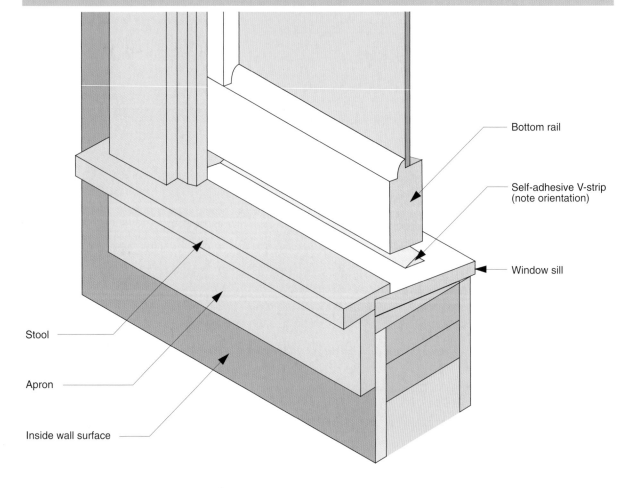

Bottom rail

Self-adhesive V-strip (note orientation)

Window sill

Stool

Apron

Inside wall surface

Meeting Rails

The two meeting rails (top of lower sash and bottom of upper sash) are beveled, so when they come together there should be a tight fit. Perform the dollar-bill test (see p. 244) with the sash lock fully engaged. If the window is old, chances are excellent that either: (1) you can't fully engage the lock, or (2) when locked, the joint is still loose.

If you can't fully engage the sash lock, the fixed half of the lock (the part at the bottom of the top sash) needs to be shimmed. Small pieces of shirt cardboard or matchbook covers are of convenient thickness and easy to cut. Remove the screws from the lock, insert shim(s), and replace the screws. Use longer screws if necessary.

To apply the weatherstripping:

1. Raise the bottom sash just enough to be able to reach the mating surface of the upper meeting rail.

2. Clean the surface where the V-strip will be applied with detergent, followed by a fresh-water rinse. Let dry.

3. Measure the width of the sash and cut the V-strip about ⅛ in. shorter.

4. Fold the V-strip and remove the self-adhesive strip.

5. Press the strip into place.

6. Lower the sash and engage the sash lock. The pressure from the sash lock will keep the V-strip from disengaging.

Weatherstripping the Meeting Rails

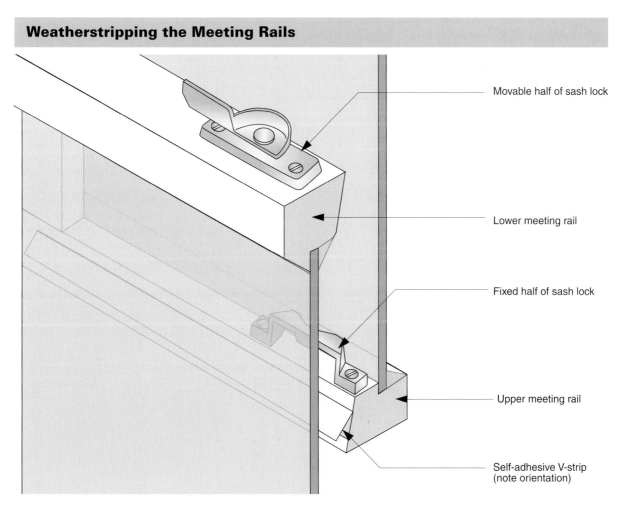

Movable half of sash lock

Lower meeting rail

Fixed half of sash lock

Upper meeting rail

Self-adhesive V-strip (note orientation)

Adding Glazings

Windows are unique thermal components in a building's envelope. While floors, walls, and roofs are designed to minimize conductive heat loss, windows serve the dual functions of retarding heat loss and admitting solar radiation.

All building surfaces, including windows, lose heat by conduction whenever the outside temperature is lower than the temperature inside. During the heating season that is pretty much 24 hours per day. On the other hand, windows admit significant solar radiation only while the sun is shining directly on them, that is, when the sky is clear and the sun is on the side of the house facing the sun.

In the illustration below, we are looking down on the roof of a house with single-glazed windows in Portland, Maine. The lighter half of the gray roof is the half facing south. The four walls face due north, east, south, and west. The light blue bars show the conductive heat loss per heating season per sq. ft. of single-glazed windows on each of the walls. All of the blue bars are the same height because the temperature differences between inside and outside are the same on all four sides of the house.

The yellow bars represent, to the same scale, the amount of *solar energy gained* per heating season per sq. ft. of window. The differences in height reflect the differences in solar intensity and duration due to the changing paths of the sun through the heating season.

The illustration at bottom right combines conductive losses and solar gains to find the net heat transfer. Blue indicates a net loss, that is, conductive loss exceeds solar gain. Red indicates a net gain in energy. In other words, while windows on the north, east, and west increase the building's fuel bill, windows facing south actually lower the annual fuel bill.

The bar graphs on the facing page illustrate what happens to the solar gains and conductive losses as we add more glazings.

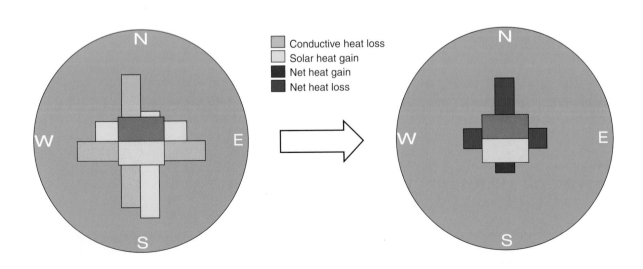

Orientation vs. Net Heat Gain/Loss of Single-Glazed Windows in Portland, ME

- Conductive heat loss
- Solar heat gain
- Net heat gain
- Net heat loss

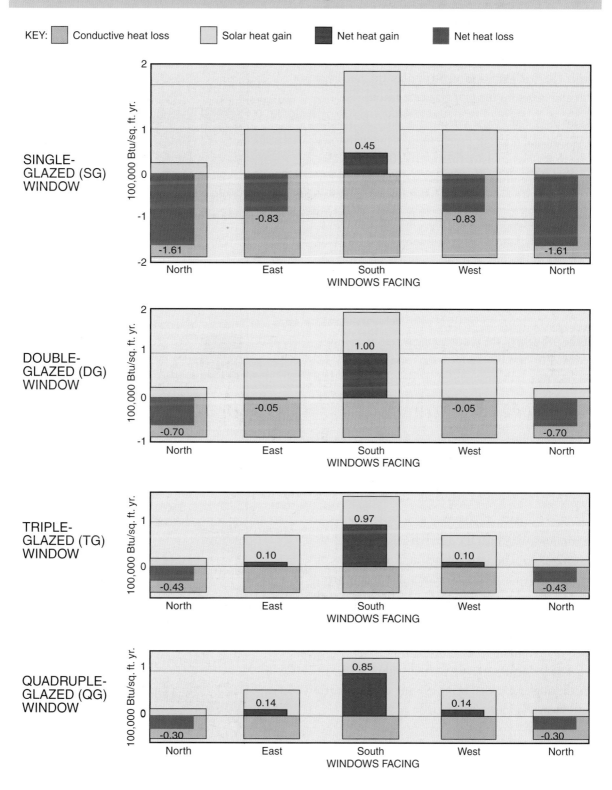

Orientation vs. Net Heat Gain/Loss of Single-Glazed Windows in Portland, ME

KEY: ☐ Conductive heat loss ☐ Solar heat gain ■ Net heat gain ■ Net heat loss

SINGLE-GLAZED (SG) WINDOW

100,000 Btu/sq. ft. yr.

North	East	South	West	North
-1.61	-0.83	0.45	-0.83	-1.61

WINDOWS FACING

DOUBLE-GLAZED (DG) WINDOW

100,000 Btu/sq. ft. yr.

North	East	South	West	North
-0.70	-0.05	1.00	-0.05	-0.70

WINDOWS FACING

TRIPLE-GLAZED (TG) WINDOW

100,000 Btu/sq. ft. yr.

North	East	South	West	North
-0.43	0.10	0.97	0.10	-0.43

WINDOWS FACING

QUADRUPLE-GLAZED (QG) WINDOW

100,000 Btu/sq. ft. yr.

North	East	South	West	North
-0.30	0.14	0.85	0.14	-0.30

WINDOWS FACING

Should You Add Glazings?

We saw on the previous page that south-facing, single-glazed windows—at least in Portland, Maine—gain more heat than they lose over the heating season. But what about double-, triple-, and quadruple-glazed windows? The bar graphs at right display the net heat gains and losses for the four glazing possibilities.

The top graph, *single-glazed*, quantifies the results we saw on the previous page. North-facing windows suffer a net loss of 1.61 therm (161,000 Btus) per sq. ft., while south-facing windows, due to high solar gain, enjoy a net gain of 0.45 therm per sq. ft.

Double-glazed windows reduce heat loss dramatically. Now the north-facing windows lose only 0.70 therm per sq. ft. net, and the south-facing windows reap a full 1.00 therm of free heat per sq. ft.

As you might expect, *triple-glazing* further decreases heat losses on north-, east-, and west-facing windows, but the net gain of the south-facing windows has now decreased from 1.00 therm to 0.97 therm per sq. ft. The decrease in heat loss is more than offset by the decrease in solar gain due to a reduction in the solar heat gain transmission by the third layer of glass.

The same trend continues for *quadruple-glazed* windows: reductions in both conductive heat losses and solar gains, with north, east, and west windows benefitting but south-facing windows suffering.

So here is the question: Should one retrofit existing windows with the DIY insert panels described on pp. 252–269? The insert panels add two layers of glazing, so if your present windows are single-glazed, compare the net gains of single- and triple-glazed windows. If they are already double-glazed, compare the results for double- and quadruple-glazed windows, and compute the annual savings. Generally, in heating climates, the payback is within a year or two, the single exception being existing double-glazed south-facing windows, which never pay back.

Net Energy Gains of Glazing Options

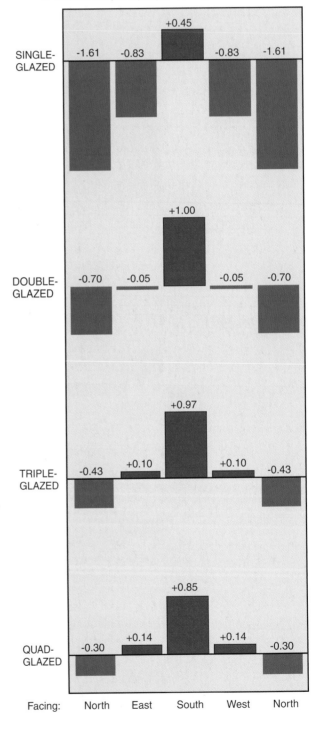

Net heat gain ■ or loss ■ of windows in Portland, ME, in 100,000 Btu per sq. ft. per heating season

SINGLE-GLAZED
-1.61 | -0.83 | +0.45 | -0.83 | -1.61

DOUBLE-GLAZED
-0.70 | -0.05 | +1.00 | -0.05 | -0.70

TRIPLE-GLAZED
-0.43 | +0.10 | +0.97 | +0.10 | -0.43

QUAD-GLAZED
-0.30 | +0.14 | +0.85 | +0.14 | -0.30

Facing: North | East | South | West | North

Calculating Years to Payback

To illustrate, we have calculated the years to payback for two common situations (insert panel over single-glazed windows and over double-glazed windows) and for two common fuels (natural gas and oil) in the same heating climate of Portland, Maine.

Payback with Natural Gas Heat

The first set of bar graphs at right is for natural gas priced at $1.33 per 100 cu. ft. or therm. The top row shows the years to pay back for panels installed over single-glazed windows. The row below shows the results for panels installed over double-glazed windows.

Example 1: How long would it take to pay back the cost of a panel installed over a single-glazed window facing east with gas heat? Looking at the top row (panel over SG window) in the Facing E column we find 3.2 years.

Example 2: How long would it take to pay back the cost of a panel installed over a double-glazed window facing north with gas heat? Looking at the lower row (panel over DG window) in the Facing N column we find 7.6 years.

Payback with Oil Heat

The bar graphs in the illustration at right are for oil heat priced at $3.70 per gallon. Again, the top row is for insert panels over single-glazed windows and the row below for panels installed over double-glazed windows.

Example 3: How long would it take to pay back the cost ($5.00/sq. ft. installed) of a panel over a double-glazed window facing south with oil heat? Looking at the lower row (panel over DG window) in the Facing S column we find "never pays back." Looking back at the graphs of net gains on the previous page we find the reason. The net gain of a double-glazed south-facing window actually decreases when the double-glazed panel converts the window to quadruple-glazing.

The costs of the panels, installed, are assumed to be $5.00 per square foot. Years to payback is calculated as the cost of the panel, divided by fuel cost per delivered therm, times the difference in net gains for the windows with and without panels.

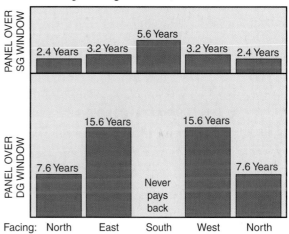

Panel Payback for Natural Gas Heat

Years to pay back $5.00/sq. ft. cost of panel assuming natural **gas heat** at $1.33/100 cu. ft.

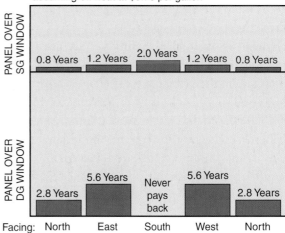

Panel Payback for Oil Heat

Years to pay back $5.00/sq. ft. cost of panel assuming **oil heat** at $3.70 per gallon

Measuring for Window Insert Panels

Determine Orientation

As we saw on p. 251, the decrease in conductive heat loss resulting from the addition of double-glazed panels over existing single- and double-glazed windows is so great the panels generally pay for themselves in a few heating seasons.

The single exception is south-facing double-glazed windows. Unshaded south-facing DG windows are "solar collectors," contributing the equivalent of a gallon of fuel oil or a therm of natural gas per sq. ft. per heating season. Adding two more glazings, however, decreases solar gain more than it does the conductive loss, so adding a south-facing panel would actually increase the fuel bill.

Which of your windows face south? South is where the sun is at noon.

Check for Obstructions

The illustration at right shows the panel installed over a double-hung window. The insert panel sits on the window sill and presses against the lower sash. Often, however, there are obstructions. Examples might be: venetian blinds, cafe curtains, plant shelves, and decorative what-nots. In such a case there are two possible solutions. Either:

1. The obstruction has to be removed, or

2. The panel has to be made larger in both dimensions so that it overlaps the window casings.

In the overlapping case, the panel is constructed 2 in. wider and 1 in. taller than the insert version, allowing it to sit on the window sill and overlap the top and side casings by 1 in. Weatherstripping installed on the panel's top and side faces compress against the top and side casings. The bottom weatherstripping is installed on the panel's bottom edge so it compresses down against the stool on which it rests.

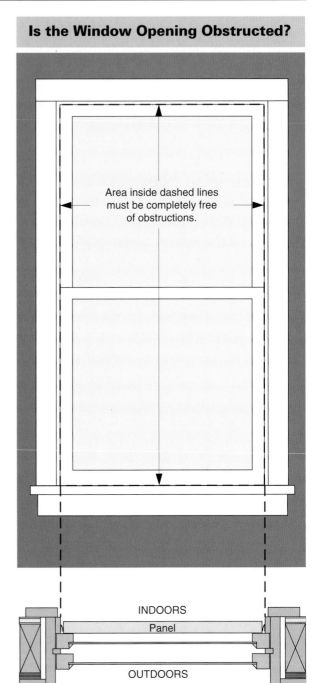

Is the Window Opening Obstructed?

Area inside dashed lines must be completely free of obstructions.

INDOORS

Panel

OUTDOORS

VIEW FROM TOP

Check Squareness of Opening

The insert panels are constructed as rectangles, each corner measuring exactly 90°. The panels are also made slightly smaller than the openings to allow weatherstripping around the edges. The maximum compression of the weatherstripping, however, is about ¼ in., so the degree to which the windows deviate from rectangles must be checked. The illustration at right shows how to measure the deviation.

Sheets of plywood are perfect rectangles. From one end of a sheet of plywood (⁵/₃₂-in. lauan plywood is recommended) cut a triangle measuring 24 in. by 48 in. Place the triangle in the opening as shown. Measure the gap between the top tip and the window frame. Repeat in the opposite bottom corner. If either gap exceeds ¼ in., the insert version will not work, and you must use the overlapping version.

If the opening is shorter than 48 in., you can use a carpenter's framing square instead of the plywood.

Option for Checking Squareness

In a perfect rectangle, the two diagonals are identical. If you have neither plywood nor a framing square, and the window is close to the average size of 30 in. by 50 in., you can use the opposite diagonals test:

1. Measure diagonal A, from the intersection of stool and casing to the intersection of top casing and opposite side casing. Record this dimension to the nearest ¹/₁₆ in.

2. Measure the opposite diagonal in the same way and record the dimension.

3. Subtract diagonal A from diagonal B. If the difference is less than or equal to ¼ in., an inset panel will work. If not, use the overlapping panel version.

NOTE: This measurement is difficult to make with a tape measure. You will find it simpler using the measuring sticks demonstrated on the next page.

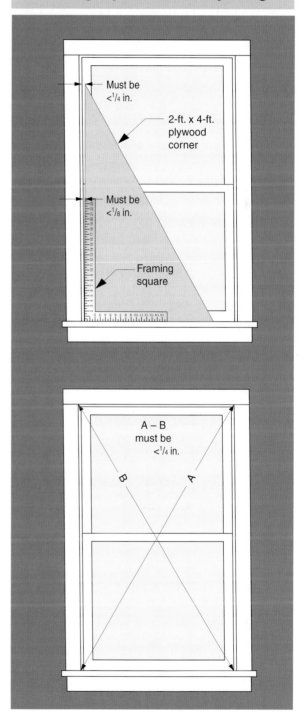

Checking Squareness of Opening

Must be <¹/₄ in.

2-ft. x 4-ft. plywood corner

Must be <¹/₈ in.

Framing square

A – B must be <¹/₄ in.

Using a Measuring Tape

If you have limited experience measuring, here is a short tutorial. First, study the section of tape measure at right. Each inch is marked by a solid line across the tape. The next longest lines indicate half inches, followed by shorter lines for quarter inches, etc., all the way down to the shortest of all lines marking thirty-secondth inches.

Below the tape are four marks labeled A, B, C, and D. Without looking at the dimensions below the marks, write down the measure corresponding to each mark. Then compare your answers to those in the illustration. If you score 100%, you are ready to measure your windows. If not, figure out why. Keep practicing until you consistently score 100%.

Another way to practice is with a partner. Measure the length of an object and write your answer while your partner looks away. Next reverse roles with your partner, then compare your answers. If the same, chances are 99% you are both correct. If different, find out why.

Using Measuring Sticks

Unless you are a professional carpenter or seamstress, measuring inside to inside with a tape measure is an uncertain business. Three different people will usually arrive at three different answers—usually different by at least ¼ in.

The stick trick shown at right is an amazingly simple, accurate woodworker's technique:

1. Find two thin sticks, each of which is shorter than the distance to be measured.

2. Gripping the sticks in both hands, slide them apart until they fill the gap being measured.

3. Transfer the sticks to one hand.

4. Hook the end of the tape over the end of one stick and read the distance at the end of the other.

Reading a Measuring Tape

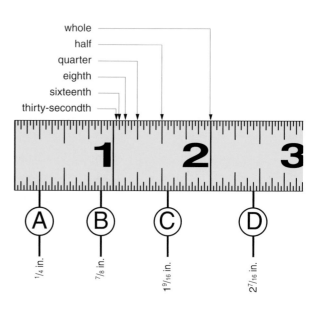

whole
half
quarter
eighth
sixteenth
thirty-secondth

A ¼ in.
B ⅞ in.
C 1⁹⁄₁₆ in.
D 2⁷⁄₁₆ in.

Using Measuring Sticks

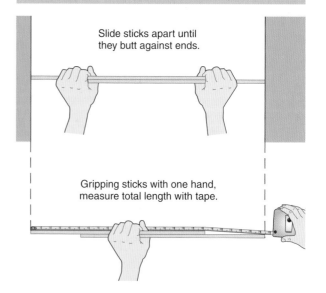

Slide sticks apart until they butt against ends.

Gripping sticks with one hand, measure total length with tape.

Recording Window Dimensions

Measuring a window for the height and width of the panel is the same for both the insert and the overlapping versions. Dimensional adjustments for the panel type and weatherstripping are made later when cutting the frame. Data is organized in a form such as the one shown below and entered into the following columns:

1. *Window Number* is the order in which windows are measured and may serve as the identifier written on both the panel and the window casing.

2. *Location* is an optional more descriptive identifier.

3. *(I)nsert or (O)verlap* specifies the type of panel mounting.

4. W_{min} is the smallest width of the window opening. It is found by sliding the pair of sticks up and down inside the opening.

5. H_{min} is the minimum height of the opening, found the same way with the pair of sticks.

Two Window Dimensions

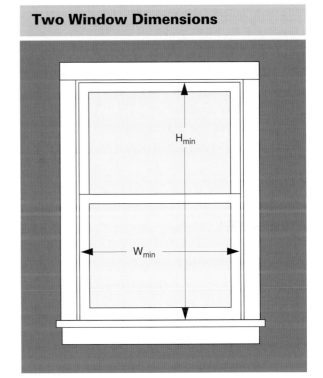

Form for Recording Window Dimensions

Window Number	Location	(I)nsert or (O)verlap	W_{min} (inches)	H_{min} (inches)
1	1st Fl, LR, NE corner	I	$29\frac{5}{8}$	$47\frac{13}{16}$
2	1st FL, LR, SE corner	O	$29\frac{9}{16}$	$47\frac{3}{4}$
3	1st Fl, DR, NW corner	I	$24\frac{5}{8}$	$47\frac{11}{16}$
4	1st FL, DR, Middle	I	$24\frac{9}{16}$	$47\frac{13}{16}$
5	1st FL, DR, SW corner	I	$24\frac{9}{16}$	$47\frac{3}{4}$

Shrink-Wrapped Insert Panels

The following fourteen pages contain instructions for constructing two different versions of the insert panel. The original shrink-wrapped panel described first was developed by Topher Belknap of the Mid-coast Green Collaborative in Maine and requires few tools and minimal skill.

Materials and Tools

All required materials and tools can be found at any big-box home center and all but the lumber at large hardware stores. An excellent source for up-to-date material sources and prices, as well as construction guidance, can be found on the web at *www.arttec.net/Thermal-Windows/index.html*.

Material Tips

1. If you don't have access to a tablesaw for ripping the 1×4 lumber, you can purchase 1×2 lumber, but at a higher cost.

2. Shrink film is available as 10-window kits including double-stick tape. Since the panel uses two layers of film, each 10-window kit provides film and tape for 5 panels.

3. The weatherstripping must be open-cell foam. Closed-cell foam will not compress enough to fill the gaps around the panel. If you have a choice of color, select gray. White foam degrades in ultraviolet and will not last as long.

Required Materials and Tools

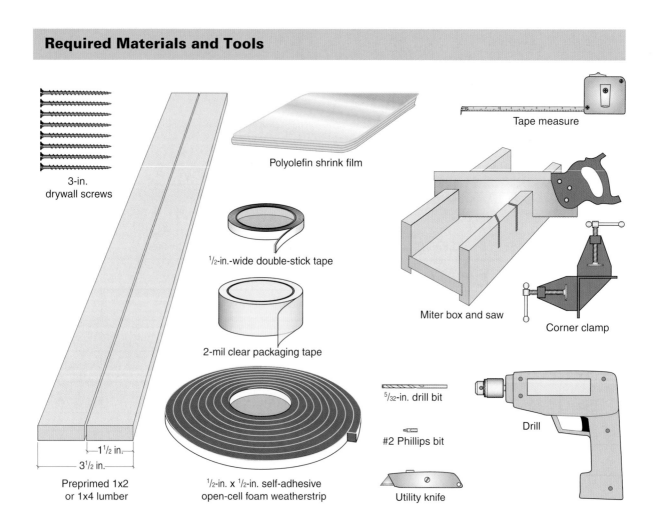

3-in. drywall screws

Polyolefin shrink film

Tape measure

1/2-in.-wide double-stick tape

2-mil clear packaging tape

Miter box and saw

Corner clamp

5/32-in. drill bit

#2 Phillips bit

Drill

1 1/2 in.

3 1/2 in.

Preprimed 1x2 or 1x4 lumber

1/2-in. x 1/2-in. self-adhesive open-cell foam weatherstrip

Utility knife

Assembling the Frame

The illustration below shows the dimensions of each piece of the frame and of the frame overall. Note that the frame is constructed ½ in. smaller in both width and height than the opening to accommodate the thickness of the weatherstripping. Also note the brace in the middle, required when the panel height is greater than 30 in., to prevent the shrink film from bowing the side members in.

If you are working with 1×4 lumber, cut the frame members to length before ripping into 1×2s so the lengths of each pair will be identical. When ripping the 1×4s, set the tablesaw fence to exactly 1½ in. This will require two passes, but will guarantee the widths of the two 1×2 strips will be the same and total 3 in.

Assemble the frame either on the floor or on a 4-ft. by 8-ft. sheet of plywood on horses. When screwing the butt joints together, a $10 corner clamp will prove invaluable.

Drill clearance holes (maximum diameter of the screw) through the first member of the joint and pilot holes (diameter of the solid part of the threaded portion) through the clearance hole into the second member. Do not overdrive the screws, or the joint will be weak.

Assembling the Panel Frame

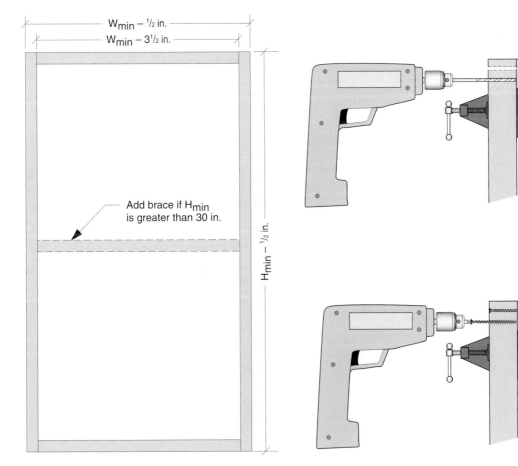

$W_{min} - \frac{1}{2}$ in.

$W_{min} - 3\frac{1}{2}$ in.

Add brace if H_{min} is greater than 30 in.

$H_{min} - \frac{1}{2}$ in.

Applying Double-Sided Tape

If you wish to make the panels as invisible as possible, now is the time to paint the frames. If you purchased preprimed lumber, then three sides of the 1×2 strips are already white. And if you were careful to assemble the frame with the sawn edges on the outside, you need paint no more.

Label the frame before you forget which panel you are working on. If you label the face of one of the members facing the window, it will be out of sight. Make sure your labeling system is good enough so there is no question where a particular panel goes when Fall rolls around each year, for instance, "Second floor bedroom, south wall." The next owner of your home may not know which bedroom you meant when you wrote "John's bedroom, south wall."

After the paint (if any) is dry, set the panel on the floor on edge and apply the double-stick tape. Start at one corner and press it down firmly all the way around the panel in one continuous strip. Don't peel the protective backing from the tape until you are ready to apply the first layer of shrink film (next page).

Applying Double-Sided Tape

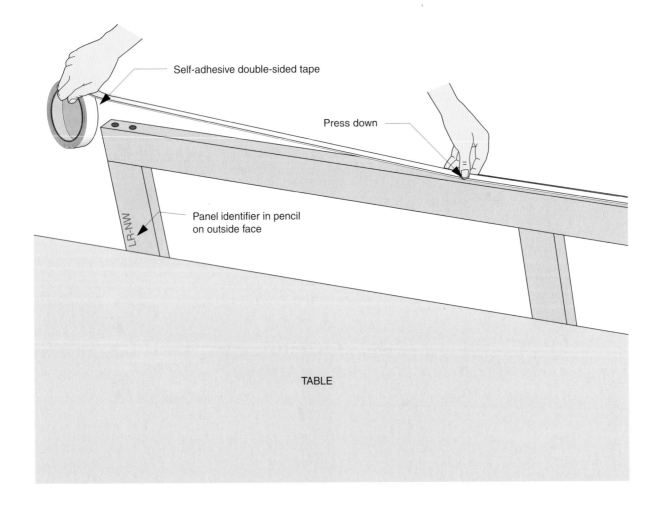

Self-adhesive double-sided tape

Press down

LR-NW

Panel identifier in pencil on outside face

TABLE

Applying the First Film

Cut the film so there is an extra 4 in. all around the frame. Lay it out flat on the table with the frame on top. Pull the edges of the film to make it lie as smoothly as possible.

Remove the backing from the double-stick tape, being careful that the film does not touch the exposed tape.

An extra person or two come in handy here. Beginning at one end, carefully lift the film up and over the frame along one edge so it sticks to the tape. Rub the edge to ensure that it is well adhered. If you can, have one person hold the frame while two other people stretch the film evenly.

Then do the opposite side. Pull the film evenly and forcefully enough to eliminate large wrinkles. On the longer sides, it is best to have two people doing this together so that you can tension the film to prevent wrinkles.

Watch for wrinkles as you go and try to pull them out before the film sticks. When pulling the final side, pull very firmly to ensure the film is stretched tight. The film will shrink only about 1% (only ½ in. across a 50-in. window).

Applying the First Film

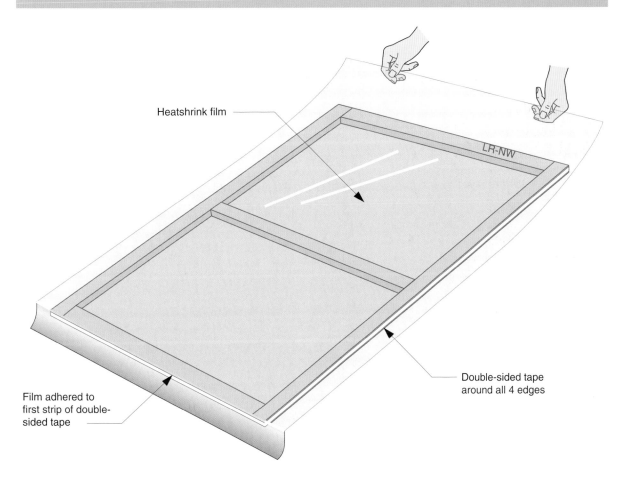

Heatshrink film

LR-NW

Double-sided tape around all 4 edges

Film adhered to first strip of double-sided tape

Trimming the Excess Film

After applying all edges of the film, cut off the excess flush with the edge. Pulling the film upward with one hand, slide a sharp utility knife along the frame to cut the film flush with the wood. A 45° angle works best with the blade resting flat on the wood. If the blade is sharp, it should glide easily without encountering resistance.

After trimming the first film, apply a second layer of double-stick tape around the edge over the first film, then apply film to the opposite side.

Wrap the entire edge of the frame with 2-in. clear packaging tape to protect it from wear. Purchase the highest quality tape you can find. The tape protects the film at the edge of the frame during handling and insertion and removal from the windows. Do each edge separately. Start by pulling out a bit of tape and wrapping it over the edges, centering the tape on the frame.

Pull the tape out to a few inches beyond the end and lay it down with the entire length centered on the frame. Cut the tape off and wrap it over the end. Now smooth the tape down along the whole edge. Finally, begin at one end and fold the tape edges down the sides. Fold the corners tightly or you will have bubbles in the tape. Trapped bubbles can be punctured with the point of a knife and rubbed out. Rub the tape down firmly so it effectively disappears.

Trimming the Excess Film

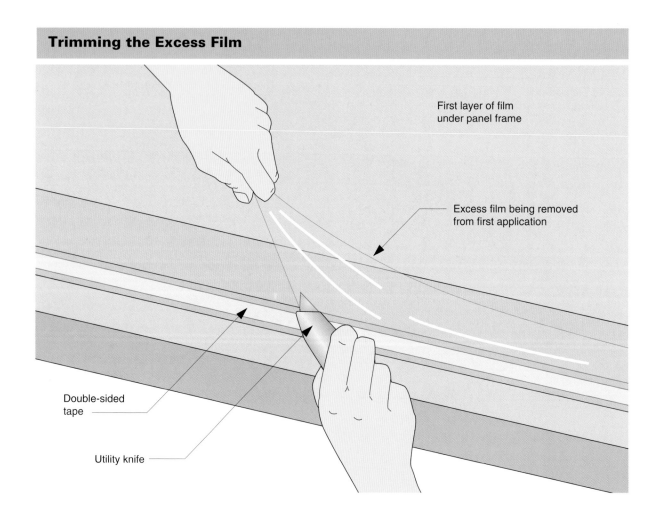

First layer of film under panel frame

Excess film being removed from first application

Double-sided tape

Utility knife

Shrinking the Film

Use a hair dryer on its "high" setting to shrink the film. Working from the middle out to the edges is the best way to remove wrinkles. Keep the hair dryer moving at all times, and be sure to heat every part of the film so you don't have loose spots or wrinkles.

If you choose to use a heat gun, be VERY careful and use only its lowest heat setting! Heat guns produce enough heat to melt right through the film. If that happens, you will have to remove the entire film and start over again. It is better to leave a few minor wrinkles in the corners than to chance burning through the film.

Shrinking the Film with a Hairdryer

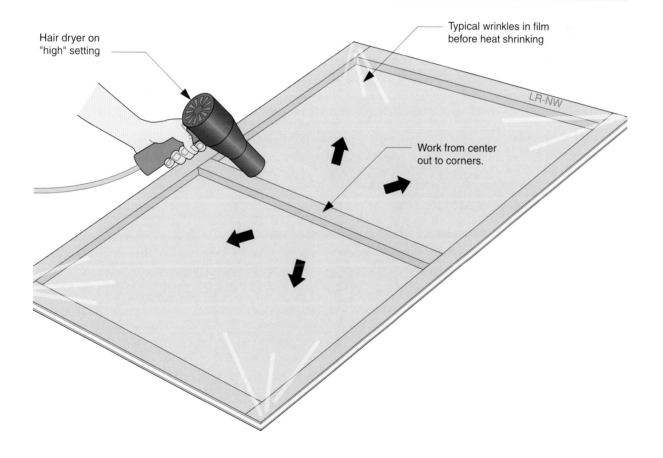

Hair dryer on "high" setting

Typical wrinkles in film before heat shrinking

LR-NW

Work from center out to corners.

Applying Weatherstripping

Before installing the foam weatherstripping, install pull tabs made from clear packing tape. The panels are very difficult to remove without the tabs. Stick short lengths of tape to the outer edges about a foot from the bottom of the panel, then fold the tape over and stick it back on itself.

Next place the panel on one of its long edges on the floor so it rests against the table, or have a helper steady it on edge. Cut a piece of foam weatherstripping about 1 in. longer than the edge.

Start peeling the protective backing off the foam tape, but be aware that it can be hard to get it to start. Although counterintuitive, the best method is to use your thumbnail to peel the foam away from the backing and not the reverse. Peel a few inches back, and stick the foam strip down to the end of the frame with a slight overhang at the end.

Slowly pull the backing tape off as you guide the foam so that it sticks in the center of the edge of the frame. One person can lead by peeling off the backing tape as the other centers the foam on the panel edge and presses it down.

Apply foam to two opposite edges first. When you apply the final two strips, trim them so they overlap and stick to the first strips, forming square corners. Wrapping the foam around the corners would leave a rounded gap that leaks air.

Applying the Weatherstripping

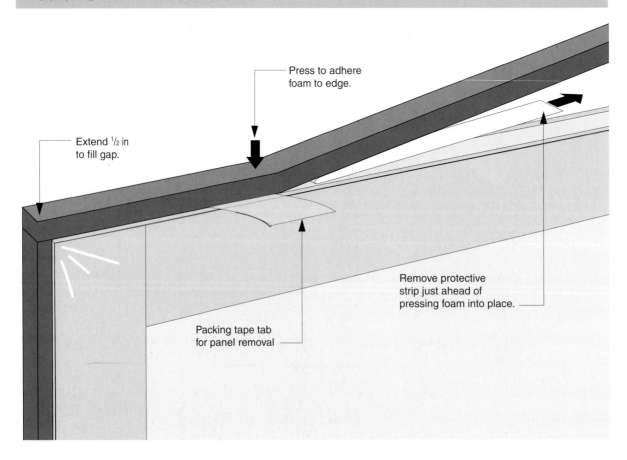

Press to adhere foam to edge.

Extend 1/2 in to fill gap.

Remove protective strip just ahead of pressing foam into place.

Packing tape tab for panel removal

Installing and Storing

To install, push the bottom of the panel down onto the stool and up against the bottom of the lower sash. As you work the panel into place, you have to apply pressure down and to one side enough to compress the foam weatherstripping nearly completely. When the panel is in place, all four pieces of weatherstripping should be compressed about half way.

If the panel resists and it appears the weatherstripping might peel off, use a spatula or wide putty knife to "shoehorn" the foam past the window casing.

If the panel is an overlap version, you will have to install panel clips, two on each vertical edge, to hold the panel in place with enough pressure to compress the mating weatherstripping slightly.

When removing the panels for the summer, bear in mind that the shrink film is strong and resilient but very fragile when exposed to sharp objects. Small tears can be repaired with clear packing tape, but larger ones will require reapplying the tape and film. Store the panels separated with pieces of cloth or paper towel to prevent film-to-film contact.

Installing the Insert Panel

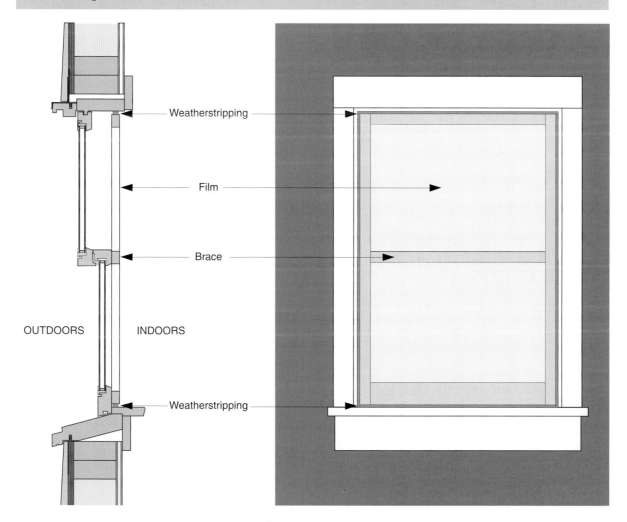

Weatherstripping

Film

Brace

OUTDOORS   INDOORS

Weatherstripping

Screen-Splined Insert Panels

The screen-splined insert panel described in the next six pages requires a tablesaw and some carpentry experience. Since the frame uses mitered corner joints, a power miter saw—often called a "chop saw"—would also prove useful, although the joints can be made with the tablesaw or with an inexpensive miter box.

Materials and Tools

All required materials and tools can be found at any of the big-box home centers, and all but the lumber at large hardware chains.

Shrink film is available as window kits including double-stick tape. The best deal is the 10-window kit.

Since the panel uses two layers of film, each 10-window kit provides film and tape for 5 panels.

V-strip is usually packaged in 17-ft. lengths—just enough to weatherstrip either a 30-in. by 80-in. exterior door or a 36-in. by 50-in. window. If you plan to make hundreds of panels, the V-strip can be purchased in bulk (11,000 lin. ft. minimum) from the manufacturer, W.J. Dennis Co.

Required Materials and Tools

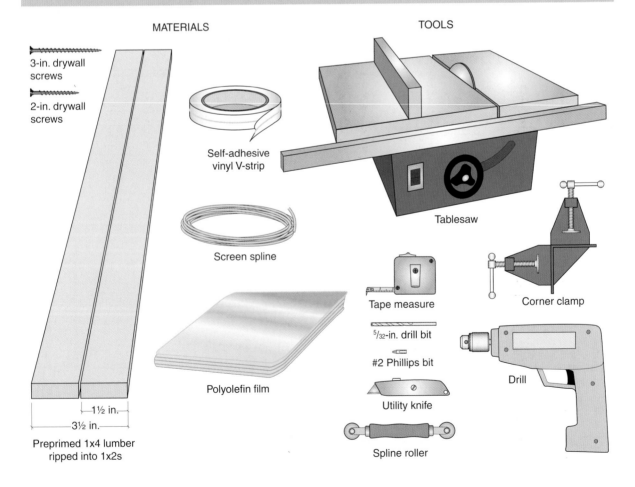

MATERIALS

- 3-in. drywall screws
- 2-in. drywall screws
- Self-adhesive vinyl V-strip
- Screen spline
- Polyolefin film
- Preprimed 1x4 lumber ripped into 1x2s (1½ in. / 3½ in.)

TOOLS

- Tablesaw
- Tape measure
- ⁵⁄₃₂-in. drill bit
- #2 Phillips bit
- Utility knife
- Spline roller
- Corner clamp
- Drill

Assembling the Frame

Note that the frame is ¼ in. less in width and ⅛ in. less in height than the opening to accommodate the thin weather strips. Also note the brace required when the panel height is greater than 36 in. to prevent the shrink film from pulling the sides inward.

When ripping the 1×4 lumber, set the tablesaw fence to exactly 1½ in. This will require two passes but will guarantee the widths of the 1×2 strips will be the same and total 3 in.

Miter the four frame members, making sure the angles are exactly 45°. Then dado each piece as shown in the cross section below. Note that both dadoes are next to the inside edge. The width of the dado will be the same as the kerf of the sawblade. The 0.125 in. shown is a common circular saw kerf. If yours is less, purchase screen spline of smaller diameter.

Assemble the frame on a large table or a sheet of plywood on horses. When screwing the corners together, a $10 corner clamp will prove invaluable.

Drill clearance holes (maximum diameter of the screw) through the first member of the joint and pilot holes (diameter of the solid shank of the threaded portion) through the clearance hole into the second member. Do not overdrive the screws or the joint will be weak.

Assembling the Panel Frame

$W_{min} - ¼$ in.

Add brace if H_{min} is greater than 36 in.

$H_{min} - ⅛$ in.

Kerf (width of cut): 0.125 in.

CROSS SECTION

¾ in.

⅜ in.

1¾ in.

Applying the First Film

Cut a piece of shrink film to just cover the frame. Lay the frame on the table, then lay the film on top, centering it carefully. Tape one corner of the film to a corner of the frame with blue masking tape. Repeat with the remaining corners to make the film lie as smoothly as possible.

Cut four lengths of screen spline to the same lengths as the four dado grooves. Drive the spline and film into the dado with the concave wheel of the spline roller. Work from the center toward the ends. When you get near an end, clip the spline to fit and finish rolling. Repeat the spline application process,

first on the opposite side of the panel, then on the two remaining sides.

No matter how careful you are, there will now be wrinkles in the film. Don't fret! That is why you are using shrink film.

Now judge whether you have the right combination of dado width and spline diameter. Imagine a gallon of milk. The force required to insert the spline should be about the same as the weight of the milk. If too little, the spline may pop out, and you need the next larger diameter spline. If too great, either stretch the spline as you roll it, or purchase the next smaller diameter.

Applying the First Film

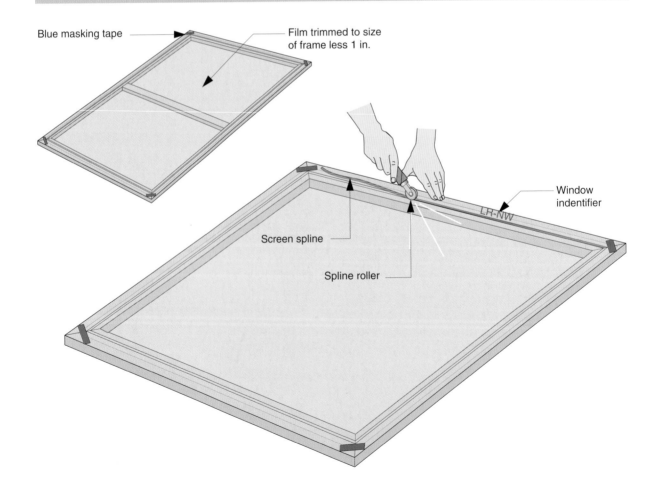

Blue masking tape

Film trimmed to size of frame less 1 in.

Window indentifier

LH-NW

Screen spline

Spline roller

Applying the Second Film

The shrink film is plastic and attracts dust. You may not see any dust now, but if dust is trapped between the layers of film, you will see it every time the sun strikes the panel—forever. So turn the panel over, and wipe the surface of the film you just applied with a damp cloth. (This will be an inside surface when you are finished.)

Apply the second film in exactly the same manner as the first film. After both films are in place, if you want the panel to be as attractive as possible, you can trim the strips of excess film.

To trim, insert a fresh blade in the utility knife. Grip the edge of the film with one hand, and slit the film just outside the spline. The illustration shows the blade vertical and slitting about ⅛ in. outside the groove. With practice, you can lay the blade nearly flat against the top of the spline and slit the film right at the top of the groove.

Applying the Second Film

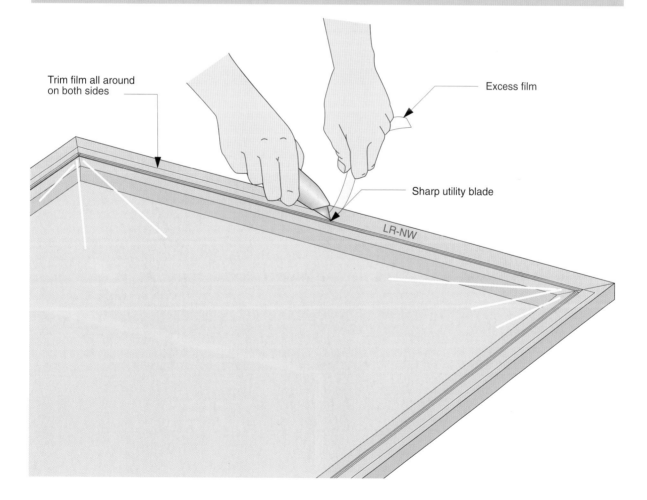

Trim film all around on both sides

Excess film

Sharp utility blade

LR-NW

Shrinking and Weatherstripping

Use a hair dryer on its "high" setting to shrink the film. Working from the middle out to the edges is the best way to remove wrinkles. Keep the hair dryer moving at all times, and be sure to heat every part of the film so you don't have loose spots or wrinkles.

If you choose to use a heat gun instead of a hair dryer, be VERY careful! Heat guns produce enough heat to melt right through the film. If that happens, you will have to replace the melted film. It is better to leave a few minor wrinkles in the corners than to chance burning through the film.

Applying the self-adhesive V-strip weatherstripping is simple. First identify the side of the panel that will face the window, because when you push the panel into the window opening the point of the V-strip has to enter first.

Cut four V-strips to match the four panel edges. Squeeze the strips between your finger and thumb to form them into V shapes. Peel the protective layer back several inches and stick a strip to the end of the panel. Align the strip with the edge and press the remaining strip in place, peeling the protective layer as you go. Apply the remaining strips the same way.

Shrinking the Film and Weatherstripping the Panel

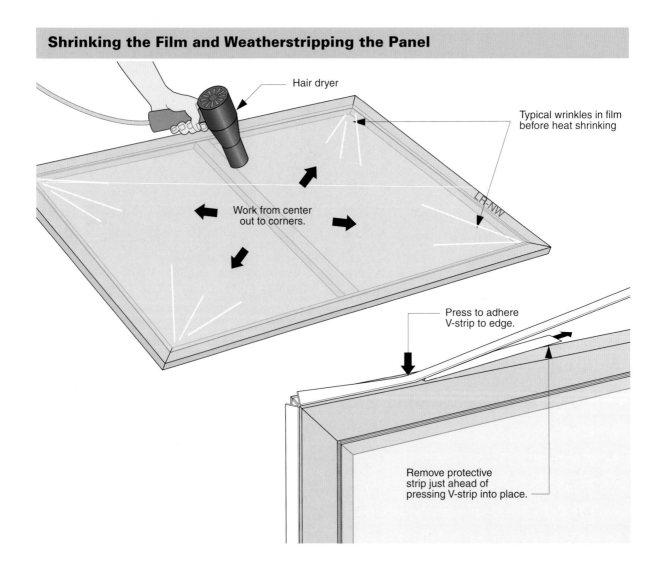

Hair dryer

Typical wrinkles in film before heat shrinking

Work from center out to corners.

Press to adhere V-strip to edge.

Remove protective strip just ahead of pressing V-strip into place.

Installing and Storing

To install, push the bottom of the panel down onto the stool and up against the bottom of the lower sash. Then gently push the panel into the window opening until it comes flush against the lower window sash. If you have measured the opening correctly, there should be little resistance. In fact, if the window is airtight, most of the resistance will be from the trapped air cushion. To prevent air gusts popping the panel out, press push pins into the window stops on both sides.

If the panel overlaps, you can either screw through the side members of the panel into the window cas-ing, or you can install panel clips to hold the panel in place with enough pressure to compress the V-strips.

To remove a panel, drive a screw into the bottom of the panel and pull straight back. When removing, handling, and storing the panels, bear in mind that the shrink film is strong and resilient but easily ripped by sharp objects. Small tears can be repaired with clear packing tape, but larger ones may require replacing the film. So store the panels on edge in an out-of-the-way location. Separate the panels with pieces of cloth or paper towel to prevent film-to-film contact.

Installing the Panel

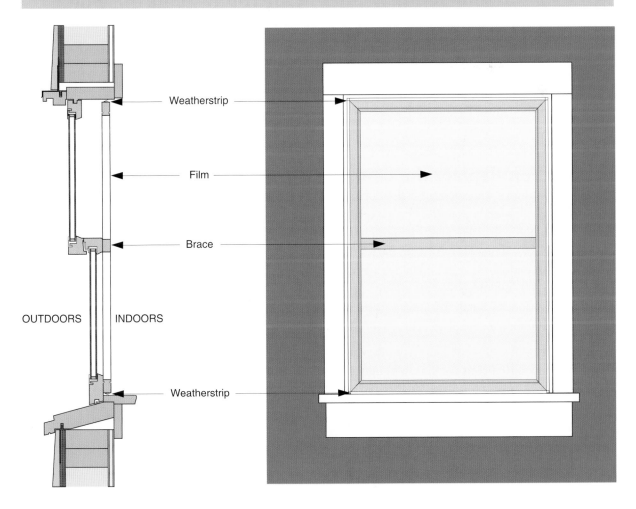

Weatherstrip

Film

Brace

OUTDOORS INDOORS

Weatherstrip

Exterior Doors

Exterior doors are the hardest-working components in your house. We expect them to:

- Let friendly people in and out easily
- Keep bad people out
- Admit large objects
- Keep driving rain out
- Let summer breezes in
- Keep summer bugs out
- Keep winter heat in
- Keep winter wind out

All are worthy of discussion, but this book is about saving energy, so it is this function we will focus on.

Fixed vs. Movable Joints

As we saw in Chapter 3, a house contains hundreds, if not thousands, of holes, cracks, and joints. Some are due to the house being built of hundreds of pieces; some are due to wear and tear; others are due to building elements designed to move. These latter movable joints are located between doors and windows and their frames.

Should You Replace the Door?

Given all the things we expect of a door, it's not surprising that they are among the most expensive elements of a house. It rarely makes sense to replace an entrance door without also replacing the frame in which it sets. A middle-of-the line prehung entry door costs about $200, and unless you are an experienced carpenter, the labor to install it will set you back an additional $200 for a total replacement cost of $400.

The average wood entrance door has an R-value of 3 and loses about 10 therms per year by conduction. Replacing it with an R-6 insulated door reduces the conductive loss to about 5 therms. At an average cost per therm of $2.50, the annual savings from replacing a door equals about $12.50.

The typical poorly weatherstripped door has a leakage area of 8 sq. in. Since the average total leakage area of homes is 144 sq. in., a single exterior door accounts for about 5% of infiltration. If infiltration accounts for half of your total fuel bill, then air leakage of the door accounts for 2.5% of your fuel bill. In northern states, the average annual heating bill is $1,400, so the leakiness of a single exterior door costs about $35. Weatherstripping the door, at a cost of $5, should save at least $25.

Of course, a new door would include weatherstripping. So your options are two:

1. Replace: cost $400.00, saving $37.50

2. Weatherstrip: cost $5.00, saving $25.00

Can You Insulate the Door?

When faced with that $300 fuel bill in February, it is tempting to simply apply a 2-in.-thick slab of foam insulation to the door. Should you?

There is nothing to stop you from applying foam to the outside—except, perhaps, the condo association or what your neighbors might say. However, the fire code requires rigid foam to be covered with 15-minute fire-rated material, so an interior application would have to be covered with ½-in. drywall or plywood.

Rehabilitating the Door

In the following pages, we will show how to weatherstrip the four edges of an exterior door well enough to eliminate air leakage. Such performance requires that the door be stable—absolutely secure on its hinges and in its latching. Therefore, before starting to weatherstrip:

1. Check the tightness of the hinge screws. If loose, remove and replace with longer screws.

2. Check the latching operation. If there is too much play, adjust or replace the latch striker plate.

Anatomy of an Exterior Door

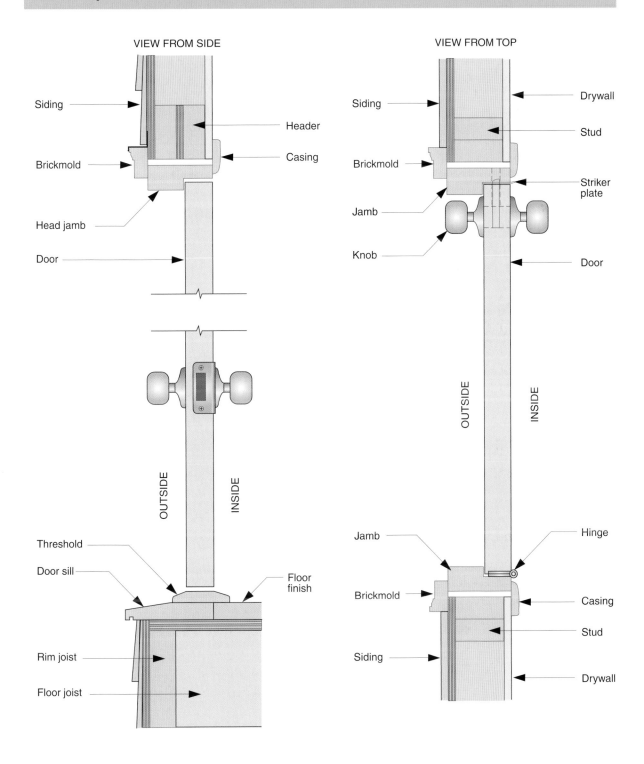

VIEW FROM SIDE

Siding

Header

Brickmold

Casing

Head jamb

Door

OUTSIDE

INSIDE

Threshold

Door sill

Floor finish

Rim joist

Floor joist

VIEW FROM TOP

Siding

Drywall

Stud

Brickmold

Striker plate

Jamb

Knob

Door

OUTSIDE

INSIDE

Jamb

Hinge

Brickmold

Casing

Siding

Stud

Drywall

Weatherstripping Exterior Doors

There are all sorts of weatherstripping: old-fashioned felt, open- and closed-cell foams, tubular vinyl, magnetic, spring bronze, and V-shaped polypropylene. The last, the "V-strip," is self-adhesive, simple to cut and apply, and applicable to every weatherstripping situation encountered in doors and windows.

Applying the Hinge Edge

As shown in the illustration below, the door's hinge edge squeezes shut with the door closed, requiring resilient weatherstripping that can compress to a thickness of $1/16$ in. The V-strip is perfect for the application.

To apply the weatherstripping:

1. Clean the surface where the V-strip will be applied with detergent and a "scrubby pad," followed by a fresh-water rinse.

2. Measure the height of the door frame and cut the V-strip $1/8$ in. shorter.

3. Orient the V-strip with the V opening toward the outdoors.

4. Peel back 6 in. of backing, position the strip, and press the very top to adhere.

5. Remove the remaining backing and, with the strip aligned, press in place.

6. Pry the V open and secure the very top and very bottom of the strip with T-50 staples.

Weatherstripping a Door's Hinge Edge

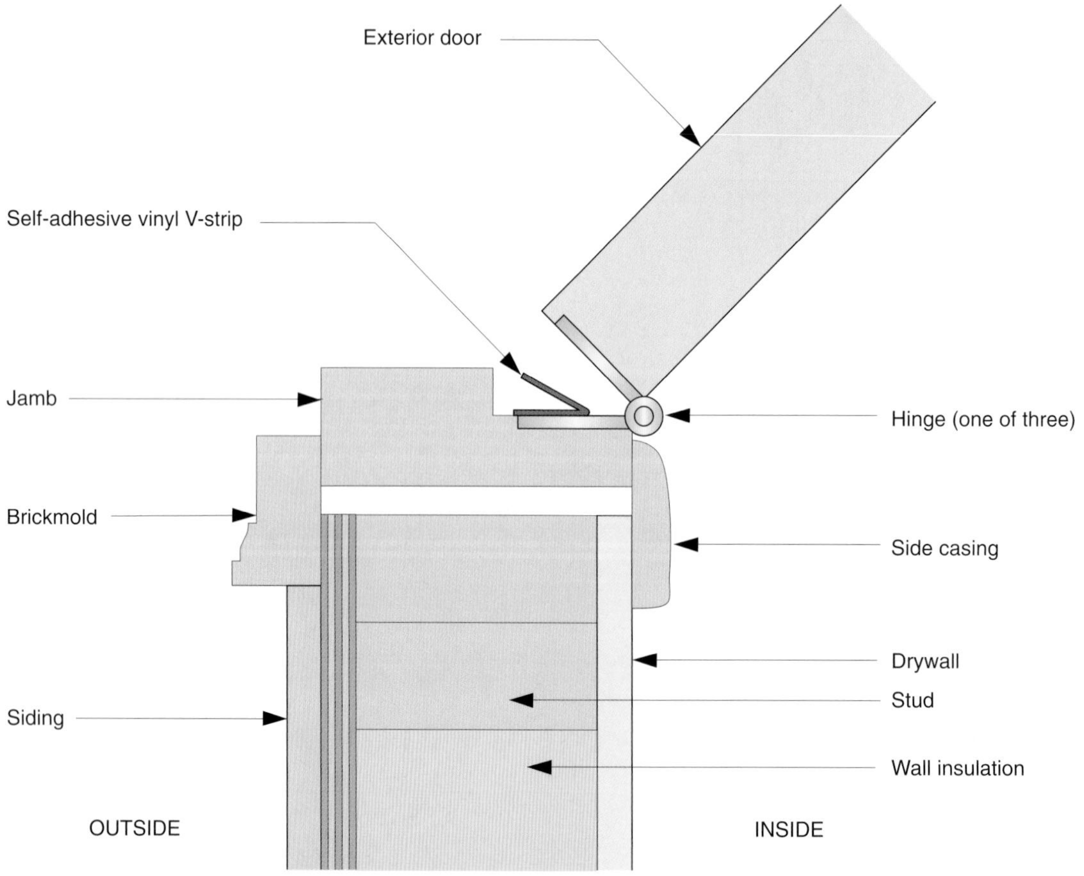

Exterior door

Self-adhesive vinyl V-strip

Jamb

Brickmold

Siding

Hinge (one of three)

Side casing

Drywall

Stud

Wall insulation

OUTSIDE

INSIDE

Applying the Latch Edge

Here is where the versatility of the V-strip becomes apparent. Instead of squeezing the weatherstripping, the latching edge of the door slides over the weather-stripping. This requires weatherstripping that is both compressible and slippery.

1. Application of the V-strip is the same as on the hinge side: clean, measure, cut, peel, align, and press into place from top to bottom.

2. After the entire strip is adhered, cut and remove the short section of V-strip covering the latch striker plate. If you don't, the door won't latch.

3. As with the hinge edge, open the V and staple each end of the two strips. The staples will prevent the strips from starting to peel off.

4. What if the door fits so tightly there isn't the $1/16$ in. of clearance required for the V-strip? You should be so lucky! In that case, the edge probably doesn't need weatherstripping.

Weatherstripping a Door's Latch Edge

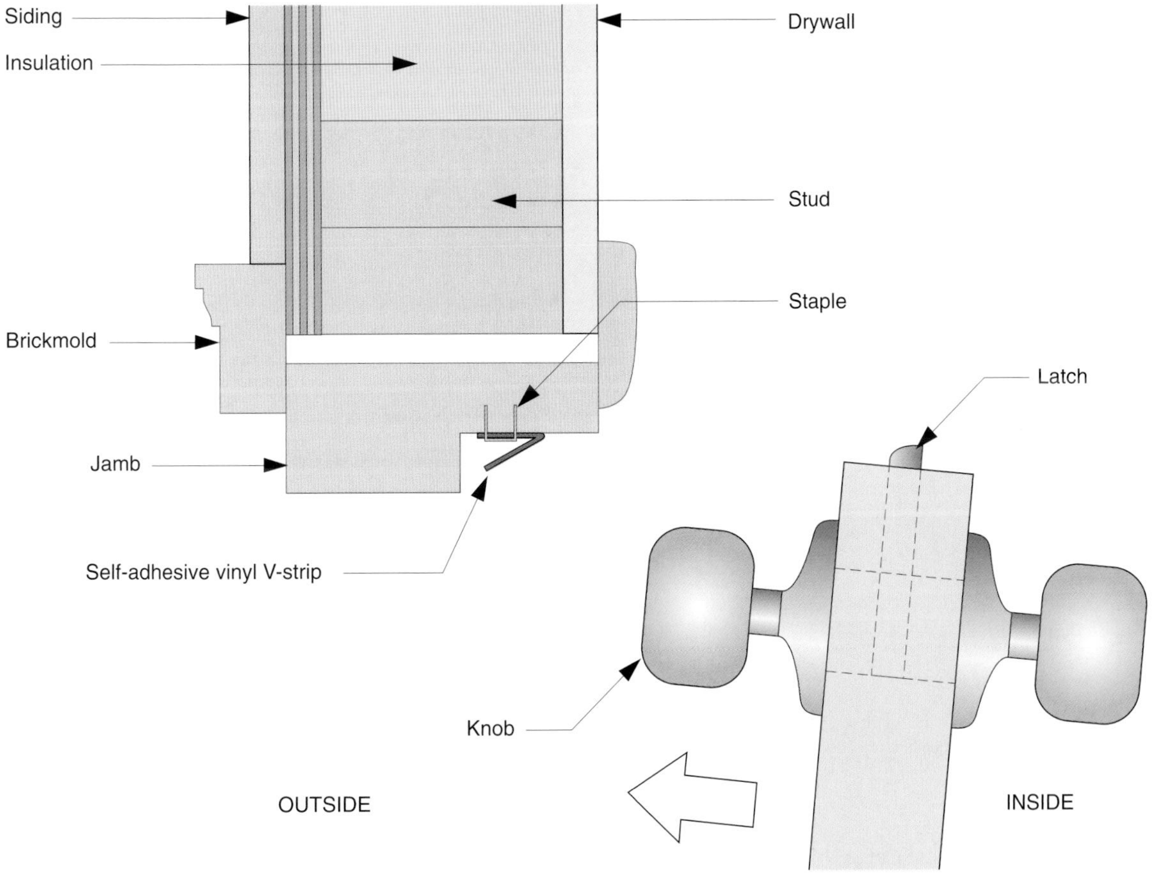

Siding
Insulation
Drywall
Stud
Staple
Brickmold
Latch
Jamb
Self-adhesive vinyl V-strip
Knob
OUTSIDE
INSIDE

Applying the Top Edge

You may have noticed that the illustrations for the latch edge and the top of the door are nearly identical. That is because the constructions are the same except for the presence of the latch and striker plate. As with the latch edge, the door compresses the V-strip as it slides over it on the way to closure.

It was suggested that you staple both ends of the V-strip in every instance to prevent the strip from starting to loosen. If perchance the strip ever does come loose, it may be stapled every six inches along its length. The strip will still compress and will remain an effective air seal as long as it remains in place.

Weatherstripping the Top Edge of a Door

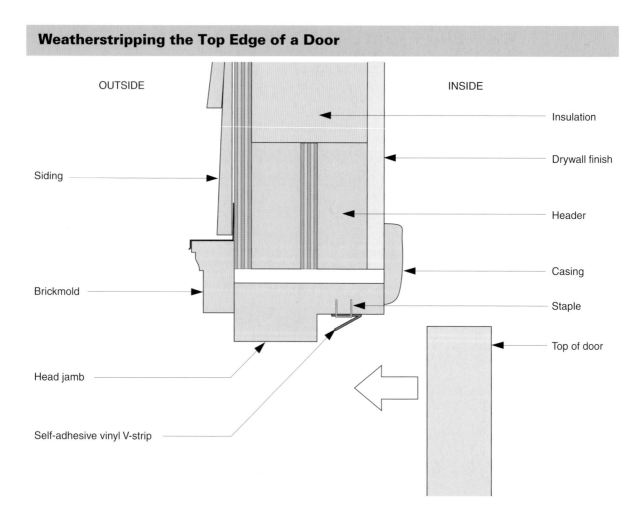

OUTSIDE

INSIDE

Insulation

Drywall finish

Siding

Header

Casing

Brickmold

Staple

Top of door

Head jamb

Self-adhesive vinyl V-strip

Weatherstripping the Bottom

The bottom of an entrance door takes considerably more abuse than the other three edges. It gets wet; it freezes; and it has to deal with dirt and debris. Clearly, a solution other than the V-strip is required.

Enter the door sweep. The illustration below shows an aluminum-extrusion/vinyl-blade version that is screwed to the bottom of the door. Another long-lasting version substitutes a nylon brush for the vinyl blade. In any case, do not accept a self-adhesive version even though it promises a simpler installation. Simpler, yes, but the adhesive will fail within months, and the sweep cannot be adjusted after installation.

To apply a door sweep:

1. Trim the sweep to the door width with a hacksaw.

2. With the door closed, hold the sweep against the door with the blade resting on the door sill. With a felt-tip pen, mark a dot in the center of each of the slots in the aluminum extrusion.

3. Drill pilot holes at each dot, and fasten the strip loosely with the supplied screws.

4. Press the strip down so the sweep deflects slightly, then tighten the screws.

5. If the sweep ever needs readjustment, loosen the screws, adjust the sweep, and retighten the screws.

Installing a Door Sweep on the Bottom of a Door

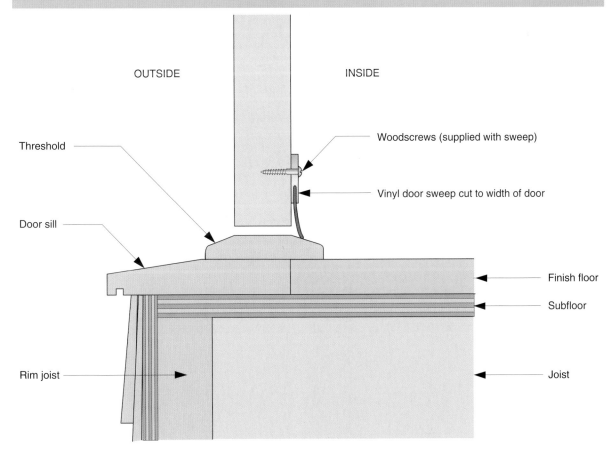

OUTSIDE

INSIDE

Threshold

Door sill

Rim joist

Woodscrews (supplied with sweep)

Vinyl door sweep cut to width of door

Finish floor

Subfloor

Joist

Air Sealing the Envelope

11

We have considered in great detail the best methods for insulating the floors, walls, ceilings, roofs, and windows of the thermal envelope. In so doing, we have treated these surfaces as if they were perfect. If they are perfect, though, why do our houses lose so much heat through infiltration? In fact, our houses are riddled with hidden holes and cracks.

We begin by offering *a field guide to air leaks*: what they look like and where to look for them. To find the leaks in your house, you have two options: (1) hire an energy auditor with leak-detection equipment (*professional leak detection*), or (2) do it yourself (*low-tech homeowner leak detection*) with simpler, less expensive equipment.

Once you have identified and marked the leaks in your envelope, read our recommendations for *sealing attic air leaks, sealing basement air leaks, sealing interior air leaks*, and *sealing exterior air leaks.*

A Field Guide to Air Leaks

Below is a similar home to the one we saw on p. 147. The previous illustration was simplified, but now we are looking at a real house with real imperfections. The 39 identified air leaks are listed in the table on the facing page with their average measured areas.

Most homes have a vented clothes dryer (Leak #34). Is the damper on yours stuck open? If so, the table shows it is equivalent to a 4-sq.-in. hole.

Does your home have a masonry chimney (Leak #3)? If so, the fire code-required 2-in. gap between it and the ceiling framing surrounding it is equivalent to a hole in the ceiling of 12 sq. in.

The total area of air leaks in the average home is an incredible 288 sq. in. You read that right, 2 sq. ft. That is effectively the same as leaving a window sash open about 12 in. all winter long!

Thirty-Nine Common Air Leaks in a Home's Thermal Envelope

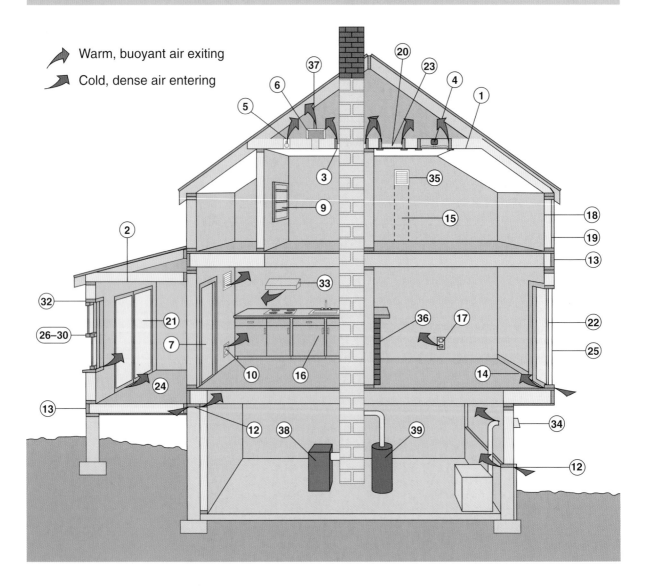

Warm, buoyant air exiting

Cold, dense air entering

Equivalent Sizes of Typical Air Leaks

Air Leak	Area, sq. in.
Ceiling	
1. General, per 100 sq. ft.	0.05
2. Dropped ceiling, per 100 sq. ft., no poly vapor barrier	78
With poly vapor retarder	8
3. Framing around chimney	12
Sealed off	1
4. Whole-house fan, louvers closed	8
Covered with weatherstripped box	0.6
5. Ceiling fixture, surface or sealed recessed	0.3
Recessed, not air-tight	4
6. Pipe or duct through ceiling	1
Caulked at ceiling	0.2
Interior Walls	
7. Pocket door	5
8. Pipe or HVAC duct in wall cavity (not shown)	2
9. Recessed cabinet	0.8
10. Electrical switch or receptacle	0.2
With foam cover plate gasket	0.03
Exterior Walls	
11. General, per 100 sq. ft. (not shown)	0.8
12. Sill on masonry foundation	65
Caulked	13
13. Box sill	65
Caulked	13
14. Floor/wall joint	27
Caulked	7
15. HVAC duct in wall	9
16. Pipe in wall	2
17. Electrical switch or receptacle	0.2
With foam cover plate gasket	0.05
18. Polyethylene vapor retarder (deduct for)	-30
19. Extruded polystyrene sheathing (deduct for)	-15
Doors	
20. Attic fold down	17
Weatherstripped	8
Insulated and weatherstripped cover	2

Air Leak	Area, sq. in.
21. Patio sliding door	16
22. Entrance	8
Weatherstripped	6
Magnetic seal	4
23. Attic hatch	6
Weatherstripped	3
24. Air-lock entry (deduct for)	-4
25. Storm door (deduct for)	-3
Windows (all weatherstripped)	
26. Double-hung	0.8
27. Horizontal slider	0.6
28. Awning	0.2
29. Casement	0.2
30. Fixed	0.2
Door and Window Frames	
31. Masonry wall (not shown)	2
Caulked	0.4
32. Wood wall	0.6
Caulked	0.1
Vents	
33. Range hood, damper open	9
Damper closed	2
34. Clothes dryer, damper open	4
Damper closed	1
35. Bathroom, damper open	3
Damper closed	1
36. Fireplace, damper open	54
Average damper closed	9
Stove insert with cover plate	2
Heat and Hot Water	
37. Ducts in unheated space	56
Joints caulked and taped	28
38. Furnace, with retention head burner	12
With stack damper	12
With retention head and stack damper	9
39. Gas/oil boiler or water heater	8

Source: *Cataloguing Air Leakage Components in Houses*, Princeton University Center for Energy and Environmental Studies, 1984.

Professional Leak Detection

The Blower Door

As shown in the illustration at right, a blower door consists of:

- An adjustable frame that fits tightly into an exterior doorway
- A variable-speed fan that can be adjusted to produce a given pressure difference between the inside and outside of a building
- Pressure gauges for measuring the inside–outside pressure difference, plus the rate of air flow in cubic feet per minute (cfm)

Preparing for the Test

The purpose of the blower door test is to discover either: (1) the natural air exchange rate of the building during the heating season or (2) individual hidden air leaks in the building's thermal envelope. After installation of the blower door, all known openings in the building envelope are tightly sealed. A partial list of openings to be sealed includes:

- Exterior doors
- Windows
- Fireplaces
- Woodstove dampers
- Kitchen and bathroom vents, if operable

Heating equipment, including furnaces, boilers, water heaters, and clothes dryers are not sealed, but are turned off.

The Test

The fan is turned on and its speed slowly increased until the inside–outside pressure difference reaches 50 Pascals. The fan's air flow is then recorded in cfm. Test results are usually reported in two ways:

1. *cfm50*—the air flow in cfm at 50 Pascals pressure difference, and

2. *ach50*—the number of building volume air changes per hour at 50 Pascals

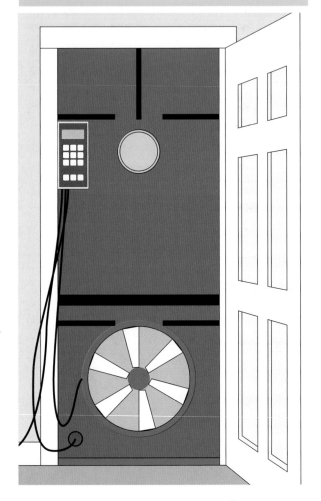

A Blower Door

Cfm50 is read directly from the blower door instrumentation. *Ach50* is calculated as:

$$ach50 = cfm50 \times 60/\text{building volume in cu. ft.}$$

The volume of a conditioned basement is usually included; an unconditioned basement is not, but the door to the basement is closed.

Interpretation of Results

Some energy auditors estimate a home's natural air change rate, *achnat*. Rules of thumb for calculating *achnat* range from *ach50*/15 in northern regions to *ach50*/30 in the southernmost states due to the natural (not wind-driven) air exchange being driven by the inside–outside temperature difference. Another factor that renders *achnat* questionable is the locations of leaks. Were a building like an upside-down bucket with all of its leaks in the basement and none in the walls and ceilings, the natural (buoyant) air exchange would be virtually zero.

The real value of the blower door in leak detection lies in its ability to magnify natural air leaks by a factor of 15 to 30 so they are more easily found.

Thermal Imagery

If heat were water, we could see it flowing into and out of a building's holes and cracks. But heat is invisible— at least to our eyes. Professional leak detectives employ another tool to "see" heat leaks. Thermal imagers (also known as infrared scanners) "see" the infrared radiation given off by surfaces. The intensity of this radiation is a function of surface temperature. Thus, the image displayed is one of temperatures, not colors.

The illustration below shows a handheld thermal imager pointed at an exterior wall with an electrical outlet. The horizontal scale below the image in the display shows the color/temperature scale: blue (50°F) to yellow (70°F).

In the image we see that the floor and wall are at a fairly uniform temperature of about 70°F. The electrical receptacle, however, appears to have a temperature close to 50°F. Assuming the imaging is being performed in winter, what we are seeing is the cooling effect of cold air infiltration around and through the outlet.

Below the outlet is a band of blue, apparently associated with the baseboard at the floor/wall juncture. What we are seeing here is the cooling effect of cold air infiltration beneath the baseboard and sill plate of the wall.

Blower doors and thermal imagers are powerful leak detection tools, but they cost thousands of dollars. Next we will show how to find heat leaks in a similar manner but at much lower cost.

Finding Leaks with Thermal Imagery

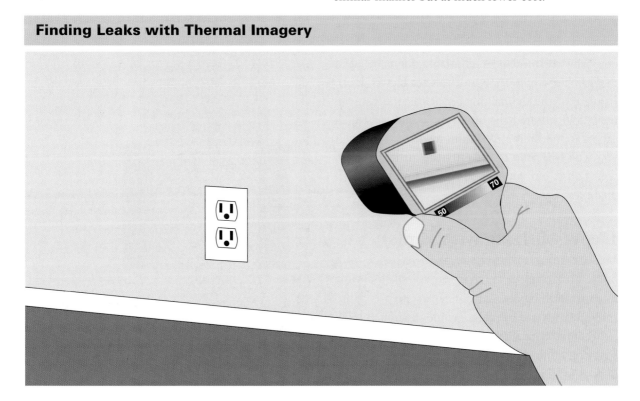

Low-Tech Homeowner Leak Detection

If your house were a boat, finding its leaks would be a simple matter of launching it and looking to see where the water gushed in. Unlike water, however, air is invisible, so finding the air leaks in your house will take a bit more ingenuity.

As we have seen, energy auditors find air leaks using a powerful fan called a "blower door" to suck the air out of the house. Then they view the interior walls, floors, and ceilings with an infrared thermal imager (see p. 281). The imager display is a picture where the temperatures of the various surfaces are shown in colors, varying from blue (cool) through red (warm) to white (hot). If it is cooler outdoors than indoors, the cooler inflowing air lowers the temperatures of the areas around cracks and holes so that they show up on the scanner as blue. Conversely, if it is a hot summer day and the house is air-conditioned, the inflowing hot air warms the cracks and holes, and they show on the display as red.

You don't have a $10,000 thermal imager and a $3,000 blower door? All is not lost. Instead of a blower door, you can use one or more 20-in. box fans (available at any big-box store for less than $20). For about $130, you can get the Air King 9166 window fan, which includes adjustable side panels and moves 3,560 cfm (60% as much air as a blower door). In place of the thermal imager or camera, you can use a $30 infrared thermometer, dozens of which can be found online. With this low-cost equipment you won't be able to quantify the air-leakiness of your house, but you will be able to find the individual leaks.

Depressurizing with Fan(s)

You are going to lower the pressure inside your house by sucking as much air out as possible using one or more window fans. The first step is to locate one or more openable windows large enough to accommodate a 20-in. box fan. These will most likely be double-hung units in the living room or bedrooms. Raise the bottom sash and set the fan on the interior window sill. The fan will be blowing out at maximum speed, so it will tend to tip back into the room. Secure the fan at the top so it doesn't tip. Seal the gaps between the sides of the fan housing and the window frame with plastic sheeting or cardboard and painter's blue masking tape.

You are looking for the unknown leaks, so your next task is to eliminate all of the leaks you do know about. Secure the sash locks on all other openable windows throughout the house, and close fireplace dampers, if there are any. If there is a fireplace with a missing damper, seal the opening with plastic sheeting and duct tape.

Some of the "invisible" air leaks are pretty obvious once you have studied "A Field Guide to Air Leaks" on pp. 278–279. For instance, you may examine the

Box Fan Installation

- 20-in. box fan
- Masking tape
- Plastic sheeting

clothes dryer vent and find that it is stuck in the open position. You may also discover that the attic access panel has no weatherstripping, so you already know that it is leaking warm air into the attic. Stuffing a rag into the dryer vent opening and sealing the attic hatch with masking tape will eliminate those two leaks, amplifying the air flow through the remaining leaks.

You probably also have one or more bathroom fans and a kitchen range hood that vent to the outside. Turning these on high may add 300 cfm to 600 cfm of air flow to that of the box fan(s) in the windows.

Before turning on any of the fans, however, *turn off any gas or oil heating equipment.* Otherwise, the vacuum created by the fans may suck exhaust fumes back into your home.

Best Times to Perform the Test

What you will be looking for with your infrared thermometer is a temperature contrast. The greater the contrast, the easier it will be to detect. Therefore, in addition to maximum air flow, you want a large temperature difference between indoor and outdoor air. The difference on a July night might be only 10°F. Compare that to the 70°F difference on a January night with the outside thermometer reading 0°F and the inside thermostat set at 70°F (see the illustration at top right).

In southern states, one could wait for a cold "norther" to come down and produce freezing temperatures. Alternatively, one might wait for a really hot summer afternoon when the outdoor thermometer reads 100°F and the air-conditioned interior is only 70°F. In this case, of course, you would be looking for air leak-induced warm spots, as shown in the illustration at bottom right.

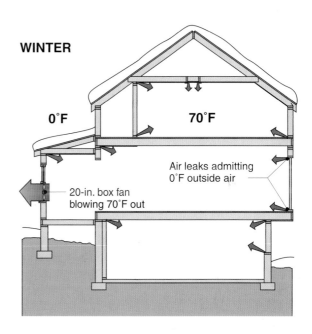

Winter Depressurization

WINTER

0°F   70°F

Air leaks admitting 0°F outside air

20-in. box fan blowing 70°F out

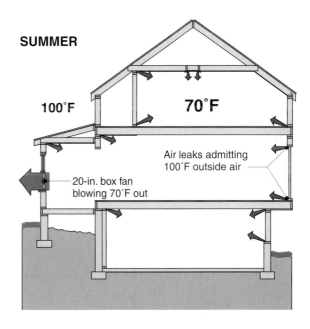

Summer Depressurization

SUMMER

100°F   70°F

Air leaks admitting 100°F outside air

20-in. box fan blowing 70°F out

The Infrared Thermometer

As mentioned on p. 6, all objects continually radiate energy. Most of this radiation is at infrared frequencies (below the frequency of visible red light). The infrared thermometer focuses this infrared radiation onto a sensor that sends a proportional voltage to a microcomputer. The computer, assuming the radiating surface to have an average emissivity of 0.94 (typical of most materials), then calculates the object's absolute temperature, converts it to either Fahrenheit or Centigrade, and displays it on an LCD screen.

When used for the purpose of measuring the temperature of ordinary building surfaces such as paint, wallpaper, and drywall, the device is quite accurate. Pointing it at ice water and boiling water, for example, will usually display 32±2°F and 212±2°F.

More important, regardless of accuracy, the sensitivity is ±0.1°F. Since, in this application, you care only about temperature differences, the device is a powerful tool.

A built-in laser beam pointer identifies the target. The user guide for each thermometer will state the device's "distance-to-spot ratio," usually 6:1. As shown in the illustration at top right, this means the area being averaged when the thermometer is at a distance of 6 ft. is a circle of 1 ft. diameter If you wish to detect the temperature of a 3-in.-diameter circle, the thermometer must be held 6 × 3 in. = 18 in. from the surface.

The illustration at bottom right shows an infrared thermometer scanning an uncaulked joint between a window casing and a wall. Remember that the temperature is unimportant. What you are looking for, as you slowly scan the length of the crack, are changes in temperature. For example, the reading is holding steady at 68–69°F when it suddenly drops to 59°F. What happened? You have found a leak allowing cold air into the house. Mark that area with a piece of blue masking tape. You will come back later and caulk it.

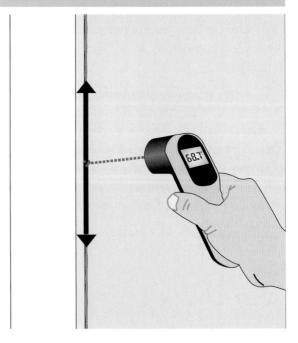

Finding the Leaks in an Insulated Attic

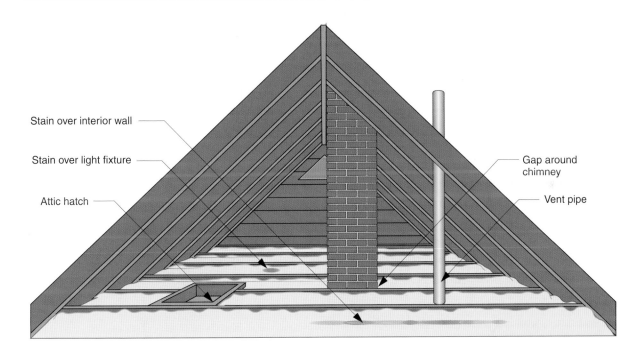

Stain over interior wall

Stain over light fixture

Attic hatch

Gap around chimney

Vent pipe

Unheated attics are different from the interiors of houses because they are on the opposite side of the thermal envelope. If a fan were sucking air out of the house, air would flow from the attic into the house and there would be no temperature difference within the attic to detect. Therefore, you want to conduct your attic test with the fan off, relying instead on the hot-air balloon effect to push warm interior air up through the leaks into the attic.

A second difference is that the hole, crack, or other gap is usually hidden under a layer of insulation. So how do you find these hidden leaks? There are three effective sleuthing techniques:

First, use the guide on pp. 278–279. As seen in the illustration above, attic hatches (through which you probably came), chimneys, and vent pipes are all obvious.

Second, use your head. While downstairs, sketch a map of the ceiling below the attic. Note the locations of all interior walls and ceiling light fixtures. Later, while in the attic, use the map to locate the tops of the walls and the fixtures under the insulation.

Third, use your eyes. As warm air flows up into the attic and through the fibrous insulation, it carries with it grease from cooking, smoke from candles, and dust. Much of this particulate matter is caught by the insulation, leaving dark stains behind. Scan the surface of the insulation with a bright light. If you see a dark spot, chances are you have found a light fixture box. If you see a linear stain, chances are you have found an open-top (without a top plate) interior wall. Of course, both should be confirmed on your map.

Note all of these suspect areas on your map of the ceiling. You will return later with the tools and materials required to seal the leaks.

Sealing Attic Air Leaks

Attic Access Panel

Did you realize that the little access panel in the ceiling is an exterior door? If you define an exterior door as one that separates the inside from the outside, then the panel is one because your attic is (or should be) ventilated and at outdoor temperature.

Cut a piece of rigid foam the exact size of the lift-out hatch panel and fasten it to the panel's attic side with either construction adhesive, long roofing nails, or long drywall screws.

Apply either V-strip or sponge rubber weatherstripping to the top of the hatch casing, as shown in the illustration at right. What you have just done will pay for itself in just a few months and will last a lifetime.

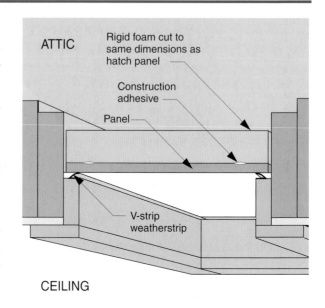

ATTIC

Rigid foam cut to same dimensions as hatch panel

Construction adhesive

Panel

V-strip weatherstrip

CEILING

Pull-Down Stairs

Many homes have attic pull-down stairs instead of a hatch hole. These are large and notoriously leaky. You can purchase a kit for insulating and sealing the stair opening, or you can make your own, as shown.

To make your own, simply cut a panel of ½-in. plywood and a matching panel of rigid foam to fit over the ceiling framing surrounding the fold-down stairs.

Attach the foam to the plywood with construction adhesive or long drywall screws.

If the depth of the framing box is insufficient to contain the folded stairs, build up the surrounding framing with ripped 2×4 stock to the required height. Apply foam weatherstripping to the top edge of the framed box.

According to the air-leak field guide on pp. 278–279, you have just reduced the size of a hole to the outside by 15 sq. in. (17 – 2 = 15).

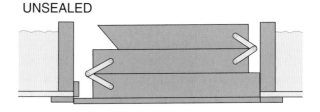

UNSEALED

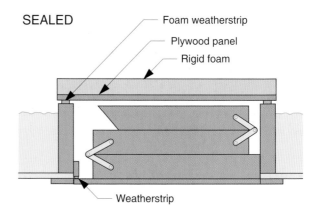

SEALED

Foam weatherstrip

Plywood panel

Rigid foam

Weatherstrip

Masonry Chimney Surround

Fire codes require a 2-in. clearance between masonry chimneys and combustible materials, including the floor and ceiling framing surrounding the chimney. Most often interior chimneys are enclosed within wood-framed walls. What you will discover if you look down around a chimney passing through the attic is a hollow passage connecting the basement and the attic. If it is winter, you will also feel a strong draft of warm air flowing up into the attic—a heat loss disaster!

The solution is to nail four strips of 26-ga. galvanized roof flashing to the joists boxing in the chimney. Butt the metal strips up against the masonry, and seal the joints with high-temperature caulk (available at most home centers).

What about stuffing the gap with unfaced fiberglass? Don't do it. The resin binding the glass fibers is flammable.

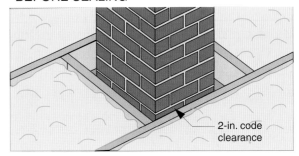

BEFORE SEALING

2-in. code clearance

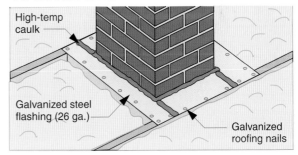

AFTER SEALING

High-temp caulk

Galvanized steel flashing (26 ga.)

Galvanized roofing nails

Vent Pipes

Plumbers are rarely finish carpenters. When they cut holes for pipes in wall framing they are interested in only one thing: a loose fit. Therefore, when you find a vent pipe passing through the attic, you will generally find it coming through an oversized hole in the top plate of an interior wall. Worse yet, you may find it passing between a pair of interior walls with the space between the walls unsealed.

In the first case, the solution is to fill the space around the pipe with a generous application of latex foam. In the second case, seal the space between the two walls with strips of 6-in. or 8-in. metal flashing. Unlike the case of the chimney space, this flashing may be aluminum, which is easily cut with ordinary scissors or a utility knife.

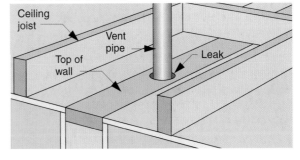

BEFORE SEALING

Ceiling joist

Vent pipe

Top of wall

Leak

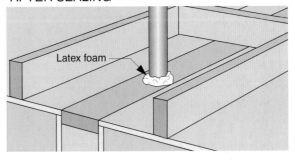

AFTER SEALING

Latex foam

Wiring Penetrations

If you find an electrical cable running across the floor of the attic, it probably connects a switch in an interior wall to a ceiling light fixture. The cable will enter the attic through an oversized hole drilled through the top plate of a wall below.

To seal the oversized hole, remove the insulation (if any) covering the area, and fill around the hole with latex foam. Then replace the insulation.

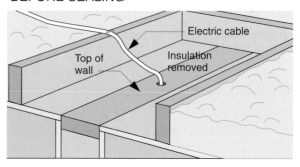

BEFORE SEALING

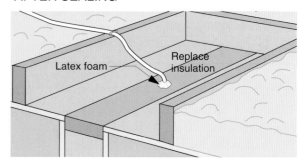

AFTER SEALING

Ceiling Light Fixtures

According to the electrical code, all wiring connections must be made within electrical boxes. Where there is a ceiling fixture, you will find an electrical box. This is usually a round or octagonal metal can fastened to a joist. Whoever designed these boxes didn't have energy conservation in mind. They are full of holes and are surrounded by an oversized hole in the ceiling. Fill all holes and gaps with latex foam.

If the box is the size of a large cylindrical coffee can and is attached to another box to one side, it is housing a recessed light. The code says there must be a 3-in. clearance between it and insulation. Unfortunately, there are only two effective solutions: (1) disconnect the fixture and seal the opening at ceiling level, or (2) replace the fixture with an expensive IC (Insulation Contact) fixture.

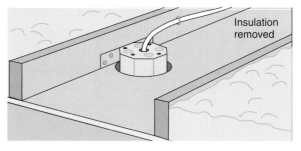

BEFORE SEALING

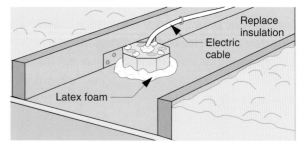

AFTER SEALING

Open Interior Walls

If your house was built prior to about 1950, chances are good that it was framed in the older "balloon frame" style. Rather than constructing interior walls with top and bottom plates connecting the tops and bottoms of studs and raising the wall into place, the interior walls were built in place with the tops of the studs nailed to ceiling joists or blocking installed between ceiling joists. This type of construction leaves the stud cavities on the top floor open to the attic. Of course, these act as miniature chimneys venting warm air into the attic.

Using your floor plan, locate the tops of the interior walls in the attic and remove any covering insulation. Fill plastic grocery bags with pieces of unfaced fiberglass batt, seal the bags by tying the bag handles together, and stuff the bags into the tops of the stud cavities. The compressed fiberglass will serve to fill the cavity, and the plastic will stop air flow.

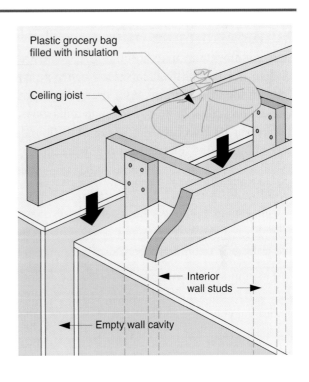

Knee Walls

If your house has top-floor rooms with knee walls (short walls with crawl spaces behind them), the sloping ceilings, knee walls, and floors of the crawl spaces are all probably insulated with fiberglass or rockwool batts. Since the floor under the room was inaccessible at the time of insulating, it was left uninsulated. Although that was standard practice when the house was built, we now realize that air between the joists in the floor is warmed from above and below and flows out into the uninsulated and vented crawl space. Essentially, the crawl space, if properly vented to the outside, is part of the outdoors.

The solution, again, is to fill plastic grocery bags with unfaced fiberglass batt, sealing the bags by tying the bag handles together, and stuffing the bags between the joists under the floor. The bags will stop the warm air escaping into the unheated crawl space.

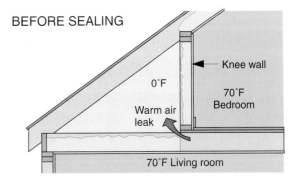

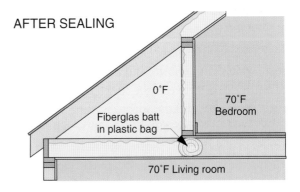

Sealing Basement Air Leaks

Foundation and Sill

Unlike lumber, concrete can be neither planed nor sanded, and it is difficult to smooth when poured between foundation forms. As a result, the tops of foundation walls can be rather rough and uneven. To prevent air leaks between the top of the foundation and the wood sill, contractors now install strips of "sill sealer"—thin strips of closed-cell foam—under the sill.

Unless your home was built recently, it doesn't have this feature. At best, it may have an ineffective and leaky strip of unfaced fiberglass.

The solution is to stuff foam backer rod into the joint with a putty knife wherever possible, followed by cleaning the wood and concrete of dust and caulking the joint.

Backer rod is used to back up the caulk used to seal joints in concrete block construction. It can be found at most stores that sell masonry construction supplies.

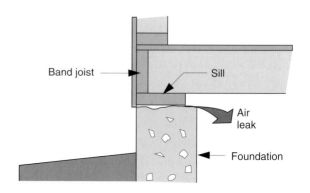

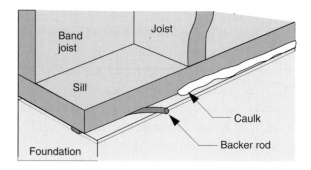

Box Sill

The building sill (Field Guide Leak #12) is not the only problem in the basement. The assemblage of wood framing (Leak #13, the "box sill") immediately above the building sill also accounts for a surprising 65 sq. in. of leakage area. In addition, as you can see from the section view in the illustration at right, the rim joist offers little in the way of R-value. Fortunately, we can solve both problems with one application.

The solution is to cut Thermax HD foil-faced rigid foam panels ⅛ in. shorter and narrower than the rectangular space between the joists and wedge them hard up against the rim joists. Stuffing ¼-in. foam backer rod into the side and top gaps will hold the panels in place and seal against moisture and air leaks. Facing the foil side into the basement should satisfy local fire code regulations.

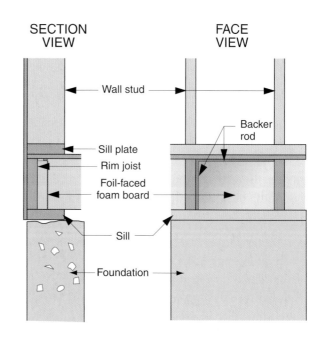

Balloon-Frame Wall Cavities

If your home was built before 1950, chances are it has a balloon frame. The name derives from the fact that the walls are framed with long studs extending unbroken from sill to rafters. Balloon framing was replaced by modern platform framing, due in part to the unavailability of long studs (up to 24 ft.) but also to the ease with which fire could spread from basement to attic through the tall flue-like wall cavities. Unfortunately, these wall cavities act like miniature chimney flues, allowing warm air to escape from the basement into the cold, ventilated attic.

From a stepladder in the basement, reach over the sill and up into the outside wall. If you can reach beyond floor level, you have a balloon frame. If so, fill plastic grocery bags with fiberglass batt, tie the handles together, and stuff the bags up into the stud spaces from below. The bags will stop the air flow.

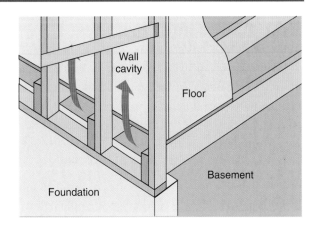

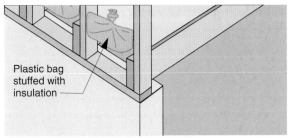

Ducts in Unconditioned Spaces

Wherever a duct runs outside of your home's thermal envelope (in the attic, crawl space, unheated garage, etc.), any air leak is also an energy loss.

Where you can reach a duct, sealing its seams is quite simple. First, clean the seam or joint with glass cleaner and paper towels, then tape the seam with 2-in.-wide UL-181 approved foil tape. Why not duct tape? Because fabric-based duct tape deteriorates quickly when heated, while foil-faced tape will last for many years.

While you are at it, insulate the ducts. Purchase R-8 fiberglass "duct wrap" or wrap foil-faced bubble wrap around the ducts, using pieces of slit foam pipe insulation at the edges to create insulating ¾-in. air spaces. Tape the joints between the wraps with clear packing tape, available at any office supply store.

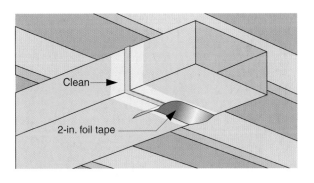

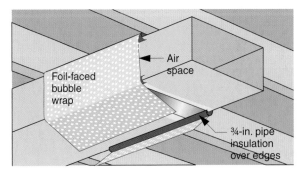

Sealing Interior Air Leaks

Receptacles and Switches

According to the air-leak field guide on pp. 278–279, a receptacle or switch plate equates to 0.2 sq. in. of leak. That's a pretty small hole, so why bother? Do you have any idea how many receptacles your home has? The average new home contains 80 receptacles, and 80 × 0.2 sq. in. = 16 sq. in.

Sealing the leaks could not be simpler. Hardware stores and home centers sell packages of foam gaskets to be installed under the cover plates. Simply remove the cover plate screw(s) and plate, fit the foam gasket over the receptacle or switch, and replace the plate. Where there are multiple receptacles or switches, trim additional gaskets to fit without overlapping.

Make sure you or your screwdriver doesn't contact anything inside the box. Those are live wires back there. To play it safe, turn off the circuit breaker serving the circuit you are working on.

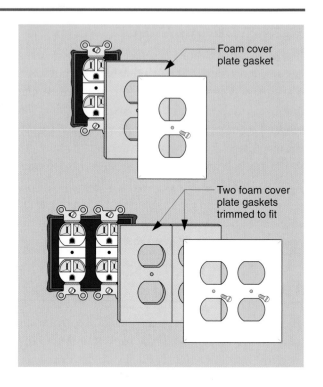

Foam cover plate gasket

Two foam cover plate gaskets trimmed to fit

Interior-Wall Electrical Boxes

OK, you have gasketed all of the receptacles and switches located on the outside walls. Why do the same for those located on interior walls? After all, those are all inside the thermal envelope, so a leak is not a loss, right?

Wrong, or at least not necessarily. Study the illustration at right. Suppose you are Mickey Mouse™, living in the basement, and you wish to visit Minnie Mouse™, residing in the attic. You find an electrical cable disappearing up through the basement ceiling. Following it through the oversized hole you find it runs up inside a wall to a switch box. Another wire exits the top of the switch box and disappears into the top plate of the wall.

You follow the wire again and, voilà, you are in the attic. The moral of the story: You never know where those wires will end up.

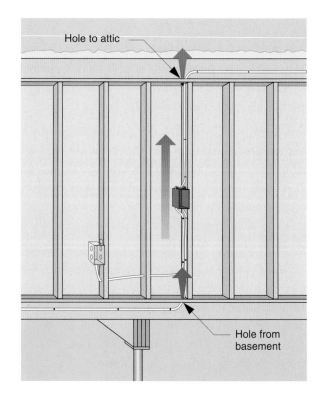

Hole to attic

Hole from basement

Pipes through Walls

As with wires in walls, without x-ray vision we have no idea where supply and drain pipes lead. We do know, however, that they ultimately run downhill to the basement. We also know that they are somehow vented through the roof. Those shiny little rings (escutcheons) plumbers place over the pipes where they disappear into a wall or floor? Those are to conceal the oversized hole the plumber drilled.

Where are these pipes found? Almost always beneath kitchen and bath sinks. Look inside the kitchen sink cabinet and inside all bathroom vanities.

Sealing a leak couldn't be simpler. If there is an escutcheon, slide it back or remove it, then fill the gap between pipe and wall or floor with easily cleaned up latex foam, and replace the escutcheon.

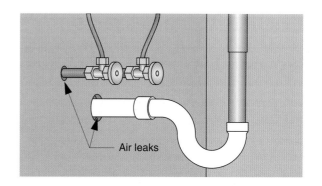

Air leaks

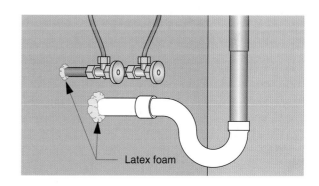

Latex foam

Pipes through Floors

Hot water baseboards and radiators are served by pipes from the basement. In very old houses, running water was added later, and the hot and cold supply pipes will be found exposed in the corner of a room or hiding in a closet. Regardless of when they were installed, the holes through which they run are oversized, creating large air leaks.

Here, relative motion is more likely, and the pipes serving baseboards and radiators are likely to become very hot. Latex foam is friable and breaks down with high heat. Therefore, seal the leaks by wrapping short lengths of foam backer rod around the pipes and stuffing them down into the hole. If you can't find backer rod, cut a 1-in.-long section of foam pipe insulation, place it over the pipe, and force it down into the gap.

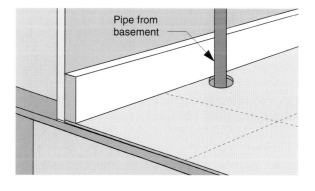

Pipe from basement

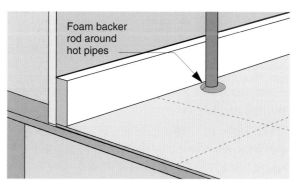

Foam backer rod around hot pipes

Exterior-Wall Baseboards

Wood shrinks when it dries. Framing and finish lumber dries after a house is occupied, resulting in myriad small cracks and joints in and between the walls and floors. Picture a $1/16$-in. crack between the baseboard and floor. For a typical 24-ft. by 40-ft. house with two floors (1,920 sq. ft. of floor area), the length of baseboard along the outside walls is 256 ft. or 3,072 in. The area of the $1/16$-in. gap would be 3,072 in. × $1/16$ in. = 192 sq. in. You can see that the effective leakage area of 27 sq. in. listed in the Field Guide on pp. 278–279 might actually be conservative.

Caulking 256 ft. of baseboard would be, at the least, messy. A better solution is to stuff $1/4$-in.-diameter foam backer rod (it is compressible) into the cracks with a putty knife wherever possible. Don't worry about the putty knife damaging the foam. It will be out of sight but still effective.

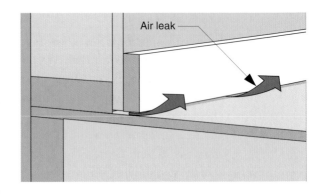

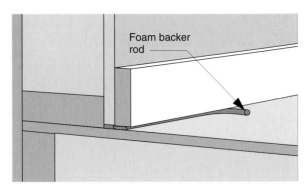

Fireplaces

Fireplaces work because hot air rises. Unfortunately, this "stack effect" continues all winter, even in the absence of a fire. The Field Guide indicates 54 sq. in. of leakage with the fireplace damper open. Is your damper open? Does your fireplace even have a damper?

To determine the status of your fireplace and damper, it is not necessary to lie with your head in the fireplace. Just activate the flash on your digital camera, reach in, point the camera up, and take a picture. The photo will clearly show the condition of both the damper and the chimney flue.

Unless the damper closes tightly, open it up and stuff the fireplace throat with fiberglass-filled plastic grocery bags. To avoid an unpleasant surprise the next time someone builds a fire, hang a conspicuous warning tag down into the fireplace opening!

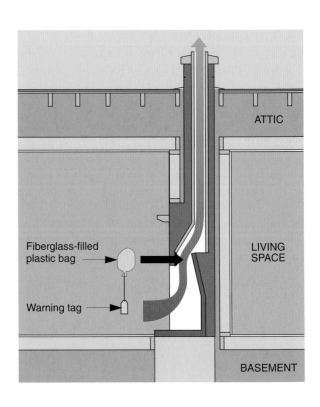

Sealing Exterior Air Leaks

Clothes Dryer Vents

Do you wonder why the inside of your clothes dryer is as cold as a refrigerator in winter? The lint filter in the dryer catches most, but not all, of the tiny lint fibers in the exhaust. When the humid, lint-carrying exhaust air hits the vent housing outdoors, some of the moisture condenses and deposits lint on the housing, the flap, and the tiny springs whose purpose is to keep the flap closed. After six months, the lint buildup is so great the flap is jammed open permanently.

The solution is to clean the housing and springs with an old toothbrush until the flapper operates easily. Post a reminder note on the dryer to clean the flapper after Labor Day every year. If you notice the dryer suddenly becoming frigid, it's time to get out the old toothbrush again.

Why not just vent the dryer into the basement? Don't do it—unless you like mold!

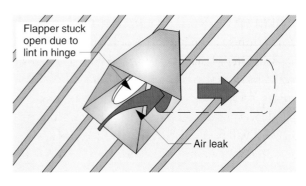

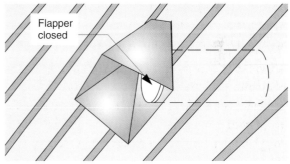

Wiring Penetrations

Especially when electrical wiring, telephone service, or television cable is added to a home, the hole the installer drills in the foundation or wall is likely to be larger than required in order to make pulling the cable through easier. This is especially true when the hole is drilled in brick or concrete.

Latex foam turns to powder when exposed to sunlight, and polyurethane is "blobby" and turns an unsightly yellow. A better solution is to stuff the gap between cable and wall with foam backer rod. If the hole is really big, fill it with backer rod to within ¼ in. of the surface, then fill the remaining space with acrylic latex or silicone caulk.

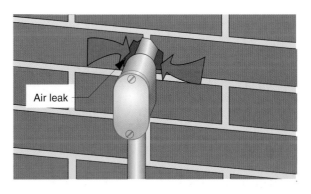

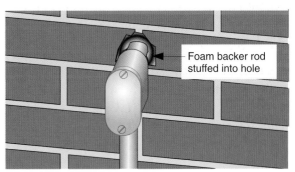

Moisture and Air Quality

12

Why moisture? As you will see, *moisture and air quality* are closely related. There is, in fact, an *optimum humidity for health*. With too little moisture, you become subject to a host of respiratory problems. With too much moisture, your home develops mold, and you fall prey to even more serious illness.

We first alert you to the *signs of excess moisture* in your home. What excess moisture you ask? We point out twelve *moisture sources in the home* you probably never think about.

One potential source is so large we show you specifically how to eliminate it, *capping the big one: basement moisture*.

A separate moisture issue is condensation. To deal with this very important and destructive problem, we need to understand the *behavior of water vapor in air*. We examine and explain both *moisture transport by air pressure* and *moisture transport by diffusion*. *Preventing building cavity condensation* requires an understanding of both transport mechanisms as well as the concepts of relative humidity and R-factor.

Finally, because air movement into and out of a building can result in both energy loss and moisture issues, we explore all of your options for controlling *ventilation*.

Moisture and Air Quality

Our desire for fresh air is well founded. The EPA reports that, unless you live downwind of a source of pollution, the air quality inside your home is worse than the quality of the air outside.

Aside from the repugnance of offensive odors, why should we be concerned about the air we breathe? The illustration at right shows the physiological reason: our complex and intricate respiratory system.

The human body is highly attuned to recognizing foreign invaders, such as viruses, bacteria, parasites, and fungi. When an invader is recognized, the body's immune system reacts by isolating or destroying it before it can multiply to a lethal level. If you doubt the effectiveness of this defense, recall what happens when an animal dies. When the animal dies, so does its immune system. Without the immune system, the body rapidly decomposes.

An obvious entrance for invaders is the respiratory system. Some invaders are filtered out by nasal hairs; others are trapped by the wet mucous membranes lining the air passages on the way to the lungs, but the invaders that make it all the way into the lungs' alveoli cause the immune system to spring into action. The illustration lists the most common foreign invaders (pollutants) and the physiological effects (not correlated to the pollutants) resulting from the immune response.

Aside from smoke, the pollutants that have the greatest potential for harm are molds. Molds are fungi that are omnipresent in nature. They are of many colors, but the most common are either black or white. They reproduce by means of tiny spores, invisible to the naked eye, that float in air.

Molds require three conditions to grow: a temperature above 40°F, relative humidity above 65%, and a surface of organic material. Of the three conditions, the only one we can eliminate in the home is relative humidity in excess of 65%. That is why the following four pages examine how we can control the moisture levels in our homes.

Respiratory Effects of Pollutants

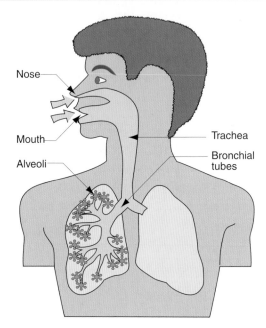

Nose

Mouth

Alveoli

Trachea

Bronchial tubes

POLLUTANTS:	EFFECTS:
Pollen	Allergies
Dust	Asthma
Mold spores	Lung disease
Dust mites	Influenza (flu)
Toxic gases	Headaches
Smoke	Dizziness
Bacteria	Common cold
Viruses	Nausea

Optimum Humidity for Health

As we saw on the previous page, too high a relative humidity in the home encourages the growth of mold. Some people are sensitive to molds, others not. For those who are sensitive, molds can cause nasal stuffiness, throat irritation, coughing or wheezing, eye irritation, or, in some cases, skin irritation. People with mold allergies may have greater, even life-threatening, reactions. Immune-compromised people and people with chronic lung illnesses, such as obstructive lung disease, may get serious infections in their lungs. For this reason, relative humidities in the home should be limited. The Centers for Disease Control (CDC) and the Institute of Medicine (IOM) suggest 60% as the upper limit.

Unfortunately, lowering air temperature results in raising its relative humidity. Shutting off heat to unoccupied rooms in winter increases their relative humidity and encourages mold to grow. Therefore, we will choose 50% relative humidity in the heated areas of the home as an optimum upper limit.

At very low relative humidities, the mucous membranes in the nose and throat dry out and become less effective at trapping invading viruses. In addition, the dry membranes are more easily irritated, resulting in coughing and sore throats. For these reasons, there is near universal agreement on 30% relative humidity as an optimum lower limit.

Finding the Optimum Humidity for Health

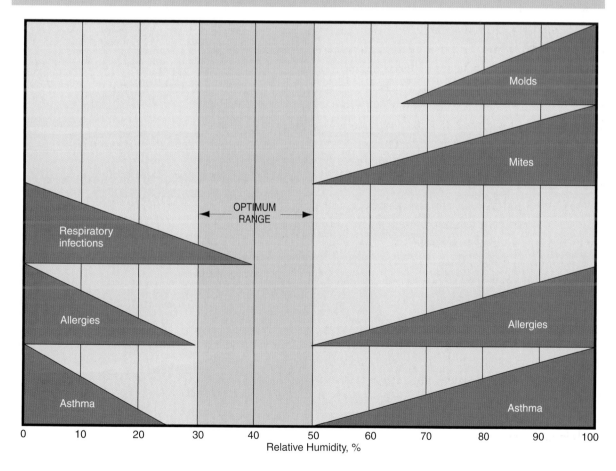

Signs of Excess Moisture

Both liquid water and the signs of excess humidity are obvious if you know where to look. Liquid water, or the damage caused by it, is readily seen in a basement: a pool of water near the perimeter, peeling paint, or a highwater line on the wall.

High humidity in a basement or crawl space is evidenced by mold or by dry rot in joists or sills.

Upstairs, mold is often found in rooms isolated from heat: closed-off bedrooms, closets on outside walls, and inside kitchen and bath cabinets.

In the attic, look for black mold on the undersides of the roof sheathing and end walls—particularly those that never receive sunlight.

Basement Water Incursion

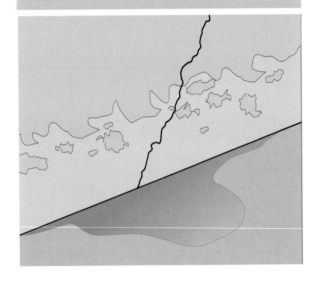

Basement Mold

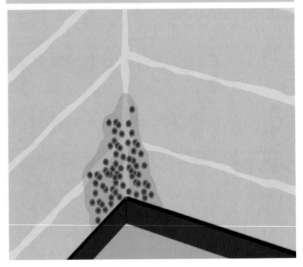

Mold in Outside-Wall Closet

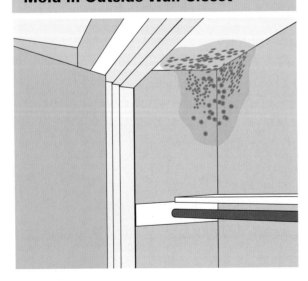

Mold in Attic

Moisture Sources in the Home

With no addition of moisture, homes tend to be too dry in winter. In fact, that is probably the most common homeowner complaint. So the question becomes: Where is this added moisture coming from?

The illustration below and the table at right show typical amounts, in pints per day, of water vapor injected into a home's air by a family of four. With a dry basement or crawl space, the total amounts to 42 pints (or lb.); for a damp basement or one with a dirt floor, 82 pints; and for standing water in the basement or crawl space, 132 pints per day!

Typical Moisture Sources and Amounts

Source	Pints/day
Respiration and perspiration	5.3
Showering (5-minute showers, no venting)	2.0
Plants (6 average)	0.9
Automatic defrosting of refrigerator	1.0
Cooking	1.4
Dishwashing by hand	0.7
Gas pilot light	0.4
Clothes dryer vented to inside	5.5
Drying 1 cord of firewood	3.3
Basements and crawl spaces: dry/damp/wet	10/50/100

Daily Moisture Addition by a Typical Family of Four

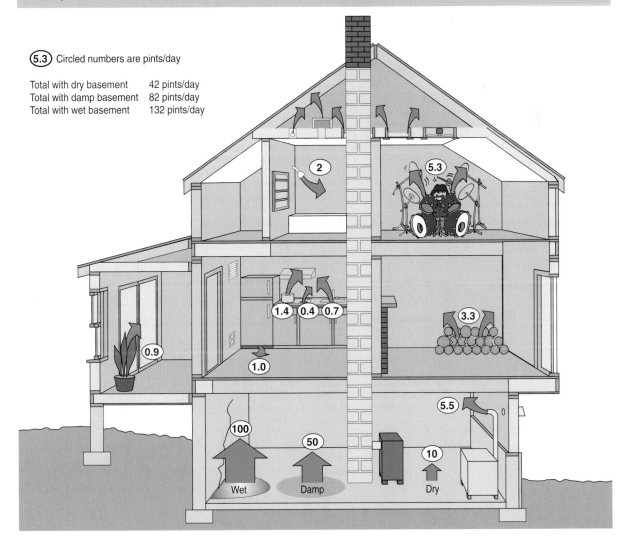

(5.3) Circled numbers are pints/day

Total with dry basement   42 pints/day
Total with damp basement   82 pints/day
Total with wet basement   132 pints/day

Capping the Big One: Basement Moisture

The table on the previous page showed the greatest source of moisture to be the basement or crawl space. With a wet basement the first question to ask is, "Why?" If you have water incursion when it rains heavily, verify that your gutters are working and that the earth around the foundation slopes down and away. If water ever rises above the floor, either you don't have a perimeter drain or it is clogged. Unclog the drain or have an interior (French) perimeter drain and sump pump installed.

However, "dry" floors, whether concrete or dirt, can be sources of water vapor as well. Concrete looks solid, but it is full of microscopic voids that wick moisture from the earth below. A simple test will determine if your basement or crawl space floor is a source of water vapor. Place a 3-ft. by 3-ft. sheet of clear plastic on the floor and tape down its edges. After 24 hours, look at the sheet. Visible condensation on the underside of the plastic proves that water vapor is rising from the floor.

The simplest solution is inexpensive and simple to effect. Buy a roll (up to 40 ft. by 100 ft.) of black 6-mil polyethylene sheeting and cut it about a foot longer and wider than the floor. Slit the sheet from one edge to immovable obstructions such as a chimney. After fitting the sheet around the obstruction, you can tape the slit edges together. Pour a strip of sand or gravel around the perimeter to hold down the edges. Protect the plastic from foot traffic with sheets of plywood. For a more permanent solution, paint the floor with epoxy paint, or install sheet vinyl flooring.

Putting a Lid on Basement Moisture

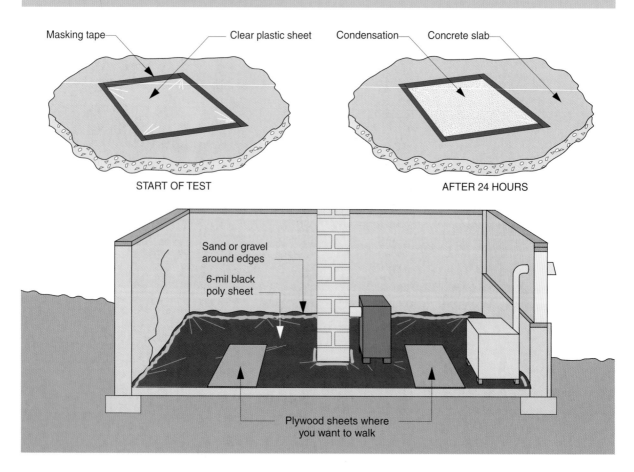

Masking tape — Clear plastic sheet

START OF TEST

Condensation — Concrete slab

AFTER 24 HOURS

Sand or gravel around edges

6-mil black poly sheet

Plywood sheets where you want to walk

Behavior of Water Vapor in Air

A psychrometric chart is the standard tool for graphing the properties of air/water vapor mixtures versus temperature. The horizontal scale shows temperature in both °F and °C. The vertical scale shows the concentration of water vapor per lb. of air. The topmost curve shows the greatest possible concentration at a given temperature—the saturation level above which water vapor is forced out of the air as condensation. This curve thus represents 100% relative humidity (100% RH), where RH is the amount of water vapor present compared to the maximum amount possible at that temperature. The red curves show lesser relative humidities in 10% increments.

The usefulness of the chart is demonstrated by the example drawn in blue. The average noon outdoor air, December–February, in Portland, Maine (32°F, 62% RH), is shown at (1). Were that air to replace the air in a home without the addition of any water vapor, the warmed interior air (2) would be at 68°F and 16% RH. Now you see why drafty houses tend to be too dry in winter.

At 68°F and 65% RH, (3) represents the air in a home with high humidity—humidity due to a wet basement or other sources shown in the illustration on p. 301. We can see on the psychrometric chart that moisture will condense (4) when the interior air cools upon contacting any surface at a temperature of 56°F or less.

Using the Psychrometric Chart to Understand the Behavior of Moisture in Air

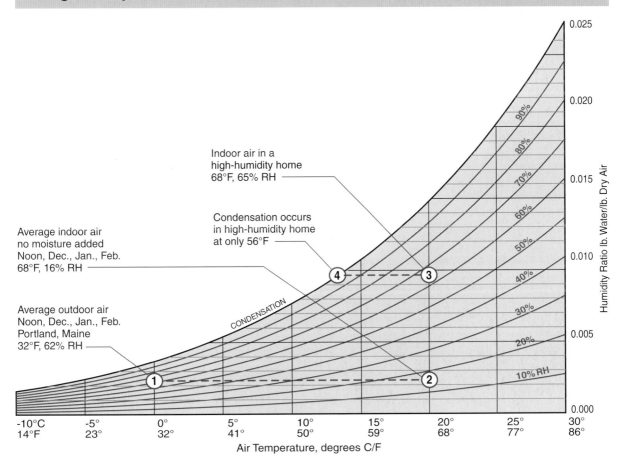

Moisture Transport by Air Pressure

In Heating Climates

As we saw in the previous chapter, heated buildings in cold climates resemble hot air balloons. Because air expands when heated, the air inside a heated building is buoyant and wants to rise relative to the surrounding colder atmosphere. This buoyant force results in heated air flowing up and out through holes and cracks in the upper half of the thermal envelope and cold air flowing in at lower levels to replace the lost warm air. The process is so powerful that the average older home in northern areas exchanges its entire volume of air every 30 minutes.

What does this have to do with moisture? Water vapor, along with oxygen and nitrogen, is a normal component of air. When the air flows, the water vapor is transported along with it. In addition to the loss of heating energy, we now have a problem of destructive condensation. When the warm, moist interior air strikes the colder surfaces of the attic roof and upper wall sheathing, it is likely to condense moisture, either in the form of water or ice.

What can be done to stop this convective transport of moisture? Plug the air leaks, and you have stopped the water vapor transport. The strategy is to caulk or gasket all holes and joints and create a continuous *air barrier* on the warm side of the envelope.

In Cooling Climates

When air is cooled it becomes more dense. Instead of the hot air balloons found in heating climates, we now find something more like water-filled balloons. The heavier air now wants to flow down and out of the lower half of the thermal envelope. To replace the escaping air, warm outside air flows into the upper half of the envelope.

In addition to the loss of valuable cooling dollars, we again face a condensation problem. Now warm, humid air flowing into the upper envelope will condense moisture on the cooler surface of the drywall (again, blue lines in the illustration at right).

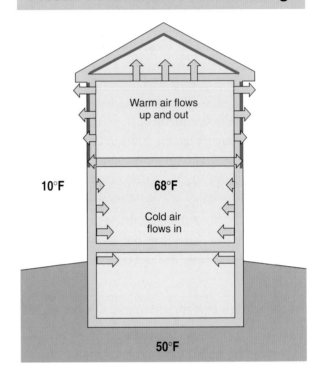

Pressure Distribution when Heating

Warm air flows up and out

10°F 68°F

Cold air flows in

50°F

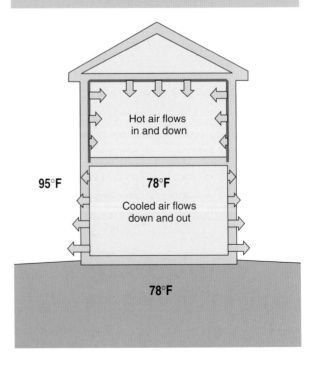

Pressure Distribution when Cooling

Hot air flows in and down

95°F 78°F

Cooled air flows down and out

78°F

Moisture Transport by Diffusion

Diffusion Mechanism

Molecular diffusion is the tendency of molecules in a fluid to distribute uniformly due to random motion. With the addition of water vapor to our homes in winter (see p. 301), there is a tendency for water vapor molecules to migrate from inside the home to the outdoors through the thermal envelope. If the humidity is high enough and the temperature in the cavity low enough, condensation may occur within the cavity (blue area in illustration at right).

In cooling climates, the diffusion is from outside to inside and the condensation occurs in the cavity on the cooled surface of the drywall. The solution to this problem, whether heating or cooling, is the creation or addition of a *vapor barrier* on the warmer side of the thermal envelope.

Vapor Barriers

A vapor barrier can be any continuous material having a permeance of 1.0 perm or less (see table below). Provided the vapor barrier is caulked, gasketed, taped, or otherwise sealed, it can also function as the *air barrier* to prevent vapor transport by air pressure.

Perm Ratings of Common Materials

Type	Material	Perms
Exterior wall	Plywood, ½ in.	0.7
Interior wall	Gypsum drywall, ½ in.	40
Insulation	Extruded polystyrene, 1 in.	1.2
	Expanded polystyrene, 1 in.	2.0–5.8
	Fibrous batt, unfaced	116
Vapor barrier	Polyethylene, 4 mil	0.08
	Foil facing on batt insulation	0.5
	Kraft facing on batt insulation	1.0
Paint	Latex primer sealer, 1 coat	6.3
	"Vapor barrier" paint, 1 coat	0.6
Wallpaper	Paper wallpaper	20
	Vinyl wallpaper	1.0
Housewrap	15-lb. building felt	5.6
	Air barrier, Tyvek®, etc.	10–40

Vapor Diffusion in Heating Climates

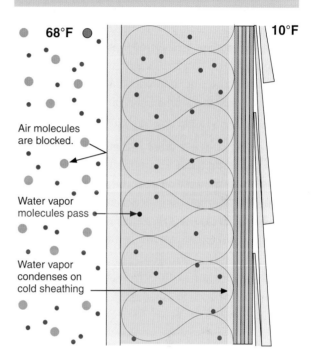

68°F   10°F

Air molecules are blocked.

Water vapor molecules pass

Water vapor condenses on cold sheathing

Vapor Diffusion in Cooling Climates

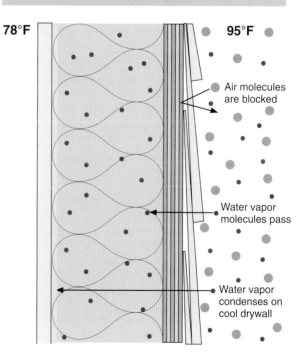

78°F   95°F

Air molecules are blocked

Water vapor molecules pass

Water vapor condenses on cool drywall

Preventing Building Cavity Condensation

Mold and structural damage from dry rot occur, not only where they can be seen, but also often inside building cavities comprising the thermal envelope. The most common areas, aside from crawl spaces and basements where they can be seen, are the stud spaces of exterior walls, unconditioned and underventilated attics, and unvented cathedral ceilings.

The previous two pages described the two mechanisms by which water vapor is transported into these spaces: convection, due to air pressure differences, and diffusion, due to vapor pressure differences. It is worth noting that building scientists believe convection to be responsible for at least 90% of the problem, so air barriers are even more important than vapor barriers.

Fortunately, there is one more thing we can do to prevent cavity condensation. The vapor pressure (relative humidity) of the interior air can be lowered,

and the temperature of the cavity can be raised above the condensation point of the water vapor that does make it into the cavity.

Lowering Relative Humidity

Below is a psychrometric chart of winter conditions in Chicago, where the average daily outdoor temperature and relative humidity for the month of January are 25°F and 74%. Let's examine what happens when 70°F interior air leaks into an exterior wall cavity.

First, assume the interior air is at the maximum recommended relative humidity, 50% (top small circle). As the air entering the cavity cools, its relative humidity increases. Following the horizontal line to the left, we find the relative humidity reaches 100% at 51°F. From 51°F to the outdoor temperature, 25°F, water vapor condenses out of the air as water or ice.

Effect of Interior Relative Humidity on Cavity Condensation

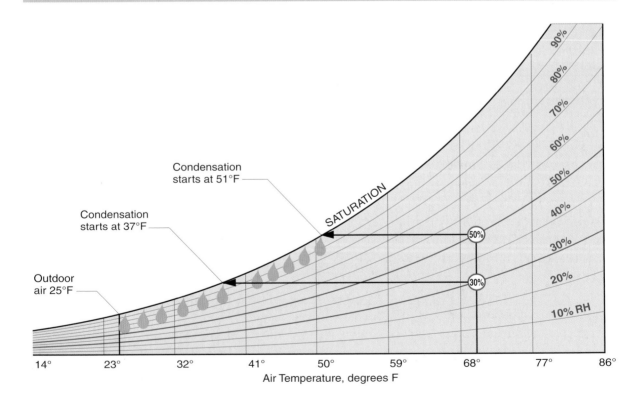

What if we reduce the interior relative humidity to its minimum recommended value, 30%? Following the horizontal line from the circle labeled 30%, we see that condensation now first occurs at 37°F.

Raising Cavity Temperatures

If you were to measure the temperature at every point through a building cavity, you would find the temperature difference across any single element to be proportional to that element's R-factor. For example, assume a total temperature difference of 50°F (70°F inside minus 20°F outside). Assume also the total R-value of the wall is 20, and the R-value of the cavity insulation is 12. The temperature drop through the insulation would then be: R12/R20 × 50°F = 30°F.

The top illustration at right shows calculated temperatures through a 6-in. stud wall containing R-19 fiberglass batts under the same temperature and humidity conditions as in the psychrometric chart on the facing page. The psychrometric chart allowed us to determine the temperatures at which condensation would first occur for interior relative humidities of 50% (51°F) and 30% (37°F). Using the temperature scale at the left of the illustration, we can pinpoint those locations within the wall cavity. Obviously, condensation will occur, the amount determined by the volume of water vapor entering the cavity.

What if we were to raise the temperature of the insulation-filled cavity? The bottom illustration shows the addition of 2 in. of extruded polystyrene between the plywood sheathing and the siding. The total R-value of the wall increases by 2 × 5.0 = 10.0. More important, about a third (R10/R30 × 45°F = 15°F) of the temperature drop now occurs within the closed-cell foam. That means the temperature at the outside face of the fiberglass (where it meets the plywood sheathing) is now 15°F warmer than before. Plotting the same condensation points shows that, at 30% relative humidity, no condensation occurs within the cavity.

The takeaway? Holding relative humidity to 30% and adding closed-cell foam to the sheathing reduces cavity condensation in heating climates.

Condensation in Standard Walls

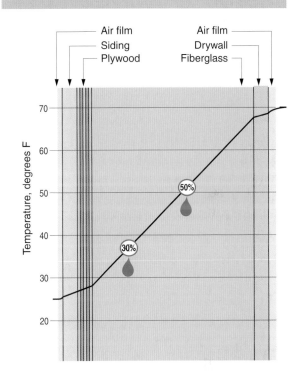

Condensation with Foam Sheathing

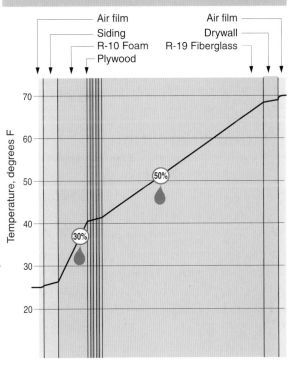

Ventilation

Who doesn't like fresh air? I like sleeping with my bedroom window open a crack—even in Maine in winter. The fresh smell of the outdoors makes me sleep like a fallen log. I also appreciate a powered ventilation fan in the bathroom, both to freshen up the air and to remove the moisture after showering.

But there are other reasons the American Society of Heating, Refrigerating, and Air-Conditioning Engineers (ASHRAE) says the conditioned volume of a home should be ventilated at 0.35 air changes per hour, minimum. Formaldehyde, volatile organic compounds (VOCs), mold, and radon gas are all detrimental to our health, while excess interior moisture may be detrimental to the health of our home's structure.

There are numerous ways to effect ventilation, ranging from the natural (holes and cracks in the house) all the way up to high-tech heat-recovery systems. Let us examine each with a view to choosing the best one for you and your home.

Natural (Accidental) Ventilation

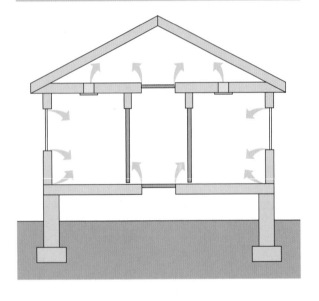

Spot (Purposeful) Ventilation

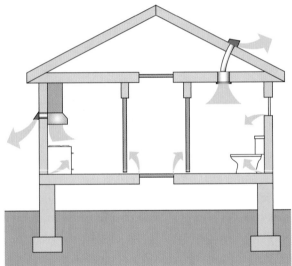

Natural Ventilation

"A house has to breathe." That was the mantra of carpenters back in the day. It was convenient because the available materials made it nearly impossible to construct an air-tight building. Unfortunately, natural infiltration is unpredictable because it depends not only on the tightness of the envelope but also on wind and outdoor temperature. During mild, calm weather, windows may have to be opened to achieve sufficient ventilation for pollutant removal. During winter, with its extreme cold and strong winds, natural ventilation is usually excessive and contributes to high heating bills.

Spot Ventilation

The use of exhaust fans (kitchen range hoods and bathroom fans) to remove pollutants at their source before they spread throughout the house is a good idea regardless of the tightness of the envelope. Exhaust fans should be an integral part of any whole-house ventilation strategy. In fact, ASHRAE recommends, as alternatives to operable windows, intermittent or continuous ventilation rates of 100 cfm for kitchens and 50 cfm for bathrooms.

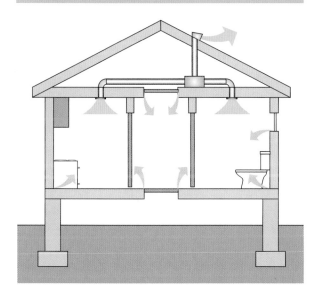

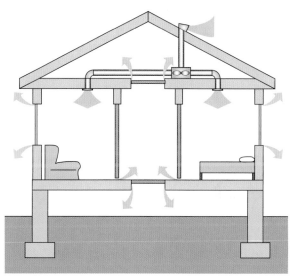

Central Exhaust Ventilation

Exhaust ventilation systems work by depressurizing the building. By reducing the inside air pressure below the outdoor air pressure, they pull indoor air out of a house, while make-up air infiltrates through leaks in the building shell and sometimes intentional passive vents.

Central exhaust systems are relatively simple and inexpensive to install in a new house. Typically, the system consists of a single fan connected to a centrally located, single exhaust point in the house. A better option is to connect the fan to ducts from rooms where pollutants tend to be generated, such as bathrooms.

Exhaust ventilation systems are appropriate in cold climates. In warm humid climates, depressurization can draw moist air into cool building wall cavities, where it may condense and cause moisture damage.

One concern with exhaust ventilation systems is that they may draw flue gases from a fossil-fuel-fired furnace, boiler, or water heater. This can happen especially when bath fans, range fans, and clothes dryers are run concurrently with the exhaust ventilation system.

Central Supply Ventilation

Supply ventilation systems work by pressurizing the building. They use a fan to pull outside air into the building, while air leaks out through holes and cracks in the thermal envelope and through kitchen, bath, and clothes dryer fan ducts. Central supply ventilation systems are also simple and inexpensive to install in new construction. A typical supply ventilation system has a fan and duct system that introduces fresh air into one or more rooms of the home that are most often occupied (bedrooms and living room).

Supply ventilation systems avoid backdrafting of combustion gases from fossil-fuel-fired appliances. Supply ventilation also allows outdoor air to be filtered to remove pollen and dust or dehumidified to provide humidity control.

Supply ventilation systems are appropriate in warm climates. Because they pressurize the house, they can cause moisture problems in cold climates. In winter, the increased interior pressure may force warm, moist interior air into exterior wall and ceiling cavities. If the interior air is humid enough, moisture may condense on exterior wall and attic sheathing where it can cause mold and decay.

Balanced Ventilation System

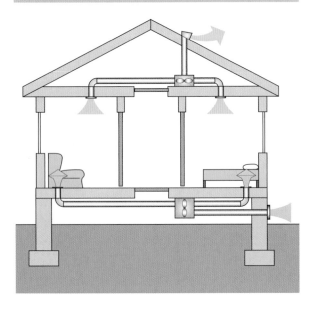

Heat-Recovery System

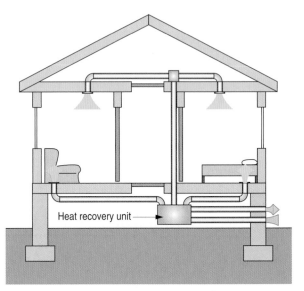

Heat recovery unit

Balanced Ventilation

Balanced ventilation systems avoid the main problems inherent in both central exhaust and central supply systems by neither pressurizing nor depressurizing the building. By supplying and exhausting approximately equal volumes of fresh outside air and polluted inside air, they avoid forcing air through wall and ceiling cavities where moisture might accumulate. Balanced systems are appropriate in any climate.

The balanced ventilation system usually has two fans and two duct systems. Supply and exhaust vents may be installed in every room, but a typical balanced ventilation system supplies fresh air to the rooms where people spend the most time (bedrooms and living rooms) and pulls air from the rooms where moisture and pollutants are most often generated (kitchen and bathrooms). Some designs may use a single-point exhaust. They also allow the use of filters to remove dust and pollen from outside air before introducing it into the house.

Balanced systems are more expensive, both to install and to operate, than supply or exhaust systems simply because they require two duct and fan systems.

Heat-Recovery Ventilation

The ultimate balanced system adds a heat-recovery unit (air-to-air heat exchanger). The heat-recovery unit saves energy by transferring heat from warm exhaust air to cold supply air in the winter, and vice-versa in the summer. Comfort is also improved because supply air is tempered before exiting supply registers.

Heat-recovery systems are more expensive to install because they are more complex and require powerful fans to overcome air flow resistance in the heat exchanger. They are most cost effective in climates with extreme winters or summers. In mild climates, the cost of powering the fans may exceed the energy savings.

A not-to-be-overlooked factor is that heat-recovery systems require more maintenance than other ventilation systems. They need to be cleaned periodically to maintain their efficiency and to prevent growth of mold and bacteria on the heat-exchange surfaces. When warm, moist air is cooled, condensate forms on cool heat-exchange surfaces and must be drained from the heat-recovery system. In cold climates, very cold air can result in frost formation in the heat exchanger, reducing efficiency and possibly damaging the unit.

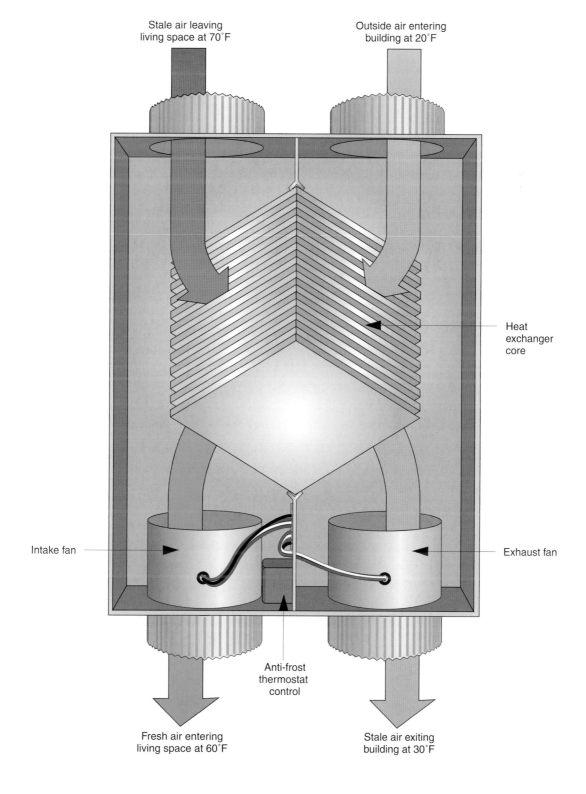

Stale air leaving
living space at 70°F

Outside air entering
building at 20°F

Heat
exchanger
core

Intake fan

Exhaust fan

Anti-frost
thermostat
control

Fresh air entering
living space at 60°F

Stale air exiting
building at 30°F

13

Lighting

We begin at the beginning, with *Edison's incandescent lamp*. After decades of no more than slight improvements, *halogen incandescent lamps* signaled the advent of energy efficiency in lighting.

Halogens remained popular for high intensity lighting, but fluorescent bulbs soon replaced incandescent forms for office and factory—even kitchens and bathrooms in the home. From there, it wasn't much of a stretch to miniaturize and coil fluorescent bulbs into *compact fluorescent lamps* as incandescent replacements. And now it appears *light-emitting diode lamps* will completely replace even the compact fluorescent.

The bottom lines with all types of lighting are *lamp efficacy* and *expected life*, which determine their *lighting life-cycle costs*.

Of course, the simplest trick for saving on your lighting bill is simply to turn lights off when they are not needed. This is easier said than done, however, so we introduce simple replacement *motion-detection switches* that turn off the lights when you leave a room.

You don't have enough money to switch all of your lighting right away? We include a utility lighting usage study that will serve as a guide to your *replacement priorities*.

Edison's Incandescent Lamp

Edison was not the first to make an electric lamp with an incandescent filament, but he was the first to make one with a filament that would burn more than a few hours. Patent No. 223,898, granted in 1880, used a carbonized bamboo fiber as its filament, which burned 1,250 hours.

Although manufacturers have switched to filaments of tungsten (which burn hotter and brighter), the ubiquitous, 50-cent, 40/60/75/100-watt light bulb hasn't changed much in the past 130 years.

That is changing. Countries around the world have already started banning the inefficient incandescent lamp in an attempt to reduce energy waste. In the United States, a 2007 law requiring light bulbs to meet an energy standard impossible to achieve with incandescent technology was stalled by politicians who felt the free market should take precedence. But all agree it is only a matter of time before the new, much higher efficiency lamps replace Edison's antique for all but a few specialty applications.

In the following pages we explain how the new halogen, compact-fluorescent (CFL), and light-emitting diode (LED) lamps work, and why you should implement your replacement plan now.

The "Old Standard" A-19 Incandescent Lamp

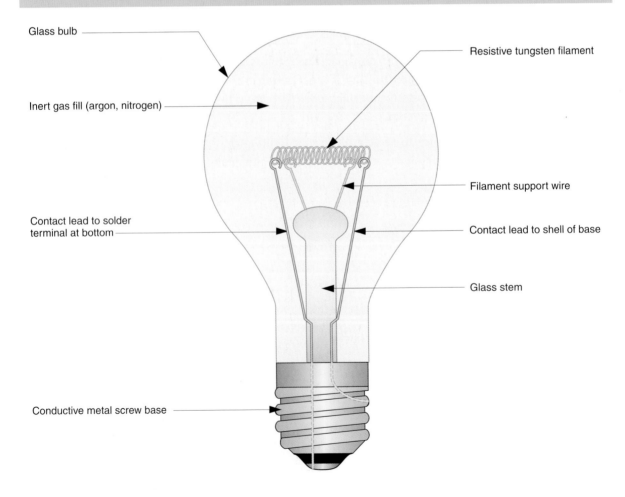

Glass bulb

Inert gas fill (argon, nitrogen)

Contact lead to solder terminal at bottom

Conductive metal screw base

Resistive tungsten filament

Filament support wire

Contact lead to shell of base

Glass stem

Halogen Incandescent Lamps

The tungsten halogen lamp is similar to the old standard incandescent lamp in that it uses a tungsten filament in an inert gas-filled bulb. It is different, however, in that the bulb also contains a halogen gas—either bromine or chlorine—which causes tungsten vaporized from the filament and deposited on the inside of the bulb to be redeposited onto the filament. The recycling of the tungsten increases the life of the filament and reduces darkening of the bulb.

Another benefit of the recycling (halogen cycle) is the ability to operate at a much higher temperature, resulting in an efficiency nearly twice that of the standard incandescent. Efficiency in a lamp is measured by its efficacy, or lumens of light output per watt of electrical input. The efficacy of all of the lamps discussed here compared on p. 320.

Halogen lamps are superior in efficiency, but they suffer from two practical drawbacks:

1. Operating at a much higher temperature, they pose a fire danger unless housed in an outer protective bulb (below) or metal cage.

2. Contaminants, especially the oil from your fingers, will cause hot spots and failure of the quartz bulb.

A Halogen A-19 Incandescent Lamp

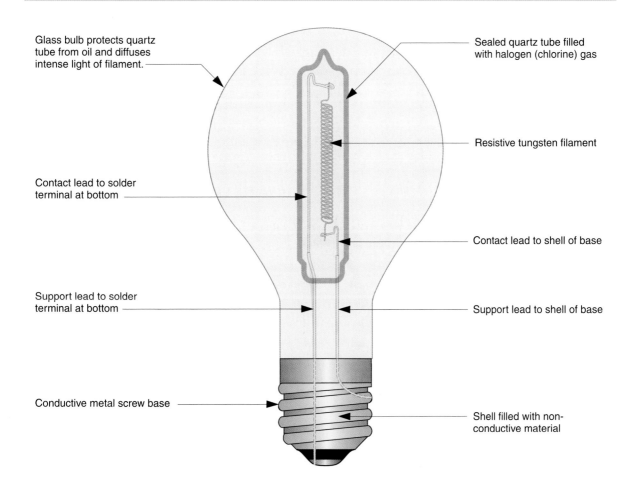

Glass bulb protects quartz tube from oil and diffuses intense light of filament.

Sealed quartz tube filled with halogen (chlorine) gas

Resistive tungsten filament

Contact lead to solder terminal at bottom

Contact lead to shell of base

Support lead to solder terminal at bottom

Support lead to shell of base

Conductive metal screw base

Shell filled with non-conductive material

Compact Fluorescent Lamps

The long fluorescent tubes we all know from our schools and offices have been around since 1941. They are roughly four times as efficient as the standard incandescent bulb, but their awkward shape makes them impractical for most residential uses.

Lighting engineers have long realized that a thin fluorescent bulb twisted into a compact spiral of about the same size and shape as the standard bulb could revolutionize residential lighting. The first commercial versions appeared in the early 1980s, but the expense of manufacturing resulted in a prohibitive price of about $15 per bulb. However, promotional programs by electric utilities have increased the volume to the point where CFLs now cost only about twice as much as standard bulbs.

A common objection to CFL bulbs is that they contain a small amount of mercury. Environmentalists point out, however, that the amount of mercury is less than that emitted by coal-fired plants in generating the amount of electricity saved by the bulb.

How a Compact Fluorescent Lamp (CFL) Works

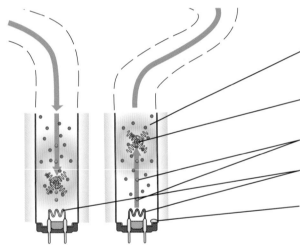

5. Photons hit a phosphor coating, resulting in more photons being re-emitted as white light.

4. When struck by electrons, atoms of mercury emit UV photons.

3. Electrons are "boiled" off the hot electrode.

2. The electronic ballast supplies low current to, and high voltage between, the two electrodes.

1. A drop of mercury provides mercury vapor (gas).

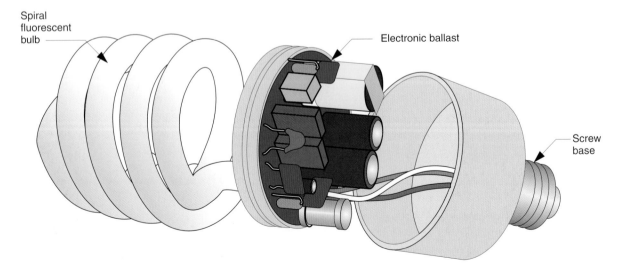

Spiral fluorescent bulb

Electronic ballast

Screw base

Efficacy

A lamp's output is measured in lumens, a measure of how bright it is perceived by the human eye. In lighting, efficiency is called efficacy, the ratio of lumens of light output to watts of electrical input. The efficacy of CFLs ranges from 50 to 70 lumens per watt, compared to just 10 to 16 for incandescents.

Life Span

The rated life span of CFLs ranges from 6,000 to 15,000 hours, compared to just 750 to 1,000 for standard incandescent bulbs. However, when turned on and off often, as in a bathroom, the life of a CFL is dramatically shortened. Because of the shortened life span and low power consumption of a CFL, the Energy Star program recommends not turning a CFL off when you will be turning it on again in fewer than 15 minutes.

Color Rendering

Our eyes are accustomed to two light sources: natural daylight (referred to as "cool") and the light produced by an incandescent bulb ("warm"). For indoor lighting, all other lamps are compared to the standard incandescent bulb. The Color Rendering Index (CRI) indicates how accurately bulbs reproduce this standard spectrum, with CRI-100 being perfect. The common "cool white" office fluorescent rates a 62, while a "warm white" CFL rates 80 to 85. Anything over 80 is considered very good.

Appearance

Another, usually unstated, objection is that the twisted bulb looks "weird." Bulb manufacturers have come to realize many customers won't buy a bulb unless it looks like the "light bulb" of their childhood. To this end, manufacturers have encased the spiral tube inside a more conventionally shaped outer shell. They have also begun to offer CFL versions of less prolific specialty bulbs such as those shown at right.

CFL Bulb Shapes

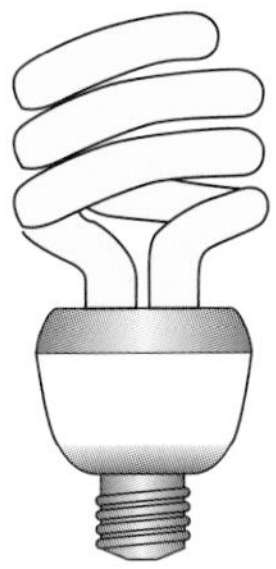

MINI-SPIRAL OR TWIST

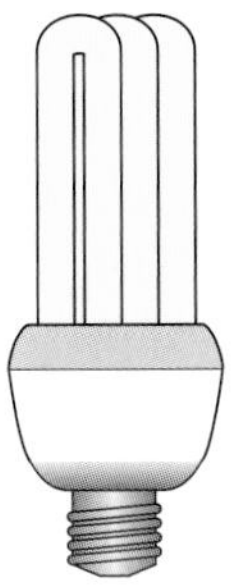

TUBE OR UNIVERSAL

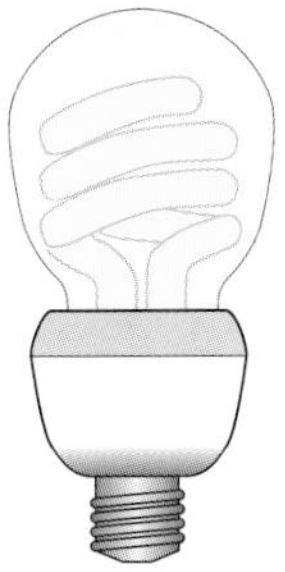

INCANDESCENT/A-LINE

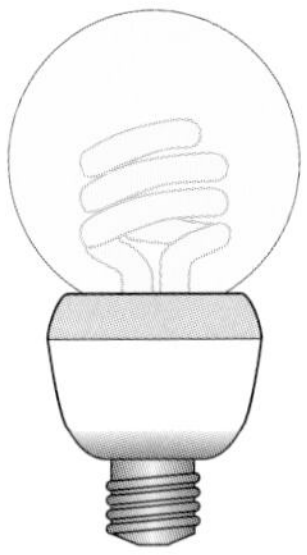

GLOBE: G25, 30, 40

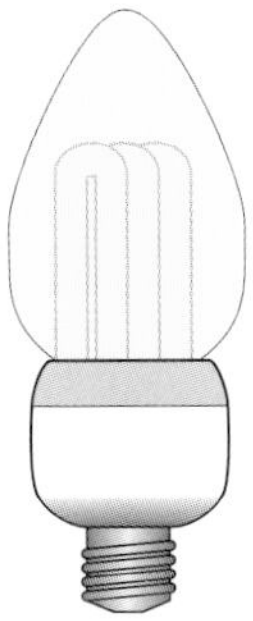

CANDELABRA OR POST

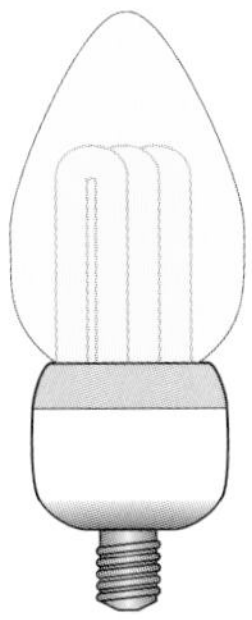

CANDELABRA OR POST

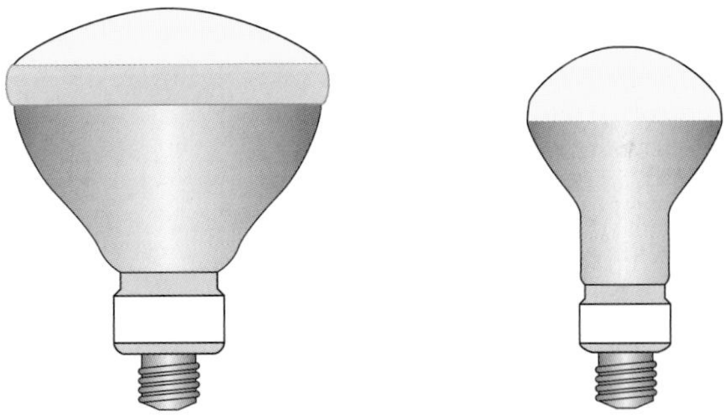

INDOOR OR OUTDOOR: R20, R30, R40, PAR38

Light-Emitting Diode Lamps

Light-emitting diodes (LEDs) are tiny solid-state chips consisting of two layers of different semiconducting materials. When a voltage is applied across the LED junction, current flows from the positive lead to the negative lead but not in the opposite direction. Electrons flowing across the junction fall from a higher energy state to a lower energy state, emitting the energy difference as photons of light.

Depending on the semiconducting materials, the photons may be red, green, or blue. A white LED can be made by combining red, green, and blue LEDs or more commonly, as shown below, by coating a blue LED with a yellow phosphor that then converts the blue light to white light.

Individual LEDs operate on 2 to 4 volts DC, depending on their color, instead of normal household 110 volts AC. In addition, the light output of a single LED is much less than that required for general residential lighting, so LED lamps combine many individual diodes in series (30 to 50 LEDs in a string). Since the light output of an LED is highly directional, the individual diodes are arranged in a cylindrical or a hemispherical pattern, as shown in the lamps on the facing page.

How a Light-Emitting Diode (LED) Works

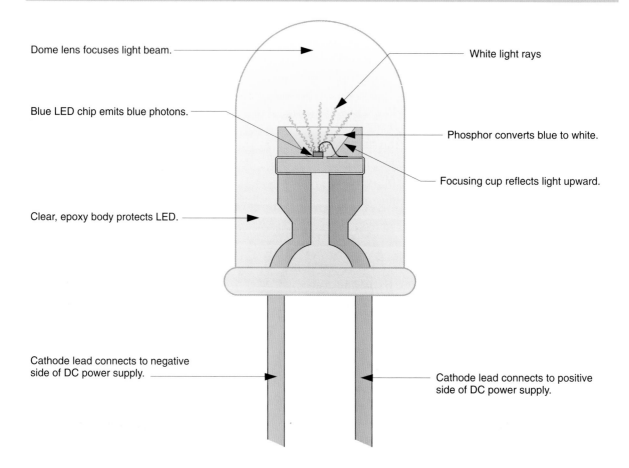

Dome lens focuses light beam.

White light rays

Blue LED chip emits blue photons.

Phosphor converts blue to white.

Focusing cup reflects light upward.

Clear, epoxy body protects LED.

Cathode lead connects to negative side of DC power supply.

Cathode lead connects to positive side of DC power supply.

Efficacy

The lumens per watt of incandescent bulbs ranges from 10 (40-watt) to 17 (150-watt). By comparison, the efficacy of CFLs (see p. 320) ranges from 50 to 70, while white LEDs achieve an even greater efficacy of 60 to 90.

Color Rendering

The LED's Color Rendering Index (CRI) can be made as near 100 (perfect) as desired, either by adjusting the relative outputs of separate red, blue, and green chips or by using of phosphors. However, high CRI comes at the cost of efficacy. A CRI 80 is the most common.

Life Spans

The rated life spans of incandescent bulbs range from 750 to 1,000 hours, while CFLs last about 10,000 hours. Because the LED is solid state, and nothing is arcing or oxidizing, its lifetime is theoretically infinite. Practically speaking you can count on at least 30,000 hours of use.

Other Advantages

In addition to superior efficiency and phenomenally long life, the LED is rugged, dimmable from 0 to 100%, and cool enough to touch.

Two LED Replacement Bulb Shapes

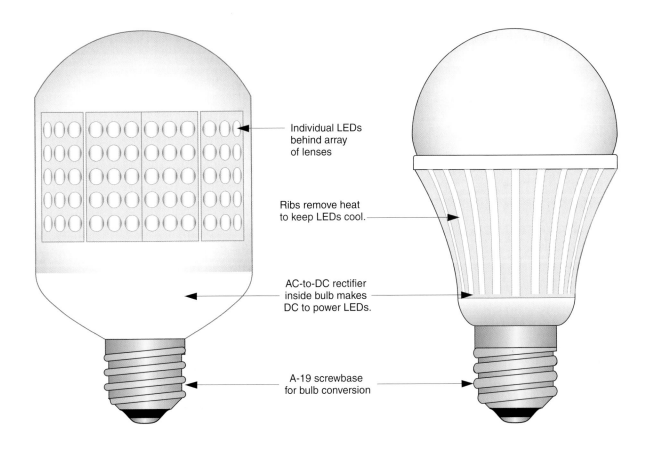

Individual LEDs behind array of lenses

Ribs remove heat to keep LEDs cool.

AC-to-DC rectifier inside bulb makes DC to power LEDs.

A-19 screwbase for bulb conversion

Lamp Efficacy and Expected Life

The chart below and table at right illustrate the tremendous improvements in efficiency and longevity that lighting manufacturers have achieved over the past twenty years.

Compared to the standard incandescent bulb, which has changed little in the past 130 years, the quartz halogen bulb uses roughly half as much electricity; the compact fluorescent a quarter; and the light-emitting diode one-sixth!

In addition to efficiency, average lamp lifetimes have increased even more dramatically. If you are tired of replacing that 750-hour incandescent light bulb in the hall, think about the 10,000-hour CFL and the 50,000-hour LED.

Lamp Efficacies

Light Out Lumens	Incandescent Watts	Halogen Watts	CFL Watts	LED Watts
450	40	22	9	6
800	60	51	14	9
1,100	75	49	18	–
1,600	100	74	25	16

Of course, CFLs and LEDs cost more than the old 50-cent incandescent bulbs, but the life-cycle cost calculations on the facing page demonstrate that homeowners who stick with the old are being "penny wise and pound foolish."

Efficacy (Lumens per Watt) of Light Sources

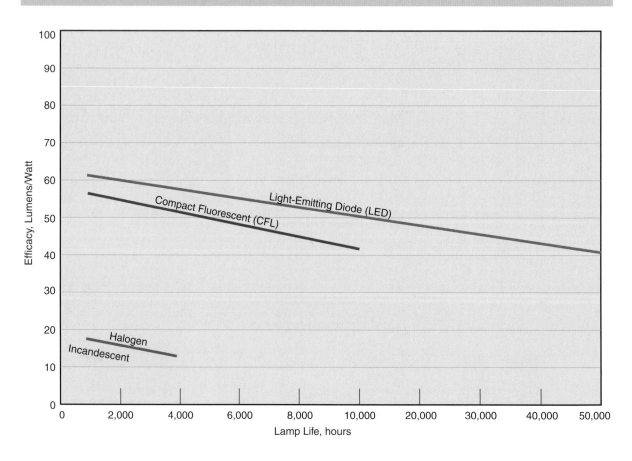

Lighting Life-Cycle Costs

Life-cycle costing is a tool used by economists and businessmen to minimize costs over a long term. The life-cycle cost of operating a single light fixture in your home consists of the cost of the bulbs, including replacements, plus the cost of the electricity consumed by the bulbs over the period. To compare our four lamp types, we will use the average life of the longest-lasting type, the LED, as our time period.

The results speak for themselves. The halogen bulb saves nothing, its single advantage a longer life. However, the CFL and LED save $284 and $303 per bulb. To see the advantage of a house-wide replacement, we multiplied the per bulb savings by 30, resulting in life-cycle savings of $8,520 and $9,090!

Lamp Efficacies

	Incandescent	Halogen	CFL	LED
Life span, hours	1,000	2,500	10,000	50,000
Bulbs used in 50,000 hr.	50	20	5	1
Cost per lamp*	$0.50	$4	$1	$15
Total cost of bulbs	$25	$80	$5	$15
Watts equivalent to 60W	60	51	14	9
kWh used in 50,000 hr.	3,000	2,550	700	450
Electricity cost @ $.115/kWh	$345	$293	$81	$52
LCC of bulbs + electricity	$370	$373	$86	$67
Lifetime saving per bulb	–	–$3	$284	$303
Lifetime saving for 30 bulbs	–	–$90	$8,520	$9,090

* 2012 prices. LED prices are expected to drop by half by 2015.

Life-Cycle Costs of Competing Light Sources

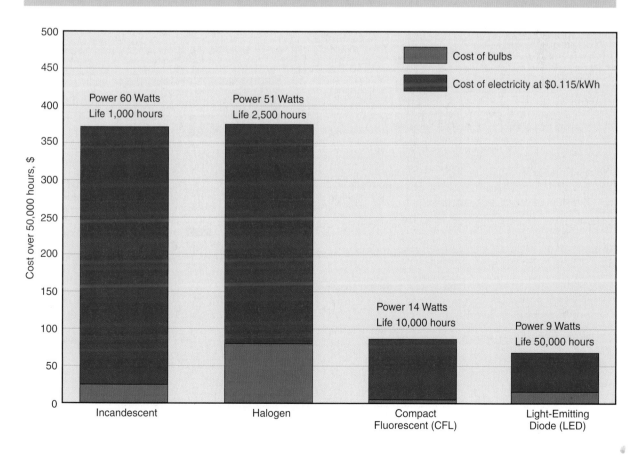

Motion-Detection Switches

You have probably experienced them in public rest rooms. You walk into the room and, without touching a switch, the lights come on. A motion-activated sensor detected your arrival and turned the lights on for you. Nice touch, but whoever installed the switch didn't have courtesy in mind. When you left the room the switch turned the lights off, saving the owner a lot of money.

The motion-detection switch contains passive infrared (PIR) sensors. These sense the infrared energy radiated by the human body. To distinguish between a moving body and objects in the room that are simply warming up to body temperature, motion detectors look not at the voltage output of an infrared sensor but at its rate of change.

The location of the switch is critical because: (1) it receives line-of-sight radiation (nothing must block its view), (2) its peripheral vision extends ±90° from ahead, and (3) its range is 20 ft.

Savings are proportional to the wattage of the lighting controlled, the number of hours the switch would otherwise be left on, and the price of electricity.

Example: A bathroom has 200 watts of installed lighting, and forgetful residents leave the light burning an average of 4 hr. per day. Electricity costs $0.18/kWh.

$$\text{Annual Saving} = kW \times Hours \times 365 \times Price/kWh$$
$$= 0.2 \times 4 \times 365 \times \$0.18$$
$$= \$52.56$$

Automatic Motion-Detection Light Switches

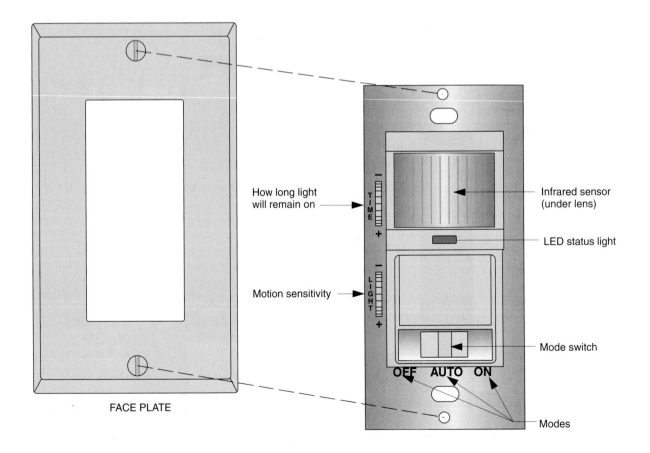

FACE PLATE

How long light will remain on

Motion sensitivity

TIME

LIGHT

Infrared sensor (under lens)

LED status light

Mode switch

OFF   AUTO   ON

Modes

Replacement Priorities

A study conducted by the Tacoma, Washington, Public Utilities determined the average consumption of electricity for residential lighting to be approximately 1,800 kWh per year. The percentage of the total consumed in each room or area of the house is shown in the graph below. Just two rooms consumed 35% of the total: the kitchen and the living room.

About 43% of the kitchen lights and 35% of living room lights were on at least 3 hours per day. Assuming an average use of 4 hours per day, annual consumption for a single 60-watt bulb would be 87.6 kWh. Substituting an equivalent 14-watt compact fluorescent lamp reduces consumption per bulb to 20.5 kWh, for an annual saving of 67.1 kWh.

At the 2011 national average electric rate of $0.115/kWh, the annual monetary saving per bulb would be $7.72. At a cost of $1.00 per bulb, payback would be just six weeks. With such a rapid payback it is obvious that it would pay to replace every bulb in your home.

At a cost of about $1.00 per CFL, funding should not be a reason to delay. If you are short of time, use the graph below as a guide to the order in which bulbs should be replaced. And speaking of time, remember that incandescent bulbs need to be replaced ten times for every CFL and fifty times for each LED.

Usage of Lighting in the Home

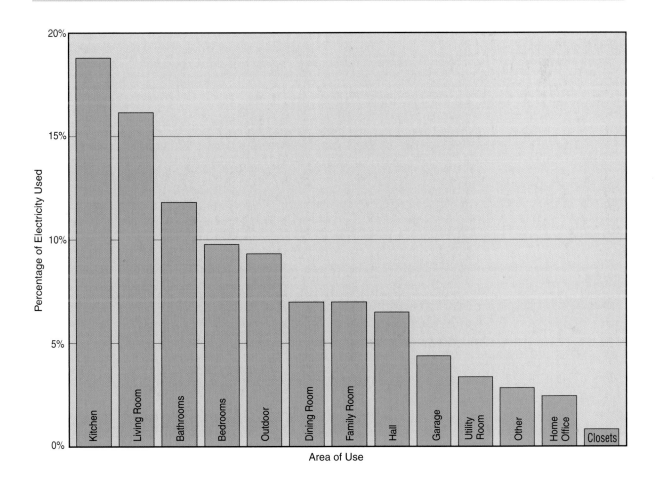

14

Appliance Efficiency

In 1992 the U.S. Environmental Protection Agency (EPA) introduced Energy Star, a trademarked, voluntary labeling program for identifying and promoting energy-efficient products. Appliances and other electrical equipment carrying the Energy Star logo generally use 20% to 30% less energy than required by federal standards.

Beyond the familiar blue-and-white Energy Star logo, what does the program offer the consumer trying to make an energy-conscious choice of appliances? It requires that all appliances carrying the Energy Star sticker also display an "Energy Guide" label showing the results of efficiency tests performed in accordance with the Department of Energy's standard procedures. The label shows the energy consumption of the particular model, compared with similar products, and the approximate annual operating costs.

In this chapter we explain the efficiency improvements in *room air conditioners, dishwashers, clothes washers*, and *refrigerators*.

Reading appliance energy guides will tell you how much that appliance will cost to run. Then, *measuring (your present) appliance electrical usage* will allow you to compute annual savings and to determine whether it is worth upgrading.

Last, but perhaps not least, we will show you a device for *reducing phantom electrical loads*—the energy consumed by many devices even while they are "off."

Room Air Conditioners

In moving heat instead of generating heat, air conditioners can be more than 100% efficient. The efficiency of a room air conditioner is given as its Energy Efficiency Ratio (EER), the ratio of output Btu/hr. to input watts of electricity. Prior to 1990, air conditioner EERs ranged from about 6.0 to 8.0. Today, a top Energy Star air conditioner rates 10.8. Even if your present room air conditioner is only 10 years old, its EER has probably dropped to 8.0 or less.

The annual saving from replacing your old air conditioner can be calculated as:

$$\text{Annual saving} = \text{Present cost} \times (1 - \text{EER}_{old}/\text{EER}_{new})$$

Example: You live in a hot climate where your room air conditioner runs 24/7 for 100 days, costing you $280 per year. Due to its age, you guess its EER is about 8.0. How long would it take to earn back the $280 price of a new AC with EER 10.8?

$$
\begin{aligned}
\text{Annual saving} &= \text{Present cost} \times (1 - \text{EER}_{old}/\text{EER}_{new}) \\
&= \$280 \times (1 - 8.0/10.8) \\
&= \$280 \times 0.26 \\
&= \$72.80/\text{year}
\end{aligned}
$$

The new AC would pay for itself in 3.8 years.

How a Room Air Conditioner Works

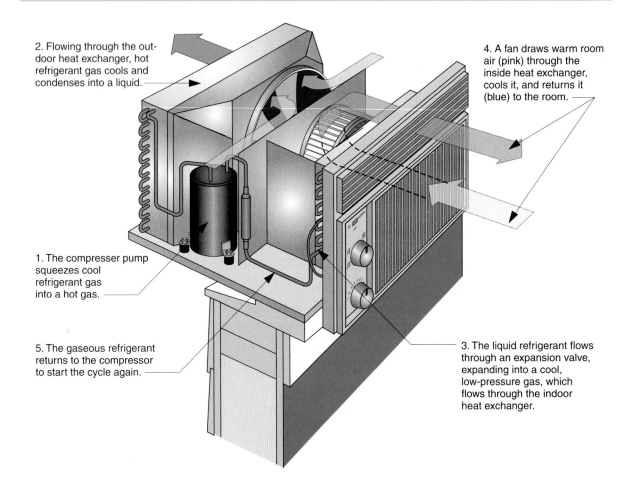

2. Flowing through the outdoor heat exchanger, hot refrigerant gas cools and condenses into a liquid.

4. A fan draws warm room air (pink) through the inside heat exchanger, cools it, and returns it (blue) to the room.

1. The compresser pump squeezes cool refrigerant gas into a hot gas.

5. The gaseous refrigerant returns to the compressor to start the cycle again.

3. The liquid refrigerant flows through an expansion valve, expanding into a cool, low-pressure gas, which flows through the indoor heat exchanger.

Dishwashers

If your present dishwasher was manufactured before 1994, it is costing you an extra $40 per year compared to an Energy Star dishwasher. The savings result from using an average of 10 fewer gallons of hot water per wash. If you run a load of dishes every day, that would amount to 3,650 gallons per year and 73,000 gallons over a 20-year lifetime.

But what if you wash your dishes by hand? While you may be breaking even now with your old machine, compared to a new Energy Star dishwasher, washing by hand costs $40 more in energy and water and 230 hours of your time! What is your time worth per hour?

Example: Disregarding the value of your time, how long would it take for a new Energy Star dishwasher to pay for itself?

Annual saving = $40

Payback years = Cost of new washer/Annual saving
= $270/$40
= 6.75 years

If that sounds like a bad investment, put it in terms of rate of return (interest rate) on your investment:

Rate of return = Annual saving/Cost of new washer
= $40/$270
= 14.8%

Inside and under the Dishwasher

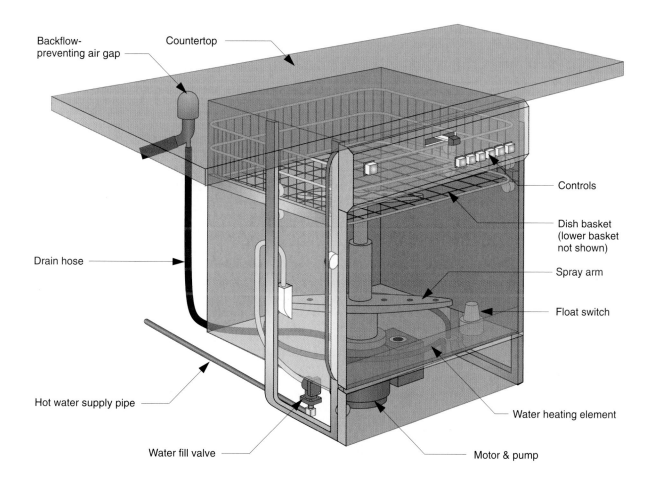

Backflow-preventing air gap

Countertop

Controls

Dish basket (lower basket not shown)

Spray arm

Float switch

Drain hose

Hot water supply pipe

Water fill valve

Water heating element

Motor & pump

Clothes Washers, Old and New

When I was growing up, the clothes washer in the basement or laundry room loaded from the top. Clothes were dumped into the perforated basket, and the machine's timer filled the tub with hot water. An agitator twisted back and forth, sloshing the clothes, water, and detergent. After a few minutes, the water was pumped out, and the whole washing process was repeated. Then the wash water was drained, and a load of fresh rinse water filled the tub. Finally, after the rinse water drained out, the machine started jumping around as the basket spun like a centrifuge. When the machine stopped, Mom lifted out the heavy, saturated clothes and placed them in the clothes dryer. Or, if you lived in a rural area, Mom hung the soggy clothes out on a clothesline to dry in the sun and wind.

If you didn't own a washing machine, you took your laundry down to the laundromat. There the machines were quite different. You loaded the machines through a front door into a basket that spun horizontally. There was no agitator. Looking through the glass door, you could see the basket turning slowly while the laundry tumbled from the top of the turning basket back into a small amount of water. After several cycles of filling and pumping out water, the basket spun wildly. When all motion ceased, you opened the door and removed your laundry. It was surprising how much lighter and dryer the clothes were.

Why do you suppose the laundromat owner installed those expensive front-loading washers? Wasn't he in business to make money? Well, now we know. The machines used a lot less hot water, and the extra cost of the machines was paid back many times over.

But now you can buy your own water- and money-saving washing machine. Every manufacturer and every retailer offers front-loading Energy Star-qualified machines (there are more efficient top-loaders now, as well). You will suffer sticker shock when you see the price difference, but it is well worth going for the efficiency, as we will now explain.

The Differences

Compared to older machines, Energy Star-qualified washing machines:

1. Use less than 270 kWh of electricity per year, versus 390 kWh, for a saving of 120 kWh.

2. Use less than 14 gallons of water per load, versus 27 gallons. Assuming 300 washer loads per year, that's a saving of 3,900 gallons per year or 43,000 gallons over an average lifetime of 11 years.

Life-Cycle Cost Using Electricity

Here is the Energy Star program life-cycle cost analysis for those using electricity both for heating water and running a clothes dryer.

	Conventional	Energy Star	Savings
Electricity, kWh	8,657	6,193	2,464
Water, gallons	133,969	62,007	71,962
Electricity cost @ $0.109/kWh	$751	$537	$214
Water cost @ $7.50/1,000 gal.	$800	$370	$430
Purchase price	$492	$750	–$258
Life-cycle cost (Total)	$2,043	$1,657	$386

Life-Cycle Cost Using Natural Gas

Here is the Energy Star program life-cycle cost analysis for those using natural gas both for heating water and running a clothes dryer.

	Conventional	Energy Star	Savings
Electricity, kWh	888	626	262
Water, gallons	133,969	62,007	71,962
Gas, therms	328	229	99
Electricity cost @ $0.109/kWh	$77	$54	$23
Water cost @ $7.50/1,000 gal.	$800	$370	$430
Gas cost @ $1.05/therm	$274	$191	$83
Purchase price	$492	$750	–$258
Life-cycle cost (Total)	$1,643	$1,366	$277

Top- and Front-Loading Clothes Washers

TOP-LOADING WASHER

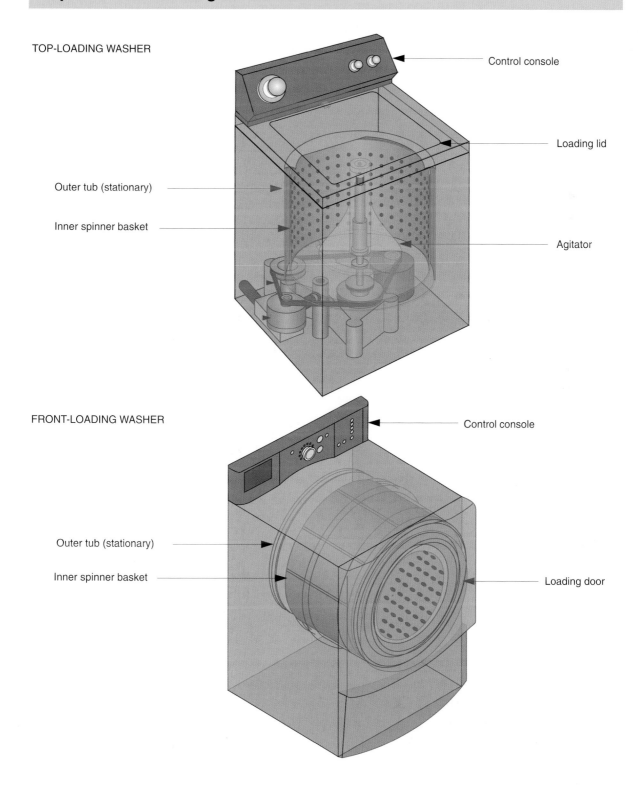

Control console

Loading lid

Outer tub (stationary)

Inner spinner basket

Agitator

FRONT-LOADING WASHER

Outer tub (stationary)

Inner spinner basket

Control console

Loading door

Refrigerators

Of all your home appliances, refrigerators have been improved in energy efficiency the most. The illustration below compares the construction of that pre-1980 "icebox" humming away in your kitchen to that of a new Energy Star-qualified unit. The three big improvements are:

1. R-7/in. foam vs. R-3/in. fiberglass insulation.

2. Elimination of metal, heat short-circuiting stiffeners by the use of the rigid foam.

3. Smaller compressor allowed by reduced heat load.

Below is a table showing the average costs of running typical 20-cu.-ft. refrigerators with top freezers.

Year manufactured	kWh/yr	Annual Cost[1]	Annual Saving[2]
Before 1980	2,215	$241	$195
1980–1989	1,709	$186	$140
1990–1992	1,285	$140	$94
1993–2000	857	$93	$47
2001–2008	537	$59	$12
New Energy Star	423	$46	—

[1] Assuming US average residential rate of $0.109/kWh.
[2] Assuming replacement with an Energy Star refrigerator.

Refrigerators, Old and New

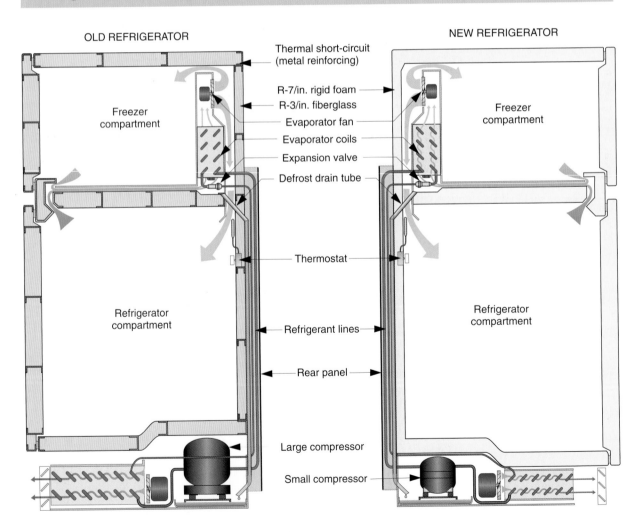

Reading Appliance Energy Guides

When you go shopping for a major appliance, you will find a bright yellow Energy Guide label stuck to the appliance. Appliance manufacturers are required to test the energy efficiency of their products using standard test procedures developed by the US Department of Energy. The test results are printed on the yellow Energy Guide label. The label estimates how much energy the appliance uses, compares its energy use to the use of other similar products, and gives the approximate annual operating costs. Note that the estimated annual cost to run assumes the cost per kWh of electricity listed at the bottom of the label. Calculate your annual cost by multiplying the estimated annual kWh listed in the middle of the label by your local cost per kWh. This can be found on your monthly electric bill or by calling your utility customer service department.

Appliance Energy Guide Label

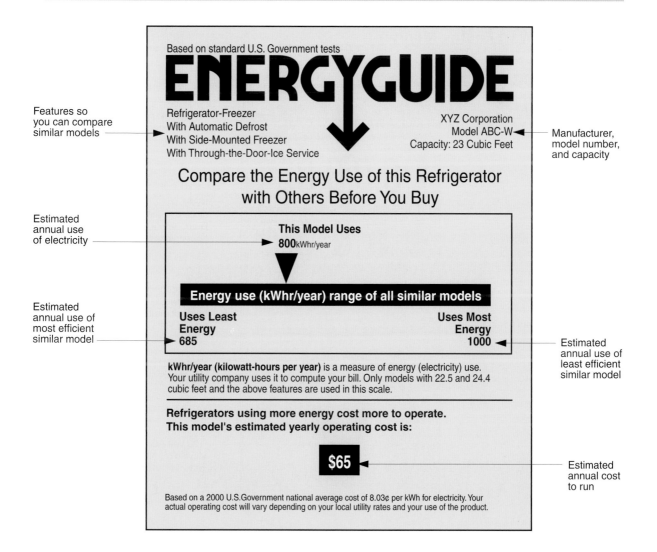

Measuring Appliance Electrical Usage

On p. 330, we listed the estimated annual electrical consumption of 20-cu.-ft. refrigerators of different ages. The calculated savings from replacing these refrigerators with new Energy Star-qualified refrigerators of the same size are dramatic—probably sufficient to convince you to take action. But if your refrigerator is of a different size or type, or if you have no idea how old it is, you may wish to measure its actual consumption. Fortunately, this will not require a degree in electrical engineering, nor will it require a laboratory full of test equipment. All you need is a P3 Kill A Watt® energy monitor (see illustration below), available on the web for less than $20.

The Kill A Watt

The device plugs into any 115 VAC outlet. To measure how much electricity any appliance or device is consuming, simply plug it into the receptacle on the front face of the Kill A Watt. Push buttons allow you to read:

- volts
- amps
- watts
- hours since last reset
- accumulated kWh since last reset

The Kill A Watt Energy Monitor

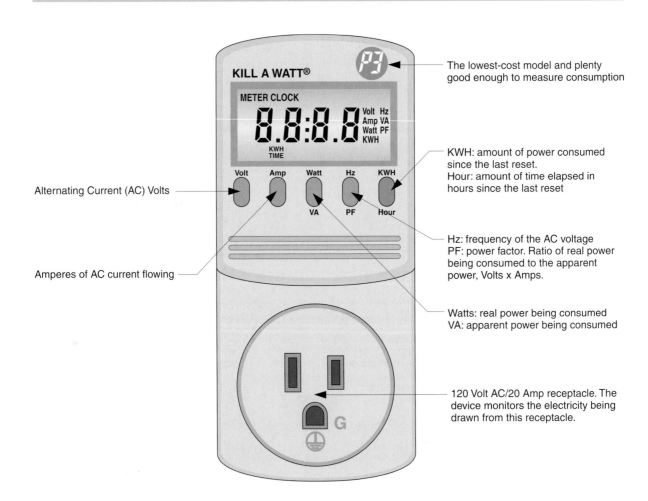

The lowest-cost model and plenty good enough to measure consumption

Alternating Current (AC) Volts

Amperes of AC current flowing

KWH: amount of power consumed since the last reset.
Hour: amount of time elapsed in hours since the last reset

Hz: frequency of the AC voltage
PF: power factor. Ratio of real power being consumed to the apparent power, Volts x Amps.

Watts: real power being consumed
VA: apparent power being consumed

120 Volt AC/20 Amp receptacle. The device monitors the electricity being drawn from this receptacle.

Using the Kill A Watt

The illustration below shows the Kill A Watt being used to determine the annual electrical consumption of a refrigerator. Here is the procedure:

1. Plug the Kill A Watt into the nearest outlet.

2. Unplug the refrigerator, and plug it into the Kill A Watt.

3. Note the time.

4. After 24 hours, press the "KWH" button and write down the kWh displayed.

5. Multiply the kWh by 365 for the annual use.

Measuring Electricity Usage of a Refrigerator

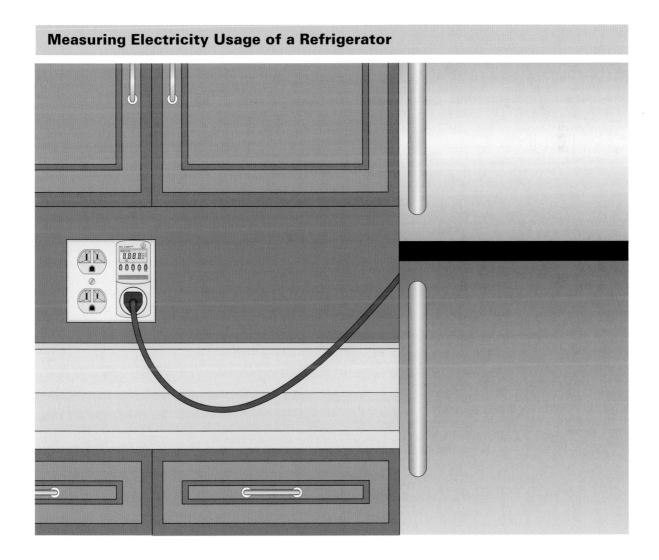

Reducing Phantom Electrical Loads

A phantom load is power being drawn, unknown to you, by an electrical appliance or other device while the device is either "off" or on "standby." As the saying goes, "Out of sight, out of mind." Until you get the bill!

What sorts of device draw phantom loads? Generally, anything with a remote control, a continuous display (including an LED clock), a soft keypad (such as your microwave), a "sleep" mode, or one of those little black power modules plugged into the wall.

Finding Your Phantom Loads

How can you tell if a device is drawing power and, if so, how much? There are two ways:

- Find it in the table at right
- Measure its draw with the Kill A Watt (p. 332)

If you use the Kill A Watt, you need not measure use for 24 hours as you did with the refrigerator because phantom loads don't cycle on and off. Just read "Watts."

Calculating the Costs

Simple. There are 8,760 hours in a year, so 1 Watt for a whole year is 8,760 Wh or 8.76 kWh. The average price of electricity is $0.115, so each Watt of phantom load will cost 8.76 kWh × $0.115/kWh = $1.00/yr.

Eliminating Phantom Loads

1. If you aren't using the device regularly, unplug it.

2. Home entertainment centers and computer set-ups usually consist of a number of separate components (like the computer setup on the facing page). Plug all the components into a single power strip so you can turn everything off with a single switch.

3. Energy Star products use minimal standby power, so when shopping for a new electrical device, look for the Energy Star label.

Life-Cycle Cost of Electricity

Lawrence Berkeley National Laboratory (LBL) has measured and compiled the standby or off power draw of nearly every type of household device. Here are the average results and estimated costs per year at LBL's assumed price of electricity, $0.115/kWh.

Device	Mode	Ave. Watts	Cost/yr
Answering machine	Standby	4.0	$4.00
Audio minisystem	Off	8.3	$8.30
CD player	Off	5.0	$5.00
Cellphone charger	Standby	0.3	$0.30
Clock on radio	Off	2.0	$2.00
Computer display, CRT	Sleep	12.1	$12.10
Computer display, LCD	Sleep	1.4	$1.40
Computer, desktop	Sleep	21.1	$21.10
Computer, laptop	Sleep	15.8	$15.80
Cordless phone	Standby	2.8	$2.80
Fax, inkjet	Off	5.3	$5.30
Garage door opener	Ready	4.5	$4.50
Microwave oven	Off	3.1	$3.10
Modem, cable	On	6.3	$6.30
Modem, DSL	On	5.4	$5.40
Multifunction device, inkjet	Off	5.3	$5.30
Multifunction device, laser	Off	3.1	$3.10
Printer, inkjet	Off	1.3	$1.30
Printer, laser	Off	1.6	$1.60
Scanner, flatbed	Off	2.5	$2.50
Set-top box, cable	Off	17.8	$17.80
Set-top box, cable with DVR	Off	44.6	$44.60
Set-top box, satellite	Off	15.6	$15.60
Set-top box, satellite with DVR	Off	28.4	$28.40
Television, CRT	Off	3.0	$3.00
Television, rear projection	Off	6.9	$6.90
VCR	Off	4.7	$4.70

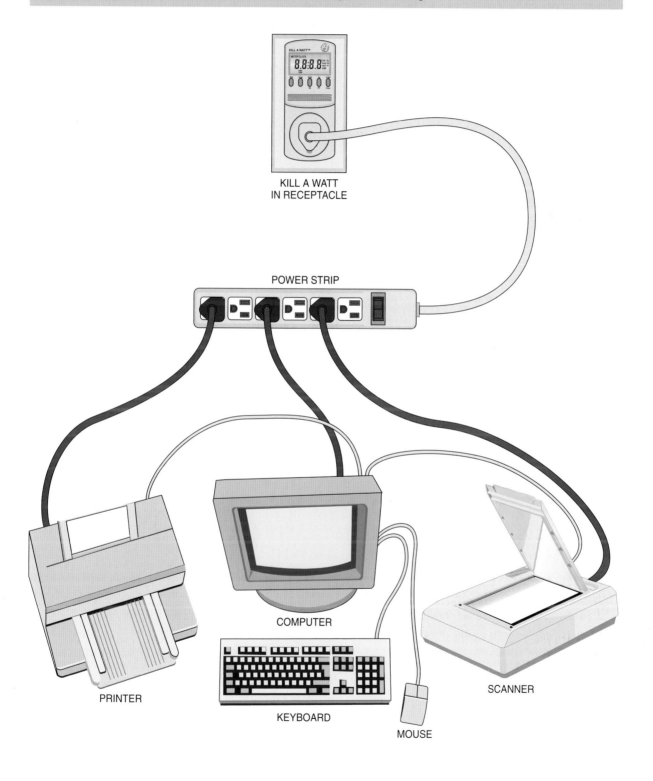

KILL A WATT
IN RECEPTACLE

POWER STRIP

PRINTER

COMPUTER

KEYBOARD

MOUSE

SCANNER

15

Solar Tempering

Since man constructed the first rudimentary shelter, he has always instinctively utilized free energy from the sun. With all of our modern materials and construction techniques, what are our *solar possibilities* today? Our first task is *determining solar access and shading* for our site. To do that, we utilize *solar path charts*, or maps of the sun's path at different seasons and latitudes.

Next we consider the effects of *glazing orientation and tilt*. We will see that good solar performance requires placing a high percentage of glazing (windows) on the south wall and little or none on the north. We also discover that ordinary vertical windows perform as well or better than tilted windows when the ground is covered with snow.

Of course, windows that gather the sun's heat in winter can also gain heat in the summer, so we look at techniques for *shading the summer sun*.

If we wish to get a high percentage of our heat from the sun, we have to take in as much radiation as possible while the sun is shining. In order that the building not overheat and that we have heat to carry us through the sunless night, we must also provide a means for *storing excess solar gain*.

Utilizing all of the tricks above, we are able to predict the solar performance of our design using a simple *design procedure for solar tempering*. The final step of the design procedure then allows us to calculate the required surface areas of various heat-storing building materials in five different *thermal mass patterns*.

Solar Possibilities

What Is Solar Tempering?

There are many techniques for reducing energy consumption in buildings. Techniques such as increasing insulation, caulking and weatherstripping, and using high-performance windows and doors have been described in previous chapters. These energy conservation techniques are primarily buffers against cold climates, reducing the rate of escape of interior heat.

There are, however, techniques that capture free energy from the sun, reducing—and in some cases eliminating—the need for conventional central heat sources. These solar techniques can be roughly divided into two categories: active and passive solar heating. Passive techniques rely upon the interrelationship of solar radiation, the mass of the building, and siting; these capture, store, and release solar energy. With little, if any, increased cost, and with no noisy equipment to maintain, passive solar has become the technique of choice.

During the past 25 years, designers have learned a lot about the actual performance of passive solar buildings. This chapter contains a condensation of that knowledge in the form of a design procedure with simple graphs and tables that allows the design of near-optimum residential passive solar buildings anywhere in North America.

Passive solar, of course, is no substitute for standard energy conservation techniques. An underlying assumption for all that follows is a very high level of energy conservation. State and local energy standards should be considered the minimum for any passive solar design.

Conservation First

Guidelines for energy conservation in conjunction with passive solar design include the following:

1. Insulate walls, roofs, and floors one step beyond the local norm; for example, if the code calls for R-19 walls, make them R-25.

2. Select triple-glazed, low-E, or heat mirror windows, and insulated doors.

3. Reduce air infiltration through the use of continuous air/vapor barriers and caulking and weatherstripping of all openings.

4. Reduce the areas of windows and doors on the north side of the building.

5. Orient the building and openings to maximize the effects of cooling summer breezes and minimize the effects of winter winds.

6. Utilize landscape elements to provide summer shade and to block winter winds.

7. If natural deciduous shading is not possible, provide overhangs and projections to shade glazings during the cooling season.

8. Ventilate roofs and attics to avoid condensation damage and summer overheating.

Direct Thermal Gain Sun Space

Of all the passive solar types, direct gain is the easiest to understand, since it is a simple variation of an ordinary house with south-facing windows. A direct-gain design is one in which the solar radiation directly enters and heats the living spaces. The building itself is the solar collector.

In the heating season during daylight hours, sunlight enters through south-facing windows, patio doors, clerestories, or skylights. The radiation strikes and is absorbed by floors, walls, ceilings, and furnishings. As anyone who has ever been in a south-facing room in winter realizes, some of the heat is transferred to the air immediately, warming the room. The rest of the heat is absorbed into the structure and objects in the room, to be released slowly during the night, filling some of the overnight heating requirement. In extreme designs, increased surface absorptivities and increased amounts of mass allow capture and storage of a full day's heat supply.

Although ceilings can be designed to store heat, common direct-gain storage materials are most easily incorporated into floors and walls, which frequently serve a structural purpose, as well. Two very simple but effective storage masses that can be incorporated into any home are a masonry, tile, or slate floor, and walls with double layers of gypsum drywall.

Open floor plans are recommended, to allow distribution of the released heat throughout the house by natural air circulation.

Thermally Isolated Sun Space

Attached sun spaces are frequently constructed as extensions to homes. They are generally considered secondary-use spaces, in which heat is either collected and vented directly to the living space or is stored for later use. The energy collected is generally used to heat both the sun space and the adjacent living space.

Sun spaces are designed for one of two basic modes of operation. In the first, the sun space is isolated from the living space (middle illustration at right) by an insulated wall and doors that may be closed. As a result of this isolation, the sun space is not treated as part of the conditioned space and its temperature is allowed to fluctuate beyond the range of human comfort.

Thermally Integrated Sun Space

In the second case, the sun space is integrated with the living space (bottom illustration at right) and its temperature is controlled with auxiliary heat or heat from the main living areas.

Integration is desirable when the space is primarily a living space. Isolation is desirable when the sun space is used primarily as a greenhouse, generating more water vapor than the house can safely absorb without causing condensation and mildew.

Sun space glazings are often tilted for maximum light penetration and collection, but this exposes the glazings to increased summer heat gain. Two solutions are planting deciduous shade trees to block direct summer sun and ventilating windows and doors left open during the summer.

In northern areas, sun space glazings should either be of a high-performance type (double-glazed with high-solar-gain low-E coating) or covered at night with a form of movable window insulation.

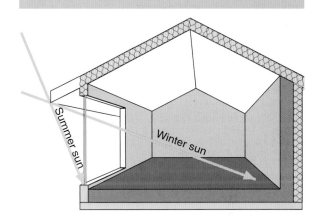

Direct Solar Gain

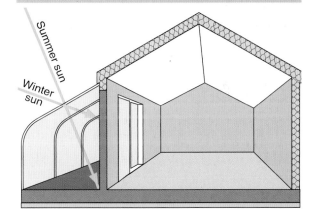

Thermally Isolated Sun Space

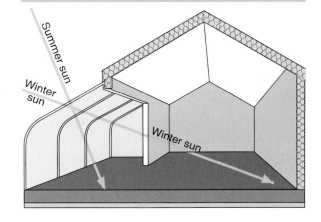

Thermally Integrated Sun Space

Determining Solar Access and Shading

The intensity of solar radiation striking glazing is affected by the glazing's orientation to the sun and the fraction of the sky blocked by permanent objects such as trees and buildings. Optimum solar access permits no shading between the hours of 8 AM and 4 PM, from September 21 through March 21. These hours and seasons are represented by the darker yellow areas in the charts on the facing page.

In planning glazing, you can plot solar access on a sun chart, a map of the sky viewed from the location of the glazing. In the pages that follow, you will find sun charts for latitudes in the United States and southern Canada.

Measuring the Position of the Sun

On the charts, the height scale, from 0° to 90°, represents *altitude*, the angle of the sun above the horizon; the horizontal scale represents *azimuth*, the number of degrees east or west of true south. To plot obstructions on your sun chart, you need to determine both their azimuths and altitudes.

To find altitude, sight the top of an object along the straight edge of a protractor with added string and weight, as shown in the top illustration at right. Read the altitude where the string crosses the outside of the scale.

To find azimuth, first determine the direction of true south. A simple method is to see where the sun is at solar noon—halfway between the times of sunrise and sunset. Then, simply use a protractor and a piece of string (red) as shown in the illustration at bottom right. Standing at the proposed location of the glazing, point the zero on the protractor toward true south and stretch the string toward the object. The string will cross the azimuth reading.

Take as many readings as you need to plot the outlines of all obstructing objects on the sun chart, as shown in the "Good Solar Access" and "Poor Solar Access" examples on the facing page.

Measuring the Sun's Altitude

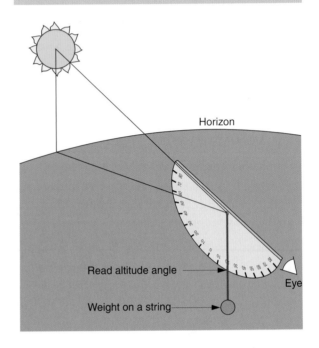

Horizon

Read altitude angle

Eye

Weight on a string

Measuring the Sun's Azimuth

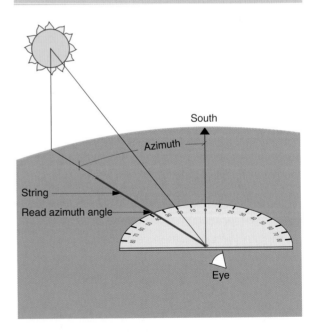

South

Azimuth

String

Read azimuth angle

Eye

Good Solar Access

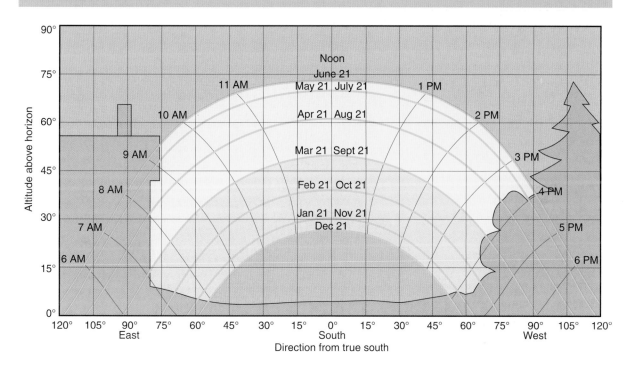

Poor Solar Access

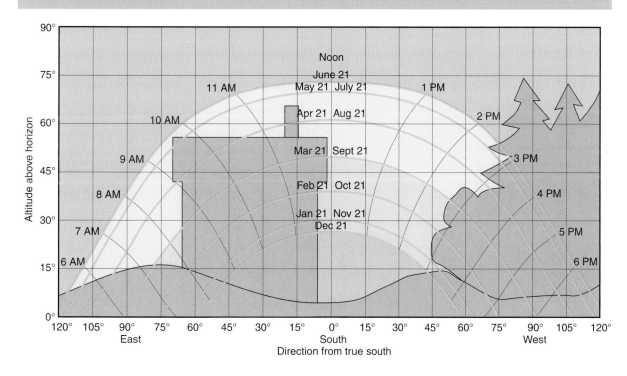

Sun Path Charts

Sun Path Chart for 24°N Latitude

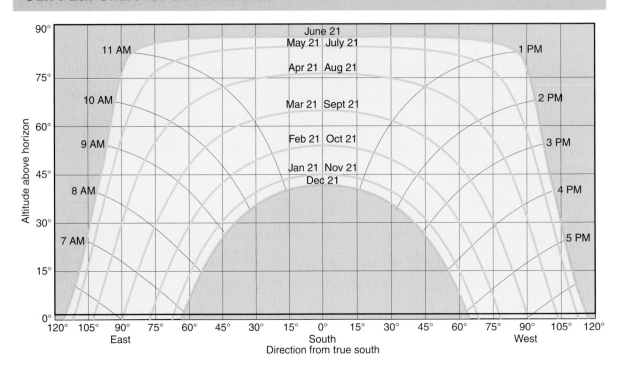

Sun Path Chart for 28°N Latitude

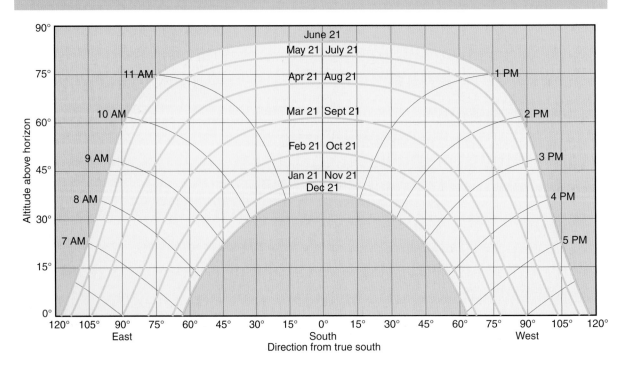

Sun Path Chart for 32°N Latitude

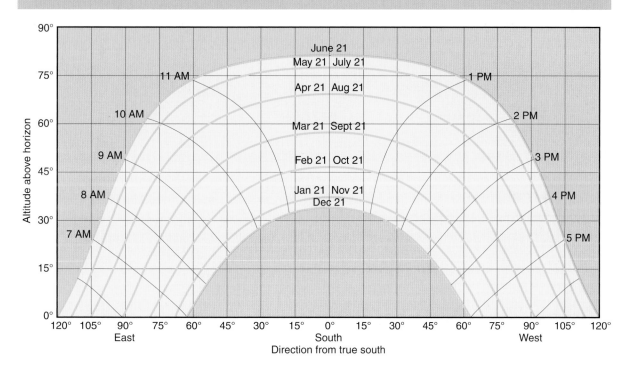

Sun Path Chart for 36°N Latitude

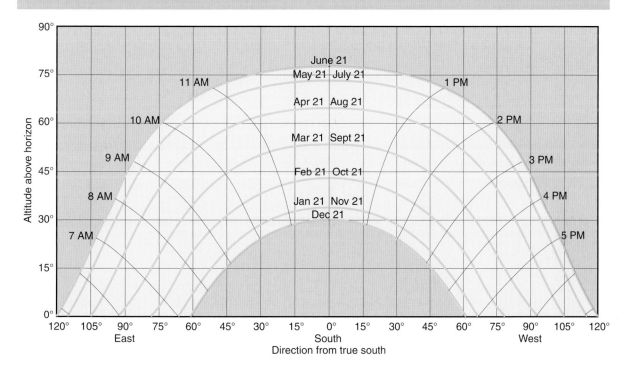

Sun Path Chart for 40°N Latitude

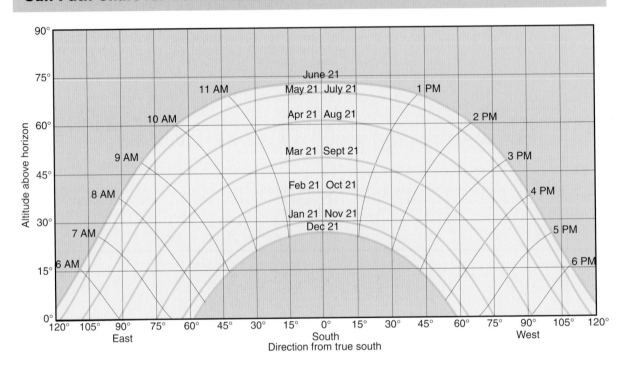

Sun Path Chart for 44°N Latitude

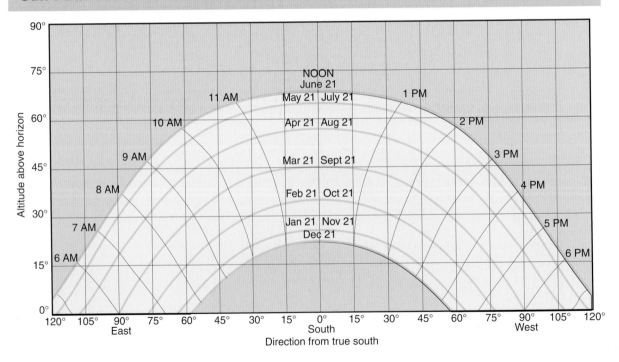

Sun Path Chart for 48°N Latitude

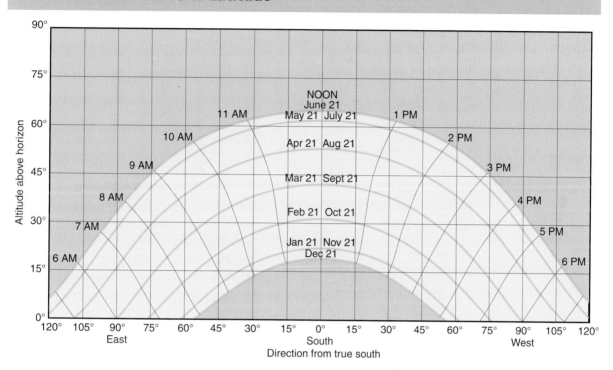

Sun Path Chart for 52°N Latitude

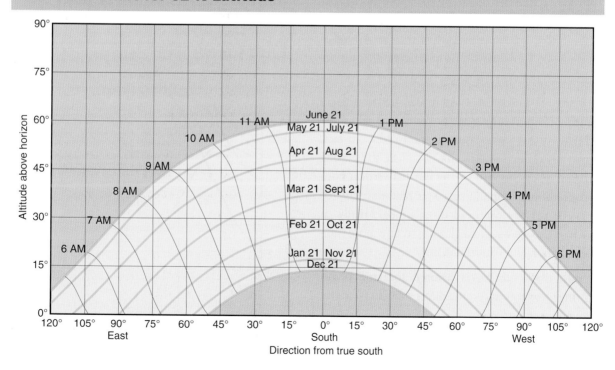

Glazing Orientation and Tilt

Glazing Orientation

A fortunate circumstance that makes solar tempering possible is the fact that the sun is lower in the southern sky in winter than it is in summer. As the graph at right shows, this results in south-facing windows receiving more solar heat in winter than in summer, while for north, east, and west exposures, the reverse is true.

This is also why solar-tempered buildings usually have 50% to 100% of their windows located on the south wall and little, if any, glazing on the north wall. Nonsolar houses traditionally have approximately 25% of their glazing on each of the four sides.

While the chart at right gives clear-day radiation at 40° north latitude, the principle applies throughout the northern hemisphere. The numbers of Btus per sq. ft.-day will change, but the general shapes of the curves will remain the same.

Glazing Tilt

Over the years, there has been controversy over the proper tilt for solar glazing. As the graph at bottom right shows, tilted glazing receives slightly more *direct* radiation than vertical glazing. But vertical surfaces receive more *total* radiation when the foreground is covered with ice or snow. The net effect is that tilt has little effect upon performance.

Moreover, tilted glazing has practical disadvantages compared with vertical glazing. Tilted glazing is more difficult to seal and is more prone to leak. In fact, most glass companies will not guarantee the glazing unit seal when installed in any but the vertical position. Additionally, building codes require tempered or safety glass for overhead installations. Finally, as the chart also shows, tilted glazings receive more summer radiation and require shading.

Still, tilted glazing is favored for true plant-growing greenhouses because direct sunlight is needed throughout the structure.

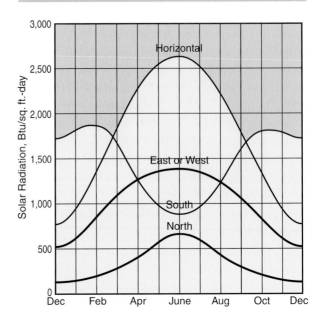

Clear Day Radiation on Vertical Glazings at 40°N

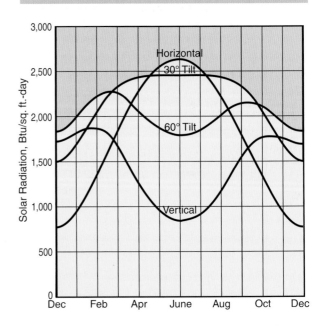

Clear Day Radiation on Tilted South-Facing Glazings at 40°N

Shading the Summer Sun

As discussed on the previous page, south vertical glazings must be shaded to prevent summer overheating. You can use a variety of awnings and inside or outside shades and shutters. But the most practical, attractive, and maintenance-free methods of providing shade are deciduous trees and roof overhangs.

Save existing shade trees and incorporate them into the siting of the building. If trees prove insufficient, roof overhangs can be incorporated into the building design. Use the formula and table below to find the proper overhang projection for south-facing glazings from the latitude of the site and the height of the eaves above the window sill. Use the May 10 to August 1 shade factor in the table if you have no shade trees on the south side of the house.

$$OH = H \times F$$

where:

OH = overhang's horizontal projection
H = height from eaves to window sill
F = factor found in the table

Example: What is the required horizontal projection of eave (beyond the plane of the glazing) to fully shade, on June 21, a south-facing window located at 40° north latitude if the window sill is 7 ft. 2 in. lower than the eaves?

H = 7 ft. 2 in.
 = 86 in.
F = 0.29
OH = 86 in. × 0.29
 = 25 in.

Roof overhangs are not practical for shading windows facing east or west or for tilted south-facing windows.

Geometry of a South Overhang

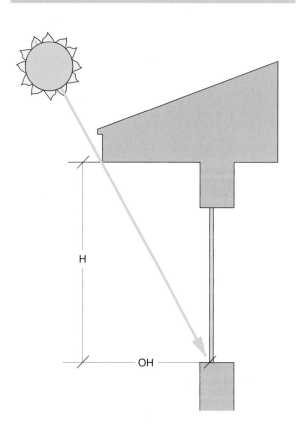

Factors for South-Facing Overhangs

North Latitude	For 100% Shading	
	June 21 Only	May 10–Aug 1
28	0.09	0.18
32	0.16	0.25
36	0.22	0.33
40	0.29	0.40
44	0.37	0.50
48	0.45	0.59

Storing Excess Solar Gain

Solar Absorptance

Once through the glazing, transmitted solar energy that strikes an interior surface can do one of two things:

1. be reflected to another room surface or back through the glazing, or

2. be absorbed (converted from radiant energy to sensible heat) by the surface.

The percentage not reflected, but converted to heat, is termed the *absorptance* of the surface. The choice of absorptances of room surfaces is more complicated than one might assume. If all light were absorbed, all of the light would be from a single direction, and the room would suffer from glare. If little of the light were absorbed in the first several reflections, much of the radiation could escape back through the windows. And light absorbed by lightweight surfaces results in heated air and little thermal storage.

Solar designers therefore recommend the following rules of thumb:

- Lightweight objects should be light in color to avoid overheating of the room air, promote more even light distribution, and reflect radiation onto more massive surfaces.

- Massive objects, such as concrete slabs and fireplaces, should be dark in color and located in direct sunlight in order to efficiently collect and store heat.

- Ceilings should be white, and deep rooms should have light-colored back walls to diffuse light more evenly.

- Masonry floors receiving direct sun should not be covered with rugs or wall-to-wall carpeting.

Example 1: A room has both wood-paneled and brick walls. Make the paneled walls light in color and the brick walls dark.

Example 2: A combined living/kitchen space has both wood and slate floors. You may carpet the wood floor, but leave the slate floor uncovered.

Solar Absorptance of Surfaces

Material	Solar Absorptance
Flat black paint	0.95
Water	0.94
Gloss black paint	0.92
Black concrete	0.91
Gloss dark blue paint	0.91
Stafford blue bricks	0.90
Dark gray slate	0.90
Dark olive drab paint	0.89
Dark brown paint	0.88
Dark blue-gray paint	0.88
Dark green lacquer	0.88
Brown concrete	0.85
Medium brown paint	0.84
Silver gray slate	0.80
Medium light brown paint	0.80
Medium rust paint	0.78
Light gray oil paint	0.75
Red oil paint	0.74
Red brick	0.70
Uncolored concrete	0.65
Light buff bricks	0.60
Medium dull green paint	0.59
Medium orange paint	0.58
Medium yellow paint	0.57
Medium blue paint	0.51
Kelly green paint	0.51
Light green paint	0.47
White semigloss paint	0.30
White gloss paint	0.25
White unpainted plaster	0.07
Aluminum foil	0.03

Heat Storage Capacity of Materials

Thermal mass is the amount of heat absorbed by a material as its temperature rises, expressed as Btu/°F. The *specific heat* of a material is its thermal mass per pound. Note that the specific heat of water is, by definition, exactly 1.00. Coincidentally, it is also the highest for all natural materials.

As shown in the graph at right, the benefit of building thermal mass into a house is that the house becomes less responsive to outdoor temperature swings. This means the house won't get as hot during the day or as cold at night as it would without the added mass. In the graph, the outdoor temperature swings from an overnight low of 60°F to a daytime high of 80°F. An ordinary well-insulated house's interior temperature might swing from 65°F to 75°F, but the same house with added mass would swing only from 68°F to 72°F. The wider the outdoor temperature swing, the more beneficial the mass.

The table at right shows that there is little reason to turn to exotic materials. Masonry floors and walls, exposed wood, and extra-thick gypsum drywall can all be used effectively as storage masses. Water has been included in the table and in the design procedures at the end of the chapter, in case you wish to go supersolar.

You have already seen how material and color can affect the effectiveness of thermal mass. A third factor is thickness. When it comes to thermal mass, thicker is not necessarily better. When a wall is too thick, it remains always too cool to become a heat source. If too thin, it warms too quickly and begins returning heat before evening, when it is most needed.

Optimum thicknesses for common heat storage materials are:

- adobe   8 in. to 12 in.
- brick   10 in. to 14 in.
- concrete   12 in. to 18 in.
- water   6 in. or more

Temperature Swing vs. Thermal Mass

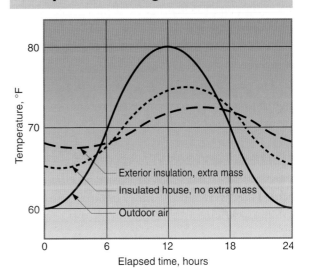

Heat Capacities of Materials

Material	Specific Heat Btu/lb. °F	Density lb./cu. ft.	Heat Capacity Btu/cu. ft. °F
Air (at 75°F)	0.24	0.075	0.018
Asphalt	0.22	132	29.0
Brick	0.20	123	24.6
Cement	0.16	120	19.2
Clay	0.22	63	13.9
Concrete	0.22	144	31.7
Copper	0.09	556	51.2
Glass	0.18	154	27.7
Gypsum drywall	0.26	78	20.2
Iron	0.12	450	54.0
Limestone	0.22	103	22.4
Marble	0.21	162	34.0
Sand	0.19	94.6	18.1
Steel	0.12	489	58.7
Water	1.00	62.4	62.4
White oak	0.57	47	26.8
White pine	0.67	27	18.1

A Design Procedure for Solar Tempering

The tables in this section provide a simple method for designing solar-tempered buildings. Initial sizing of both window area and storage mass can be quickly achieved knowing only location, floor area, building insulation level, and glazing R-value.

The procedure yields the area of south-facing glazing, amount and placement of storage mass, and estimated reduction in winter heating bills.

Percent Savings vs. Area of Glazing

Extensive computer simulations have been performed by researchers at Los Alamos Laboratory for solar-tempered homes in the cities listed in the table on the facing page. Interpretation of the table is simple:

"A south-facing glazed area of between XI and X2 percent of the floor area can be expected to reduce the winter heating bill of a home by Y1 to Y2 percent."

The smaller glazed areas and fuel-saving percentages (X1 and Y1) correspond to ordinary homes with ordinary areas of window, with the exception that the windows have all been moved to the south wall. The larger figures (X2 and Y2) give the maximum recommended target percentages for the location.

The predicted fuel saving depends on the type of glazing: double-glazed (DG), triple-glazed or equivalent R-3 glazing such as low-E (TG), or double-glazed with R-9 night insulation (DG+R9).

Example: In Boston, Massachusetts, a south-facing window area of 15% to 29% of floor area can be expected to reduce the winter fuel bill by 17% to 25% if double glazed, 26% to 39% if triple glazed, or 40% to 64% if double glazed with R-9 night window insulation.

Assumed Heat Loss

The predictions assume a building heat loss of 6 Btus per sq. ft.-day of floor area, corresponding roughly to R-19 walls, R-38 ceilings, double glazing, and an infiltration rate of three-quarters air change per hr.

Customizing the Design

You can customize your analysis with different building styles, insulation levels, and any of the glazing types described in Chapter 10 by running the interactive online Lawrence Berkeley Laboratories' Home Energy Saver™ program (*hes.lbl.gov/consumer*). This will also give you more accurate results.

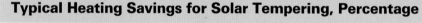

Typical Heating Savings for Solar Tempering, Percentage

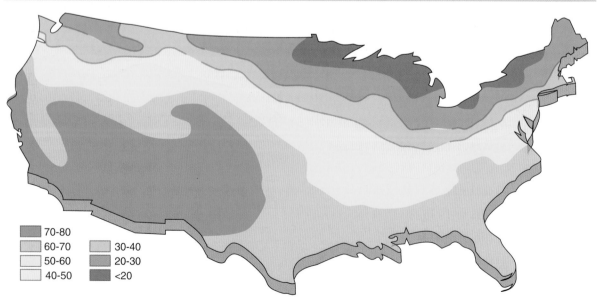

70-80
60-70
50-60
40-50
30-40
20-30
<20

Glazed Area vs. Solar Savings

State, City	Glazed Area[1] X1 - X2	Percentage Savings[2] for DG Y1 - Y2	TG Y1 - Y2	DG+R9 Y1 - Y2
AL, Birmingham	9–18	22–37	34–58	34–58
AZ, Phoenix	6–12	37–60	41-66	48-75
AR, Little Rock	10-19	23-38	28-47	37-62
CA, Los Angeles	5-9	36-58	39-63	44-72
CO, Denver	12-23	27-43	34-54	47-74
DE, Wilmington	15-29	19-30	26-42	39-63
DC, Washington	12-23	18-28	25-40	37-61
FL, Orlando	3-6	30-52	33-56	37-63
GA, Atlanta	8-17	22-36	26-44	34-58
ID, Boise	14-28	27-38	35-50	48-71
IL, Chicago	17-35	17-23	27-39	43-67
IN, Indianapolis	14-28	15-21	23-35	37-60
IA, Des Moines	21-43	19-25	30-44	50-75
KS, Topeka	14-28	24-35	32-48	45-71
KY, Louisville	13-27	18-27	24-39	35-59
LA, Baton Rouge	6-12	26-43	29-49	34-59
ME, Portland	17-34	14-17	25-36	45-69
MA, Boston	15-29	17-25	26-39	40-64
MI, Detroit	17-34	13-17	23-33	39-61
MN, Duluth	25-50	Not Rec	24-33	50-70
MS, Jackson	8-15	24-40	28-47	34-59
MO, St. Louis	15-29	21-33	28-45	41-65
MT, Great Falls	18-37	23-28	35-46	56-77
NE, North Platte	17-34	25-36	34-51	50-76
NV, Las Vegas	9-18	35-56	40-63	48-75
NH, Concord	17-34	13-15	25-35	45-68
NJ, Newark	13-25	19-29	26-42	39-64
NM, Albuquerque	11-22	29-47	35-57	46-73

State, City	Glazed Area[1] X1 - X2	Percentage Savings[2] for DG Y1 - Y2	TG Y1 - Y2	DG+R9 Y1 - Y2
NY, Syracuse	19-38	Not Rec	20-29	37-59
NC, Greensboro	10-20	23-37	28-47	37-63
ND, Bismarck	25-50	Not Rec	27-36	56-77
OH, Columbus	14-28	13-18	21-32	35-57
OK, Tulsa	11-22	24-38	30-49	41-67
OR, Salem	12-24	21-32	27-33	37-59
PA, Pittsburgh	14-28	12-16	20-30	33-55
RI, Providence	15-30	17-24	26-40	40-64
SC, Columbia	8-17	25-41	29-48	36-61
SD, Pierre	22-43	21-33	35-44	58-80
TN, Nashville	10-21	19-30	24-39	33-55
TX, Dallas	8-17	27-44	31-51	38-64
UT, Salt Lake City	13-26	27-39	31-51	48-72
VT, Burlington	22-43	Not Rec	23-33	46-68
VA, Richmond	11-22	21-34	27-44	37-61
WA, Seattle	11-22	21-30	28-41	39-59
WV, Charleston	13-25	16-24	22-35	32-54
WI, Madison	20-40	15-17	28-38	51-74
WY, Caper	13-26	27-39	38-53	53-78
AB, Edmonton	25-50	Not Rec	26-34	54-72
BC, Vancouver	13-26	20-28	27-40	40-60
MB, Winnipeg	25-50	Not Rec	26-34	54-74
NS, Dartmouth	14-28	17-24	27-41	45-70
ON, Ottawa	25-50	Not Rec	28-37	59-80
QC, Normandin	25-50	Not Rec	26-35	54-74

[1] Glazed area as percentage of heated floor area.

[2] Percentage reduction in annual heating bill from that of an equivalent house having uniform distribution of windows of area totaling 15% of heated floor area.

Thermal Mass Patterns

Thermal Mass Sizing and Placement

All buildings have some amount of thermal mass in their floors, walls, ceilings, and furnishings. If they didn't, they'd all overheat on sunny days. The table below shows the approximate maximum areas of south-facing windows in average-insulated and well-insulated wood frame homes before overheating will occur.

**South Glazing Area Limits
(glazed area as percentage of floor area)**

Degree-Days[1]	Ave. Jan. Temp, °F	Average House[2]	Well-Insulated House[3]
4,000	40	11	6
5,000	30	13	6
6,000	25	13	7
7,000	20	14	7

[1] See Chapter 3 for heating degree days, base 65°F.
[2] R-11 walls, R-19 ceiling, double-glazed windows.
[3] R-25 walls, R-38 ceiling, triple-glazed windows.

Example: With no additional mass, what is the maximum allowed area of south-facing window for a 1,800-sq. ft. home in Boston (6,000 DD_{65}) constructed with R-25 walls, R-49 ceiling, and R-3 windows? The energy efficiency of the home is close to that of the well-insulated house in the table, so the appropriate percentage is 7, and the maximum south-facing glazed area is 0.07 × 1,800 sq. ft. = 126 sq. ft.

The example above was a typical nonsolar home. To realize the higher fuel savings listed in the table on the previous page, a much greater window area would be required. For example, the suggested window percentage for Boston is 15% to 29%, or two to four times the percentage in the example. Such a home would require additional storage mass.

Adding Thermal Mass

In the pages that follow, five distinctly different storage mass patterns are shown. For each, an accompanying table specifies the material, thickness, and surface area of mass required for each square foot of glazing in excess of the norm.

Example: Assuming you wish to achieve 25% solar savings for the home in Boston, you will need about 15% of the floor area in south glazing. You therefore need additional thermal mass to compensate for (15% minus 7% equals) 8% of the floor area, or 144 sq. ft. of glazing. Using Pattern 1 and assuming a bare 6-in. concrete slab as the mass, you'll find you need 3 × 144 sq. ft., or 432 sq. ft. of slab in direct sunlight. If you don't have the required area of slab, you'll have to add mass from other patterns.

Five Mass Patterns

Pattern 1: A home with a masonry floor. The floor could be a concrete slab-on-grade, or it could consist of a masonry veneer over a wood or concrete base.

Pattern 2: A home with one or more exposed masonry walls or a home with an extra-thick plaster or drywall finish.

Pattern 3: A home with an exposed interior masonry party wall. It could also represent a very large masonry fireplace.

Pattern 4: Typically a sun space with a masonry rear wall.

Pattern 5: Any massive structure in direct sunlight that does not reach the ceiling. A masonry planter/room divider would fall into this pattern.

Pattern 1

Pattern 1 is defined as thermal storage mass with one surface exposed to the living space and in direct sun for at least six hours a day. Architecturally, this pattern combined with Pattern 2 is useful for direct-gain solar-tempered rooms.

The mass could be either a directly irradiated floor slab, as shown, or a directly irradiated outside wall (inside walls are considered in Pattern 3). As with Patterns 2 and 3, the mass element is single-sided; that is, heat enters and exits the mass from the same surface.

Example: The design procedure has identified an excess 100 sq. ft. of south-facing glass in a room with 200 sq. ft. of floor and 380 sq. ft. of windowless wall. Does a 4-in. concrete slab provide enough thermal mass to prevent overheating?

According to the table, you should provide 4 sq. ft. of 4-in. concrete slab for each sq. ft. of glazing.

Mass Sizing for Floors and Walls in Direct Sun

Mass Thickness	Sq .Ft. of Mass per Sq. Ft. of Glazing				
	Concrete	Brick	Drywall	Oak	Pine
½ in.	—	—	76	—	—
1 in.	14	17	38	17	21
1½ in.	—	—	26	—	—
2 in.	7	8	20	10	12
3 in.	5	6	—	10	12
4 in.	4	5	—	11	12
6 in.	3	5	—	11	13
8 in.	3	5	—	11	13

That would require 400 sq. ft. of slab. Increasing the slab thickness to 6 in. would still require 300 sq. ft. of slab. Therefore, you must either reduce the glazed area or add further mass, utilizing one of the other four mass patterns.

Thermal Mass Pattern 1

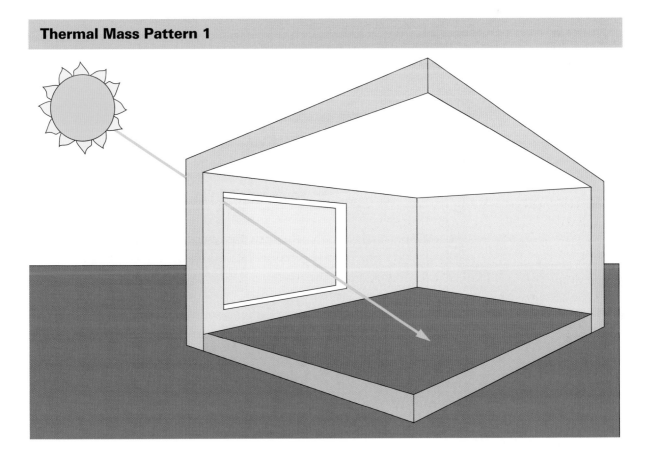

Pattern 2

The mass in Pattern 2 is like that in Pattern 1, that is, the mass is single-sided and insulated on the back side. The distinction here is that the mass is receiving not direct radiation, but reflected sun.

In a simple direct-gain space, some of the mass will be of Pattern 1 (a floor slab near the solar glazing, for example), and some mass will be of Pattern 2 (the ceiling, for example). Much of the mass in such a space will be directly irradiated some of the time and indirectly irradiated the rest of the day. In these cases, an interpolation between Pattern 1 and Pattern 2 must be carried out, as described in Pattern 1.

Example: You have decided to use an 8-in. concrete slab for the room described in mass Pattern 1. This leaves 33 sq. ft. of glazing to provide mass for. How many sq. ft. of 8-in. brick wall will be required to provide the mass?

Mass Sizing for Floor, Wall, or Ceiling in Indirect Sun

Mass Thickness	Sq. Ft. of Mass per Sq. Ft. of Glazing				
	Concrete	Brick	Drywall	Oak	Pine
½ in.	—	—	114	—	—
1 in.	25	30	57	28	36
1½ in.	—	—	39	—	—
2 in.	12	15	31	17	21
3 in.	8	11	—	17	20
4 in.	7	9	—	19	21
6 in.	5	9	—	19	22
8 in.	5	10	—	19	22

According to the table above, 10 sq. ft. of 8-in. brick wall is required to balance each sq. ft. of glazing. You therefore need 330 sq. ft. of brick wall. Since the total wall area is 380 sq. ft., this is a practical solution.

Thermal Mass Pattern 2

Pattern 3

As in Patterns 1 and 2, the mass in this pattern is one-sided. The difference is that the mass receives neither direct radiation nor reflected radiation. It is instead heated by the room air that is warmed as a result of solar gains elsewhere in the building.

This pattern is useful for mass deep within a passive building. However, solar-heated air must reach the remote mass either by natural or forced air circulation. Judgment is required here—a hallway open to a south room could be included; a back room closed off from the solar-heated space should not be included.

Example: Your remodeling plan calls for removing half of a wood-framed gypsum wall to open the south-facing kitchen to the living room. The remaining wall has an 80-sq.-ft. fireplace of 8-in. brick on the living room side. You plan to add a south-facing window

Mass Sizing for Floor, Wall, or Ceiling Remote from Sun

Mass Thickness	Sq. Ft. of Mass per Sq. Ft. of Glazing				
	Concrete	Brick	Drywall	Oak	Pine
½ in.	—	—	114	—	—
1 in.	27	32	57	32	39
1½ in.	—	—	42	—	—
2 in.	17	20	35	24	27
3 in.	15	17	—	26	28
4 in.	14	17	—	24	30
6 in.	14	18	—	28	31
8 in.	15	19	—	28	31

in the kitchen. How many sq. ft. of window will the mass of the fireplace balance? According to the table, the fireplace alone will account for a little more than 4 sq. ft. of window.

Thermal Mass Pattern 3

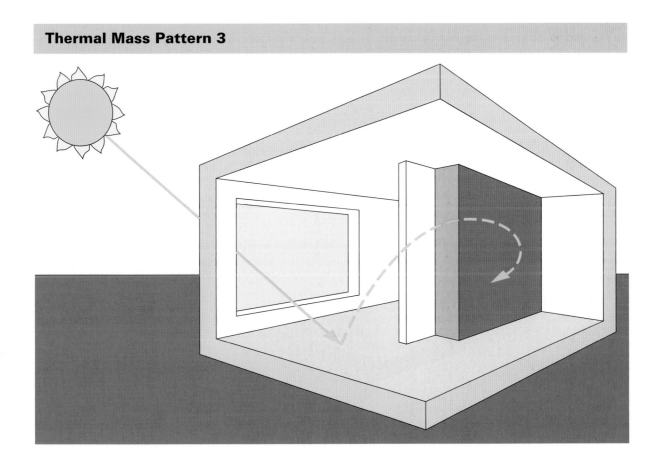

Pattern 4

Pattern 4 is a floor-to-ceiling wall of massive material that receives direct sun on one side and is exposed to the living space on the other side. In other words, the sunlit side is isolated from the living space.

This pattern is useful for isolated sun spaces and greenhouses. The storage wall may have high and low vents or be unvented, as shown, without affecting the values in the table.

The performance of the wall improves with thickness up to about 18 in. but is not very sensitive to variations in thickness within normal buildable ranges. For brick walls, higher density bricks (with water absorption of less than 6%) are recommended over bricks of lower density. Note that the mass surface area refers to the area of the sunlit side only.

Mass Sizing for Mass Wall or Water Wall in Direct Sun

Material and Thickness	Sq. Ft. of Mass Surface per Sq. Ft. of Glazing
8-in.-thick brick	1
12-in.-thick brick	1
8-in.-thick water wall	1

Example: You are considering adding an attached solar greenhouse. The primary purpose of the greenhouse will be to grow plants. The greenhouse structure should therefore be isolated to avoid excess humidity in the living space.

As the table shows, 1 sq. ft. of 8-in. brick, 12-in. concrete, or 8-in. water wall (water containers) for each sq. ft. of glazing will provide all of the required thermal mass.

Thermal Mass Pattern 4

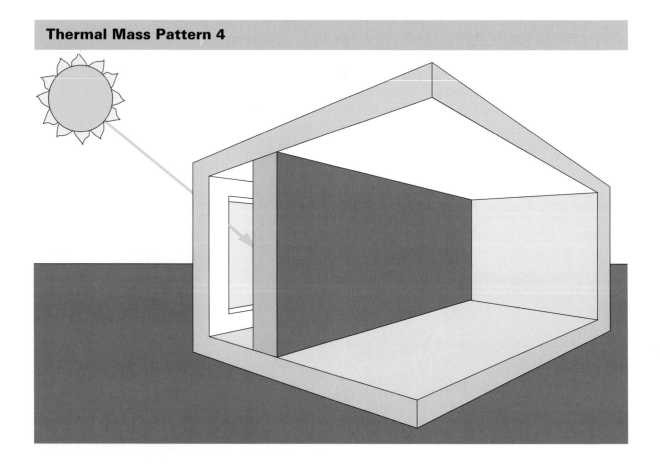

Pattern 5

Similar to Pattern 4, mass in this pattern is sunlit on one side and exposed to the living space on the other side. The distinction is that there is free air circulation around this mass material so that heat may be gained by the living space from either side of the partial wall or from all sides of the water containers.

This pattern may represent a freestanding masonry wall or a series of water containers.

The mass is assumed to be in full sun for at least 6 hours. As with Pattern 4, the wall thicknesses listed are not very sensitive to variations, and the wall surface area listed is for one side of the wall only. Water containers are listed in the table as gal. per sq. ft. of glazing.

Example: You plan to add a sun space with 160 sq. ft. of south-facing glazing. Unlike the example in Pattern 4, however, you plan to use the space for living rather than growing. You'd like the sun space to be open to the adjacent kitchen. Will a 3-ft.-high by 20-ft.-long room divider constructed of 8-in. brick provide sufficient thermal mass?

The area of the room divider exposed to direct sunlight is 60 sq. ft. According to the table, the room divider alone will account for only 30 sq. ft. of glazing. You will need to employ a Pattern 1 brick floor, as well.

Mass Sizing for Partial Mass Wall or Water Containers in Direct Sun

Material and Thickness	Sq. Ft. of Mass Surface per Sq. Ft. of Glazing
8-in.-thick brick	2
6-in.-thick concrete	2
Water containers	7 gal. per sq. ft. of glazing

Thermal Mass Pattern 5

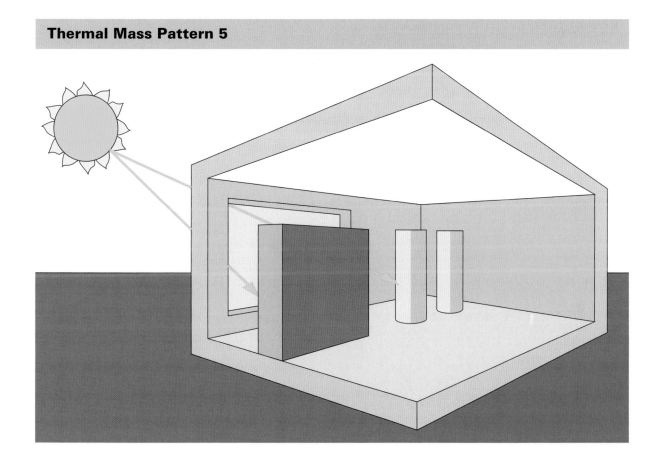

Appendices

Units and Conversion Factors

Multiply	By	To Get
LENGTH		
Centimeters	0.3937	Inches
Centimeters	10	Millimeters
Centimeters	0.01	Meters
Inches	2.54	Centimeters
Inches	0.0278	Yards
Feet	30.48	Centimeters
Feet	0.3048	Meters
Feet	12	Inches
Yards	91.44	Centimeters
Yards	0.9144	Meters
Yards	36	Inches
Yards	3	Feet
Meters	39.37	Inches
Meters	3.281	Feet
Meters	1.094	Yards
Meters	100	Centimeters
Meters	0.001	Kilometers
Kilometers	3,281	Feet
Kilometers	1,094	Yards
Kilometers	0.6214	Miles
Kilometers	1,000	Meters
Miles	5,280	Feet
Miles	1,760	Yards
Miles	1.609	Kilometers
AREA		
Square centimeters	0.1550	Square inches
Square centimeters	100	Square millimeters
Square centimeters	0.0001	Square meters
Square inches	6.4516	Square centimeters
Square inches	0.0069	Square feet
Square inches	7.72×10^{-4}	Square yards
Square feet	929	Square centimeters
Square feet	0.0929	Square meters
Square feet	144	Square inches
Square feet	0.1111	Square yards
Square yards	8,361	Square centimeters
Square yards	0.8361	Square meters

Multiply	By	To Get
Square yards	1,296	Square inches
Square yards	9	Square feet
Square meters	1,550	Square inches
Square meters	10.765	Square feet
Square meters	1.1968	Square yards
Square meters	10,000	Square centimeters
Square meters	1.0×10^{-6}	Square kilometers
Square kilometers	1.076×10^{7}	Square feet
Square kilometers	0.3861	Square miles
Square kilometers	1.0×10^{6}	Square meters
Square miles	2.788×10^{7}	Square feet
Square miles	640	Acres
VOLUME		
Cubic centimeters	0.0610	Cubic inches
Cubic centimeters	1,000	Cubic millimeters
Cubic centimeters	1.0×10^{-6}	Cubic meters
Cubic inches	16.387	Cubic centimeters
Cubic inches	5.787×10^{-4}	Cubic feet
Liters	0.2642	Gallons, US
Liters	1.0568	Quarts
Liters	1,000	Cubic centimeters
Gallons, US	0.0238	Barrels (42 gallon)
Gallons, US	4	Quarts
Gallons, US	231	Cubic inches
Gallons, US	3,785	Cubic centimeters
Cubic feet	2.832×10^{4}	Cubic centimeters
Cubic feet	0.0283	Cubic meters
Cubic feet	1,728	Cubic inches
Cubic feet	0.0370	Cubic yards
Cubic yards	7.646×10^{5}	Cubic centimeters
Cubic yards	0.7646	Cubic meters
Cubic yards	4.667×10^{4}	Cubic inches
Cubic yards	27	Cubic feet
Cubic meters	6.102×10^{4}	Cubic inches
Cubic meters	35.320	Cubic feet
Cubic meters	1.3093	Cubic yards
Cubic meters	1.0×10^{6}	Cubic centimeters
Cubic meters	1,000	Liters

Multiply	By	To Get
MASS		
Pounds	4.448	Newtons
Pounds	32.17	Poundals
Tons, US short	2,000	Pounds
Tons, US long	2,240	Pounds
Tons, metric	2,205	Pounds
Tons, metric	1,000	Kilograms
Grains	0.0648	Grams
Grains	64.8	Milligrams
Grams	15.43	Grains
Drams	0.0625	Ounces
Grams	2.205×10^{-3}	Pounds mass
Grams	0.001	Kilograms
Grams	15.432	Grains
Ounces	16	Drams
Ounces	28.35	Grams
Ounces	437.5	Grains
Ounces	0.0284	Kilograms
Ounces	0.0625	Pounds
Pounds	453.6	Grams
Pounds	0.4536	Kilograms
Pounds	16	Ounces
Kilograms	35.28	Ounces
Kilograms	2.205	Pounds mass
Kilograms	1,000	Grams
Tons, US	0.9070	Tons metric
Tons, US	907	Kilograms
Tons, US	2,000	Pounds
Tons, metric	1.102	Tons, US
Tons, metric	2,205	Pounds
Tons, metric	1,000	Kilograms
TEMPERATURE		
C Degrees	1.8	F Degrees
F Degrees	0.5556	C Degrees
K Degrees	1	C Degrees
Degrees C	1.8 ($^{\circ}$C+32)	Degrees F
Degrees F	0.556 ($^{\circ}$F-32)	Degrees C
Degrees K	($^{\circ}$K-273)	Degrees C

Multiply	By	To Get
ENERGY		
Btus	1,055	Joules
Btus	252	calories
Btus	0.252	kilocalories
Btus	0.252	Calories (food)
Btus	0.293	Wh
Btus	0.000293	kWh
Ergs	1.0×10^{-7}	Joules
Joules	1	Newton-meters
Joules	1.0×10^{7}	Ergs
Joules	0.2389	Calories
Joules	9.48×10^{-4}	Btus
Joules	0.7376	Foot-pounds
Calories	3.97×10^{-3}	Btus
Btus/hour	0.293	Joules/second
Btus/hour	252	Calories/hour
Therms	100,000	Btus
Therms	29.31	kWh
Btus	0.00001	Therms
kWh	0.03412	Therms
POWER		
Watts	1	Volt-Amperes
Watts	0.001	Kilowatts
Watts	1.0×10^{-6}	Megawatts
Watts	3.412	Btus/hour
Watts	859	calories/hour
Watts	1	Joules/second
Watts	0.001341	Horsepower
Watts	0.0002843	US refrigeration tons
Kilowatts	3,412	Btus/hour
Kilowatts	1,000	Watts
Kilowatts	1.34	Horsepower
Kilowatts	0.259	US refrigeration tons
Btus/hour	0.2931	Watts
Btus/hour	252	calories/hour
Horsepower	746	Watts
US refrigeration tons	12,000	Btus/hour
US refrigeration tons	3.517	Kilowatts

Glossary

AAHE: air-to-air heat exchanger.

Absolute zero: temperature at which matter has zero internal kinetic energy.

Absorptance: ratio of energy absorbed by a surface to the amount striking it.

Active solar collector: mechanical system for collecting solar heat.

Aerator: a device for introducing air into water.

AFUE: annual fuel utilization efficiency–the percentage of energy in a fuel transferred to the home averaged over the entire heating season.

Air barrier: material or surface designed to prevent passage of air, but not water vapor.

Air-dry: no more than 20% moisture content.

Air-source heat pump: mechanical device that transfers heat from outdoor air to a building interior.

Altitude: vertical angle of the sun above the horizon.

Annual heat load: total heat loss of a building over the heating season.

ASHRAE: American Society of Heating, Refrigerating, and Air-Conditioning Engineers.

Azimuth angle: horizontal direction to the sun, usually measured from true north. Solar azimuth is measured east or west from true south.

Backer rod: foam rope used to fill large gaps before caulking.

Balloon frame: wood frame in which studs are continuous from the sill to the top plate of the top floor.

Blocking: short member bracing between two longer framing members.

Boiler: central heating appliance which generates either hot water or steam.

Bow window: same as a bay window, except the projection approximates a circular arc.

British Thermal Unit (Btu): amount of heat required to raise the temperature of 1 lb. of water 1°F.

Building code: rules adopted by a government for the regulation of building.

Capillarity: movement of water through small gaps due to adhesion and surface tension.

Casing: inside or outside molding covering the space between a window or door jamb and a wall.

Catalytic: employing a substance which increases the rate of a chemical reaction without itself undergoing any permanent chemical change.

Cavity wall: masonry wall with a continuous space between the inside and outside bricks which acts as a capillary break.

CDC: Centers for Disease Control, an agency of the US Department of Health and Human Services.

Cellulose insulation: loose-fill insulation consisting of shredded and treated newspaper.

Celsius: new name for the Centigrade temperature scale.

Centigrade: temperature scale defined by 0° and 100° at the freezing and boiling points of water at 1 atmosphere air pressure.

CFL: compact fluorescent lamp.

Comfort zone: range of temperatures and relative humidities in which the average lightly-clothed person feels "comfortable."

Condensation: process of water vapor turning to liquid water.

Conduction: transfer of heat through an opaque material. Also the transfer of electrons (current) through a material.

Convection: heat transfer through either the natural or forced movement of air.

Cooling degree days: positive difference between the average of daily high and low temperatures and a fixed temperature—usually 65°F.

Cooling degree hours: positive difference between the average hourly temperature and a fixed temperature—usually 65°F.

Cord (of wood): a stack of fire wood measuring 128 cu. ft.

Crawl space: space beneath a building not high enough for a person to stand in.

Damper: valve designed to control the flow of air or smoke.

Degree-day: difference between the average of daily high and low temperatures and a fixed temperature—usually 65°F.

Design heat load: rate of heat loss from a building per hour when the outside temperature is at the design minimum temperature.

Design maximum temperature: outdoor temperature exceeded 2.5% of cooling season hours.

Design minimum temperature: outdoor low temperature exceeded 97.5% of heating season hours.

Dew point: air temperature at which water vapor begins to condense as either water or ice (frost).

Diffuse radiation: solar energy received from a direction different from that of the sun.

Diffusion: the process whereby liquid or gaseous molecules mix as the result of their thermal energy and move from regions of higher to regions of lower concentration.

Direct gain: system in which energy received from the sun directly enters and heats the living spaces.

Direct venting: discharging flue gas without use of a chimney.

DOE: US Department of Energy.

Draft: air pressure difference between the inside and outside of a chimney. Also the rate of flue gas or combustion airflow.

Dry-bulb temperature: air temperature registered by a dry thermometer.

EER: Energy Efficiency Rating—the ratio of Btus moved to watts of electricity consumed by an air conditioner.

Effective R-value: an R-value which accounts for parallel heat paths and the dynamic heat storage effects of mass.

Efficacy (lighting): the ratio of luminous flux in lumens to power in watts.

EIA: US Energy Information Administration.

EIFS: Exterior Insulation Finishing System.

Emissivity: the ratio of energy radiated by the surface of a body to the energy radiated by a black body at the same temperature.

Energy Guide: DOE-mandated yellow label affixed to appliances which estimates annual energy use, compares energy use to the use of other similar products, and gives the approximate annual operating cost.

Energy Star: a voluntary program under the Department of Energy and the Environmental Protection Agency for identifying and promoting energy-efficient products and buildings.

EPA: US Environmental Protection Agency.

EPS: extruded polystyrene foam insulation.

EXP: expanded polystyrene foam insulation, also known as beadboard.

Fahrenheit: temperature scale defined by the freezing (32°F) and boiling (212°F) points of water.

Fenestration: the area, design, and placement of windows in a building.

Flashing: material used to prevent leaks at intersections and penetrations of a roof.

Flue: passage in a chimney for the venting of flue gases or products of combustion.

Flue gases: mixture of air and the products of combustion.

Fluorescent light: lamp which emits light when an electric discharge excites a phosphor coating.

Forced-air system: heat transfer system using a blower.

Foundation: section of a building which transfers the building load to the earth.

FSEC: Florida Solar Energy Center.

Fuel efficiency: percentage of energy in fuel converted to useful energy.

Furnace: appliance that generates hot air.

Glazing: glass or other transparent material used for windows.

Ground-source heat pump: mechanical device which transfers heat from the ground to a building interior.

Gypsum drywall: rigid paper-faced board made from hydrated gypsum and used as a substitute for plaster and lath.

Halogen: one of five chemically related elements: fluorine, chlorine, bromine, iodine, and astatine.

Halogen lamp: an incandescent lamp containing a small amount of iodine or bromine which can be operated at higher temperatures and efficiencies than ordinary incandescent lamps.

Hardwood: wood from a deciduous tree.

Heat-absorbing glass: glass containing additives which absorb light in order to reduce glare, brightness, and solar heat gain.

Heat capacity: quantity of heat required to raise the temperature of 1 cu. ft. of a material 1°F.

Heat pump: mechanical device which transfers heat from a cooler to a warmer medium.

Heat trap: device which prevents convective heat loss from a water heater.

Heating degree days: negative difference between the average of daily high and low temperatures and a fixed temperature—usually 65°F.

Humidifier: appliance for adding water vapor to air.

Hydronic: method of distributing heat by hot water.

Ice dam: ridge of ice at roof eaves.

ICF: insulated concrete form.

IECC: International Energy Conservation Code.

Incandescent: heated to the point of giving off light.

Induction: the production of an electrical current in a conductor exposed to a varying magnetic field.

Infiltration: incursion of outdoor air through cracks, holes, and joints.

Infrared radiation: radiation of a wavelength longer than that of red light. Also known as heat radiation.

Insulating glass: factory-sealed double or triple glazing.

Insulation: material having high resistance to heat flow.

IOM: Institute of Medicine, part of the National Academy of Sciences.

Kilowatt: 1,000 watts. Abbreviated *kW*.

Kilowatt-hour: unit of electrical energy consumed. One thousand watts of power for a 1-hour duration. Abbreviated *kWh*.

Latent heat: heat absorbed or given off during a change of phase of a material.

LBL: Lawrence Berkeley National Laboratory.

LED: light-emitting diode.

Life-cycle cost: Sum of recurring and non-recurring costs over the life span of an appliance or structure.

Low-E: low thermal emissivity—the quality of emitting (radiating) a low percentage of radiant energy.

Lumen: measure of total light output. A wax candle gives off about 13 lumens, a 100-watt incandescent bulb about 1,200 lumens.

Microclimate: local area or zone where the climate differs from that of the surrounding area.

Moisture barrier: material or surface with the purpose of blocking the diffusion of water vapor. The same as a vapor barrier.

Moisture content: amount of moisture in a material, expressed as the percentage of dry weight.

Natural ventilation: air movement in a building due only to natural pressure differences caused by air temperatures.

NCDC: National Climatic Data Center.

NFRC: National Fenestration Rating Council.

Orientation: placement relative to the sun, wind, view, and so forth.

ORNL: Oak Ridge National Laboratory.

OSB: oriented strand board, a type of sheathing panel.

OVE: Optimum Value Engineering, also called Advanced Framing, is a framing system developed by NAHB which uses less lumber and results in greater effective R-values.

Passive solar collector: a system for collecting solar energy without use of mechanical devices such as fans or pumps.

Perlite: expanded volcanic glass. Used as an insulator and as a lightweight additive to concrete.

Perm: 1 grain of water vapor per square foot per hour per inch of mercury difference in water vapor pressure.

Permeability: ability to transmit water vapor, measured in perms.

Phantom electrical load: power being drawn by an electrical device while the device is either off or on standby.

PIC: polyisocyanurate foam insulation.

Plenum: ductwork chamber serving as a distribution point for airflow.

Prescriptive R-value: R-value required by a building energy code.

Present value: value today of an amount of money in the future.

Primary transmittance: fraction of radiation passing directly through a glazing. See also *visible transmittance* and *secondary transmittance*.

Psychrometric chart: graph showing the properties of water vapor in air.

Radiant heating: method of heating whereby much of the heat transfer is accomplished by radiation through space from warm building surfaces such as floors, walls, or ceilings.

Radiation: the transfer of electromagnetic radiation through space.

Reflectance: decimal fraction of light incident on a surface reflected and not absorbed. Absorptance equals 1 minus reflectance.

Reflective glass: glass treated to reflect a fraction (the reflectance) of incident light.

Reflectivity: (see reflectance).

Relative humidity: amount of water vapor in air compared with the maximum amount possible, expressed as a percentage.

Retrofit: to upgrade a structure using modern materials.

Return duct: ducting returning air to furnace for reheating.

Ridge vent: continuous, prefabricated outlet ventilator placed over an opening at the ridge of a roof.

R-value: measure of resistance to heat flow.

Secondary transmittance: fraction of radiation absorbed in a glazing. See also *VT (visible transmittance)* and *primary transmittance*.

Sensible heat: heat required to raise the temperature of a material without changing its state.

Shading coefficient: ratio of solar gain to the solar gain through a single layer of clear, double-strength glass.

Sheathing: layer of boards over the framing but under the finish.

Shelter belt: band of trees and shrubs planted to reduce wind speed.

SHGC: solar heat gain coefficient—the fraction of total solar radiation received at the surface of the earth that passes through a glazing.

Siding: exterior finish for a wall.

Sill: lowest horizontal member in a frame. Also the bottom piece of the window rough opening.

SIP: structural insulating panel.

Skylight: window set into or onto a roof.

Slab-on-grade: concrete slab resting directly on the ground at near-grade level.

Slider: window which slides horizontally. Also called a *sliding window*.

Soffit: underside of a roof overhang, cornice, or stairway.

Soffit vent: inlet vent in a soffit. It may be individual or continuous.

Softwood: wood from an evergreen tree.

Solar absorptance: the ratio of the amount of total solar radiation absorbed by a surface to the amount of radiation incident upon it.

Solar radiation: total electromagnetic radiation from the sun.

Solar-tempered heating: deriving a significant fraction of the heating requirement of a building from the sun.

Specific heat: ratio of the heat storage capacity of a material to that of an equal weight of water.

Stack effect: buoyancy of warm gases within a chimney.

Stile: vertical outside frame member in a door or window sash.

Stool: interior horizontal, flat molding at the bottom of a window.

Stop (molding): thin molding for stopping doors on closure or holding window sash in place.

Storm door or window: removable, extra door or window for reducing winter heat loss.

Temperature: a measure of the concentration internal kinetic energy of a mass.

Therm: 100,000 Btu.

Thermal envelope: the set of contiguous building surfaces separating the conditioned (heated and/or cooled) interior of a building from the outdoors and the earth.

Thermal mass: the amount of heat absorbed by a material as its temperature rises, expressed as Btu/°F.

Thermostat: a temperature sensing device which turns an electrical circuit on or off when a particular temperature is reached.

Tilt angle: angle of a collector or window from the horizontal.

Ultraviolet radiation: radiation of wavelengths shorter than those of visible radiation.

U-value: inverse of R-value.

Vapor barrier: material or surface designed to block diffusion of water vapor.

Vent: pipe or duct allowing inlet or exhaust of air.

Vermiculite: mica which has been expanded to form an inert insulation.

VT: visual transmittance.

Weather strip: thin, linear material placed between a door or window and its jambs to prevent air leakage.

Weep hole: hole purposely built into a wall to allow drainage of trapped water.

Wet-bulb temperature: temperature registered by a thermometer whose bulb is encased in a saturated wick and is spun rapidly in air. A dry-bulb and wet-bulb pair of thermometers comprise a sling psychrometer having the purpose of determining humidity.

Additional Resources

Blower Door Testing

An excellent article covering all aspects of using blower doors in air-sealing a home.
www.greenbuildingadvisor.com/blower-door-basics

Building Energy Codes

2012 International Energy Conservation Code
http://shop.iccsafe.org/codes/2012-international-energy-conservation-code-soft-cover.html

US Department of Energy Status of State Energy Code Adoption. Interactive site displays the status of both residential and commercial energy codes in each state.
www.energycodes.gov/adoption/states

Building Science Guides

Detailed theory and practice for building energy-efficient structures:
• Builder's Guide to Cold Climates
• Builder's Guide to Hot-Humid Climates
• Builder's Guide to Hot-Dry & Mixed-Dry Climates
• Builder's Guide to Mixed-Humid Climates
www.buildingsciencepress.com

Climatic Maps and Data

Climate maps of the lower 48 states (color PDF), including:
• first/last frost date
• high temperature by month
• low temperature by month
• heating degree days
• cooling degree days
• precipitation
• snow
• sky cover
• wind speed and direction
cdo.ncdc.noaa.gov/cgi-bin/climaps/climaps.pl

Tables by city and state of:
• highest temperature and date
• lowest temperature and date
• warmest month and date
• coldest month and date
• snowfall records
• rainfall records
weatherrecords.owlinc.org

DIY Energy Audit

The free Home Energy Saver (HES) interactive energy audit computes a home's energy use online using software developed at the US Department of Energy's Lawrence Berkeley National Laboratory. Heating, cooling, water heating, major appliances, small appliances, and lighting are all included. HES generates a list of energy-saving upgrade recommendations for the user's consideration.
hes.lbl.gov/consumer

Energy Statistics

DOE Buildings Energy Data Book
www.onlineconversion.com

Foundation Insulation

The Foundation Design Handbook is a comprehensive source for the principles and details of construction for slabs, crawl spaces, and full foundations
www.ornl.gov/sci/buildings foundations/handbook/

Heat Load Calculations

Build It Solar Home Heat Loss Calculator—calculates:
• design heat load in Btu/hr.
• annual heat loss in Btu/yr.
• annual heating bill in $/yr.
• carbon footprint in lb. CO_2/yr.
www.builditsolar.com/References/Calculators/HeatLoss/HeatLoss.htm

Home Energy Efficient Design Software (HEED)

Free, easy-to-use, downloadable software shows how much energy and carbon you can save with design or remodeling changes to your home. You draw the floor plan then drag windows to their correct location on each wall. You select from lists of standard wall and roof construction, and you can add high mass to temper indoor temperatures. Passive heating and cooling options include ventilation, evaporative cooling, and passive solar heating. HEED automatically downloads climate data for thousands of locations around the world. HEED works on non-networked Windows XP or Mac OS X 10.6 or newer systems.
www.energy-design-tools.aud.ucla.edu

Home Energy Magazine

Directed toward the buildings and energy professional, including energy auditors, builders, and retro-fitters, *Home Energy* covers every aspect of energy conservation in the home. Subscriptions (1-year/6 issues): print $75, online $45.
www.homeenergy.com

Home Power Magazine

Published since 1985, *Home Power* Magazine offers the widest range of in-depth articles about generating your own sources of energy. Topics:
• Solar electricity
• Solar water heating
• Wind power
• Microhydro power
Subscriptions (1-year/6 issues): print, $14.95, online $9.95.
www.homepower.com

Landscaping for Energy

"Shelterbelts" adapted from *Plants, People, and Environmental Quality* (Washington, DC: US Department of the Interior, National Park Service, 1972).

"USDA Plant Hardiness Map" adapted from *American Horticultural Society USDA Plant Hardiness Zone Map* (Alexandria, VA: American Horticultural Society, 2003).

"Trees for Shade and Shelter" from *Landscaping Your Home* (Urbana-Champaign, IL: University of Illinois, 1975).

Life-Cycle Cost Calculators

All of the calculators below run in Microsoft Excel and can be downloaded for either Windows or Macintosh at:
www1.eere.energy.gov/femp/ technologies/eep_eccalculators.html
• Gas furnaces
• Central air conditioners
• Air-source heat pumps
• Programmable thermostats
• Electric/gas water heaters
• Solar water heaters
• Dishwashers
• Clothes washers
• Refrigerators

Moisture Control for Builders and Designers

Professional-level exploration of the building science of avoiding moisture damage in residential construction in all climates. Includes both theory and practical construction details.
www.buildingscience.com/documents/ digests/bsd-012-moisture-control-for- new-residential-buildings/files/bsd- 012_ moisture_control_new_bldgs.pdf

Mold

An excellent, in-depth article for homeowners in hot-humid climates describing how mold grows and what to do to keep it out of your home.
www.fsec.ucf.edu/en/consumer/ buildings/basics/moldgrowth.htm

Photovoltaic Calculator

An excellent online calculator from the National Renewable Energy Laboratory for computing the dollar value of electricity generated by any size PV array in any location in North America. The calculator allows customization of any system variable.
gisatnrel.nrel.gov/PVWatts_Viewer

Recommended R-Values

The interactive ORNL ZIP-Code Insulation Program calculates the most economic (optimum) insulation level for new or existing homes.
www.ornl.gov/~roofs/Zip_2002/ ZipHome.html

REScheck–Web automates trade-off calculations for the International Energy Conservation Code (IECC).
www.energycodes.gov/adoption/states

Solar Water Heating

In-depth article explains every detail of heating water by the sun:
• How different systems work
• Step-by-step installation guidance
• Interpreting collector ratings
• A payback calculator for Florida locations (but may be used for other locations with similar climates). *www.fsec.ucf.edu/en/consum- er/solar_hot_water/homes/index.htm*

Unit Conversions

Conversions between 5,000 units
www.onlineconversion.com

Water Heating

Selecting a New Water Heater.
energy.gov/energysaver/articles/ selecting-new-water-heater

Sizing a New Water Heater.
energy.gov/energysaver/articles/ sizing-new-water-heater

Energy Star Gas Storage Water Heater Product List, March 27, 2013
downloads.energystar.gov/bi/qplist/ Water_Heaters_Product_List.pdf

Estimating Costs and Efficiency of Storage, Demand, and Heat Pump Water Heaters
energy.gov/energysaver/articles/esti- mating-costs-and-efficiency-storage- demand-and-heat-pump-water- heaters

Estimating the Cost and Energy Efficiency of a Solar Water Heater
energy.gov/energysaver/articles/ estimating-cost-and-energy-efficiency- solar-water-heater

Weatherization

Insulate & Weatherize, by Bruce Harley. The best book on air sealing and insulating for do-it-yourselfers.
www.tauntonstore.com

Window Efficiency

Description of new window technologies plus an online calculator for selecting the best window for your climate.
www.efficientwindows.org

Index

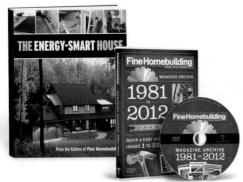